D1562033

Praise for *Jewish Revival*

"In the light of the radical focus on Central European Jewish identity with the Russian invasion of Ukraine in 2022, where a Jewish president was falsely accused of being at the helm of a Nazi state, a comprehensive study of how Jewish identity has been transformed in our global world was needed; the present volume with its reach from Israel to Germany to (indeed) Ukraine, more than fulfills the bill. This is an important addition to our understanding of the debates about the intersection of religious, ethic, and political images of the Jew in the modern world."

—Sander Gilman, coauthor of *Cosmopolitanisms and the Jew*

"A bold and global approach to today's complex Jewish experiences. Looking beyond the two demographic centers of Jewish life, it includes foci on Europe, where communal continuity was devastated, and Asian-inspired hybrid spiritualities emerging in North America or encountered by young Israelis traveling eastward. Recommended for those willing to rethink assumptions about the contemporary meaning of the adjective 'Jewish.'"

—Harvey Goldberg, emeritus professor, Hebrew University of Jerusalem

"The rhizome of ethoses and practices of Jewishness unraveled in *Jewish Revival Inside Out* transcends cultural and national boundaries to suggest an evergreen dynamic of thriving Jewish identities in a post-Holocaust era. The mélange of embodiments of Jewish affiliations and associations vibrantly depicted in the book testifies to the diasporic decentralization of all manner of Jewishly inspired living among various circles and communities. The authors of this volume, while addressing different manifestations of this move, daringly and originally argue that through reclaiming and remaking Jewishness, an excitingly budding cultural turn emerges. It heralds new ways of surviving a self-contradictory, yet hybridized world, compounding secularization, fundamentalism, globalization, and nationalism."

—Haim Hazan, professor emeritus of social anthropology, Tel Aviv University

"What a feast this is, drawn from an eclectic and refreshingly global menu of contemporary cultural performances of Jewish revival. For those who take pleasure in accounts of Jewish innovations, both enduring and ephemeral, here are the inside stories, thoughtfully parsed, with an abundance of judicious, yet still juicy detail."

—Vanessa Ochs, professor of religious studies, University of Virginia

Jewish Revival Inside Out

Raphael Patai Series in Jewish Folklore and Anthropology

GENERAL EDITOR

Dan Ben-Amos

University of Pennsylvania

JEWISH REVIVAL INSIDE OUT

Remaking Jewishness in a Transnational Age

Edited by Daniel Monterescu and Rachel Werczberger

WAYNE STATE UNIVERSITY PRESS
DETROIT

Library of Congress Control Number: 2022944876

ISBN 978-0-8143-4917-5 (paperback)
ISBN 978-0-8143-4918-2 (case)
ISBN 978-0-8143-4949-6 (e-book)

Published with support from the fund for the Raphael Patai Series in Jewish Folklore and Anthropology.

Cover design by Mindy Basinger Hill.

Wayne State University Press rests on Waawiyaataanong, also referred to as Detroit, the ancestral and contemporary homeland of the Three Fires Confederacy. These sovereign lands were granted by the Ojibwe, Odawa, Potawatomi, and Wyandot Nations, in 1807, through the Treaty of Detroit. Wayne State University Press affirms Indigenous sovereignty and honors all tribes with a connection to Detroit. With our Native neighbors, the press works to advance educational equity and promote a better future for the earth and all people.

Wayne State University Press
Leonard N. Simons Building
4809 Woodward Avenue
Detroit, Michigan 48201-1309

Visit us online at wsupress.wayne.edu.

In memory of Régine Azria (1948–2016) and for the
futures of our own intimate Jewlennials—
Hillel, Gaia, Adam, Naomi and Ella

The Jews are not a historical people
and not even an archeological people—the Jews
are a geological people with rifts
and cave-ins and strata and fiery lava.
Their history must be measured
on a different scale.

Yehuda Amichai, *The Jews* (1994)
Translated by Rick Black, *The Amichai Windows*,
Turtle Light Press (2017)

Contents

PART III.
Bodies

PART IV.
Retrospects

Acknowledgments

This book started on two rooftops 3,000 miles away from each other—one in Dharamsala, India, and the other in Budapest, Hungary. During a backpacking trip in India, Rachel took part in an ad hoc Rosh Hashanah prayer service conducted at a rooftop restaurant that included a neo-Hasidic rabbi, a group of Israeli backpackers, half a dozen young American Jews, and a Jewish-Buddhist monk from a nearby monastery. In this exceptional moment, spirituality of different kinds—Jewish and non-Jewish—was seamlessly integrated. In Budapest, on another rooftop, Daniel marveled at the liberty young Hungarian Jews take in reformulating the Sukkot ritual in an improvised sukkah overlooking the infamous Jewish ghetto wall. Guided by his co-author and native Budapestan, Sara Zorandy, he witnessed the rise of a young millennial generation juggling Jewish form and content in unorthodox ways.

Such experiences, complemented by the insights of actors and critics across the globe, turned our attention to the manifold Jewish landscapes and lifestyles as they evolve before our eyes. We pondered the global transformations of contemporary Jewishness, which give renewed meaning to identity, tradition, and politics in our postsecular world. In the process, everyday Jewish subjectivities and official doctrines seem to diverge and intersect in profound ways.

Our respective observations soon evolved into intellectual synergy exercised in a productive academic workshop that took place in Florence, Italy, in June 2013. Under the Tuscan sun and the generous auspices of the Robert Schuman Center for Advanced Studies at the European University Institute, sixteen scholars convened to present, debate, and further develop their work on Jewish revival, an event that enhanced our collective endeavor considerably and eventually facilitated the publication of this volume.

We wish to thank all participants who contributed to these significant gatherings for their unrelenting enthusiasm and commitment to the project throughout the process. Special thanks are due to the ReligioWest ERC project run by Olivier Roy and Nadia Marzouki for making this event possible. We are grateful to Sophie Zimmer, Magdalena Waligórska, Erica Lehrer, Lewis R. Gordon, Benjamin Beit-Hallahmi, Sally Berkovic, Michael Miller, and Isabel Frey for their insightful and illuminating input. In Florence, Régine Azria made a substantial contribution to our thinking by distinguishing between Jewish revival and renewal and their respective temporalities. Her untimely passing in 2016, before the volume came into fruition, arrived as a shock to us all. We thus dedicate this volume to her groundbreaking work.

Like most edited volumes, this project took a long time to materialize. We are indebted to our authors for their enduring patience during the process of revision and production. Daniel Monterescu acknowledges with thanks the financial support of the Central European University and the helpful comments of the faculty and students in the Department of Sociology and Social Anthropology. At Wayne State University Press we were fortunate to work with an experienced, committed, and highly professional team. We wish to thank Marie Sweetman, the acquisitions editor, as well as Kristin Harpster, the project editor and EDP manager, Carrie Teefey, the senior production editor, and copyeditor Mimi Braverman for their excellent work and dedication and for making the process so smooth, efficient, and enjoyable.

Introduction

Riding the Jewish Renaissance: Survival, Revival, and Renewal

Rachel Werczberger and Daniel Monterescu

If we are part of a movement then this movement has a lot of power right now. . . . This movement has a huge task in front of her: to rebrand God!

Yitz Jordan (in *Punk Jews*, 2012)

Jewish Present, Continuous and Progressive

A dazzling array of cultural initiatives, institutional modalities, and individual practices, grouped together under the labels "Jewish revival" and "Jewish renewal," emerged at the end of the second millennium. From Chabad's global tactics of outreach into new social spaces, through alternative cultural projects that are often dubbed Jewish spirituality, to local, community-based educational activities, these enterprises are realigning the contours of Jewish identity, engagement, and affiliations across the three geographic centers of contemporary Jewish life. Centered largely in Europe, North America, and Israel, projects of revival have also recently extended to uncharted territories in Asia and Latin America.[1] Indeed, the trope of a Jewish renaissance

---

1. The world's core Jewish population was estimated at 14,707,400 in 2019. In Europe, out of a population of 827 million, Jews numbered 1,340,000, or 0.16% of the total population (Dashefsky and I. Sheskin 2020). Two countries, the United States (39% of the world total) and Israel (45%), including the West Bank (2%), account for 84% of those recognized as Jews or of sufficient Jewish ancestry to be eligible for citizenship in Israel under its Law of Return. Nine percent lived in Europe (predominantly in France, Germany, the United Kingdom, and Hungary), 5% in other North American and Latin American countries (Canada, Argentina, and Brazil), and 2% in the former Soviet Union and other continents (DellaPergola 2020).

has become both a *descriptive category* of an increasingly popular public and scholarly discourse across the globe and a *prescriptive model* for social action. The urgent call to revive Judaism has engulfed all realms of Jewish culture, education, and modes of devotion, replacing older categories of practice with the promise of innovation, authenticity, and relevance.

Against the gloomy forecast of "the vanishing Diaspora" (Wasserstein 1996), which prophesied the dissolution of European Jewry in the wake of World War II, since the 1990s the Jewish revival discourse has posited an alternative future beyond the flourishing communities in Israel and the United States. In her internationally debated policy paper, *A New Jewish Identity for Post-1989 Europe*, historian Diana Pinto claimed that post–cold war Europe could be turned "into the third pillar of a world Jewish identity at the crossroads of a newly interpreted past, and a pluralist and democratic future" (Pinto 1996, 15). Reflecting Pinto's call to animate a "Jewish space," in the 1990s Jewish NGOs and philanthropic organizations, the Orthodox *teshuva* (return to the fold) movement and its well-known emissary, Chabad-Lubavitch Hasidism, and alternative cultural initiatives that promoted what can be termed "lifestyle Judaism" (Monterescu and Zorandy, this volume) or "identity à la carte" (Kovács et al. 2011) attempted various forms of communal and religious revival. This spectrum between institutionalized revival movements and ephemeral event-driven projects circumscribes a diverse space of creative agency and calls out for a bottom-up empirical analysis of cultural creativity and the reinvention of Jewish tradition worldwide. To address this loose assemblage of social movements and cultural initiatives, in this volume our contributors provide a more comprehensive portrait of what is now a full-fledged transnational field.

Projects of revival offer different articulations of the temporal and affective relations with the Jewish past and history and project them into the Jewish future. On one end of the spectrum, Orthodox forms of Jewish revival devise new ways to promote what they deem historically authentic Judaism and call for the revival of age-old traditions. For instance, in a lecture titled "Rethinking What We Know About the Universe," Chabad rabbi Levi Teldon proposed a "revolutionary" mode of existential reflection: "Drawing on the wisdom of Chassidic teaching, the most basic building blocks of existence are reexamined from the bottom up, revolutionizing our understanding of life, reality, and our place in the world."[2] On the other

2. See https://www.chabadsa.com/templates/articlecco_cdo/aid/4013109/jewish/What-Is .htm (accessed February 25, 2021).

end of the spectrum, alternative cultural actors, such as the "unorthodox Orthodox" artists documented in the film *Punk Jews* in New York City and Marom and Moishe House in Budapest, creatively define postdenominational religious and cultural modalities: secularized but not assimilated, liberal yet adhering to "tradition" as they understand it. By reconfiguring the concepts of tradition, culture, and religion, they remake new ways of "being Jewish." Likewise, espousing the New Age credo of "embodied, earth-based transformative Jewish ritual," the Kohenet Hebrew Priestess Institute announces, "We create ritual as a transformative force in Jewish and human life. We practice spiritual leadership as an act of holding sacred space, time and soul."[3]

Defined here as the practices of transmission, social adaptation, and cultural innovation of religion *qua* "discursive tradition" (cf. Asad 1993), the terms *Jewish revival* and *Jewish renewal* should be first critically recognized as emic and normative concepts, often used by political and religious actors. Despite their differences, contemporary revival and renewal movements are driven by similar states of dissatisfaction with the present reality, be it the collective survival of the Jewish people, the safety of Jews in the Diaspora, or the solvency of Judaism (Magid, this volume). These diverse, often hybrid efforts have emerged in response to the synchronic challenge of global modernity and the diachronic plurality of Jewish life.

However, as analytic concepts, the terms *Jewish revival* and *Jewish renewal* remain vague. To make sense of this wide basis of social action, we propose the following tripartite definition of Jewish revival in temporal, ritual, textual, and communal terms:[4]

1. The attempt to answer the call for urgent adaptation and reformulation of Jewish practice in temporal terms from the perspective of the communal present continuous.
2. The framing of social action in terms of Jewish memory and tradition through textual or ritual reinterpretation.
3. The effort to seek new social and communal frameworks for Jewish life.

---

3. See Rock-Singer (this volume) and https://www.youtube.com/watch?v=4HRovbSp4BM (accessed July 2, 2020).
4. For the sake of simplicity, we use the term *Jewish revival* as an umbrella concept for a range of projects, including those defined as Jewish renewal or renaissance by their actors.

Jewish Revival Inside Out seeks to reframe the interdisciplinary scholarship about the emergent transnational social field of Jewish revival from a
global perspective. Transcending the standard demarcations between center
and periphery, Orthodox and Liberal Judaism, Ashkenazi and Sephardic
(Mizrahi) movements, we offer a broad outlook on the plurality of Jewish
revivals in terms of time and space, text and context, body and ritual. More
specifically, we unpack the dialectic notions of Jewish survival, revival, and
renewal and ask how the attempts at a physical and concrete revival of Jewish
life relate to projects of cultural renewal and the calls for a spiritual revival.
Ultimately, what can be learned from these essays about the conceptualization of Jewish temporality by different social actors and about the different
outlooks of Orthodox, traditional, liberal, and secular Jews regarding the
Jewish past, present, and future?

In the following section we explore the history of Jewish revival as a
dynamic discursive frame whose meanings changed over the course of the
twentieth century. We then examine the modalities of revival as a communal practice: its temporalities, spatialities, subjectivities, and degrees of
institutionalization.

The Newness of Oldness: Historicizing Revival

The concept of Jewish revival has had a checkered history in Europe, Israel,
and the United States. As an analytic starting point, we conceptualize
the distinctions between revival, renewal, and survival based on the different perspectives on Jewish temporality invoked by each one of these
terms. It should be stressed that these categories are ideal types and can be
mixed in practice, as demonstrated in Nila Ginger Hofman's ethnography
of Jewish Croatia (Hofman 2006).[5] We propose the following tripartite
definition:

> *Survival* addresses a state of emergency, always in the traumatic pres-
> ent, that calls for the physical survival of the Jewish people and
> the communal salvage of Jewish heritage and material culture

---

5. Nila Ginger Hofman subtly argues that "the 'disappearance thesis' is belied by the experiences of many Croatian Jews, who continue to derive meaning from Jewish community life, notwithstanding their lack of religious commitment and cultural hybridization"
(Hofman, 2006, 6).

(e.g., the reconstruction of Jewish cemeteries and synagogues in extinct European communities).

Revival refers to a commitment to tradition and continuity, predicated on a past-oriented temporality (e.g., the Chabad and Breslov Orthodox revival movements).

Renewal emphasizes present- and future-oriented temporality, where the past provides an adaptable inspiration source prone to radical creative alterations without the shadow of hegemonic tradition (e.g., New Age movements, secular yeshivas, urban individualistic initiatives).

Against the ideology of survival and a preoccupation with continuity, blood, and kinship, the categories of revival and renewal manifest the Janus face of Jewish life between past and future. "For many generations," write Amos Oz and his daughter Fania Oz-Salzberg, "Jews stood in the river of time with their faces to the past and their back to the future, until the modern age arrived, shook them and turned them to the opposite direction. Oftentimes it was the condition for their survival" (Oz and Oz-Salzberg 2012, 148). Indeed, such a sweeping assertion "naturalizes a highly contingent linear temporality" (Boyarin, this volume). Yet the historicization of Jewish revival in relation to modernity also shows that past, present, and future orientations are always mutually implicated in such projects.

Throughout Jewish modernity (Traverso 2016) the idea of a Jewish revival shaped, motivated, and gave meaning to disparate calls for the reawakening of Jewish culture, faith, nationhood, community, and identity. For modern Judaism the idea(s) of revival, renewal, and renaissance have fired powerful and enduring imaginations—"fantasies," however, "that cannot be reduced to nostalgia or the naïve longing" for a "golden past," but should be viewed as a "moral task" (Biemann, this volume). Historically, a systematic reflection on Jewish revival was first introduced by the German philosopher Martin Buber in his 1901 essay "Jüdische Renaissance." According to Biemann, the notion called for Jewish revival, which Buber saw as more than a mere call for national reawakening. It called for a comprehensive self-transformation of Jewish culture and existence firmly rooted in romanticist, modernist, and thoroughly aestheticizing sensibilities. It was aimed at "restoring a positive and unified sense of Jewishness *outside* the traditional tenets of Judaism" (Biemann 2001, 60). What Buber expected for the new renaissance of Judaism was akin to what he believed the "old" Renaissance had mastered for its own age: A "return" that spelled radical innovation; spontaneous "rebirth" to a "new life" that promised freedom from decline and inward decay. In this respect, the Jewish renaissance echoed and expanded the call for *techiya* (rebirth) that had come from the Hebrew renaissance in Eastern Europe; and it echoed no less the development of cultural or spiritual Zionism, as whose cousin—and corrective—it often posed. But it also resonated with a broader longing for a "new renaissance" that was common among European intellectuals at the fin de siècle and during the three decades to follow (Biemann 2009, 2).

World War II, the Holocaust, and the near demise of European Jewry pushed many communities to the defensive mode of survival, and some have remained in such a state of existential emergency to this day (notably in Europe). The founding of the State of Israel in 1948 and the waves of emigration that followed left most of the residual Jewish communities in the Middle East and North Africa dwindling and vulnerable (Levy 2015; Baussant 2011). At the same time, the experience of displacement and trauma also endowed the concepts of rebirth and revival with new meanings: the actual physical rebuilding of Jewish life. Consequently, the idea of revival functioned as a powerful *figura* of thought to interpret an event as final and irreparably destructive as the Holocaust as both radical break and continuity—not mere and effortless continuance but *conscious* continuity. Jewish life after the Shoah did not just "go on," writes Biemann, it was "reborn," "restored," and made anew.

Concurrently, in the United States, Jewish discourse reflected an ongoing anxiety about the physical survival of the Jewish people, that is, a projected fear of annihilation through assimilation that resonated with the Holocaust, the plight of Soviet Jews, and the Six Day War. It heralded what Magid (this volume) calls Jewish survivalism, the so-called American Jewish obsession with demography and continuity. Survivalism has constituted a "culture of enumeration" that has become the ideology of American Jewish leadership (Kravel-Tovi and Dash Moor 2016). Yet, among many young American Jews in the 1960s and 1970s, a complementary move reformulated a renewed Jewish identity that was as much about renewing Judaism as it was about the survival of the Jewish people (Dollinger 2000; Staub 2020; Prell 1989). According to Magid (this volume), although Jewish revival in its survivalist sense is intent on the preservation of the *Jewish* people, Jewish renewal in its non-Orthodox, liberal sense focuses on the transformation of *Judaism* from a state of atrophy to a state of vitality.

In the last few decades, new Jewish venues have embraced gender diversity, with synagogues and community centers opening their gates to LGBTQ members (Shokeid 2002).[6] The heated debate on race in America (Itzkovitz 2005) now calls to include Jews of color—a pan-ethnic term that is used to identify Jews whose family origins are in African, Asian, or Latin American countries—into Jewish communal space.[7] Together with the controversy on intermarriage (Sarna 2007) and the place of Mizrahi and Sephardic Jews in Jewish history, these debates animate the field of Jewish revival by bringing global Jewish trajectories, colonialism, and migration into the conversation.

In Israel the economic neoliberalization and deregulation of the 1980s and the concurrent decline of the hegemonic Zionist narrative and its social carriers—the veteran, socialist, secular, and Ashkenazi elites—gave rise to new identity politics, which triggered ethnic and religious revival movements (Ram 2013; Leon, this volume). In this new cultural regime, Shas (the Mizrahi ultra-Orthodox party that calls to "return the crown to its former glory") and non-Orthodox secularized Jewish renewal projects (such as the Alma College for Hebrew Culture and Beit Midrash Elul) reclaimed Jewish practice heretofore monopolized by the (Ashkenazi) rabbinic establishment (Lehmann and Siebzehner 2006; Werczberger and Azulay 2011). These claims for the return of Jewish life, however, are not immune to nationalist connotations, as demonstrated by the urban settler movement in Jaffa, Israel, operating under the banner of a "re-jew-venated Torani community." Featuring the figure of Rabbi Kook, one of the founders of religious Zionism and the rabbi of Jaffa in 1904–1916, the movement calls for ridding ethnically mixed towns of their Arab legacy and restoring Jewish dominance (Monterescu and Shmaryahu-Yeshurun 2021).

6. In *Queer Theory and the Jewish Question*, editors Daniel Boyarin, Daniel Itzkovitz, and Ann Pellegrini explain, "While there are no simple equations between Jewish and queer identities, Jewishness and queerness are bound up with one another in particularly resonant ways. This crossover also extends to the modern discourses of antisemitism and homophobia, with stereotypes of the Jew frequently underwriting pop cultural and scientific notions of the homosexual. And vice versa" (Boyarin et al., 2003, 1).
7. A recent politicized discourse that self-identifies as the BIJOCSM Network (Black Indigenous Jews of Color, Sephardim, Mizrahim) engages the question of Palestine through the lens of race and ethnicity. See https://act.jewishvoiceforpeace.org/a/2021-05-palestinian-liberation-black-lens (accessed January 17, 2021).

Modalities of Revival: Jews, Jewishness, Judaism

Today, the ideas of Jewish revival and renewal have come to denote multiple and often contradictory social-historical processes, meanings, and motivations: from the physical national revival of the Jewish people in the nation-state of Israel and the reconstruction of Jewish communal and cultural life in Eastern Europe, through the revival of Marrano identities in Portugal, to the philanthropy-based identity projects and individualized forms of Jewish spirituality in North America. These revival projects are predicated on four modular building blocks: temporality (past, present, future), subjectivity (the scope of the historical subject), institutionalization (the degree of organizational structure), and spatiality (local, national, regional, and global). The relational arrangement of these foundations produces a mosaic of modalities, movements, and initiatives and offers different frame alignments (Snow and Benford 1988) for Jewish action and social mobilization.

Temporality

As a cultural idiom, the term *revival* reflects a sense of crisis and discontent with the present state of Judaism (often deemed "stagnant") and a wish to rectify and transform it. It marks a turning point and rupture, "a symbolic template of collective self-recognition at the moment of turning between old and new" (Geertz 1973, 219). We identify two temporal articulations of the present with the past and the future: past-oriented and future-oriented. In terms of the past, movements of renewal use the past as "an infinite and plastic symbolic resource, wholly susceptible to contemporary purposes" (Appadurai 1981, 201). Thus, although some Orthodox revival tends to submit the past to strict discursive and ritual constraints, other strands of Orthodox traditionalism are New Age or messianic, hence future oriented. Similarly, some Reform and Reconstructionist trends of Judaism are very much oriented toward the past (Werczberger 2011).

For instance, in an article titled "What Is Chabad" (2012), the Hasidic global organization defines Jewish belonging through the connection between past and present.

> By means of a rare combination that blends traditional Judaism with modern day techniques, Chabad has found the formula to develop a

rapport with the most alienated of Jews and to enhance their outlook. By arousing an intellectual and/or emotional interest in our faith, Chabad has become the catalyst to connect Jews with their Jewish roots and revive the sparks of Jewish consciousness in the hearts and minds of each Jew. . . . You do not have to be a member at Chabad, you do not even have to agree with everything Chabad says or does—you just have to be Jewish—and you automatically belong.[8]

Like other Orthodox revival projects, Chabad offers here a temporality that is primarily backward looking ("traditional Judaism") yet up-to-date. Fully committed to the traditions of the past, the present is understood as its direct continuation, through an instrumental use of "modern day techniques."

Conversely, the notion of renewal applied by the transdenominational North American Jewish Renewal movement or the Kohenet Hebrew Priestess Institute embraces a forward-looking perspective, one that is bent on transformation of the present for the sake of the future (Rock-Singer, this volume). Here the past is framed as an adaptable source of inspiration, prone to radical creative changes and modification without the constraints of hegemonic rabbinic tradition. Similarly, in postsocialist Europe at the turn of the twenty-first century, the "Judapest" initiative rebelled against the outmoded official institutions (Mazsihisz) and focused on the "here and now" of young liberal urbanites: "a wholly homegrown and grassroots online and offline community aiming to uncover the Stimulating, the Relevant and the Cool in the Hungarian Jewish experience" (Monterescu and Zorandy, this volume).

The Subjectivity of Revival

The scope of the historical subject defines the contours of projects of revival, ranging from the abstract to the concrete, from the collective to the individual, and from the plural to the singular. As Ruth Ellen Gruber (this volume) shows, the different inflections, punctuations, and permutations of Jewishness entail radically different intentionalities and ambitions. Although Orthodox projects of revival often claim to speak for Judaism or for Jewish

8. https://www.chabadni.com/templates/articlecco_cdo/aid/1545922/jewish/About
-Us.htm/fbclid/IwAR1bRbkfJCKTIcVAj79FnV0-vaARpT0C7Q3LyrUbVBmULsEN5k
kG3lQbJGQ (accessed January 17, 2021).

tradition, alternative movements opt for more inclusive plurality (Jews and Jewishness). Some stress the physical continuity of the collective (the Jewish people), as a national or ethnic imagined community, whereas others focus on an individualistic reframing of Jewish identity.

The scope of revival movements attests to varying degrees of cultural essentialism and competing claims for authenticity. Thus, in her ethnography of the Jewish scene in Kraków, Erica Lehrer uses the concept of "vicarious identity" to come to terms with Christian Poles who identify with or pass as Jewish: "The Jewish-identified Poles I met in Kazimierz do not identify themselves *as* Jewish in conventional terms. But they clearly identify *with* Jewishness in a variety of ways that deserve attention. . . . These Jewish-identified Poles, in the confusion and consternation they create (whether actively or passively), also function as a form of cultural education and cultural critique" (Lehrer 2007, 95). In this context, Jewish music and the klezmer revival of the 1970s open up a space of engagement that Waligórska (2013) describes as the "dynamics of encounter."

Questions of race and ethnicity also expand the field of revival. Although much of Jewish studies reproduces the divide between Ashkenazi and Sephardic cultures (Bilu and Mark 2012), movements of revival can be equally observed among Mizrahi and Sephardic communities in the United States, Europe, and Israel. Thus Breslov and Chabad, originally Ashkenazi factions, now turn to secular and Sephardic publics and position themselves as bottom-up popular movements (Leon, this volume; Baumgarten 2012). One strategy used by Chabad in public events is the use of Arabic and Mizrahi music remixed and rendered with Jewish content. Thus the hit "Hashem Melech" (God is King) by Gad Elbaz and Beni Elbaz draws on Algerian Cheb Khaled's blockbuster "C'est la Vie."[9] More recently, Gad Elbaz joined forces with African American Hasidic rapper Nissim Black, taking to the streets of New York City to perform a new rendition of "Hashem Melech." Likewise, Israel saw ongoing hybridization of what was traditionally deemed Mizrahi or Ashkenazi religiosity with movements such as Breslov Hasidism and Shas, crossing Litvak and Hasidic practices for Mizrahi practitioners (Bilu and Mark 2012).

---

9. See the two versions at https://www.youtube.com/watch?v=5dWeeUIZFgA&index=1& list=RDRvK19xgAxSU and https://www.youtube.com/watch?v=w-Y_5brDUSM.

Institutionalization

Complicating their differences in temporal orientations and subject positions, initiatives of revival display variable scales of institutionalization, ranging from loose and improvised ad hoc local initiatives to highly structured state-sponsored or philanthropic projects on a regional or global scale. Grassroots bottom-up initiatives run by urban "ethnic entrepreneurs" (Gitelman et al. 2003) and "professional Jews" often reject defunct institutional structures and strive for diversity, relevance, and inclusiveness. The offline and online transnational exchanges of ideas and organizational models between activists from all walks of Jewish life are crucial for establishing a local Jewish scene and an active sense of Jewishness. For instance, Café Sirály (now Auróra), Budapest's "non-official Jewish urban space" and the Marom Masorti Jewish community center offer young urbanites a European sense of Jewishness—diasporic by choice, cosmopolitan yet endowed with a local grassroots agenda. Sensitive to the trends imported from Berlin, London, or New York, these loosely knit communities are built on the concept of cool-and-happens-to-be-Jewish. Such initiatives blend together a mission to "re-interpret Jewish cultural heritage" with liberal values such as multiculturalism, gender equality, and environmentalism.[10] These modes of action, like much of popular culture in late modernity, mobilize social media as part of what Campbell (2015) has termed digital Judaism. For Nathan Abrams and colleagues, "Social networking sites, such as Facebook, offer the ideal opportunity in twenty-first century Jewish life to explore and experiment with religious self-definition, meaning, congregation and even being itself, insofar as in Facebook one's being can be literally reinvented in way without 'stifling' religiosity by forcing it to conform" (Abrams et al. 2013, 143).

The figure on the next page visualizes heuristically some of the modes of Jewish revivals across a temporal and a social axis. A fuller understanding of the positionality of Jewish revival actors would also include further dimensions such as spatial and degree of institutionalization.

---

10. See https://marom.hu/. The 2015 "refugee crisis" in Europe forged new connections between Jewish activists and migrant support associations (Kallius et al. 2016).

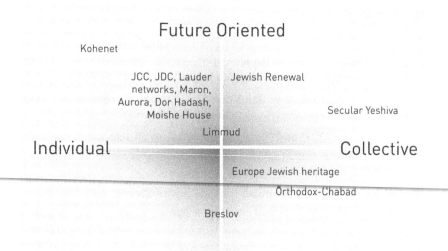

The field of Jewish revival across temporal and social axes.

Spatiality

After the fall of the Iron Curtain, historian Diana Pinto put forth the term *Jewish space* to describe social and cultural sites of Jewish life in reviving post-1989 Europe: "There is now a new cultural and social phenomenon: the creation of a 'Jewish space' inside each European nation with a significant history of Jewish life. The first is the gradual integration of the Holocaust into each country's understanding of its national history and into twentieth-century history in general. And the second is the revival of 'positive Judaism'" (Pinto 1996, 6). Almost a decade later, Gruber (2002) showed how non-Jews "fill" Europe's so-called Jewish space. She coined the term *virtually Jewish* to describe how non-Jews adopt, enact, and transform elements of Jewish culture and how they use Jewish culture at times to create, fashion, or trace their own identities. Other scholars have extended Pinto and Gruber's conceptualizations to describe Jewish space as a spatial environment in which "things Jewish happen" and "Jewish activities are performed" (Brauch et al. 2008; Gantner and Oppenheim 2014).

Since the 1990s, Jewish spaces have multiplied exponentially, both in form and content, and are now if anything global. By crossing national boundaries far beyond "the three poles of Judaism" (Pinto 1996), Jewish spaces bridge the conventional geographies in the Old and New World. Notably, Chabad houses emerged in India, China, and South America, catering to tourists and local Jews who want to rediscover their roots (Maoz and Beckerman 2010). At the same time local projects of revival operate on a microscale in many cities, reflecting different cultural, physical, communal, and religious concerns.

Thus, in postsocialist Europe, Monterescu and Zorandy (this volume) identify what they call the Jewish triangle—Budapest, Berlin, and Kraków—which displays three different modalities of revival: exogenous, endogenous, and virtual. Berlin was first, witnessing some of the fastest growth of Jewish demographics in Europe (from 10,000 in the 1970s to 30,000 today); next was Budapest, which remains the largest residential center of Jews in continental Europe (circa 100,000); and finally Kraków emerged, a city with no substantial Jewish community to speak of but that hosts one of the largest festivals of Jewish culture in the world (which some have described as a Jewish Woodstock). The community in Berlin after reunification consists mainly of ex-Soviet immigrants and, more recently, young Israeli migrants; Budapest draws on native Jewish Hungarians who recast their identity, and Kraków hosts a bustling scene of heritage tourism. These cities form a field of exchange and connectivity, as demonstrated by such projects as BBLU Salon (Budapestberlinsalon), which brought together Jewish activists in Budapest and Berlin to "display the multicoloured and diverse nature of the city." As one artist in the German fusion band Jewdyssee poignantly remarked, "Jew is the feeling of metropolitan people who come from everywhere."

The Book Outline

Jewish Revival Inside Out unravels the cultural tension inherent in projects of revival, renewal, and survival. The contributors explore the dialectic between continuity and change, dissolution and creative transformation, by offering a fresh outlook on the tribulations of Jewish life and its protean agency in the face of an uncertain future. They explore notable cases of Jewish revival grounded in concrete geographic, cultural, and material realities.

Part I frames the diverse theoretical ways of understanding Jewish revival movements. It provides the analytic vocabulary for the reader to better grasp the specific cases that follow. This part consists of three essays that explore the notion of Jewish revival from a conceptual and historical perspective. Historian Asher Biemann draws from modern and contemporary thought to trace the ideas of revival, renewal, and renaissance as normative concepts in Jewish modernity. The call for a renaissance emerged as a response to crisis and self-alienation. As such, projects of Jewish renewal also constitute forms of collective introspection; their programs often resemble a call for cultural *teshuva*, a return or turning that is akin to collective repentance. Drawing on North American public discourse, Shaul Magid proposes an analytic distinction between the two categories of survival and renewal. Both are embedded in the Hebrew Bible and rabbinic traditions and emerged from different iterations given specific social and political contexts throughout Jewish history. Both survivalism and renewal frame the present as a state that threatens the health of the collective. Yet survivalism is more focused on Jews and the collective, whereas renewal stresses the individual and Judaism. In that sense they serve opposite ends; the first is physical continuity, and the second is spiritual flourishing. Ruth Ellen Gruber highlights the case of post-Soviet Europe and the new Jewish-style religious culture that has become part of the mainstream and branded Jewishness as a recognized and recognizable commercial commodity. Although heritage tourism and the creation of Jewish spaces produce new authenticities, Jews themselves are increasingly becoming stakeholders in the development of novel definitions of Jewishness.

Part II engages in the richness and resilience of Jewish life in radically different contexts. Projects of place making from Europe to Asia rescale the transnational field of Jewish revival from the individual experience to communal initiatives, national projects, and global scales of action. This part consists of six chapters that follow various instantiations of Orthodox and non-Orthodox revival across the three centers of Jewish life: North America, Europe (Eastern, Central, and Western), and Israel. Analyzing the strategies and practices by which different social movements, NGOs, informal groups, and individuals take the liberty to create and often improvise new communal frameworks, the contributors reveal the predicament of religious minorities and fears of assimilation alongside the intense desire to transform Judaism and enhance its spiritual relevance for contemporary Jews.

Daniel Monterescu and Sara Zorandy look at the emergence of a particular kind of Jewish civil society in Budapest since 1989. Home to the largest surviving Jewish community in continental Europe after World War II, Budapest presents a case of indigenous revival, which draws on native Hungarians who recast their Jewish identity. Against a history of strategic invisibility of the Jews in Hungary, Monterescu and Zorandy investigate patterns of community formation and identity discourses, which produce unique cultural institutions, religious claims, and grassroots activities that are vastly different from traditional structures and assimilative ones alike. In calls to reinvent tradition, initiatives such as Judapest, Marom, and Moishe House distance themselves from Orthodox, Neolog, or Reform institutions and promote a cultural project of lifestyle Judaism. Geneviève Zubrzycki discusses the significant revival of Poland's small Jewish communities and institutions since the fall of communism, a process occurring in tandem with non-Jewish Poles' soul searching about their role in the Holocaust and the development of their interest in Jewish culture and in Poland's Jewish past. As part of Poland's Jewish turn, Zubrzycki shows how these multipronged phenomena are related to a broader secularization process of Polish national identity and the building of pluralism in contemporary Poland. Zvi Gitelman assesses the challenges to the creation of public Jewish life in the former Soviet Union. Attempts at revival were made possible by the removal of all restrictions against Jews and organized Jewish communities, a large infusion of funds and personnel dedicated to reestablishing Jewish life, and a manifest interest in doing so among significant numbers of self-identified Jews. However, this project has been vitiated by massive emigration, especially of the young, the absence of traditions of volunteerism and self-organization, and widespread ignorance of Judaism and any form of "thick" Jewish culture. As a result, despite the efforts of foreign Jewish "ethnic and religious entrepreneurs" who began their activities in the late 1980s, there has been no religious revival or great upsurge of Jewish secular culture. With the destigmatization of Jewishness, ethnicity is no longer a mark of shame, but neither is it a driving force in the lives of post-Soviet Jews. Hannah Tzuberi proposes a postsecular critique of revival politics in contemporary Germany caught between philo-Semitic desires and state policies. She argues that today it is primarily liberal Protestant conceptions of Jewishness that shape notions of "proper" morality and modernity. Focusing on the process of becoming Jewish (*giyur*), she shows that, paradoxically, after the attempted annihilation of Jews in Europe, the desire for a return or revival of Judaism works to delegitimize and marginalize non-Protestant notions of Jewish distinction. Moving from Berlin to Paris, geographer Lucine Endelstein focuses on the spatial effects of the ultra-Orthodox revival in Jewish neighborhoods in Paris. The practice of *eruv* illustrates both the blurring of ethnic boundaries between Ashkenazim and Sephardim and the emergence of new boundaries inside the ultra-Orthodox world. Remaining in the ultra-Orthodox revival field, Nissim Leon focuses on the ethnic determinants of the Breslov Hasidic movement in Israel, highlighting the reasons for its unprecedented popularity among Mizrahi Jews. Drawing on long-term ethnographic research on the Haredi revival movement, Leon identifies a number of elements that have awarded Breslov its prominent place in the sphere of Haredi religious outreach. These include the enterprises headed by the charismatic rabbis Schick and Berland, the blurring of ethnic identity, and the strategic engagement with secular public space in all Israeli cities.

Part III explores the intersection of Jewish identity and renewal with the body and the self. This exciting front of Jewish performativity takes the reader on a tour of the creative cutting edge of Jewish renewal, from New Age Jewish spirituality to feminist forms of Jewish shamanism. Rachel Werczberger studies two Jewish New Age communities that were active in Israel at the turn of the millennium. Undergirded by their critique of mainstream Judaism, the two communities attempted to renew Jewish life through ritual creativity and religious eclecticism and by fusing various traditional elements, especially Kabbalah and Hasidism, with New Age practices. She shows how a hybrid discourse manipulates several claims of authenticity: descriptive-essentialist, prescriptive, and existential. These layers fuse the personal and highly subjective search for the authentic self with the quest for an authentic form of Jewish spirituality. Shlomo Guzmen-Carmeli presents an ethnography of the BINA secular yeshiva located in southern Tel Aviv. This yeshiva is one of the hubs of the Jewish Israeli renewal movement, working out varied and sometimes contradictory values: pluralism, Jewish studies, Zionism, secularization, and humanism. In the yeshiva the canonical Jewish texts are viewed as a cultural tool kit and students are encouraged to debate, deconstruct, and reassemble them in accordance with their liberal values. Thus the yeshiva seeks to cultivate a textually based reflexive and individualistic Jewish self. The students use their regained authority over the Jewish texts to subvert the traditional Orthodox interpretive framework. Cara Rock-Singer's ethnography explores a radical form of individualized

Jewish renewal in North America: the Kohenet Hebrew Priestess Institute. Combining elements of earth-based spirituality, neo-Hasidism, and feminist neopaganism, Kohenet's spiritual leadership training program crafts an authentic tradition that integrates traditional practice with new forms of textuality, prayer, and ritual. Focusing on the contentious use of an altar, conceived by Kohenet's members as a ritual technology, Rock-Singer suggests that the altar serves as a window into the gendered politics of Jewish authenticity and, by extension, to the gendered limits and possibilities of Jewish revivals.

The volume concludes with Part IV. In excerpts from a previously published interview with Rabbi Michael Paley, Paley details from personal experience the emergence and subsequent dissolution of Havurat Shalom. This *havurah* was the first countercultural Jewish community in the United States and set the precedent for the national *havurah* movement. Founded in 1968, it was also significant in the development of the Jewish Renewal movement and Jewish feminism. Jonathan Boyarin closes the volume with a critical epilogue and an overview of the stakes of Jewish revivals. Reviewing the individual contributions, Boyarin provides a lucid analysis of the ongoing challenges facing Jewish revival movements in the twenty-first century.

References

Abrams, Nathan, Sally Baker, and B. J. Brown. 2013. "Grassroots Religion: Facebook and Offline Post-Denominational Judaism." In *Social Media and Religious Change*, ed. Marie Gillespie, David Eric John Herbert, and Anita Greenhill, 143–63. Berlin: Walter de Gruyter.

Appadurai, Arjun. 1981. "The Past as a Scarce Resource." *Man* 16(2): 201–19.

Asad, Talal. 1993. *Genealogies of Religion*. Baltimore: Johns Hopkins University Press.

Baumgarten, Eliezer. 2012. "Between Uman and Morocco: Ethnic Identities in Bratslav Hasidism." *Pe'amim* 131: 147–78. [Hebrew]

Baussant, Michèle. 2011. "Heritage and Memory: The Example of an Egyptian Jewish Association." *International Social Science Journal* 62: 45–56.

Biemann, Asher D. 2001. "The Problem of Tradition and Reform in Jewish Renaissance and Renaissancism." *Jewish Social Studies* 8(1): 58–87.

Biemann, A. D. 2009. *Inventing New Beginnings: On the Idea of Renaissance in Modern Judaism*. Palo Alto, CA: Stanford University Press.

Bilu, Yoram, and Zvi Mark. 2012. "Between Tsaddiq and Messiah: A Comparative Analysis of Chabad and Breslav Hasidic Groups." In *After Spirituality: Studies in Mystical Traditions*, ed. Philp Wexler and Jonathan Garb, 47–78. New York: Peter Lang.

Boyarin, Daniel, Daniel Itzkovitz, and Ann Pellegrini, eds. 2003. "Strange Bedfellows: An Introduction." In *Queer Theory and the Jewish Question*, ed. Daniel Boyarin, Daniel Itzkovitz, and Ann Pellegrini, 1–18. New York: Columbia University Press.

Brauch, Julia, Anna Lipphardt, and Alexandra Nocke, eds. 2008. *Jewish Topographies*. Farnham, UK: Ashgate.

Buber, Martin. 1901. "Jüdische Renaissance." *Ost und West* 1(1): 1–10.

Campbell, Heidi A., ed. 2015. *Digital Judaism: Jewish Negotiations with Digital Media and Culture*, vol. 2. London: Routledge.

Dashefsky, A., and I. Sheskin, eds. 2020. *American Jewish Year Book 2019*. Cham, Switzerland: Springer.

DellaPergola, Sergio. 2020. "World Jewish Population, 2019." In *American Jewish Year Book 2019*, ed. A. Dashefsky and I. Sheskin. Cham, Switzerland: Springer, 263–353.

Dollinger, Marc. 2000. *Quest for Inclusion: Jews and Liberalism in Modern America*. Princeton, NJ: Princeton University Press.

Gantner, Eszter, and Jay K. Oppenheim. 2014. "Jewish Space Reloaded." *Anthropological Journal of European Cultures* 23(2): 1–10.

Geertz, Clifford. 1973. *The Interpretation of Cultures: Selected Essays*. New York: Basic Books.

Gitelman, Zvi, Barry Kosmin, and András Kovács, eds. 2003. *New Jewish Identities: Contemporary Europe and Beyond*. Budapest: Central European University Press.

Gruber, Ruth Ellen. 2002. *Virtually Jewish: Reinventing Jewish Culture in Europe*. Berkeley: University of California Press.

Hofman, Nila Ginger. 2006. *Renewed Survival: Jewish Community Life in Croatia*. Lanham, MD: Lexington Books.

Itzkovitz, Daniel. 2005. "Race and Jews in America: An Introduction." *Shofar: An Interdisciplinary Journal of Jewish Studies* 23(4): 1–8.

Kallius, Anastiina, Daniel Monterescu, and Rajaram Prem Kumar. 2016. "Immobilizing Mobility: Border Ethnography, Illiberal Democracy, and the Politics of the 'Refugee Crisis' in Hungary." *American Ethnologist* 43(1): 25–37.

Kovács, András, Barna Ildiko, Sergio DellaPergola, and Barry Kosmin. 2011. *Identity à la Carte: Research on Jewish Identities, Participation, and Affiliation in Five Eastern European Countries*. Oxford, UK: JDC International Centre for Community Development.

Kravel-Tovi, Michal, and Deborah Dash Moore, eds. 2016. *Taking Stock: Cultures of Enumeration in Contemporary Jewish Life*. Bloomington: Indiana University Press.

Lehmann, David, and Batia B. Siebzehner. 2006. *Remaking Israeli Judaism: The Challenge of Shas*. London: Hurst.

Lehrer, Erica. 2007. "Bearing False Witness? Vicarious Jewish Identity and the Politics of Affinity." In *Imaginary Neighbors: Mediating Polish-Jewish Relations After the Holocaust*, ed. Dorota Glowacka and Joanna Zylinska, 84–109. Lincoln: University of Nebraska Press.

Levy, Andre. 2015. *Return to Casablanca*. Chicago: University of Chicago Press.

Maoz, Dary, and Zvi Bekerman. 2010. "Searching for Jewish Answers in Indian Resorts: The Postmodern Traveler." *Annals of Tourism Research* 37(2): 423–39.

Monterescu, Daniel, and Yael Shmaryahu-Yeshurun. 2021. "The Hebronization of Jaffa." *Haaretz*, April 29.

Oz, Amos, and Oz-Salzberger, Fania. 2012. *Jews and Words*. New Haven, CT: Yale University Press.

Pinto, Diana. 1996. *A New Jewish Identity for Post-1989 Europe*. JPR Policy Paper no. 1. London: Institute for Jewish Policy Research.

Prell, Riv-Ellen. 1989. *Prayer and Community: The Havurah in American Judaism*. Detroit: Wayne State University Press.

Punk Jews. 2012. Documentary film directed by Jesse Zook Mann. https://www.youtube.com/watch?v=5c29lJ3U_A0&t=115s.

Ram, Uri. 2013. *The Globalization of Israel: McWorld in Tel Aviv, Jihad in Jerusalem*. London: Routledge.

Sarna, Jonathan B. 2007. "Intermarriage in America: The Jewish Experience in Historical Context." In *Ambivalent American Jew: Charles Liebman in memoriam*, ed. Stuart Cohen and Bernard Susser. New York: Jewish Theological Seminary of America, 125–33.

Shokeid, Moshe. 2002. *A Gay Synagogue in New York*. Philadelphia: University of Pennsylvania Press.

Snow, David A., and Robert D. Benford. 1988. "Ideology, Frame Resonance, and Participant Mobilization." *International Social Movement Research* 1(1): 197–217.

Staub, Michael E. 2020. "Thirteen Ways of Looking at a 'Jewish Continuity Crisis.'" *American Jewish History* 104(2): 229–33.

Traverso, Enzo. 2016. *The End of Jewish Modernity*. London: Pluto Press.

Waligórska, Magdalena. 2013. *Klezmer's Afterlife: An Ethnography of the Jewish Music Revival in Poland and Germany*. Oxford, UK: Oxford University Press.

Wasserstein, Bernard. 1996. *The Vanishing Diaspora: The Jews in Europe Since 1945*. London: Penguin.

Werczberger, Rachel. 2011. "Memory, Land, and Identity: Visions of the Past and the Land in the Jewish Spiritual Renewal Movement in Israel." *Journal of Contemporary Religion* 26(2): 269–89.

Werczberger, Rachel, and Na'ama Azulay. 2011. "The Jewish Renewal Movement in Israeli Secular Society." *Contemporary Jewry* 31(2): 107–28.

I

CONCEPTS

In the face of calamity and the threat of extinction, how do Jewish thinkers and ordinary community members define the Jewish condition and their own Jewishness? The contributors in Part I draw the contours of modern Jewish vitality by historicizing and theorizing the oscillations between survival, revival, and renewal throughout the twentieth century. Intellectual historian Asher Biemann traces the European emergence of the revival discourse to the early twentieth century and the writings of Martin Buber, who highlighted the specific temporality that marks the Jewish renaissance in relation to the early modern renaissance. As a form of reflexive introspection and critical break, the notion of revival redefines collective Jewish subjectivity and urges Jews to reclaim their cultural autonomy and historical accountability. By contrast, philosopher Shaul Magid focuses on post–World War II North American Jewry and highlights the spectrum between two complementary forces: survivalism, which seeks to ensure the physical continuity of the Jewish people; and renewal, which seeks the spiritual flourishing of Judaism. The tensions between individuals and the collective, Jews and Judaism, continue to nourish these concerns to this day.

Whereas the first two chapters focus on the historical temporality of Jewish revival, in the third chapter Ruth Ellen Gruber, writing from the perspective of an investigative journalist and a researcher, provides a grounded and critical observation of the cultural interstices of Jewish borders and boundaries after 1989. In postsocialist Europe and beyond, traditional essentialism transformed into virtuality and old authenticities gave way to new authenticities and Jewish-style commodification. The various inflections of Jewish subject positions mark the potentialities of revival and self-definition in an ever-globalizing world.

1

Revival as Imperative

Reflections on the Normativity of Jewish Renaissance

Asher Biemann

"Why," Heinrich Heine wondered in 1841, "this great desire for the time of the Renaissance, for rebirth, or rather, resurrection? Does our age feel a sort of elective affinity with that period of history, which, like ours, searched in the past for a rejuvenating font, thirsty for a refreshing elixir of life?" (Heine 1975, 375)

"He is thirsty, dreadfully thirsty, dying of thirst," the French historian Lucien Febvre wrote a century later about Jules Michelet, the inventor of the Renaissance. "He is so much in need for rejuvenation, refreshment, renewal," until suddenly the "whole of Italy opens up before him with its beautiful girls under the bright sky," and the word Renaissance *springs from his lips as a "total renewal of life, as well-being and hope."* (Febvre 1973, 264)

"What is the great Malheur of dying?" Michelet meditated in his History of France. *"Is it not the price to pay to be reborn to better life?"* (Michelet 1975b, 50)

New Beginnings

To be "reborn to better life" is the subject of this essay. But it is a subject of neither metaphysics nor religious faith. I will not write of "rebirth" or "resurrection" as literal events belonging to the factual world, even if classical

Jewish tradition and theology have occasionally mandated such beliefs as creedal doctrine.[1] If I speak of revival, renewal, and renaissance, then it is with a "secular" and rather unsentimental mind. There is nothing refreshing about death. Dying is a great *malheur* indeed, and as in history, so we must sometimes in our lives accept tragedy and senseless suffering for all their plain and blatant mockery of human meaning and otherworldly justice.

And yet the cluster of concepts, whose family resemblance signifies new beginnings, cannot be altogether reduced to metaphor. Stripped of their transcendental promise, revivals are still replete with meanings of immanence. The acts of beginning and beginning anew, as Hannah Arendt observed, belong to our fundamental human condition, to our existence between natality and mortality: "Because they are initium, newcomers and beginners by virtue of birth, men take initiative, are prompted into action" (Arendt 1998, 177). To Arendt, every one of our initiatives replicates the beginning of birth and gives us agency in our otherwise beginningless lives. But it also opens a pathway to beginning anew, to acts of self-revision and continuity despite repeated ruptures. "The new beginning inherent in birth," writes Arendt, "can make itself felt in the world only because the newcomer possesses the capacity of beginning something anew, that is, of acting" (9). In the spontaneity of our beginnings, then, lies the potential for human freedom.

But freedom can be a frightful thing if left to what Arendt calls the bewildering "abyss of pure spontaneity." Thus new beginnings rarely champion radical novelty, and even if their task is one of foundation, like the foundation of ancient Rome, their understanding of the new most often acts as an "improved re-statement of the old" (Arendt 1978, 1: 211, 216). And thus history is replete with resurrections of the past, with rebirths and renaissances, renewals and revivals, with beginnings beginning elsewhere. And as much as we may find individual resurrections fictitious and obsolete, we must, therefore, take seriously the reality of renaissances as historical phenomena, even epochal events, that are, at the same time, cultural self-expressions. For, after all, there *is* an age of the Italian Renaissance, a certain Quattrocento; there *is* a phenomenon we call the Harlem Renaissance of the 1920s, or the Jewish Renaissance in Weimar Germany, or the

---

1. For traditional views on resurrection in Judaism, see Gillman (1997, esp. 215–41) and Levenson (2006). On the crisis of resurrection in modern Judaism, see Petuchowski (1983) and Batnitzky (2009).

Irish Renaissance of the 1890s, or the Catalan Renaixença of the Romantic period, and there *is*, as most historians agree, a period of renewal or revival in American Jewish history after 1945.

Metanoetic Action

Thus a long and ongoing series of empirical phenomena and events allow us to view certain periods of time under the aegis of revival, renewal, or, to speak with Heine, the great desire for rebirth. To be sure, historians tend to label time periods and ages in retrospect, for how else would we know the limits of an age and its particular characteristics or its inherent spirit, as it were? Yet some ages seem to emerge not only from the historians' craft but also from their self-awareness. Some ages know themselves, whereas others are driven by the desire to *be* themselves. Thus modernity, however elusive a concept, is conceived as both a historical classifier and a condition, a form of consciousness, an unfinished state of mind. The Enlightenment, if we follow Ernst Cassirer's reading, was both an age—the *siècle des lumières*—and a specific way of thinking, a *Denkform*, a *figura* of thought. And likewise, the Renaissance, as it emerged from nineteenth-century historical imagination, was understood not merely as an epochal concept but also as a worldview, a comprehensive way of being: It was an idea and, as such, not confined to its own epoch but retrievable and renewable in every generation.

Renaissances tend to have their own renaissances. Their rebirth differs from historical neologisms: We speak easily of neoclassicism, neomedievalism, neo-Gothic, neo-Orthodoxy; but it would be somehow unfitting to speak of neorenaissances, neorevivals, or neorenewals—though I am, of course, aware that architectural historians are accustomed to referring to certain stylistic elements of nineteenth-century historicism as neo-Renaissance. As a style of thought, however, renaissance is precisely *not* the citation of a previous age but, as Michelet already insisted, its "re-creation"—a new creation, sometimes even ex nihilo: "It emerged from nothing; it was the heroic impetus of an immense volition" (Michelet 1975b, 51–52; Febvre 1973, 265).

I begin, then, from a simple premise: that renaissance is not only a concept but a *mode of thought*. We think of and about a renaissance, but we think also *in* renaissance. Because thinking is itself a form of action, renaissance frequently appears as a form of doing, an *energeia*, as Cassirer put it, a *momentum*, concerned less with ideal contents than with agency itself.[2] The idea of renaissance, as Nathan Birnbaum wrote in 1902, is a "poetic force" (Birnbaum 1910, 1: 163). But I argue more: that renaissances not only are but *ought to be*; that renaissance, as our example of modern Judaism will illustrate, became not only a possibility but also a cultural *postulate*; that, as a mode of thought, renaissance acts as a regulative idea, as an imperative claiming its own normativity. With that normativity in mind, I argue my final point: that renaissances belong to a class of cultural concepts and behavior we might call *metanoetic*.[3] They are collective self-revisions with a restorative orientation turning introspection and sometimes even atonement into poetic forces of rebirth.

Reform and Renaissance

Now we are ready to approach the historical phenomenon of what is commonly known as the German Jewish Renaissance between 1900 and 1933 (see especially Brenner 1996; Batnitzky 2011, 73–90). It is justifiably called a Jewish Renaissance because it *viewed itself* as such. Thus Martin Buber wrote in 1903:

> We are speaking of the Jewish Renaissance. By this we understand the peculiar and basically inexplicable phenomenon of the progressive rejuvenation of the Jewish people in language, customs, and art. We justifiably call it "renaissance" because it resembles—in the transfer of human fate to national fate—the great period that we call Renaissance above all others, because it is a rebirth, a renewal of the entire human being like this Renaissance, and not a return to old ideas and life forms; [it is] the path from semi-being to being, from vegetation to productivity, from the dialectical petrification of scholasticism to a broad and soulful perception of nature, from mediaeval

---

2. Cf. Cassirer (1943, 56). See also Panofsky (1969, 1–41) and Gombrich (1979, 51). It is telling that the Jewish Women's Renaissance Project, founded in 2008 by the Utah 8, changed its name to Momentum in 2019.

3. This theme, along with its resurrectionist qualities, was developed between 1945 and 1946 by the Japanese Heideggerian (and Buberian) Tanabe Hajime. Tanabe viewed metanoetics as both a critical and a constructive project of transformation and "rebirth" that was intimately connected to his personal and national atonement after the war. See Tanabe (1986, li, lvi–lix).

asceticism to a warm, flowing feeling of life, from the constraints
of narrow-minded communities to the freedom of the personality,
the way from volcanic, formless cultural potential to a harmonious,
beautifully formed cultural product. (Buber 1999, 176)

What Buber formulated was, in essence, a Jewish rewriting of Jacob Burckhardt's Italian Renaissance. What he expected was nothing less than a complete self-transformation of Judaism through cultural productivity "in quite
the same fashion," as he wrote in 1909, "as the Italians of the fourteenth
century" (Buber 1993, 711). Where Burckhardt had seen the Renaissance
state as a work of art, Buber conceived of the Jewish people as a work of art.
Where Burckhardt found the liberation from the medieval veil of delusion,
Buber charted the path from petrifying scholasticism to free-flowing life.
And where Burckhardt celebrated the discovery of the individual, Buber
articulated a new freedom of personality and self-creation. Indeed, echoing
Michelet, Buber's renaissance claimed to be a "creating anew" (*Neuschaf-
fen*) rather than a "return" (*Rückkehr*), a celebration of the "becoming" (*das
Werdende*) rather than an adoration of the "rigid monuments of protective
tradition" (Buber 1916, 10). "In the confusion of our days," Buber writes
in another essay of 1901, "there have emerged men in our midst, who at
the time when the ax is laid upon the roots and new life is breaking from the
earth, proclaim the living fire and prepare the way to the becoming future"
(Buber 2001–2020, 1: 159). This renaissance will be completely new, so new
that its culture will no longer resemble an "image made by human hand"
but a "newborn creature" (*neugeborenes Wesen*) that "cannot be compared
to any existing thing" (157–58). Here, then, Buber's renaissance no longer
views itself as a rebirth but as a truly new birth, a spontaneous breaking forth
of hidden energies: "New and unexpected things emerge from its hands and
become more powerful than [the culture that forms them]" (157).

Buber's concept of renewal and renaissance thus sought to differ considerably from the discourse of gradual reformation. "By renewal," Buber writes
in 1909, "I do not mean anything gradual, an accumulation of small changes,
but something sudden and awe-some; not continuation and improvement but
return and revolution" (Buber 1993, 28). Along with the ideologues of Zionism, as well as the generally non-Zionist exponents of German Jewish neo-
Orthodoxy, Buber shared a bitter distaste for the liberal and assimilatory
tendencies of German Reform Judaism; Buber rejected the idea of Reform

as weak and "undernational," calling its adherents in an open letter to Hermann Cohen a "characterless [artlos], memory-less, and unsubstantial marginal brood [substanzloses Randgezücht]" (280).

Polemical as it was, Buber's attack against Jewish Reform unwittingly replicated the language of Reform Judaism itself. Consider what Abraham Geiger wrote in 1837: "Reform . . . is not . . . the mere casting off of all that is cumbersome. . . . The call for reform is now a different one: a transformed, new total form [Gestalt], a rejuvenated life, and forms that are saturated with and penetrated by the spirit! The difficult and the easy, the whole and the part, shall have meaning and significance, shall elevate the spirit, warm the heart, and bear on the entire expression of vitality" (Geiger 1875, 465).

Ignoring the deeply renaissancist aspirations of early and, to be fair, present-day Reform Judaism, Buber rearticulated Burckhardt's critique of the Christian Reformation as a "negation of the past" and "break with everything historical," arguing instead for a "genuine renewal" that resembled an "awakening" and would usher in a radically different "mode of existence" (Existenzweise). What Burckhardt quipped about the Reformation could have applied to Buber's understanding of Reform Judaism as well: "Reformation is the belief of all those who prefer not to have to do something anymore" (Burckhardt 1988, 130).

Buber's real critique of Jewish Reform, however, was not its lack of observance (Buber, in good Paulinic faith, considered not keeping the Law far more difficult than keeping it) but its lack of memory or, rather, its lack of creative memory. One might think of Aleida Assmann's distinction between the passive memory of "storage" and the active memory of "retrieval," where memory ceases to be an effort to preserve something against time to become, rather, a "renewal of the remembered" (Assmann 1999, 27–28). One might also think of her analysis of "eschatological" memory as a form of "awakening" (Assmann and Harth 1993, 22). Indeed, in a 1932 address to the Berlin School of Jewish Youth, Buber reminded his audience that each generation is a "community of memory" (Erinnerungsgemeinschaft), whose continuity was established not by a "sentimental looking back or nostalgia [Rücksucht]" or by a "mystical" remembrance that would continue "on its own" (von selber) but by an "awakening power," by a renewal of the "age-old bond of memory" (Buber 2001–2020, 8: 220, 221, 222). Thus each new generation must remember anew—or "put itself into" (er-innern)—the mnemic objects that the previous generation left behind. In his 1934 speech "Teaching and Deed,"

Buber directly characterizes the putting oneself into the event of passing on as an "organic" process of giving and taking (*Übergabe und Übernahme*), an act of uninterrupted yet also initiative transmission that was tantamount to a "creating anew and rebirth" (Buber 1936, 61). For Buber, being in tradition thus meant not living according to what tradition says but living in the *mode of transmission* itself, in the mode of remembering, in the mode of repairing anamnesis—in the mode, then, of renaissance.

The Revival of Worldliness

Buber's call for a specific renaissance of Judaism was, of course, not unique. Echoes and parallel Jewish renaissances existed in revolutionary Russia and among Italian Jewish youth movements, such as Pro Cultura, which was established in 1907 (see especially Bettin 2010, 79–96, 139–51; Apter-Gabriel [1988]). It also had nineteenth-century precursors, such as the Hebrew renaissance movement (*techiyat ha-safa*), the proto-Zionism of Moses Hess, who repeatedly spoke of Judaism's "striving for rebirth" (1905, 5), and the spiritual nationalisms of Shimon Dubnow and Ahad Ha'am (1930, 6), who advocated for cultural rebirth and called for a resurrection of the hearts (*techiyat ha-levavot*) rather than recultivation of the soil.[4] Across the Atlantic a separate Jewish renaissance was popularized in periodicals such as the *American Hebrew* or, later, the *Menorah Journal*. Indeed, already in 1879—long before the paradigmatic German Jewish Renaissance took hold—the Young Men's Hebrew Associations of Philadelphia and New York called for a "Grand revival" of Jewish holidays, and by 1887 it was already obvious to their members that it had brought about "something of a renaissance" (quoted in Fishbane and Sarna 2011, 64). In 1919, Mordecai Kaplan, the spiritual founder of Reconstructionism, announced the founding of the Society for the Jewish Renascence, which encouraged its members to attend synagogue services on the Sabbaths and festivals and to devote weekly time to the study of Jewish history and the "consideration of social, civic, and economic problems" (1920, 6–7).[5]

----

4. Ahad Ha'am even invokes a resurrection from the dead (*techiyat hametim*). For an earlier version of a *renaissance du coeur*, see Michelet (1975a, 399).

5. Reprinted in Mel Scult, "The Society for the Jewish Renascence: A Forgotten Chapter in Denominational History (Proto-Conservative or Proto-Reconstructionist?)," https://kaplancenter.org/belonging/the-society-for-the-jewish-renascence/ (accessed March 5, 2021).

What these Jewish renaissances on both sides of the Atlantic had in common was their cultural agenda, a program of revived "worldliness," whose vehicle was a collective sense of self-formation, or *Bildung*.[6] This agenda did not necessarily exclude the simultaneous efforts of Zionism (though occasionally it did); it viewed itself as preceding, even *preparing*, them. "True cultural work," Martin Buber wrote, "is also one of the most essential means of achieving the territorial goal" (Buber 2001–2020, 3: 191). The Jewish Renaissance viewed itself as transcending "merely" national aspirations, transcending also what it identified as the root cause of political Zionism: anti-Semitism. "Since the Jewish people still has the power to resurrect itself," wrote Nathan Birnbaum, "it will do so also without, and after, anti-Semitism" (Birnbaum 1910, 1: 171).

And yet a perception of crisis was not unimportant to this renaissance as well: The crisis of assimilation, the crisis of culture, the crisis of stasis and petrification (not unlike Petrarch's *tenebrae* or Burckhardt's Middle Ages), and, finally, a loss of self, however elusive, were necessary justifications for revival, for *resuscitare le cose morte*. "Crises," Jacob Burckhardt once wrote with a typical historian's nonchalance, "clean up," for they remove "lifelessness and fear of change" (Burckhardt 1949, 188). Renaissances, then, belong in the human inventory of crisis management, because they belong to the idea of *kairos* and "turning." They are principal forms of introspection. "A generation of Jews, who were relatively free from the anxiety of social climbing," writes Shulamit Volkov of the German Jewish Renaissance, "was beginning to look inward . . . seeking a new definition for one's identity, and often also a new self-respect" (Volkov 1985, 211).

Repentance and Rebirth

"Halting at the brink" and looking "backward and inward," as Volkov suggests, are not merely historical observations. They also evoke a language of repair and self-revision that touches on one of the most fundamental moral ideas: the idea of repentance. Repentance, like renaissance itself, is rooted in a religious conception of resurrection, redemption, and immortality. "Resurrected souls," Erwin Panofsky writes of the spirit of the Renaissance, "are somewhat intangible, but they have the advantage of being immortal and

---

6. For the Enlightenment roots of this ideal, see Mosse (1985, 1–20).

omnipresent" (Panofsky 1944, 228). "Rinascimento," Fritz Mauthner once wrote in letter to Martin Buber, "is a blasphemous reinterpretation of the rebirth in Christ."[7] Yet it was Panofsky who celebrated the Renaissance as a complete metamorphosis that was more even than a "change of heart" (Panofsky 1969, 37), and it was the German philologist and neohumanist Karl Burdach who already understood the Renaissance to be a "concrete turning around of the entire inner life," as the historical manifestation of baptism and atonement, the *sacramentum regenerationis* and the *sacramentum resurgentium*.[8]

The Renaissance, in other words, represented an age of repentance, of turning, metanoia, *teshuva*, a *conversio*—the "purging of the mind of the grossness of the past," as Giorgio Vasari already remarked (Vasari 1965, 45). Renaissance is the historical *reformatio* that resembles repenting self-revision. Max Scheler, writing during the final years of World War I, spoke of the possibility of *Gesamtreue* (collective atonement) preceding and making possible a collective "rebirth": The creation of a "new heart" rising from the "ashes of the old." Scheler, then writing in his "Catholic" period, considered repentance an act of cultural self-knowledge and, ultimately, liberation: "Not utopianism but repentance is the most revolutionary force in the moral world," for repentance rescues "the self from suffocation under the weight of history" to enable the "rebirth of the new man" (Scheler 1954, 50). Renaissance, to Scheler, was the "sociological form" of individual atonement, an entire epoch's "remorseful change of conscience" (*reuevolle Sinneswandlung*). "Whenever an individual, or indeed, an entire age," writes Ernst Cassirer, "is prepared to abandon itself completely to another, always, it has found itself in a new and deeper sense" (Cassirer 2001, 116).[9] The Jewish philosopher Hermann Cohen argued that turning (*Umkehr*) was the twin concept of introspection (*Einkehr*) (Cohen 1924, 132). "Rome would be resurrected," muses Petrarch, "if it only recognized itself" (Mommsen 1969, 176). "L'homme s'y est retrouvé lui-même," writes Michelet of the period he names "Renaissance": Man has found himself again (Michelet 1975b, 51).

---

7. Mauthner to Buber, January 8, 1911, Martin Buber Archive, MS. Var. 481.21. Cited in Biemann (2009, 289–91).
8. Panofsky invokes here William James's notion of the "twice-born" man. See also Burdach (1918, 43).
9. See also Cassirer (1943, 49–56), where he develops the idea of renaissance in greater detail.

Self-recognition thus weaves together a structural relationship between repentance, renaissance, and modernity. Hans Blumenberg placed the self-awareness of the Renaissance as *being* a renaissance at the threshold of the modern age, which, "in contrast to the Middle Ages, appeared no sooner than its self-interpretation [*Selbstauslegung*]" (Blumenberg 1975, 19). Modernity, in Blumenberg's thesis, begins with its self-recognition and its need for self-affirmation (*Selbstauslegung*). Working from a similar—deeply Hegelian—paradigm a century earlier, Johann Droysen had called all epochs of history "stages of self-recognition" (Droysen 1974, 357). Friedrich Schelling, in his *Ages of the World*, invoked a "coming-to-oneself" (*Zu-Sich-Selber-Kommen*) in the re-remembrance of the "first origin of things" (Schelling 1946, 169, 112). Nathan Birnbaum, finally, characterized the Jewish Renaissance as "great reconsideration" (*große Wiederbesinnung*) (Birnbaum 1913, 245). Renaissance, then, functioned itself as the paradigm of self-recognition, a return at the moment of crisis, a forward repetition in the Kierkegaardian sense.

Conscious Continuity

Here we can also better understand why, in 1918, writing in the immediate aftermath of World War I, the New York rabbi of Temple Emanu-El, Joseph Silverman, published his sermons under the title *The Renaissance of Judaism*, whose motto was Ezekiel's vision of the dry bones. What Silverman demanded was not only a "Revival of Jewish idealism" but also an *idealism of Jewish revival*: "Israel has died a thousand deaths, but its idealism has survived. . . . Brute force may destroy life and material things, but when the smoke of the battle is cleared away, then will arise, phoenix-like from the embers of destruction, a new world based on justice and humanity, liberty, equality, and fraternity for all mankind" (Silverman 1918, 118–19).

Silverman, of course, could not have imagined in his sermons what would come to pass only a few decades later. Alfred Döblin, however, saw the writing on the wall when, in 1933, he published a German book on Jewish renewal, and Ludwig Lewisohn saw the same runes from afar, when he published, in 1935, his Jewish anthology *Rebirth*.[10]

---

10. Döblin (1933); Lewisohn (1935). This is also the time when Salman Schocken started the influential *Schocken Bücherei* and when Willy Leven began publishing the *Bücher der Erneuerung*. Renewal thus functioned as a form of *intellectual resistance*. For a critique of German Jewish renewal and *teshuva* in 1933, see Arendt (2007, 42–45).

Even the most urgent and tragic sense of crisis did not, it seems, challenge the idea of revival. In fact, to speak, as Cecil Roth (1954, 385) did, of a period of "catastrophe and resurrection" is a remarkable leap of imagination, which another scholar, describing the years after the Shoah, expressed even more radically, using an all but prophetic cliché: "The skeletons began to move; life was renewed" (Feld 1991, 150).

"What a resurrection!" Isaac Deutscher gasped in 1966. "I would have preferred the six million men, women, and children, to survive and Jewry to perish" (Deutscher 1968, 50). Yet it was precisely the image of Judaism "eternal" that formed the Jewish imagination. Whether it was the just established State of Israel or the rebuilding of Jewish life in Europe, which the historian Salo Baron, writing in 1945 (!) envisioned as a great "awakening" and "cultural resurrection of European Jewry . . . the emergence of some new vital spiritual and religious forces out of its untold suffering" (Baron 1945, 2), the image of revival and rebirth functioned as a powerful *figura* of thought to interpret an event as final and irredeemably destructive as the Holocaust as both a radical caesura and a mere interruption of continuity.

"Continuity," Karl Löwith wrote in 1949, "is more than mere going on, because it implies a conscious effort in remembering and renewing our heritage"; it implies—and Löwith specifically referred to Jacob Burckhardt—renaissances and revivals (Löwith 1958, 22). It requires, in short, the idea of renaissance as a *protest* against the present and a protest against the merely historical character of history. Renaissance is no effortless continuance. It is *conscious* continuity. Jewish life after the Shoah did not just go on: It was reborn, restored, and made anew. Only in the idea of renaissance could skeletons begin to move again and Jewish life could be renewed.

Continuous Rebirth

Revival, renaissance, and renewal are, as I have tried to argue, ideas before they are historical events, and ideas *despite* historical events. They belong to the forces of "immense volition," as Michelet put it for us. They are, to some extent, concrete utopian movements, existing in the realm of imagination, both individual and collective. They oscillate between fact and fantasy, owing their enduring significance precisely to the kinship to the counterfactual and their expression of desire. But they are also *regulative* ideas, modes of historical apperception that *defy* history itself.

Hegel's axiom that a "people cannot go through multiple phases . . . , that it cannot make history twice" (Hegel 1955, 180) and Spengler's pessimistic view of the "inescapable destiny of culture" to end in "closure" (*Abschluß*), "petrification" (*Starrheit*), and death (Spengler 1980, 43) found their a priori contradiction already in Burckhardt's conviction that "what makes a civilization a *great* civilization is its ability to undergo renaissances" (Burckhardt 1949, 67).

For Leo Baeck, one of the most important spiritual leaders of German Jewry during its darkest time, this ability constituted the essence of Jewish history. "One cannot write Jewish history in its total course," Baeck remarked in one of his last lectures before his death in 1956, "without regarding it as a history of continuous rebirth: Rebirth from epoch to epoch, rebirth that created epochs of its own—epochs of giving old ideas a new expression" (Baeck 1974, 127). Like Burckhardt, whom he greatly admired, Baeck considered renaissances the hallmark of great civilizations. But in Judaism, renaissance was not merely a sociocultural phenomenon repeating itself from time to time, testifying to the inner vitality of the nation. For Baeck, it was a prophetic frame of mind, a *Denkweise*, a "commandment" and "task" to be observed in every generation. Only when this mode of thought, only when thinking in renaissance had been internalized, did Judaism "find itself again"—only then was it "reborn" (128). For Baeck, the conscious continuity of rebirth weaves a "continuous thread" (*Leitfaden*) that enables us to not only recognize and write Jewish history in its own rhythm and periodicity but also to liberate it from the irreversible verdict of historicism. Retrieving the original meaning of *period* as *peri hodos*, which might best be rendered as the Goethean *circum-gress* and which is suggestive also of Vico's concept of *ricorso*, Baeck interprets the periods of Jewish history not as abstract and retroactive divisions in an evolutionary process of change, inevitably allowing for ideas of national decline or Hegelian *Aufhebung*, but as revolutionary turning points that mirror, by analogy, the "ability of a young individual to build for itself a world, a second life, a second I: to fashion an ideal I" (28).[11] Because the individual has the capability to create itself anew, to begin again and yet also become "totally new," a nation too can fashion an "ideal I," an ideal "we," as it were, whose "renewal" is a mode of becoming oneself again.

---

11. For Baeck's understanding of "period," see Baeck (1974, 15). Also see Vico (1946, 175–77). For a similar notion of historical periods, see Nachman Krochmal's *Guide of the Perplexed of Our Time* (1847) in Rawidowicz (1924, esp. 40).

Still in 1996, the American Jewish thinker Michael Wyschogrod noted that the "future of Judaism must include renewal" (Wyschogrod 1996, 230).

Cultural Reawakenings

What I hope has become transparent is that revival, renewal, and renaissance have functioned in modern Judaism as powerful and enduring imaginaries—imaginaries, however, that cannot be reduced to nostalgia or the naïve longing for a bygone age but should be viewed as *imperatives* facing the future. For modern Judaism, renaissance represented a moral task and postulate. The return to beginnings, for Hermann Cohen, was not the return to a golden past but the return to beginning itself, the act of a beginning anew. And thus preservation (*Erhaltung*), to Cohen, meant "incessant rebirth" (*unaufhörliche Wiederbelebung*) and "incessant re-creation of the mind"—"Man's humanity begins from his rebirth which follows the recognition of sin" (Cohen 1929, 119, 247). Return, then, was an act of self-improvement but also an act of self-preservation, of *Forterhaltung*, despite the powerful flux of modern time. Only a history including rebirths could become prophetic history. Only a history including the possibility to be oneself again can resist the perils of cultural pessimism. Renaissance is a form of historical optimism claiming the role of history's reconstitution.[12]

Thus emerges not only a distinctly modern but also a distinctly *normative* dimension of renaissance. Renaissances, for better or worse, make moral claims. Accordingly, William McLoughlin has argued that cultural reawakenings are by no means merely pathological but can work, rather, in "therapeutic" and "cathartic" ways (McLoughlin 1978, 2). John Hutchinson compared the phenomenon of cultural reawakenings to forms of "moral regeneration." Distinguishing political from cultural nationalism, he views this moral regeneration as an "integrative" return to the "creative life-principle of the nation" (Hutchinson 1987, 30). For Hutchinson, cultural nationalists are "moral innovators" conscious of the regenerative power of conflict, crisis, and profound ambivalence. They admire tradition but reject the narrow boundaries of traditionalism; they admire modernity but disavow the self-effacing course it seems to necessitate. Cultural nationalism thus typically serves as a corrective of both radical ethnocentrism and

---

12. Hence Hermann Cohen considered optimism the "practical reform of our worldly existence" (Cohen 1929, 20–21).

radical self-dissolution. If it remains in this corrective in-between, cultural nationalism emerges as the "good" kind of nationalism enabling "backward" cultures, as Hutchinson puts it, to modernize themselves without relinquishing what they consider their collective heritage and destiny.

Tikkun and *Teshuva*

"Conscious historical continuity constitutes tradition and frees us in relation to it," wrote Karl Löwith of Burckhardt's Renaissance (Löwith 1958, 22). The attractiveness of revivals, renewals, and renaissances lies precisely in their double constitution of freedom and tradition. Unlike revolutions and complete ruptures, renaissances, renewals, and revivals seek to preserve and restore lost continuities. They are refoundations, as I argued at the beginning of this essay, "improved restatements of the old," as Arendt put it for us, less, however, out of actual *respect* for the old than for fear of the violent "abyss of pure spontaneity." For Arendt, their art of foundation lies in overcoming the "perplexities inherent in every beginning." In this respect, renaissances maintain a "conservative" agenda that renders them distrustful of fresh beginnings, completely severing them from the past—distrustful, then, of modernity itself. Here lies also the darker side of modern renaissances.[13] Yet, presupposing historical rupture as mere *interruptions* and inventing dark ages in between, renaissances also trust that nothing in history is beyond repair.

This confidence, which has now emerged as an imperative, helps us explain the return of the paramount theme of *tikkun* in contemporary Judaism. *Tikkun*, Emil Fackenheim wrote in 1982, using an unmistakably Heideggerian tone, is the "recovery of Jewish tradition—a 'going back into the possibilities of [Jewish] *Dasein* that once was *da*'" (Fackenheim 1982, 310), a recovery that resembles the "recuperation from illness" yet is also a certain "fragmentariness." Recovery, to Fackenheim, is always the risk of lapsing into an "irrelevant past." But it is a risk without which Judaism has no future, for it is the risk of returning, of *teshuva*, itself. Fackenheim continues: "If the real Jewish people, while often without peace, were rarely

---

13. Naturally, renaissances and revivals have been claimed by unabashed racists (Arthur Gobineau), *völkisch* nationalists (Julius Langbehn), and religious reactionaries (Josef Müller's Catholic monthly *Renaissance*). This only proves the truism that concepts are empty until they are put to use.

without vibrant life, it is because of the ever-renewing, ever-rejuvenating power of *Teshuva*" (318).

A similar tone has entered contemporary Jewish thought, where *teshuva* has become synonymous with postmodernism. "Jewish postmodernism means a kind of *teshuva*, a return," writes Steven Kepnes. "Modern Judaism and modern Jewish thought involved a repression and destruction of Judaism; postmodern Judaism is its repair, return, and rehabilitation" (Kepnes et al. 1998, 25). Likewise, Robert Gibbs reminds his readers of the task of repentance and *teshuva*: "For post-modernists, this means turning back to traditions of practice from which modernity has cut itself off" (38).

Our brief survey, however, helps us realize that modern Jewish thought thought no differently about itself than postmodern Jewish thought did twenty years ago and that the idea of renaissance has been equally prominent to both. Modern in their own right, postmodern renaissances accuse the failures of modernity, speaking with both conservative and liberal minds. In 1952 Leo Strauss, the alleged "father" of the neocons, advocated *teshuva*, repentance, and return, against the perils of progress and beginnings (Strauss 1981, 17–19), and Michael Lerner, arguably one of the most progressive Jewish liberals in the United States, could at once attack the same neocons and argue that the prophets viewed themselves as "conservatives attempting to bring back the people to the essence of the religion." These prophets "were the first creators of the Jewish-renewal movement" (Lerner 1994, 132).

Lerner's chatty writings on renewal may not be in a league with previous writers of the Jewish renaissance, but they do epitomize the very ideological characteristics I have sketched in this essay: "Jewish renewal is the process, repeated throughout Jewish history, in which Judaism is 'changed' back to its origins as the practice of healing, repair, and transformation" (Lerner 1994, 20). It is a "substantively conservative process," which Lerner also terms "revolutionary," and as such indeed a renaissance of the renaissance (xvii). More recently, Shaul Magid, another progressive Jewish voice, has called for a similar renewal to "reconstruct Judaism in a post-Judaism era," a renewal that would also act as a "critique" and, in fact, as a revision of what he considers the "romantic/nostalgic" phase of earlier renaissances (Magid 2013, 240).

Reclaiming such evocative terms as *tikkun* or *teshuva*, Jewish renaissances today have indeed relinquished their nineteenth-century roots in the Italian Renaissance to reroot themselves in traditional Jewish language. But they have not relinquished their indebtedness to the idea of renaissance itself. When, in 2008, Edgar Bronfman, former president of the World Jewish Congress, recalled how he "dreamed up" the phrase "Jewish Renaissance" to save the vanishing Jewish youth of America in the 1990s, we can measure the continuous "invention" of this idea and its remarkable versatility. "A call for renaissance," wrote the late Bronfman, "is a call for rebirth, not for a restoration of an earlier age or a continuation of what we were doing before. Jewish renaissance must challenge the Jewish community to see where outdated ideas and structures must be discarded, and our Jewish story created anew" (Bronfman and Zasloff 2008, 22).

Creating the Jewish story anew has, as the new itself, a long tradition (to paraphrase Harold Rosenberg). The Jewish philosopher and Hebraist Simon Rawidowicz called this long tradition the anxiety of the "ever dying people." "Filled with the fear of its end, it seeks to make a new beginning," he wrote in 1948, and he concludes his famous essay with an astounding line: "Our incessant dying means uninterrupted living, rising, standing up, beginning anew" (Rawidowicz 1998, 63). In modern Judaism the tradition of renaissance has been one of the most prevalent collective imperatives and, besides memory and nostalgia, perhaps the only mitzvah still universally accepted as a commandment (rather than a good deed).[14] But it is a tradition with surprisingly little content. Indeed, the new Jewish renaissances we encounter in Europe and North America have not advanced far beyond where previous Jewish renaissances left off—or were cut short by more sinister ideologies of revival. Their object of return remained equally elusive, and their resistance to halakhic Judaism prohibitive. But if the history of renaissance teaches us anything concrete, then it would be precisely that that renaissance is really *renaissancing*, a return without a specific destination, perhaps no more than the feeling, the consciousness, and the imperative of turning, a disposition equipped, as Franz Rosenzweig wrote, with "nothing but the empty forms of preparedness" (Rosenzweig 2002, 67); or as Martin Buber put it in 1921: "We have called for turning . . . not for completion" (Buber 1993, 311).

---

14. For nostalgia as a modern Jewish mitzvah, see Eisen (1998, 156–87) and, more recently, Gross (2021).

References

Ahad Ha'am. 1930. *Al Parashat Drakhim*, vol. 1. Berlin: Jüdischer Verlag.

Apter-Gabriel, Ruth. 1988. *Tradition and Revolution: The Jewish Renaissance in Russian Avant-Garde Art, 1912–1928*. Jerusalem: Hamakor Press.

Arendt, Hannah. 1978. *The Life of the Mind*, 2 vols. New York: Harcourt Brace Jovanovich.

Arendt, Hannah. 1998. *The Human Condition*. Chicago: University of Chicago Press.

Arendt, Hannah. 2007. *The Jewish Writings*, ed. Jerome Kohn and Ron H. Feldman. New York: Schocken.

Assmann, Aleida. 1999. *Erinnerungsräume: Formen und Wandlungen des kulturellen Gedächtnisses*. Munich: C. H. Beck.

Assmann, Aleida, and Dietrich Harth. 1993. *Mnemosyne: Formen und Funktionen der kulturellen Erinnerung*. Frankfurt: Fischer.

Baeck, Leo. 1974. *Epochen der jüdischen Geschichte*. Stuttgart: Kohlhammer.

Baron, Salo. 1945. "At the Turning Point." *Menorah Journal* 33(1): 1–10.

Batnitzky, Leora. 2009. "From Resurrection to Immortality: Theological and Political Implications in Modern Jewish Thought." *Harvard Theological Review* 102(3): 279–96.

Batnitzky, Leora. 2011. *How Judaism Became a Religion: An Introduction to Modern Jewish Thought*. Princeton, NJ: Princeton University Press.

Bettin, Cristina. 2010. *Italian Jews from Emancipation to the Racial Laws*. New York: Palgrave Macmillan.

Biemann, Asher. 2009. *Inventing New Beginnings: On the Idea of Renaissance in Modern Judaism*. Stanford, CA: Stanford University Press.

Birnbaum, Nathan. 1910. *Ausgewählte Schriften zur jüdischen Frage*, 2 vols. Czernowitz: Birnbaum & Kohut.

Birnbaum, Nathan. 1913. "Das Erwachen der jüdischen Seele." In *Vom Judentum: Ein Sammelbuch*, ed. Verein jüdischer Hochschüler Bar Kochba, 239–49. Leipzig: Wolff.

Blumenberg, Hans. 1975. *Aspekte der Epochenschwelle: Cusaner und Nolaner*. Frankfurt: Suhrkamp.

Brenner, Michael. 1996. *The Renaissance of Jewish Culture in Weimar Germany*. New Haven, CT: Yale University Press.

Bronfman, Edgar, and Beth Zasloff. 2008. *Hope, not Fear: A Path to Jewish Renaissance*. New York: St. Martin's.

Buber, Martin. 1916. *Die jüdische Bewegung: Gesammelte Aufsätz und Ansprachen, 1900–1915*. Berlin: Jüdischer Verlag.

Buber, Martin. 1936. *Die Stunde und die Erkenntnis: Reden und Aufsätze, 1933–1935*. Berlin: Schocken.

Buber, Martin. 1993. *Der Jude und sein Judentum: Gesammelte Aufsätze und Reden*. Gerlingen: Lambert Schneider.

Buber, Martin. 1999. *The First Buber: Youthful Zionist Writings of Martin Buber*, ed. and trans. Gilya G. Schmidt. Syracuse: University of Syracuse.

Buber, Martin. 2001–2020. *Martin Buber Werkausgabe*, 21 vols., ed. Paul Mendes-Flohr, Peter Schäfer, and Bernd Witte. Gütersloh: Gütersloher Verlagshaus.

Burckhardt, Jacob. 1949. *Weltgeschichtliche Betrachtungen*. Stuttgart: Kröner.

Burckhardt, Jacob. 1988. *Historische Fragmente*, ed. Emil Dürr. Nördlingen: Greno.

Burdach, Karl. 1918. *Reformation, Renaissance, Humanismus: Zwei Abhandlungen über die Grundlage moderner Bildung und Sprachkunst*. Berlin: G. Paetel.

Cassirer, Ernst. 1943. "Some Remarks on the Question of the Originality of the Renaissance." *Journal of the History of Ideas* 4: 49–56.

Cassirer, Ernst. 2001. *Zur Logik der Kulturwissenschaften*. Hamburg: Felix Meiner.

Cohen, Hermann. 1924. *Jüdische Schriften*, vol. 1, ed. Bruno Straus. Berlin: Schwetschke.

Cohen, Hermann. 1929. *Religion der Vernunft aus den Quellen des Judentums*. Frankfurt: Kauffmann.

Deutscher, Isaac. 1968. *The Non-Jewish Jew and Other Essays*, ed. Tamara Deutscher. London: Oxford University Press.

Döblin, Alfred. 1933. *Jüdische Erneuerung*. Amsterdam: Querido.

Droysen, Gustav. 1974. *Historik: Verlesungen über Enzyklopädie und Methodologie der Geschichte*, ed. Rudolf Hübner. Munich: Oldenburg.

Eisen, Arnold. 1998. *Rethinking Modern Judaism: Ritual, Commandment, Community*. Chicago: University of Chicago Press.

Fackenheim, Emil. 1982. *To Mend the World: Foundations of Future Jewish Thought*. New York: Schocken.

Febvre, Lucien. 1973. *A New Kind of History*, ed. Peter Burke. New York: Harper & Row.

Feld, Edward. 1991. *The Spirit of Renewal: Crisis and Response in Jewish Life*. Woodstock, VT: Jewish Lights.

Fishbane, Eitan, and Jonathan Sarna. 2011. *Jewish Renaissance and Revival in America*. Hanover, NH: Brandeis University Press.

Geiger, Abraham. 1875. *Nachgelassene Schriften*, vol. 2, ed. Ludwig Geiger. Berlin: Louis Gerschel.

Gillman, Neil. 1997. *The Death of Death: Resurrection and Immortality in Jewish Thought*. Woodstock, VT: Jewish Lights.

Gombrich, Ernst. 1979. *Ideals and Idols: Essays on Values in History and in Art*. London: Phaidon.

Gross, Rachel B. 2021. *Beyond the Synagogue: Jewish Nostalgia as Religious Practice*. New York: New York University Press.

Hegel, Georg F. W. 1955. *Vorlesungen über die Philosophie der Weltgeschichte*, vol. 1, ed. Johannes Hoffmeister. Hamburg: Meiner.

Heine, Heinrich. 1975. *Gesammelte Schriften*, vol. 5, ed. Klaus Briegleb. Munich: Hanser.

Hess, Moses. 1905. *Jüdische Schriften*, ed. Theodor Zlocisti. Berlin: Louis Lamm.

Hutchinson, John. 1987. *The Dynamics of Cultural Nationalism: The Gaelic Revival and the Creation of the Irish Nation State*. London: Allen & Unwin.

Kaplan, Mordecai. 1920. *Society for the Jewish Renascence: Platform and Fundamental Duties*. New York: n.p.

Kepnes, Steven, Peter Ochs, and Robert Gibbs. 1998. *Reasoning After Revelation: Dialogues in Postmodern Jewish Philosophy*. London: Routledge.

Lerner, Michael. 1994. *Jewish Renewal: A Path to Healing and Transformation*. New York: Harper Collins.

Levenson, Jon. 2006. *Resurrection and the Restoration of Israel: The Ultimate Victory of the God of Life*. New Haven, CT: Yale University Press.

Lewisohn, Ludwig. 1935. *Rebirth: A Book of Modern Jewish Thought*. New York: Harper & Brothers.

Löwith, Karl. 1958. *Meaning in History*. Chicago: University of Chicago Press.

Magid, Shaul. 2013. *American Post-Judaism: Identity and Renewal in a Postethnic Society*. Bloomington: Indiana University Press.

McLoughlin, William. 1978. *Revivals, Awakenings, and Reform: An Essay on Religion and Social Change in America, 1607–1977*. Chicago: University of Chicago Press.

Michelet, Jules. 1975a. *La Mer*. Paris: Michele Lévy Frères.

Michelet, Jules. 1975b. *Oeuvres complètes*, vol. 7. Paris: Flammarion.

Mommsen, Theodor. 1969. "Der Begriff des 'Finsteren Zeitalters' bei Petrarca." In *Zu Begriff und Problem der Renaissance*, ed. August Buck, 151–79. Darmstadt: Wissenschaftliche Buchgesellschaft.

Mosse, George. 1985. *German Jews Beyond Judaism*. Bloomington: University of Indiana Press.

Panofsky, Erwin. 1944. "Renaissance and Renascences." *Kenyon Review* 6(2): 201–36.

Panofsky, Erwin. 1969. *Renaissance and Renascences in Western Art*. New York: Harper & Row.

Petuchowski, Jacob. 1983. "'Immortality—Yes; Resurrection—No!' Nineteenth-Century Judaism Struggles with a Traditional Belief." *Proceedings of the American Academy for Jewish Research* 40: 133–47.

Rawidowicz, Simon. 1924. *Kitvei Ranak (Rabbi Nachmal Krochmal)*. Berlin: Ayanot.

Rawidowicz, Simon. 1998. *State of Israel, Diaspora, and Jewish Continuity*, ed. Benjamin C. I. Ravid. Hanover, NH: Brandeis University Press.

Rosenzweig, Franz. 2002. *On Jewish Learning*, ed. Nahum Glatzer. Madison: University of Wisconsin Press.

Roth, Cecil. 1954. *A History of the Jews*. New York: Schocken.

Scheler, Max. 1954. *Gesammelte Werke*, vol. 5, ed. Maria Scheler. Bern: Francke.

Schelling, Friedrich. 1946. *Die Weltalter: In den Urfassungen von 1811 und 1813*. Munich: Felix Meiner.

Silverman, Joseph. 1918. *The Renaissance of Judaism*. New York: Bloch.

Spengler, Oswald. 1980. *Untergang des Abendlandes: Umrisse einer Morphologie der Weltgeschichte*. Stuttgart: Deutscher Bücherbund.

Strauss, Leo. 1981. "Progress or Return? The Contemporary Crisis in Western Civilization." *Modern Judaism* 1(1): 17–45.

Tanabe, Hajime. 1986. *Philosophy as Metanoetics*, trans. Takeuchi Yoshinori. Berkeley: University of California Press.

Vasari, Giorgio. 1965. *Lives of the Painters*, trans. George Bull. New York: Penguin.

Vico, Giambattista. 1946. *La scienca nuova*, vol. 3, ed. Giovanni E. Barié. Milan: Garzanti.

Volkov, Shulamit. 1985. "The Dynamics of Dissimilation: Ostjuden and German Jews." In *The Jewish Response to German Culture: From the Enlightenment to the Second World War*, ed. Jehuda Reinharz and Walter Schatzberg, 195–211. Hanover, NH: University Press of New England.

Wyschogrod, Michael. 1996. *The Body of Faith: God in the People Israel*. London: Jason Aronson.

2

From Kiruv to Continuity

Survivalism and Renewal as Competing Categories in Judaism

Shaul Magid

Exaggeration on the path to truth is progress.
—Jonathan Z. Smith, *Map Is Not Territory*, 308

That religion should again become the affair of the individual and of his own person feeling was inevitable when the Church became corrupt in doctrine and tyrannous in practice.
—Jakob Burckhardt, *The Civilization of the Renaissance in Italy*

"The world makes many images of Israel, but Israel has only one image of itself: that of being constantly on the verge of ceasing to be, of disappearing. . . . Almost from the first meeting in the desert between Moses and Israel, when the prince of prophets uttered the dread admonitions of Deuteronomy, to the pseudoprophetic outbursts of Bialik in the twentieth century, seers and mentors in Israel have time and again pronounced the dire warning, 'Israel, thou art going to be wiped off from the face of the earth; the end is near, unless and if . . .' There were many 'ifs' and yet they were always the same" (Rawidowicz 1986, 53).

This is how Simon Rawidowicz begins his seminal essay "Israel: An Ever-Dying People," a Jewish meditation on the psychic nature of impending and yet never fulfilled doom. Rawidowicz traces this psychic trope from ancient Israel to twentieth-century secular Zionists, figures such as Hayim

Nahman Bialik, Yosef Hayyim Brenner, and Yosef Micha Berdichevsky. Even the promise and ultimate establishment of a Jewish nation-state could not usurp the deeply seated notion that each generation of Jews fashioned itself to be the last. Jews seem to habitually envision themselves as taking their last breath—over and over again, and not only in times when such fear is warranted.

This mentality of immanent finality, even (and ironically) in light of the divine promise of salvation and survival (*nezah yisrael lo yeshaker*, "the eternity of Israel will not be belied"), has produced many different kinds of responses from Jews throughout history, stretching from Maimonides' plea to the Jews of Lunel that they alone are responsible for the survival of Judaism since it has been abandoned elsewhere, to Meir Kahane's civil Jewish survivalism encapsulated in the advertisement "We are talking about Jewish survival" in the founding of the Jewish Defense League in the spring of 1968.

Traditionally, the fear of Jewish erasure was less prominent than the fear of forgetting the Torah that marks the very justification for the rabbinic choice to write the Oral Law.[1] In some sense, then, Judaism itself, the extent to which it is produced by rabbinic literature, is the product of the fear of its own erasure, even though God promised that the Torah would not be forgotten and the sages say that even if it were forgotten, they would have the power to restore it.[2] In some sense, then, Judaism exists as a last ditch effort to prevent its nonexistence. Even divine and rabbinic assurance cannot uproot that feeling of doom. Rawidowicz concludes his essay, "If it has been decreed for Israel that it go on being a dying people, let it be a people that is constantly dying, which is to say, incessantly living and creating" (Soloveitchik 1976, 213). Okay, fair enough, but what does this fear of erasure produce in a historical people?

In this essay I explore in some detail the contours that exist between what I am proposing are two operational yet arguably incompatible categories of Jewish existence: survivalism and renewal. Both are to some extent driven by similar states of uneasiness or dissatisfaction with the present reality, be it the safety of the Jews or the solvency of Judaism. But they differ

---

1. B.t. *Shabbat* 138b and *Ketubot* 103b.
2. See the discussion of Rabbis Haninah and Hiyya in b.t. *Baba Meziah* 85b. This notion of the Torah being forgotten becomes a common trope in Jewish thinking. For example, when Rabbi Joseph Dov Soloveitchik discussed the contribution of his ancestor Rav Hayyim of Brisk to Torah scholarship, he wrote, "Were it not for him, Torah would have been forgotten from Israel" (Soloveitchik 1976, 213).

in that survivalism is a material concern, whereas renewal is a spiritual one. Survivalism sees everything, even or especially Judaism, as a means to a tangible end (surviving as a collective), whereas renewal fights against the obsolescence of religious practice and purpose. Renewal is not as obsessed with erasure as much as irrelevance, as survivalists paint us as no different from any other earthly creature. Survivalism feeds a natural instinct, whereas renewal nurtures a quest for purpose. In that sense, only renewal is particular to human beings. Both survivalism and renewal resist the present understood as a state that threatens the health of the collective, albeit for different reasons. Finally, both survivalism and renewal are embedded in the Hebrew Bible and rabbinic tradition and emerge in different iterations given specific social and political contexts throughout Jewish history.

My claim is that in our contemporary world survivalism and renewal have congealed as two different responses to the challenges of the post-modern and postsecular world, both in Israel and in the United States. And both take on secular and religious formations, often interlaying secularity with religion and vice versa, indicative of the postsecular moment.[3] Moreover, I argue that survivalism is more focused on the Jews and the collective (think of Jack Wertheimer's survivalist essay "What Happened to the Jewish People?"), whereas renewal is more focused on the individual and Judaism (Wertheimer 2006).[4] In that sense they serve opposite ends: physical continuity for survivalism and spiritual flourishing for renewal. Although there is certainly considerable overlap, these programs have different procedures and goals. I suggest that focus on survival serves as a foundation of American civil religion and has yielded the contemporary obsession with what has become known as continuity,[5] whereas renewal, which has its own history in modern Judaism, largely focuses on what postwar Jews have called *kiruv*, the move to bring Jews (as individuals) back to some form of tradition, a notion that has also yielded the rise of some nontraditional forms of Jewish piety. Even though the survival of Jews (survivalism) and the survival of Judaism (*kiruv* being one form) certainly overlap, with the survival of Judaism often used as a vehicle for the survival of the Jews, I suggest that the orientation

---

3. On postsecularism, see Habermas (2008).

4. On renewal's focus on the individual, George Wilkes said, "The more radical spiritual forms of Jewish renewal have been the most attentive to the needs of the individual in the face of the fragmentary nature of contemporary society" (Wilkes 2005, 118–19).

5. Here I am influenced by Woocher (1986), although I take issue with some of his conclusions.

of both forces are not identical and even serve countervailing anxieties that are worthy of exploration.

Jewish Survivalism

Perhaps it was Will Herberg who most succinctly, albeit somewhat histrionically, captured the American Jewish obsession with survival: "Never in all recorded history has the collapse of the hopes of a civilization taken place so suddenly, almost in the sight of one generation. . . . Our fathers were concerned with fashioning the good life; for us today, the all-absorbing problem is life itself, bare survival" (Herberg 1951, 3).

What is Jewish survivalism? To begin to answer this question, one must differentiate between survivalism in America and that in Israel in the postwar period, as each collective faced different sets of challenges even as they increasingly became intertwined after 1967 and 1973 and then, of late, have arguably become more distinct. My focus is on American Jewry. In the 1980s Jewish sociologists began reassessing the survivalist motivations behind Jewish institutions in America. Jonathan Woocher offers this assessment in a 1983 essay.

Assuming that "Jewish survivalism" has become the ideology of American Jewish leadership, how is it expressed concretely in that leadership's perceptions of communal problems, its priorities for the allocation of communal resources and energies, and its definitions of what it means to be a Jew on a personal behavioral level? Does survivalism have clear and constant implications in these areas that will enable us not only to speak in broad terms of a "turning inward" but also to define the specific patterns of concern likely to shape the communal agenda and of Jewish identity likely to be reflected among community leaders? (Woocher 1983, 291–92).

Woocher's point, one that he develops further in *Sacred Survival: The Civil Religion of American Jews* (1986), is that by the late twentieth century the notion of survival had become a kind of American civil religion: "Ensuring that survival has become the polity's and civil religion's consuming passion . . . Jewish survival is what the Jewish polity is about. Commitment to Jewish survival is an unqualified demand of its civil religion" (Woocher 1986, 72–73). Tradition is certainly one of the tools of this survivalist project, but what is being "saved" is not Torah but the Jews. Although Woocher notes that survival must be "creative survival" and "meaningful survival" and that the Torah is used to protect the Jews from assimilation, the subject of this American project is still arguably the physical survival of the Jews (74). In 1955 Will Herberg argued in *Protestant, Catholic, Jew* that religion was losing its hold on American Jews and that without it there would be nothing left to keep the Jewish collective afloat. Therefore they had to find "religion" or they would likely disappear. Jewish socialism could not easily maintain itself without a shared Jewish language (Yiddish) and basic Jewish literacy, both of which American Jews did not have in sufficient numbers.[6]

Herberg was right in his diagnosis but wrong in his prognosis. By the 1960s religion largely ceased serving as the predominant anchor of American Jewish identity. Most American Jews were, and remain, secular. American civil religion is largely a "religion without theology" (Herberg and Dalen 1989, 91–94). But many Jews remained identifiably Jewish nonetheless, and by the late 1960s, largely as a result of the focus on minority communal needs of the Great Society, the New Left, the movement for Soviet Jewry, the rise of the Black nationalist movement, and second-wave feminism in the early 1970s, many young Jews began rethinking their Jewish identity (Staub 2004).[7] Included in this mix is the Six Day War, which, aside from the anxiety of survival, put Israel on the radar of many American Jews.

This renewed interest in Jewish identity did not necessarily mean a return to traditional religion, although the *baal teshuva* movement in the 1970s does constitute part of what I am calling this survivalist turn, even though it may be closer to the renewal model I discuss later (Danzinger 1989). Like other minorities, especially after the celebrated TV series *Roots* in 1972, Jews began a slow process of disassimilation, not as a rejection of their Americanism or secularism but as a move toward a renewed identity that was more perspectival rather than rooted in belief.[8] The crowd around *Commentary Magazine* is but one form, preceding the rise of neoconservatism, which was not a "Jewish movement" but was certainly influenced by Jews and their newfound Jewishness (Balient 2010). Another form of survivalism enveloped in identity that arose at about the same time was Meir

---

6. We must recall that Herberg began as a Marxist and only later found his Judaism (Herberg and Dalen 1989).

7. On the relationship between Jewish identity and Black nationalism, see Dollinger (2018), Forman (1998), and Sundquist (2009).

8. The hyphenated American and the notion of ethnic pride became a major issue during this period (Jacobson 2006, 206–311).

Kahane's Jewish Defense League.[9] Originally founded to protect Jews at risk in inner-city neighborhoods in New York City, Kahane's larger program was to instill a renewed pride in being Jewish, using the term *hadar* (beauty) to inspire Jewish pride, what he also called, borrowing from the Black nationalists, "Jewish power" (Kahane 1975, 175–226; Sundquist 2009, 311–80). The focus in these and other iterations of renewed Jewish survivalist identity was a conception of Jewish ethnicity more than of Judaism as a religion. "Being Jewish" was exercising one's birthright and not necessarily fidelity to a divine calling. Religious acts such as wearing a *kippah* were often adopted by these new ethnocentrists but functioned more like the black beret of the Black Panthers than the religious articles of religious Jews. It said to the world, "I am a proud Jew. Deal with it!"[10]

The centerpiece of this new identitarian ethnocentrism was in part a response to anti-Semitism. The anti-Semitism of some on the New Left pushed some onetime Jewish liberals to the right and helped give birth to neoconservatism.[11] The anti-Semitism in the Black nationalist movement that became national news with the Ocean Hill–Brownsville, Brooklyn, teachers strike in 1968, covered in *The New York Times*, gave birth to the Jewish Defense League and soon made Kahane a household name.[12]

My point here is to argue that the rise of positive Jewish identity among many young American Jews in the 1960s and 1970s was based on three principles. First, it was very much in line with post–New Left America more generally; these newly proud Jews were following an American trend. Second, it was secular in orientation, although its use of religious articles and symbols (e.g., the *kippah* or the Star of David) already gestured toward a kind of postsecularism. And third, it was founded on physical survival, the projected fear of annihilation that resonated with the Holocaust, the plight of Soviet Jews, and the Six Day War. The subheading of the Jewish Defense

9. For perhaps the best study of the Jewish Defense League, see Dolgin (1977). For a massive documentary history of the group until 1981, see Russ (1981).

10. This focus on survivalism was not solely the province of the Jewish right represented by Kahane. Those on the Jewish left in the late 1960s and early 1970s who were resisting the New Left's cosmopolitanism in favor of a newfound sense of Jewish identity also sometimes sounded a survivalist chord. See, for example, Kenan (1973, 60).

11. The birth of neoconservatism is a much more complex phenomenon. I only want to point out the role of anti-Semitism as part of its construction (Vaisse 2011).

12. Kahane was a guest on many national talk shows and merited an interview in *Playboy* in October 1972. A *Life* magazine poll in the early 1970s showed that one in four American Jews polled had a positive opinion of the Jewish Defense League.

League advertisement, "We are talking about Jewish survival," captured a sentiment that was much larger than Kahane's small group of hooligans; it became, as Woocher argues, a kind of American Jewish civil religion and to my mind drove the increasing urgency of what is now called continuity, a gentler and more sober alternative to "survival." In practice, however, I think in our less tumultuous times, continuity is merely a substitute for survival.

Although Woocher focused on the ways that Jewish institutional life began to alter its programming to procure this new survivalism in the 1960s and although at about the same time Kahane began to advocate violence as a tactic of identity formation to raise "tough Jews," Jews whom the Gentile would fear, other consequences of Jewish survivalism in America require further exploration.[13] Suffice it to say that one of the components that interests me here is the extent to which survivalism demotes religion to an auxiliary place in the life of the Jew. It is not that religion plays no role; rather, it is that religion serves the physical survival of the Jews often, albeit not always, to the diminishment of Judaism as a system of beliefs and practices. If the goal is the physical survival of the Jews at all costs, religion will take any form that will ensure that goal.

But when did Jews become obsessed with their physical survival separate from the survival of Torah? And why should Jews survive?[14] Woocher notes that "civil Judaism does not often speak at length about why Jewish survival is important; the validity of the goal is given" (Woocher 1986, 75). But it is certainly legitimate to ask when the survival of the Jews became separated from the survival of Torah and whether Torah can be strengthened even if the Jewish people become smaller.[15] Even Rawidowicz's narrative of the ever-dying Jew has the Jew and Torah intertwined. But by the time we get to late-twentieth-century America, where, as Will Herberg predicted in his *Protestant, Catholic, Jew*, American Judaism has given way to ethnic identity, it seems that, though Torah has not been forgotten, it is relegated to a second-class status, a vehicle for other ends: the physical survival of the Jews. Contemporary uses of the term *continuity* refer mostly to the continuation of the Jewish people, not necessarily the continuation of Torah.

---

13. The tough Jew motif extended far beyond, and preceded, Kahanism (Breines 1990).
14. Rabbi Michael Goldberg in fact wrote a book asking this very question (Goldberg 1996).
15. On this second question, see my response to Wertheimer and Cohen (2014) at http://zeek .forward.com/articles/118426/.

Charles Liebman, one of the most astute observers of American Jewry in the postwar period, argued that American Jews are caught in a double bind that manifests as perennial ambivalence founded on the pursuit of ostensibly contradictory ends.[16] On the one hand, "Americanness" is viewed as a virtue that has attained almost doctrinal status (Feingold 1991, 71). On the other hand, survival as a distinct unit in American Jewish society—the fight against assimilation—often views that very Americanness with some suspicion (see, e.g., Lang 2005; Sarna 1998). For example, most American Jews would vociferously oppose any legislation prohibiting Jews from marrying non-Jews in America. Not only would that be anti-Semitic, but it also would arguably make Jews less than American. And yet they want Jews *not* to marry non-Jews, and Jewish institutions pour enormous resources toward that end. That is, many American Jews want to live in a society where Jews *can* marry non-Jews yet choose not to. Although not an unsolvable contradiction, it certainly needs to be theorized more carefully because it is simply one aspect of a built-in ambivalence of the American Jewish experience. What I will argue later is that this ambivalence, born from seemingly contradictory aspirations, manifests differently in different social settings. I have suggested survival and renewal, or continuity and *kiruv*, as terms to describe the fluctuation of this ambivalence and map its territory. Even though both always remain operational, American Jewish leaders and institutions turn from one to the other depending on how they view the challenges (real or contrived) of their present station in history.

Jewish Renewal

Turning to the concept of renewal in Judaism, I examine its articulation in two sources: Martin Buber's 1911 essay "Renewal of Judaism" and Zalman Schachter-Shalomi's notion of paradigm shift Judaism (Buber 1967, 34–55; 1999, 30–34). Writing decades apart, Buber and Schachter-Shalomi offer overlapping but distinctive visions of renewal that help us to better understand renewal as it functions in today's world.

Perhaps the earliest extended discussion of renewal in modern Judaism is Mortiz Lazarus's (1824–1903) slim volume *Renewal of Judaism* (Wilkes

---

16. David Biale calls this phenomenon "double consciousness" (borrowing the term from W. E. B. DuBois), which is distinct from the more European notion of "dual allegiance" (Biale 1998, 18).

2005, 114–25; Biemann 2009, 63–105). Lazarus's study is little more than a classic German Reform call to reinstate "prophetic Judaism," something Buber found wholly unsatisfactory in large part because, for Buber, Lazarus's focus on faith rather than deed missed the point of renewal entirely. Buber was certainly a fan of the prophets and renewing the prophetic spirit, but the Reform articulation of "ethical monotheism" was not to his liking.[17] This is one reason I think Buber turned to Hasidism as the necessary compendium to prophetic theology.[18]

I am particularly interested in how Buber's concept of renewal in "Renewal of Judaism" contributes to the more contemporary discussion at the end of the twentieth and beginning of the twenty-first century, especially regarding the relationship between the collective and the individual, between survival and renewal. Buber sometimes uses the word *renaissance*, borrowing the term from his mentor Ahad Ha'am, but in the 1911 essay he switches to *renewal*, which may speak to Nietzsche's early influence on him. Buber begins his essay by distinguishing between evolutionary and revolutionary models of Jewish existence.[19] The distinction is really between preservation and transformation. Preservation is more accustomed to an evolutionary process in which change is regulated so as not to upset the rhythm of normative Jewish existence. Transformation, on the other hand, is an act that is willing to subvert convention for the sake of seeking the roots of the tradition, often buried as a result of the historical exigencies that survival requires. Renewal for Buber is about the possibility of "an ontological sense of inner origin," a return to authentic being (Batnitzky 2003, 346).

Preservation, as Buber presents it, functions similarly to survivalism, as I articulated it earlier, in that it maintains the most basic element of existence necessary to ensure continuity. One could point to the concept of ethnicity as an example. Being Jewish today often boils down to the womb one inhabited. Renewal, on the other hand, is conceived as a radical intervention to

---

17. See Buber (2015). Buber's disdain for Reform Judaism goes quite deep (Biemann 2001, 58–87).
18. On Buber's turn to Hasidism, see Urban (2008, 116–55). In his essay "Jewish Renewal," George Wilkes notes that before the eighteenth century we have no real reference to anything that can be construed as Jewish renewal (Wilkes 2005).
19. Much of Buber's work is founded on a series of dichotomies, for example, I/Thou and myth/history, but he doesn't quite get stuck in binaries but rather works with these dichotomies to offer innovative readings of their interrelation (Shapira 1999, 17–40; Batnitzky 2003, 338).

the very definition of what it means to be a Jew, not focused primarily on saving, or even defining, the Jewish people per se but rather directed toward liberating and transforming Judaism from a state of atrophy to a state of vitality.[20] This intervention might in the short run be detrimental to survival, as its radical nature can be alienating and certainly unsettling to many who have become accustomed to the status quo of continuity. As a cultural Zionist, Buber envisioned renewal in collectivist terms. Yet the changes renewal would bring could affect, and even alter, the collective through a spiritual process that he believed reached the essence of Jewish existence. For him, renewal had three components: "the idea of unity, the idea of the deed, and the idea of the future (messianism)" (Buber 1967, 40).

One of the great examples of renewal in Judaism for Buber is the Jesus movement, whose renewal he believed reemerged again in a different form in Hasidism: "At the same time, however, the ritual law became more rigid and alienated from life, whereupon the movement spread from the self-segregated communities to the very core of the people and set ablaze the revolution of ideas that today, erroneously and misleadingly, is called early, original Christianity . . . but it [Christianity] flickered and burned around the becrowned corpse of the law, until another great movement arrived, a movement that cut to the very core of truth and stirred the very core of the people: Hasidism" (Buber 1967, 46–48). Both original Christianity and early Hasidism were renewals for Buber because they embodied what was for him the core of Judaism: "the unconditionally of the deed," the ability to use the deed as a vehicle of devotion (*devotio*) and not sacrament, the deed as the path toward an expression of divine unity. Thus Buber takes seriously Jesus's claim in Matthew 5:17 that he does not come to abolish the law but to fulfill it. And its fulfilment is never solely about creating something new but also about restoring the old, "to release it [the law] from the straits of prescriptions that had become meaningless, in order to free it for the holiness of an active relationship with God, for a religiosity of the deed" (Buber 1967, 46).[21]

---

20. In *I and Thou* Buber sees himself as writing his renewal works during a "time of sickness," where society has lost its sense of connectedness to the absolute (Buber 1958, 53). Batnitzky notes that here Buber shares much with Heidegger's notion of the "existential sickness" of humanity resulting from the adherence to modern philosophy that has forgotten experience and favored pure cognition (Batnitzky 2003, 344).

21. The notion of the new as a restoration of the ancient is an old trope in Jewish mysticism. See Matt (1993, 181–207).

Renewal for Buber is always future oriented (hence it is by definition messianic) but not in a survivalist mode: "The next generation, even before it becomes conscious of itself, is in turn charged with the task of taking care of still another generation, so that all reality of existence is dissolved in the care of the future" (Buber 1967, 50). This future is never in doubt but is rather "the fullness of time." It is the future that is promised; the Talmudic adage that God will not allow the Jewish people to disappear is taken seriously. The only question is when they will reach their fulfillment. This notion of messianism as the promise of the absolute future in some sense makes survivalism superfluous, because survivalism, on a base level, always casts the future in doubt, giving birth to the anxiety of survival. Buber's messianic future has no anxiety of survival; in fact, it is built on the *promise* of survival. Authentic futurity for Buber "must originate in [the] deeper recesses of the people's spirit, where the great tendencies of Judaism were once born" (Buber 1967, 53). Jews certainly matter but are not intrinsic to themselves. Rather, in a renewal mode they are carriers of a world spirit that promises an absolute future. Original Christianity understood this, even if, on Buber's count, it erred in other ways. The prophets did as well. As did the Hasidic masters. For Buber, the rabbis of the Talmud were the ones who ossified the deed in the act of obligation (the sacrament of the law), understandably to create a coherent community that could physically survive, but the price was that the spirit could not bear the weight of such survival, and renewal in the form of Christianity, Sabbateanism, and later Hasidism emerged.[22] On this reading, renewal is sometimes, perhaps even often, a reaction against survivalism.

Survival in general is wed to tactics. What can we do to prevent physical harm or spiritual erasure through assimilation? What can we *do* to survive? This was certainly the program of one of the first proponents of modern Jewish survivalism, Meir Kahane. Renewal is more of an act of spiritual resistance. It seeks to transform Judaism and thus is not primarily tactical. Buber claims that "Judaism can't be renewed in bits and pieces. Renewal must be all of one piece"; it is not an attitude that looks inward toward preservation, as survival often does, but one that looks outward, "a new attitude toward the world" (Buber 1967, 54). Alternatively, it is precisely *renewal* that looks inward, in the way that Jakob Burckhardt claimed that the Italian

---

22. Leora Batnitzky puts it this way: "Buber adds a more particular claim that rabbinism and Jewish law represent objectifying forces that, like modern philosophy and the modern study of history, cut off the life force of being itself" (Batnitzky 2003, 345).

Renaissance was an inward-looking movement (see, e.g., Burckhardt 1990, 98–119). For Buber too, renewal looks inward, not toward preservation but rather toward the authentic self, toward the inner being of Judaism. Survival, on this reading, gazes *outward*, not to embrace the world but to protect Jews from the dangers of the world. Continuity is then an outward-looking phenomenon, asking, How can we preserve ourselves outwardly? Its questions may be existential, but they are not ontological. Although religious symbols and even practice are part of its toolbox, its goals are in this sense antithetical to renewal.

Survival and continuity ask how we can maintain stability. Renewal is about instability, shaking the foundations that invariably will have a price with regard to maintenance. Although renewal may be holistic ("Renewal must be all of one piece"), it can never hope to be all-inclusive. It will always be an alternative that segments of society will reject. Renewal never takes everything with it, wherever it goes. I think this is implied in Buber's notion of renewal's futurity. It is always looking beyond where it is. The tactics of survival are much more presentist, what must we do *now* to make sure we survive *now*. In that sense survivalism has no messianism and thus undermines, for Buber anyway, one of the precepts of Judaism. For survivalists the future is not about transformation but about simply *being there*. It is a materialist nonmessianic notion of the future. Any movement of renewal for Buber sees its job as future oriented: How can I transform the status quo in a way that will move our project more toward its fulfillment? Jews are certainly the carriers of that project, but they are not its subject. Mistakes will be made, and as I discuss later, pietistic heresy is the occupational hazard of any renewal. But as Jonathan Z. Smith said, "Exaggeration on the path to truth is progress" (Smith 1978, 308). As we will presently see with Schachter-Shalomi, his vision of renewal follows Buber but takes a much more global and less national perspective.

Moving from Buber's "Renewal of Judaism" to the Jewish Renewal movement founded by Zalman Schachter-Shalomi in the 1970s constitutes, historically speaking, a fairly short span of time. But in reality what stands in between are arguably two of the most significant moments in post–70 CE Jewish history: the Holocaust and the founding of the State of Israel. Buber was responding in part to the increasingly dire situation of the Jews in Europe while trying to keep alive the spirit of Eastern European Hasidism that was still aflame in his youth. He viewed Zionism as a kind of renewal, an exercise in spiritual collectivism. Here he was part of a larger circle that included the likes of Hillel Zeitlin and Gustav Landauer, who offered very different but also overlapping visions of Jewish renewal.[23] Buber reconstructed Hasidic spirituality by merging it with socialism to create a radical political theology, thus bringing Buber solidly into the Zionist orbit of his time even as he remained a sharp critic of hypernationalism and the hazards of political Zionism.[24] For Buber, the nucleus of renewal was the experiment of Jewish sovereignty in its homeland. He surprisingly wrote little about the Holocaust, although Richard Rubenstein's *After Auschwitz* (1966) was published a year after Buber's death. But the collapse and subsequent destruction of European Jewry certainly had an impact on Buber's theological work.

Schachter-Shalomi grew up in Vienna but spent his teen years in Belgium and later France during the war. He spent time in a displaced persons camp in Marseilles after liberation (where he first met a young Chabad rabbi named Menachem Mendel Schneerson, who would later become the seventh Lubavitcher rebbe) until his family secured passage to America through the Caribbean (Schachter-Shalomi 2012, 13–52). In a response to my essay "Between Paradigm Shift Judaism and Neo-Hasidism," dictated a few days before his passing—a kind of final and brief offering of his life's work—Schachter-Shalomi wrote the following (Magid 2015, 11–22): "Elsewhere I have pointed out in the strongest terms how the Holocaust, the moon walk, and seeing Earth from outer space created an immense shift in consciousness for us. After these events, the reality map we had used up until that time could no longer be maintained. Since then we have been forced to rearrange the way in which we integrate the magisterium of Torah with the emerging cosmology" (Schachter-Shalomi 2015, 16).[25]

There is much to say about these few lines, which suggest a distinction between Buber and Schachter-Shalomi's visions of renewal, that will become relevant to our discussion. The reach from the Holocaust to the moon walk and photos of the Earth as a beautiful blue ball floating in space captures Schachter-Shalomi's spiritual and theological reach. Many of the responses to the Holocaust—Zionism and the creation of the State of Israel being two

---

23. For a collection of Zeitlin's writings in translation, see Zeitlin (2012). On Landauer, see Mendes-Flohr and Mali (2014).
24. See, for example, Buber's letters to Ben Gurion and his letters on Zionism, Arabs, and Jewish nationalism collected and introduced by Mendes-Flohr (2005).
25. On reality maps, see Schachter-Shalomi (2013, 299–308) and Magid (2013, 57–73).

of them (even though Zionism preceded the Holocaust)—looked inward toward a survivalism that is captured in the title of Meir Kahane's breakout book *"Never Again!"* or in Ruth Wisse's *Jews and Power* (Wisse 2007). In a different register, for Buber, Zionism's new collectivism held the potential for a Jewish cultural and spiritual renaissance. Another model might be David Hartman, who argued in his essay "Auschwitz or Sinai?" that although the memory of the Holocaust looms large over the entire Zionist project, we cannot allow it to become what drives it forward (Hartman 2013).

Buber and Hartman both constitute a form of Jewish renewal. Although Schachter-Shalomi also viewed the State of Israel as beneficial for the Jews, he saw the Holocaust through the lens of the floating Earth in space. That is, we all must coexist on this fragile planet and our religion(s) must reflect that new reality map. Inwardness was not the answer. Survivalism was not the answer.[26] Rather, Schachter-Shalomi's answer was in some sense the reverse, what was called in New Age jargon "Gaia consciousness." That is, a belief that the Earth is a living organism and we are all part of that organic life and must collectively contribute to its well-being (see, e.g., Lovelock 2016).[27] Adopting the notion of an age of Aquarius, Schachter-Shalomi believed we lived on the cusp of a changing paradigm that would require a radical revision of our religion, as was done in previous ages (Pisces, Taurus, etc.). Reality maps are lenses and ways we understand our world and our relationship to God or the gods. Reality maps are also the lenses through which we create, and then change and adapt, our religion. The devastation of the Holocaust in 1945 and the exuberance and almost miraculous nature of the moon landing in 1969 were the two points from which a new reality map was formed; the first was an attempt to destroy a human population through genocide, and the second was the reality of the Jews being a part of a global community.

Like Buber, but toward different ends, Schachter-Shalomi also found Hasidism a vital tool to construct his version of renewal. He certainly read Buber's work on Hasidism carefully and was influenced by his thinking. For Schachter-Shalomi, Hasidism had to be turned inside out, literally and metaphorically. In what he called "the fourth turning of Hasidism," he believed

26. Buber also did not envision his Zionism as survivalism but rather as a project of Jewish renewal that could produce a new kind of Jewish life, culture, and spirituality through collective sovereignty. See the essays collected in Buber (1997).
27. Schachter-Shalomi was influenced by Lovelock's work as a foundation for his paradigm shift Judaism.

that we had entered a new phase in human history in which Judaism would become a world religion.[28] To do so, it would have to rethink its notion of triumphalism (divine election) and its relationship to the law that separates the Jew from the non-Jew (resulting in the renewal movement's version of "post-halakhic" or "post-triumphalist" Judaism) and separate devotion from legalism. That is, Schachter-Shalomi conceived Jewish devotion as an art form and not a legal science.[29] Like Buber, Schachter-Shalomi rejected Reform's accommodationalist renewal and preferred a renewal that understood the need for a radical spiritual transformation that was systemic and could provide Jews with a meaningful spiritual practice that was beyond legalism (traditional Halakha) and would not exclude non-Jews. The need to preserve the integrity of the collective as a conduit to expand outward to the world was an expression of what begins with the Holocaust and ends with the iconic photo of the Earth from space.

In his final written words, Schachter-Shalomi suggests that perhaps "paradigm shift" is "misleading as it suggests an abrupt shift from one reality map to another. I would rather emphasize an 'axial turning,' the process of shifting and the long arc of transition from one paradigm to another—with people at the leading edge, people still very much connected to the past, and a vast multitude in the middle" (Schachter-Shalomi 2012, 16). This appears to pull back from the more radical Age of Aquarius Judaism that dominated the late 1960s and early 1970s and propelled him into his paradigm shift model, opting for a more inclusive notion of an axial turning, an idea first proffered by philosopher Karl Jaspers to describe global shifts in consciousness that happened simultaneously in disparate cultures. This axial turn would include those at the forefront of radical change as well as those holding onto an older paradigm and those who live largely unaware, and uninterested, in this progression. Schachter-Shalomi often said that if Lubavitch is God's army (ziva'ot Ha-Shem), Jewish renewal is God's CIA. That is, it works underground to cultivate change and create conditions for the new age. He envisioned Jewish renewal as spies for the Jewish future, not unlike the spies who were sent to scout out the land in Numbers 13.

---

28. Schachter-Shalomi describes this fourth turning in a short pamphlet published a few years before his death (Schachter-Shalomi and Miles-Yepez 2014).

29. On Schachter-Shalomi's noting of davening, viewing prayer as an artistic and aesthetic act, see Schachter-Shalomi and Segel (2012).

In these two instantiations of renewal in Judaism, the subject is Judaism and not the Jewish people. The Jewish people serve as the body on which Judaism is renewed. The survival of the Jewish people does not appear to be the central concern of either Buber or Schachter-Shalomi. Rather, each views the state of Judaism in their time as in need of radical reconceptualization because it failed to meet the needs of the time. By way of conclusion, in the final section I briefly return to continuity and *kiruv*, two practical and operative categories of survivalism and renewal.

Continuity and *Kiruv*

We did not hear the term *continuity* used much in American Jewish circles until the last decades of the twentieth century. Since then it has arguably become the central concern of American Jewry. In the opinion essay "What Do We Mean by Jewish Continuity?" (2015), Letty Cottin Pogrebin asks the classic survivalist question: "We all want Jewish grandchildren—but are we going about it the right way?" She then quotes Adin Steinsaltz, who doubles down on the survivalist fear by making the provocative claim that "a Jew is not one whose grandparents are Jewish but one who wants his or her grandchildren to be Jewish" (L. C. Pogrebin 2015). Stated otherwise, Jewishness is not (only) determined through lineage but by the extent to which one enacts a survivalism that will do everything in its power to ensure such lineage continues. If you are not focused on Jewish survival, your Jewishness is blemished. Pogrebin correctly notes that this survivalism that we now call continuity is in large part driven by increasing rates of intermarriage. Organizations such as Birthright Israel are devoted to this survival and continuity project. Its goal is not to present its members with any real meaningful religious practice or new vision of Judaism. Its stated goal is to offer young American Jews a short and intense Israel experience so that when they return to their lives in America, there will be an increased chance they will marry a Jew (Kelner 2012, 21–46, 191–206). Pogrebin suggests that the Jewish community needs to offer "attractive, visible programs that will give them direct access to their heritage, as part of the lives they are leading right now," as opposed to boring religious school or moribund synagogues (think of the Coen brothers' *A Serious Man*) that are more likely to show young Jews the exit than give them an entry point to their heritage enough to commit to marrying one of the tribe. Statistical studies suggest that if those Jews who choose the exit marry Jewish, it will largely be by accident.

What is telling about Pogrebin's suggestions is that they offer no new vision of Judaism, no spirit of renewal, no futurity. They are practical suggestions to increase the likelihood of more Jewish grandchildren. They are survivalist in their tone and in their goals. This is true of many who weigh in on the continuity question. I chose to focus on Pogrebin because in the early 1970s she was part of a revolutionary movement known as second-wave feminism. She founded *Ms.* magazine. Pogrebin didn't just want equal pay; she wanted to change American society on the question of gender. And she and her colleagues were largely successful. But here we do not see any call to change, to revolutionize Jewish society. We see a call to creatively think of ways to enable young Jews to feel Jewish enough to marry Jews.[30] Survivalism will always be mired in the practicalities of perpetuating the tribe and, as a result, will often have nothing new to offer, no future vision for Judaism, no "messianism" (as Buber articulated it). On this reading the price of survival may be the future of Judaism. As a means toward a survivalist end, Judaism will become whatever is needed to procure that result, whatever is needed to enable Jews to feel just Jewish enough (but not too Jewish) to marry Jews. If the goal of survivalism is Jewish grandchildren, the price paid may be the obsolescence of renewal as an operative category.

In the early 1970s many young Jews, inspired by the ethnic revival of the times, began to encounter and explore Judaism in new ways. The project of *kiruv rekhokim* (bringing those alienated from Judaism back into the fold) initiated in large part by the vision of Rabbi Menachem Mendel Schneerson of Lubavitch became a cottage industry in both America and Israel. Special yeshivas for *baalei teshuva* (new returnees) were established; the Artscroll Press catered to newly religious Jews, and it all had a kind of messianic aura about it. Some seismic change seemed to be happening in the Jewish Diaspora that was not exclusively about Israel. Orthodoxy met the counterculture in Shlomo Carlebach's House of Love and Prayer in San Francisco.[31]

---

30. Interestingly, Pogrebin's daughter, Abigail Pogrebin, recently published a book that samples a variety of Jewish religious and cultural practices across America and is interested more in Judaism or how Jews "do" Judaism than in maximizing Jewish grandchildren. See A. Pogrebin (2017).

31. One of the reasons for the founding of the Aquarian Minyan in Berkeley was that some in the House of Love and Prayer were against the existence of the *mehiza*. On the House of Love and Prayer, see Coopersmith (2011, 11–80) and Ariel (2003, 139–65).

New forms of Judaism began to take form in Havurat Shalom in Somerville, Massachusetts, and Schachter-Shalomi's P'nei Or in Philadelphia. The three-volume *Jewish Catalogues* were published in the early 1970s, and the Manhattan Havurah and Fabrangen Minyan in Washington, DC, were thriving. What I find interesting in this new movement of *kiruv* in all its myriad forms is that it was not primarily about "continuity" in terms of the survival of Jews; it was about a renewal or revival of Judaism. Schneerson's messianic vision of Jews keeping mitzvot and Schachter-Shalomi's radical revision of Hasidism (its "fourth turning") and even the establishment of Artscroll Press, a Lithuanian "yeshivish" form of renewal, sought to revive new forms of Jewish life and practice for a generation who had become alienated from Judaism but were now seeking spiritual sustenance as a result of their exposure to the counterculture.

It is certainly true that when *kiruv* was fully operative in the 1970s, the intermarriage rates were climbing but had not reached the proportions of the 2013 Pew Poll (58%). But survivalism was not born solely from that empirical anxiety. Part of survivalism was born from the anxiety following the Six Day War in 1967 and the Yom Kippur War in 1973. Survivalism is not just a response to a real fear of extinction; it is also an exercise that creates that fear. And for survivalism to persist, fear needs to be continuously justified.

Kiruv and continuity have shared space in the American Jewish psyche for some time. They are often viewed as two expressions of a similar sentiment. Here I have argued that, in fact, both are expressions of quite different, often contradictory, sentiments. *Kiruv* is focused primarily on Judaism; continuity is focused primarily on Jews. *Kiruv* is generally not driven by any existential crisis but by a crisis of religious meaning. Continuity (or survivalism) is a response to an existential crisis, real or imagined, that is often envisioned as perennial.

Both renewal and survivalism have occupational hazards. The occupational hazard of renewal is heresy; the occupational hazard of survivalism/continuity is faithlessness. Renewal is always in danger of overextending itself, reaching too far and thus breaking too radically with the past. This is what I think underlies Schachter-Shalomi's walking back his paradigm shift in favor of axial turning in his final words before leaving us. Axial turning slows down the process of change, enabling it to be more transitional and more inclusive of those who do not hear its call to futurity. The danger of continuity is that it is too often founded on a fundamental lack of belief in the covenant, which includes a divine promise not to destroy the Jewish people. It is one kind of collective response to the Holocaust. The fear of erasure, except in specific circumstances, is to some extent a consequence of faithlessness. And when that disbelief becomes endemic to the entire project, when it becomes a foundation of American Jewish civil religion, the very notion of Jews' intrinsic value as carriers of the Torah is undermined. When religion becomes simply a tool of survival, it potentially loses its value as an end in itself.

As Jews continue onward in the twenty-first century, they will continue to confront the two models of survival and renewal as different models of thinking about the Jewish future. Understanding their differences, and the hazards that await each, may help those who will make collective decisions in the future better prepared to face the unknown realities.

References

Ariel, Yaakov. 2003. "Hasidism in the Age of Aquarius: The House of Love and Prayer in San Francisco, 1967–1977." *Religion and American Culture* 13(2): 139–65.

Balient, Benny. 2010. *Running Commentary: The Contentious Magazine That Transformed the Jewish Left into the Neoconservative Right*. New York: Public Affairs.

Batnitzky, Leora. 2003. "Renewing the Jewish Past: Buber on History and Truth." *Jewish Studies Quarterly* 10(4): 336–50.

Biale, David. 1998. "The Melting Pot and Beyond." In *Insider/Outsider: American Jews and Multiculturalism*, ed. D. Biale, S. Heschel, and M. Galinsky, 17–33. Berkeley: University of California Press.

Biemann, Asher. 2001. "The Problem of Tradition and Reform in Jewish Renaissance and Renaissancism." *Jewish Social Studies* 8(1): 58–87.

Biemann, Asher. 2009. *Inventing New Beginnings: On the Idea of Renaissance in Modern Judaism*. Stanford, CA: Stanford University Press.

Breines, Paul. 1990. *Tough Jews: Political Fantasies and the Moral Dilemma of American Jewry*. New York: Basic Books.

Buber, Martin. 1958. *I and Thou*, trans. R. G. Smith. New York: Charles Scribner's Sons.

Buber, Martin. 1967 [1911]. "Renewal of Judaism." In *On Judaism*, by Martin Buber, 34–55. New York: Schocken.

Buber, Martin. 1997. *On Zion: The History of an Idea*. Syracuse, NY: Syracuse University Press.

Buber, Martin. 1999. "Jewish Renaissance." In *The First Buber: Youthful Zionist Writings of Martin Buber*, ed. and trans. Gilya Schmidt, 30–34. New York: Syracuse University Press.

Buber, Martin. 2015. *The Prophetic Faith*. Princeton, NJ: Princeton University Press.

Burckhardt, Jacob. 1990. *The Civilization of the Renaissance in Italy*. New York: Penguin.

Coopersmith, Aryae. 2011. *Holy Beggars; A Journey from Haight Street to Jerusalem*. San Francisco: One World Lights.

Danzinger, Herbert, M. 1989. *Returning to Tradition: The Contemporary Revival of Orthodox Judaism*. New Haven, CT: Yale University Press.

Dolgin, Janet. 1977. *Jewish Identity and the JDL*. Princeton, NJ: Princeton University Press.

Dollinger, Marc. 2018. *Black Power/Jewish Politics*. Waltham, MA: Brandeis University Press.

Feingold, Henry. 1991. "The American Component of Jewish Identity." In *Jewish Identity in America*, ed. D. Gordis and Y. Ben-Horin, 69–80. Los Angeles: Wilstein Institute.

Forman, Seth. 1998. *Blacks in the Jewish Mind: A Crisis of Liberalism*. New York: NYU Press.

Goldberg, Michael. 1996. *Why Should the Jews Survive? Looking Past the Holocaust Toward a Jewish Future*. New York: Oxford University Press.

Habermas, Jurgen. 2008. "Notes on a Postsecular Society." *New Perspectives Quarterly* 25(4): 17–29.

Hartman, David. 2013 [1982]. "Auschwitz or Sinai?" Shalom Hartman Institute, February 1. https://www.hartman.org.il/auschwitz-or-sinai/.

Herberg, Will. 1951. *Judaism and Modern Man: An Interpretation of Jewish Religion*. Philadelphia: Jewish Publication Society.

Herberg, Will. 1955. *Protestant, Catholic, Jew*. New York: Doubleday.

Herberg, Will, and David Dalen. 1989. *From Marxism to Judaism: The Collected Essays of Will Herberg*. Princeton, NJ: Marcus Weiner.

Jacobson, Matthew Frye. 2006. *Roots Too: White Ethnic Revival in Post–Civil Rights America*. Cambridge, MA: Harvard University Press.

Kahane, Meir. 1972. *Never Again*. New York: Pyramid Books.

Kahane, Meir. 1975. *The Story of Jewish Defense League*. Hawthorne, CA: BN Publishing.

Kelner, Shaul. 2012. *Tours That Bind: Diaspora, Pilgrimage, and Israeli Birthright Tourism*. New York: NYU Press.

Kenan, Amos. 1973. "To All Good People." In *Jewish Radicalism*, ed. Jack Porter and Peter Drier, 55–63. New York: Grove Press.

Lang, Berel. 2005. "Hyphenated Jews and the Anxiety of Identity." *Jewish Social Studies* 12(1): 1–15.

Lazarus, Moritz. 1909. *Renewal of Judaism*. Berlin: Georg Reimer.

Lovelock, James. 2016. *Gaia: A New Look at Life on Earth*. New York: Oxford University Press.

Magid, Shaul. 2013. *American Post-Judaism*. Bloomington: Indiana University Press.

Magid, Shaul. 2015. "Between Paradigm Shift Judaism and Neo-Hasidism." *Tikkun* 30 (winter): 11–22.

Matt, Daniel. 1993. "'New-Ancient Words': The Aura of Secrecy in the Zohar." In *Gershom Scholem's Major Trends in Jewish Mysticism 50 Years After: Proceedings of the Sixth International Conference on the History of Jewish Mysticism*, ed. Joseph Dan and Peter Schäfer, 181–208. Tubingen: Mohr Siebeck.

Mendes-Flohr, Paul. 2005. *A Land of Two Peoples: Martin Buber of Jews and Arabs*. Chicago: University of Chicago Press.

Mendes-Flohr, Paul, and Anya Mali. 2014. *Gustav Landauer: Anarchist and Jew*. Berlin: De Gruyter Oldenbourg.

Pogrebin, Abigail. 2017. *My Jewish Year: 18 Holidays, One Wandering Jew*. Bedford, NY: Fig Tree Books.

Pogrebin, Letty Cottin. 2015. "What Do We Mean by Jewish Continuity?" *Moment Magazine*, November 3, 2015. https://momentmag.com/opinion-what-do-we-mean-by-jewish-continuity/.

Rawidowicz, Simon. 1986. *Israel: An Ever-Dying People and Other Essays*. Madison, NJ: Fairleigh Dickenson University Press.

Rubenstein, Richard. 1966. *After Auschwitz*. New York: Macmillan.

Russ, Shlomo. 1981. "The 'Zionist Hooligans': The Jewish Defense League." PhD diss., CUNY.

Sarna, Jonathan. 1998. "The Cult of Synthesis in American Jewish Culture." *Jewish Social Studies* 5(1–2): 52–79.

Schachter-Shalomi, Zalman. 2012. *My Life in Jewish Renewal: A Memoir*. Lexington, KY: Rowman & Littlefield.

Schachter-Shalomi, Zalman. 2013. *Paradigm Shift: From the Jewish Renewal Teachings of Reb Zalman Schachter-Shalomi*, ed. Ellen Singer. Lanham, MD: Jason Aronson.

Schachter-Shalomi, Zalman. 2015. "Jewish Renewal: Building Closeness to God." *Tikkun* 30 (winter): 16. https://doi.org/10.1215/08879982-2834058.

Schachter-Shalomi, Zalman, and Netanel Miles-Yepez. 2014. *Foundation of the Fourth Turning of Hasidism: A Manifesto*. Boulder, CO: Albion-Andalus Books.

Schachter-Shalomi, Zalman, and Joel Segel. 2012. *Davening: A Guide to Meaningful Jewish Prayer*. Woodstock, VT: Jewish Lights.

Shapira, Avraham. 1999. *Hope for Our Time: Key Trends in the Thought of Martin Buber*, trans. Jeffrey M. Green. Albany: SUNY Press.

Smith, Jonathan Z. 1978. *Map Is Not Territory: Studies in the History of Religions*. Chicago: University of Chicago Press.

Soloveitchik, Joseph, B. 1976. "Mah Dodekh me-Dod." In *Be-Sod Ha-Yahid ve Ha-Yahad*, ed. Pinhas Peli, 189–254. Jerusalem: Orot.

Staub, Michael E. 2004. *Torn at the Roots: The Crisis in Jewish Liberalism in Postwar America*. New York: Columbia University Press.

Sundquist, Eric. 2009. "Black Power, Jewish Power." In *Strangers in the Land: Blacks, Jews, Post-Holocaust America*, by Eric Sundquist, 311–81. Cambridge, MA: Harvard University Press.

Urban, Martina. 2008. *Aesthetics of Renewal: Martin Buber's Early Representation of Hasidism as Kulturkritic*. Chicago: University of Chicago Press.

Vaisse, Justin. 2011. *Neoconservatism: A Biography of a Movement*. Cambridge, MA: Harvard University Press.

Wertheimer, Jack. 2006. "What Happened to the Jewish People?" *Commentary Magazine*, June 1. https://www.commentarymagazine.com/articles/jack-wertheimer/whatever-happened-to-the-jewish-people/.

Wertheimer, Jack, and Steven Cohen. 2014. "Why the Jewish Now (and Future) Can't Be Confined to the Paradigms of the Past." *Zeek*, November 20. http://zeek.forward.com/articles/118426/.

Wilkes, George, R. 2005. "Jewish Renewal." In *Modern Judaism: An Oxford Guide*, ed. Nicolas de Lange and Miri Freud-Kandel, 114–26. New York: Oxford University Press.

Wisse, Ruth, R. 2007. *Jews and Power*. New York: Schocken.

Woocher, Jonathan. 1983. "Jewish Survivalism as Communal Ideology: An Empirical Assessment." *Journal of Jewish Communal Service* 54(4): 291–92.

Woocher, Jonathan. 1986. *Sacred Survival: The Civil Religion of American Jews*. Bloomington: Indiana University Press.

Zeitlin, Hillel. 2012. *Hasidic Spirituality for a New Era: The Religious Writings of Hillel Zeitlin*, trans. Arthur Green and Joel Rosenberg. Mahwah, NJ: Paulist Press.

3

Jewish. Jewish? "Jewish" Jewish!

New Authenticities amid Post-Holocaust, Postcommunist Europe's Jewish Revival

Ruth Ellen Gruber

In April 2018 the Jewish Telegraphic Agency ran an article whose headline read "In Kraków, Jews Celebrate Their Community's 'Revival' amid Rising Xenophobia" (Liphshiz 2018). Putting the word *revival* in quotes, both in the headline and also in the body of the article itself, appeared—at least to this reader—to call into question or in some way even disparage a phenomenon that those of us who have chronicled or participated in Jewish developments since or even before the fall of communism in 1989–1990 have in many ways felt was by now a given—a still fragile given, perhaps, and one whose eventual outcome is still unknown, but a given nonetheless. It gave me pause, however. The article was written by a 30-something Israel-born grandson of an Auschwitz survivor who little more than a year earlier had written about his own anti-Polish bias as a Jewish journalist (Liphshiz 2017). He probably was not even born when I made my first reporting forays to the then-moribund Communist-era Jewish communities in Romania, Bulgaria, Hungary, and elsewhere in the late 1970s—an era when the Jewish presence in Central and Eastern Europe was basically considered a closed chapter. That was a time when anything written about Jews in that part of

This essay is an updated version of a paper presented at a June 2013 conference organized by the editors, "The Jewish Revival in Europe and North America: Between Lifestyle Judaism and Institutional Renaissance." It does not encompass a full treatment of the most recent developments.

the world included some variant of the words *last* or *final*. There was the exhibition and photographic essay by Laurence Salzmann, "The Last Jews of Radauti" (1976); the text and photo book by Chuck Fishman and Earl Vinocour, *Polish Jews: The Final Chapter* (1977); and later, *Remnants: The Last Jews of Poland*, by Malgorzata Niezabitowska and Tomasz Tomaszewski (1986), not to mention *The Last Jews of Eastern Europe* (1987) by Yale Strom and Brian Blue. One exception might be the special exhibit on Communist Hungary's contemporary Jewish community, mounted in the summer of 1983 at the state Ethnographic Museum in Budapest. Called "And Tell This to Your Sons," the show included about 100 color photographs by award-winning Budapest photographer Tamás Féner and resulted in a book by the same name, published in several languages. I wrote at the time, "It portrays a hidden but vibrant life most Hungarians have no idea exists" (Gruber 1983).

Things have changed dramatically since those days. Since the early 1990s, the ongoing transformations in this region have taken its Jews and their non-Jewish compatriots on an extraordinary—and, given the previous half-century, unexpected—ride. What we call the Jewish revival has taken different forms at different speeds in different countries, depending on local history and conditions. Changes are still going on, influenced both from within Jewish realities and from without.

What is clear, however, is that the idea of Jewish revival is not strictly tied to numbers of people. The Holocaust happened—more than three generations ago—and it was followed by decades of repression (or suppression) under communism. This in turn was followed by a postcommunist mass exodus of Jews from the former Soviet Union. The number of Jews in most of Europe, particularly Eastern and Central Europe, represents a mere small fraction of those who lived in this region before the Shoah. It is also clear that normal demographics—births, deaths, intermarriage, migration—mean that many of the small Jewish communities that exist today, regardless of whether they are dynamically "active" or irrevocably dwindling, will not manage to survive.

But revival means more than physical bodies. In addition to regenerated Jewish communal life, there has been a revival of attitudes, of concepts, of identity, of possibility, of recognition—among Jews but also in mainstream society. A revival of awareness, of creativity, of options. Most basically, per-haps, a revival of consciousness—consciousness of history, consciousness of heritage, consciousness of identity, consciousness of memory. But con-sciousness, too, of the challenges and pitfalls, of the still fluid present, of a future whose course is still in flux. This too forms part of the general sense of today's Jewish experience.

Definitions

I have given this essay a title that reflects some of the nuances of the changes that have taken place since the fall of communism regarding individual Jews, Jewish communities, and the Jewish world at large. It recalls the title of a best-selling book that came out some years back: *Eats, Shoots & Leaves* (Truss 2003). That book was about the power of punctuation, how a comma or other punctuation mark can radically change the meaning of a sentence. "Eats, Shoots & Leaves," which more or less describes a mob hit in a restaurant, has a quite different meaning from "Eats Shoots & Leaves," which describes the diet of an herbivore.

The title of this essay, thus, is the repetition of one word, *Jewish*, qualified by four types of punctuation to indicate shifting definitions of this word—this term, this concept—amid the changing conditions of the Jewish reality in Europe and, for the purposes of this essay, primarily postcommunist Europe.

What, indeed, does the word *Jewish* signify in today's East-Central Europe? Does it mean someone who believes in and practices Judaism, and, if so, what form of Judaism and what degree of practice? Or does it mean simply a person who can trace his or her genealogy back to Jewish ancestors; but how far back do you go, and does it matter if the ancestors are on the maternal or paternal side? Does "Jewish" refer to kosher food produced under a *mashgiach*'s supervision, or to any dish created according to an Ashkenazi, Sephardic, or Israeli recipe, or to commercial hybrids with such names as "rabbi's pocket" that are served in new, sometimes highly commercialized "Jewish" cafes and restaurants but mix meat and dairy and even might include pork? Does "Jewish" mean something sepia-toned and nostalgic that harkens back to the prewar past, or something that is "cool," "Jewcy," here and now? Does it means "Israeli" (and all those fraught and loaded connotations)? Does it mean Holocaust victim in iconic "striped pajamas"? Or all of the above? Or more? A few years ago I asked a waiter in the highly commercial Ariel café restaurant in Kraków's historic Jewish Kazimierz district why the establishment sold refrigerator magnets bearing stereotype profiles of Jews that looked straight out of the Nazi propaganda sheet *Der Stürmer*. He shrugged and replied, "They're Jewish."

Katka Reszke, in her 2013 book, *Return of the Jew*, which deals with what she calls the third generation of post-Holocaust Jews in Poland, writes:

It is of great significance that the discoveries of Jewish roots that brought about the unexpected third generation of post-Holocaust Jews are set against the background of the discovery of Polish Jewish cultural performativity. The "memory work" which accompanies contemporary representations of the Jewish past is interrelated with the "identity work" performed by individuals seeking a Jewish affiliation in Poland.

The "return of the Jew" is multilayered—there is the return to the Polish landscape (the intellectual and artistic landscape) of "the Jew" in discourse and in imagery, but there is also the "return" of real live Jews. And the "memory work" and "identity work" of both the Jewish and the non-Jewish Poles condition each other in profound ways and have by now become inseparable. (Reszke 2013, 219)

This phenomenon has not been true just in Poland. Major changes have become manifest in the years since my 2002 book, *Virtually Jewish: Reinventing Jewish Culture in Europe*, was published and introduced terminology that to some extent has become shorthand for describing ways in which non-Jews and the non-Jewish world enact, interact with, embrace, appropriate, question, and sometimes abuse (if not attack) the concept and manifold realities of Judaism and Jewishness.

Other terminology, of course, has emerged since then, as outside researchers, participant observers, philanthropic foundations, journalists, internet trolls, and, yes, local Jews and non-Jews themselves examine and try to make sense out of shifting paradigms and generational and other changes that contribute to the formation or at least the evolution of what I have come to call new authenticities and indeed new realities regarding Jewish presence and identity. Because, yes, the concepts of "real" and "authentic," though problematic, are and have been intrinsic in the evolution, if not the revival, of the way that Jews and others think of themselves and of the concept of what is, was, and even should be understood as "Jewish." In punctuation terms, one person's affirmative *Jewish!* Is another's skeptical or even dismissive *Jewish?* This is not news by any means; debates have been going on for centuries over what makes someone or something Jewish or what defines Jewish culture or Jewish art. Halakha of course lays down pretty clear strictures defining who is a Jew and who is not. Today's Jewish establishment in Europe can follow this through in ways that can narrow the very concept of Jewish "community" as many of us understand it, limiting it to officially recognized organizations and sometimes cutting off access to Jewish bodies, associations, individuals, or even congregations that operate outside the officially established framework.

In the mid-1990s, when I myself applied to join the Jewish community in Rome—and I had to apply with written proof of being Jewish—my application was summarily, and rather brusquely, rejected. The proof I had provided was the certificate from my naming ceremony in the American synagogue where I grew up, signed by our rabbi. Why was I refused? Because the rabbi in question was Conservative; in Italy, Orthodox Judaism is the only officially recognized stream. Even today, only a few small Reform congregations operate outside the Italian Jewish establishment, and, in a country where the rate of intermarriage is high, Orthodox Italian rabbis have tightened the procedures for conversion and thus formal affiliation. Partly because of this, the number of formally affiliated Jews has plummeted. Against this background, an American rabbi, Barbara Aiello, has run what she calls a pluralistic congregation in her ancestral village in Calabria since 2006. It is aimed at the descendants of *anusim*, or forced converts of 500 years ago. Aiello, who declares herself to be descended from *anusim*, is described as Italy's first and only woman rabbi, but she operates on her own, independent of and unrecognized by mainstream Italian Jewry. (Since 2017 her congregation has been a recognized member of the Reconstructionist movement.)[1]

Only more recently has the established Jewish umbrella organization in Italy (the Union of Italian Jewish Communities, or UCEI), aided by Shavei Israel, an Israel-based group that seeks out "hidden Jews" in countries ranging from Poland to India, broadened its own outreach in the south. Some years back I met a man from Calabria who told me that he had converted to Judaism three times: first by Rabbi Aiello, then in Switzerland, and finally through Orthodox conversion in Italy.

In a different sort of twist, there have been cases where non-Polish Jews living in Poland, including religiously observant Orthodox Jews, were barred from joining the established Jewish religious community because they were not Polish citizens; the postcommunist formal regulations governing Jewish relations with the state stipulated that only Jews who were Polish

1. See Aiello's website, http://rabbibarbara.com/.

citizens could formally join a Jewish religious community that is part of the officially recognized Union of Jewish Religious Communities.

To go back to the punctuation marks. Regardless of later rejection in Rome, *Jewish* period or full stop is how I, as an American growing up in the second half of the twentieth century, understood my identity and the identity of my family. We were—we are—simply Jewish: Conservative, not very observant Jews amid a broader Jewish community around us that included, and includes, an array of streams and beliefs, or nonbeliefs. I had no cause to question who—or what—I was. Nor did I even consider the potential question marks around the word until I began interacting with Jews and Jewish communities in Europe.

My first interaction with Jews in post-Holocaust Poland vividly brought this home in a way that, until then, I had never imagined. The experience dates back to September 1980, back in those days of "last" and "final," when I was a foreign correspondent with United Press International. I was in Warsaw to cover the birth of the Solidarity movement. Although I am not observant, on the eve of Yom Kippur I searched for, and found, a makeshift group of Jews, mostly elderly Holocaust survivors, gathered for prayer in a shabby meeting room. There was no rabbi and no operating synagogue in Warsaw at the time; little if any Jewish infrastructure existed at all. The Nożyk Synagogue—the only surviving synagogue in Warsaw—still stood, but it was dilapidated and empty. At that Yom Kippur gathering, three of the few young people in attendance came up afterward and asked who I was. When I told them, they appealed to me: "You're a real Jew," they said. And they asked me to come home with them and tell them what they should be doing to keep the holiday. When I protested that I was not observant, did not speak Hebrew, keep kosher, or even go much to synagogue, their response was, "No, but you have known all your life you are Jewish, and we are just finding out." So I went home with them. It was a powerful reminder of the present that their tiny apartment was located in a prefab apartment house built in the 1960s on the ruins of the destroyed Warsaw Ghetto. Later, they brought me into the so-called Jewish Flying University, a semi-clandestine group of Jews—and non-Jews—who were teaching themselves not simply Jewish ritual, traditions, and history but also, in a poignant way, the Jewish intangibles, the collective memories, the quirks of language and even sometimes of physical or facial expression that even assimilated Jews often retain.

Several years later, these then-young people, my generation, appeared in some of the pictures and text of Niezabitowska and Tomaszewski's book *Remnants: The Last Jews of Poland*. They were depicted as part of that last chapter: youthful; hopeful, perhaps, but with no real hope for a Jewish future in Poland. Several years after that, however, these same young people became the anchors of what was to become, in the 1990s, the postcommunist Jewish revival in Poland. I recall so vividly the distrust manifested by members of the Holocaust-survivor generation toward these newly emerging, questioning Jews, these young Jews claiming or reclaiming long hidden or suppressed identity. The survivors simply did not recognize them as Jews. "You guys are a fraud, a literary fiction," Marek Edelman, one of the leaders of the Warsaw Ghetto Uprising, told Jewish Flying University member Konstanty (Kostek) Gebert. "The Jewish people is dead, and you have simply thought yourselves up, looking for originality and exoticism" (Gebert 1994, 165).[2] For some of those older people, their own fervent identity was that as "the last Jews of Poland." Their passing, they believed, would be the final chapter in a 1,000-year history.[3] For some of them, thus, the emergence of "new Jews" shook the roots of their own self-definition, in effect, challenging who and what they felt themselves and their role to be—and what they felt their Jewishness to represent.

Today, it is the generation of the children and even grandchildren of people my own and Kostek's age who are setting the parameters of Jewish definitions and practice: Katka Reszke's third (or now, even fourth) post-Holocaust generation. Many have known all their lives that they are Jewish and feel confident enough now to embrace, abandon, or deal with that identity on their own and in their own ways, whether in Poland or elsewhere.

Some of the dozens of these people whom Reszke interviewed for her book had been born into families that already in the 1980s and 1990s had undergone the often anguishing experience of coming out and claiming or reclaiming Jewish identity. Others have staked their own claims and paths. Reszke, a third-generation Polish Jew herself, documents how most of her informants feel that their attraction to Jewishness has not been a conscious

---

2. Gebert went on to comment that "there was some truth in this, although less and less with the passage of time."

3. Few dreamt that, in 2014, twenty-five years after the end of Communist rule, the award-winning POLIN Museum of the History of Polish Jews would open, largely financed by the state and on a site atop the ghetto ruins donated by the city, with a state-of-the-art exhibition telling the story of those 1,000 years.

choice but an intrinsic part of their selfhood. "Being Jewish in Poland is not a matter-of-fact experience," she writes.

> It is intense. Jewish leaders around the world like to use the qualifying notion of a "strong Jewish identity," as if identity was a "thing" or a power of some kind, a fixed feature. But if we agree that identity is a process of becoming rather than of being, that it is never fixed, and that it is dialogic in nature, then the notion of a "strong identity" can be reduced to an idle slogan. The Jewish identity experience in Poland illustrates precisely the very unfinished nature of the process. Jewishness in Poland . . . is an identity that hosts questions and contradictions. And its authenticity is that of a conversation rather than a text. (Reszke 2013, 225)

So *Jewish* with a question mark, many question marks. And *"Jewish"* in skeptical quotation marks too; but ultimately, *Jewish!* as an affirmation. A publication that came out in Hungary in 2011 tackled some of these issues head-on. Bluntly titled *What Does It Mean to Be Jewish?* it listed on its first two pages a series of further subquestions qualifying that main one. Does being Jewish mean: Jewish holidays? Going to synagogue? Reading books about Jewish subjects? Listening to klezmer music? Being part of a community? Lighting candles on Friday evenings? Having Jewish ancestors? Emotional bonds to Judaism? The brightly illustrated, 32-page publication is more of a booklet than a book, and it is not a scholarly treatise. It is, in fact, a children's book. But, says the author, Linda Verő Bán, its "hidden" target is parents and other older generations who struggle with the same issues and do not know how to answer or (like the fourth son in the Haggadah) even ask the questions (Verő Bán 2011).[4]

Hungary is said to have a Jewish population of about 100,000, but even three decades after the fall of communism, the vast majority—as much as 90%—have nothing whatsoever to do with organized Jewish life or outward Jewish identification. For some, expressions of Jewish identity can come down to eating *sólet* (cholent) or having certain books on their bookshelves—not religious books but certain novels and intellectual nonfiction by certain

---

4. Verő Bán's book *What Does It Mean to Be Jewish?* was originally written in Hungarian and is one of a series of children's books by this author. Several have been translated into English and other languages. See http://zsidongo.hu/en/.

authors. Many self-identifying young Jews reject established Judaism, and in the 2000s some gravitated toward a loose, "alternative" Jewish youth scene that focused on cafés and cultural events in the newly trendy downtown Jewish quarter, the Seventh District. In recent years, as Hungary's politics have shifted to the right, toward what the increasingly authoritarian prime minister Viktor Orbán has described as an "illiberal democracy," some young Jews who were active in the alternative Jewish youth scene have more forcefully embraced opposition political, civic, and social activism. Others have left the country, if not for Israel then for elsewhere in the European Union. Others have gravitated to Chabad-Lubavitch and its active associated movement, the Unified Hungarian Jewish Congregation (EMIH), which maintains good relations with the government and has carried out high-profile openings of synagogues and other outreach.

Against this background, Verő Bán's book tackles questions regarding religious and secular Jews, having people of various religions in one family, whether you can tell someone is Jewish by looking at them, and whether you have to believe in God to be Jewish. On its back cover, as a sort of introduction, Verő Bán writes:

> Countless parents have difficulty talking to children about Judaism because they are full of unanswered questions themselves. I would like to create opportunities for all members of the family—grandparents, parents, step-parents and children, Jews and non-Jews, believers and non-believers alike—to talk to each other openly and honestly about Judaism, without taboos, expectations or prescribed answers. (Verő Bán 2011)

Verő Bán, who was born in 1976, is a Jewish educator who has been a protagonist in the postcommunist Jewish revival in Hungary for most of her life. Her father was for years the European director of the Ronald S. Lauder Foundation, which began in the late 1980s to promote Jewish education and youth programs in many postcommunist countries and became a powerful force in the Jewish revival. Verő Bán herself took part in key identity-building programs, such as the international Jewish summer camp at Szarvas, in southern Hungary, a project of the Lauder Foundation and the Jewish Joint Distribution Committee. Today, she is a *rebbitzin*; her husband, Tamás Verő, is the soft-spoken rabbi of Budapest's Frankel Leo Synagogue, one of a handful of Budapest synagogues that have seen an upsurge in membership and communal engagement in recent years. Led by rabbis who came of age after the fall of communism, they are attempting to engage young families within the organized mainstream and promote the synagogue congregation as the focus of community, learning, and long-term Jewish commitment.

Much attention was paid to the alternative Jewish youth scene that emerged in Budapest in the 2000s. A report on Jewish life in Hungary, published by the Institute for Jewish Policy Research in 2011, described the scene as "a fairly broad and loosely-connected young Jewish crowd," a "network of a few thousand people [that] has arisen completely spontaneously and independently from the organized Jewish community, although it will, from time to time, attend certain Jewish cultural events and appear at street festivals even though it does not join in the activities of Jewish organizations in any systematic fashion" (Kovács and Forrás-Biró 2011, 33). The young people tended to congregate in some of the new cafes and "ruin pubs" that opened in Budapest's inner-city Seventh District, once the main downtown Jewish quarter. The key player in this loose network was Marom, the youth organization of the Masorti (or Conservative) Jewish stream, founded in 2002 by Jewish university students. Its office was on the upper floor of a café called Sirály, which opened in 2006 on Király Street on the border of the Sixth and Seventh Districts. With a big mezuzah on its door and Marom upstairs, Sirály aimed to be an alternative Jewish culture center as well as a pub. Marom organized various events and activities there, ranging from lectures and exhibits to Purim parties, community seders, and klezmer/hip-hop/fusion concerts. Noteworthy were the annual Hanukkah Quarter 6 Quarter 7 Festival, founded in 2009, that involved other local venues, and Bánkitó, a youth arts and music festival held at a lake near Budapest. In the late 2000s some participants organized an informal nontraditional congregation, Dor Hadash, which met for Shabbat services and Friday night dinners; for several years their meeting place was Moishe House, which opened a few blocks from Sirály in 2009.

The alternative scene, geared mainly to single people in their 20s, gained much attention, including in the foreign media, but it drew criticism as well as praise. The 2011 Institute for Jewish Policy Research report quoted a Jewish community member as stating, "The pub-renaissance taking place in the Jewish quarter in the sixth and seventh districts . . . creates a totally individualized Jewish community and does not nurture any Jewish communal sensibilities in the classical sense. On the contrary: it rejects such sensibilities; a postmodern, strangely multicultural and strangely uncommitted community has been emerging that may be familiar with the basics of Jewish traditions, but rejects them" (Kovács and Forrás-Biró 2011, 34).

In 2013 Verő Bán also expressed skepticism about the lasting impact of the youthful "alternative" Jewish set. "Judaism, or active participation in Jewish life, is a period in their lives," she said. "They don't have a 'next generation'—there is no 'refill'; the continuity is missing."[5] In short, she said, they can grow out of it and move on to something else. What happens, she said, is that when young singles interested in continuing their active involvement with Judaism marry and have children, they tend to join one of the established congregations, such as Frankel Leo, which is oriented to serve young families.[6]

The Budapest authorities cracked down on Sirály, which had been operating as a squat, and closed it down in 2012 in a move that was interpreted as having more to do with right-wing politics than anti-Semitic bias. Two years later, Marom moved its activities to a multipurpose venue called Auróra in the rundown Eighth District (also a historic Jewish neighborhood). Off the beaten track of tourism, trendy pubs, and ruin bars, Marom and its activists at Auróra, now in their mid- or late 30s—or even older—have focused more intensively on social justice and civil society projects. Auróra hosts a number of NGOs, including Marom and the Dor Hadash progressive Jewish community, as well as Roma, LGBT, and other NGOs focusing on "marginalized and stigmatized groups." The English-language "About Us" page on Auróra's website does not mention the word *Jewish*. Rather, it describes Auróra as "a social enterprise which was created to connect cultural programs, civil and activist organizations work, community building and fun in an open community."[7]

5. Personal conversation, May 2013.
6. See Gruber (2012).
7. See https://auroraonline.hu/en/aboutus/. Also see the Marom Facebook page (https://www.facebook.com/marombudapest/) and the Aurora Facebook page (https://www.facebook.com/auroraunofficial/).

Dim Puff of Stardust

The British scholar Bernard Wasserstein famously scoffed at the notion of a Jewish renaissance in Europe, east or west. He articulated his deeply pessimistic vision most fully in his controversial 1996 book, *Vanishing Diaspora*, in which he cited drastically negative demographic statistics. "At best," he wrote, "the Jews in Europe face slow diminution, at worst virtual extinction." It was, he wrote, a "realistic forecast" that "within a few generations [Jews] will disappear as a significant element in the life of the continent" (Wasserstein 1996, vii). Consciously or not, Wasserstein's worst-case scenario has provided a constant and unsettling subtext to the efforts of newly emerging Jews and Jewish communities in the East to revive and/or renew Jewish life; to the efforts of established Jewish communities in the West, such as in the United Kingdom and Italy, that see numbers dwindling through intermarriage, apathy, and assimilation; and also to the efforts of Jewish organizations and international players and funders that have tried to chart strategy.[8]

The recreated, refound Jews in East-Central Europe are well aware that the proof of the success of their revival, whatever form it takes, does not rest with the first generation of Jews who reclaimed their identity and affiliation in the immediate aftermath of the fall of communism but with their children and grandchildren. What concerns them is keeping up the momentum. The challenges that exist in many cases exist now across the board: east, west, north, south. Many challenges facing Jews in Europe, including postcommunist Europe, are the same ones that confront Jews in North America and even Israel. In no particular order, these include such internal issues as:

> How to deal with the friction and sometimes bitter polarization between Orthodox and non-Orthodox Jews, between religious and secular Jews, between official established Jewry and nontraditional forms of Jewish worship and expression, between official local Jewish bodies and powerful imports such as Chabad, and between young generations and the entrenched mainstream.
> How the high inter-marriage rate should be regarded: as a bridge or as a barrier to affiliation? And what about the resulting questions of who can be considered a Jew and who can be admitted into

8. A major Jewish demographic survey published in 2020 bore out at least some of Wasserstein's predictions in statistical terms. See DellaPergola and Staetsky (2020).

an established Jewish community? What, indeed, constitutes a Jewish community? Does it matter?

How to stretch limited resources to support both communal activities and grass-roots initiatives, and also to promote and preserve Jewish heritage. In postcommunist countries in particular, how can a culture of local philanthropy, responsibility, and personal commitment be fostered so that it can lead to enhanced self-sufficiency?

How to confront what some perceive as a crisis and (in some cases) corruption in often entrenched Jewish leadership, on local, national, and Europe-wide levels (in 2013 it was telling to see the ouster of almost the entire leadership of Hungary's official Jewish umbrella organization just days after it proudly hosted the World Jewish Congress assembly), and how to make the European Jewish voice matter in today's Europe.

To these and other internal, even intensely personal questions are added broader societal issues highlighted amid increasing political polarization and shake-ups in the postcommunist European international order, for example, the impact of emboldened right-wing extremism and the success of right-wing, populist, and xenophobic parties that have come to power in, say, Poland and Hungary. The scale, impact, and mutating forms of anti-Semitism remain concerns, today often fueled by internet memes and colored by anti-Semitism linked, particularly on the left, to hatred of Israel. These new and changing circumstances, however, also include a growing resident presence of expatriate Israelis in some places, with Berlin a particular center. What will be the evolution of European Jewry's relationship to Israel as Europe's own relationship to Israel undergoes changes?

Holocaust denial and revisionism play shifting roles too, particularly with the passing of the survivor generation and the questioning of historical facts, aided by the easy spread of falsehood on social media and nationalist political moves that seek to sanitize the historic narrative. A law passed by Poland's ruling right-wing Law and Justice Party in early 2018 that criminalized attributing to the Polish state or nation complicity in the crimes committed by Nazi Germany during the Holocaust prompted protest by Israel and others but also unleashed waves of anti-Semitism, online and off.

Months later, the law was amended to eliminate criminal penalties (including prison) for violators.

The Facts of Life

So dramatic were the changes in the Jewish world in the first decade after the fall of communism that the Paris-based historian Diana Pinto dubbed the 1990s the "Jewish decade." It was an exciting, optimistic time, when everything seemed possible. But in 2001 Pinto declared that "the Jewish decade is over" and asked a gathering of European Jewish leaders, "What are the challenges beyond?"[9]

To go back to the question posed at the beginning of this essay, can—or should—we still speak about the Jewish trajectory in terms of revival? More than a generation after the fall of communism, more than two decades after the close of the "Jewish decade," the Jewish revival in Eastern and Central Europe has become a Jewish presence; it is tiny and still weak in many places and, I fear, not sustainable everywhere, but it is a presence that nonetheless is a real, functioning, authentic fact of life. What (and how long) does it take for the concept of revival to give way to something else? Anna Chipczyńska, a Jewish activist in Warsaw, feels that the time is now. She put it this way in an interview in November 2017, when she was president of the Warsaw Jewish community: "I don't call it a Jewish revival or renaissance—I call it the Jewish existence." The target of today's uncertainties, she said, "is not the Jewish revival but the Jewish existence" (Hoare 2017).

And this existence—this Jewish presence—means, as I noted earlier, much more than just numbers. Jewish heritage, Jewish culture and cultural expression, Jewish traditions, Jewish memory and history—these all form inextricable parts of the European tapestry. How do we foster them? How do we preserve them? How do we acknowledge them? How do we engage with mainstream society?

For better or worse, we increasingly are witnessing "normal" demographic shifts in Jewish populations rather than the immediate effects of the outside disasters of the Holocaust and communism. With much of Europe borderless now, Jews are free to move where they like on the continent. This

---

9. She spoke at a session of the General Assembly of the European Council of Jewish Communities, Madrid, Spain, June 2–3, 2001.

can be determined by economic possibilities or political exigencies, but also by religious ones: Israel is not necessarily the immediate choice for Jews who want to move somewhere to take advantage of Jewish educational, cultural, or religious opportunities.

Increasingly in Eastern and Central Europe there is a new, young generation of Jews who were born into Jewish identity at birth and did not suffer the restrictions of communism. Although some have embraced traditional religious observance to one degree or another, others chafe under the templates of Jewish identity and practice as introduced in the 1990s and laid down by the established Jewish authorities and international institutions (or even simply by their parents). They live in the present and future and reject Jewish identity based on Holocaust memory or anti-Semitism. Increasingly, and with the help of the omnipresent internet and easy international exchanges, they can seek their models elsewhere, whether in the iconoclastic and variegated Jewish lifestyles found in London, New York, or Tel Aviv or in the welcoming Orthodox religious world of Chabad.

Back in the mid-1990s, just as Bernard Wasserstein was scoffing at the idea of a Jewish renaissance, Diana Pinto coined the term *Jewish space* to describe the place occupied by Jews, Jewish culture, and Jewish memory in mainstream European society, regardless of the size or activity of the local Jewish population: "Indeed," she wrote, "it is possible that the larger the 'Jewish space' the smaller the number of actual Jews" (Pinto 1996, 7). This was—and remains—a groundbreaking concept that I believe is still quite valid. Yet Pinto offered up another definition in 2002, declaring Jewish space to be "an open cultural and even political agora where Jews intermingle with others *qua* Jews, and not just as citizens. It is a virtual space, present anywhere Jews and non-Jews interact on Jewish themes or where a Jewish voice can make itself felt" (Pinto 2002, 251).[10]

The future of European Jewry will depend on whether and how Jews in Europe, however they define themselves, collectively or as individuals, use that voice, those voices; and on whether and how they seize the opportunities presented to them and on how they recognize and confront the challenges they now face: external challenges to be sure, but internal challenges as well—within the Jewish world, within Jewish mind-sets and, perhaps most important, within individual Jewish minds.

10. On other aspects of Jewish space, see, for example, Brauch et al. (2008).

Back in those heady 1990s, Pinto also described Jews in Europe as "voluntary Jews" who make a conscious personal commitment to identify as Jews—culturally, religiously, or whichever other way suited them—and remain in European societies as such. But they could, she stated, "just as easily disappear into anonymity, stop being Jews, and they are of course free to do so: it is one of their rights in a pluralistic democracy" (Pinto 1996, 5). The changes since the days of "last" and "final" when I first made contact with Jews in then-communist Europe, and the more recent changes reflecting new global political realities in Europe, Israel, and also the United States, have dramatically demonstrated the difficulties in predicting, for better or for worse, the course of the Jewish experience in this part of the world.

A ceremony I attended in Poland in 2014 can be seen as an illustration of this. It was a wedding, billed as the first Jewish wedding in fourteen years in the town where it took place. Both the bride and the groom had grown up until their teenage years not knowing they were Jewish, but both embraced an active Jewish identity as adults. They announced their marriage as a symbol of the Jewish revival in Poland and made the event a public festival, with media coverage, to emphasize the import. Two Orthodox rabbis officiated, and an announcer used a PA system to describe each step, from the *ketubah* signing to the seven blessings to the breaking of the glass at the end of the ceremony. It was a joyous, optimistic occasion. But neither the euphoria nor the marriage lasted. Within three years, the couple was divorced, the groom had remarried—to a non-Jewish woman—and the bride had found happiness in a same-sex relationship. Both, however, remained publicly committed to their Jewish identities and Jewish activism; and this, perhaps, is where the lesson lies.

Jewish? Jewish.

Whatever the ultimate outcome, more than a generation on, the post-communist Jewish revival today is a complexity of Jewish lived experience: Jewish reality in its myriad religious, secular, rejected, exultant, dwindling, vital, and not necessarily predictable forms.

References

Brauch, Julia, Anna Lipphardt, and Alexandra Nocke, eds. 2008. *Jewish Topographies: Visions of Space, Traditions of Place.* Farnham, UK: Ashgate.

DellaPergola, Sergio, and L. Daniel Staetsky, eds. 2020. *Jews in Europe at the Turn of the Millennium: Population Trends and Estimates*. London: Institute of Jewish Policy Research.

Gebert, Konstanty. 1994. "Jewish Identities in Poland: New, Old, and Imaginary." In *Jewish Identities in the New Europe*, ed. Jonathan Webber, 161–70. London: Littman Library of Jewish Civilization.

Gruber, Ruth Ellen. 1983. "Photo Exhibit Shows Jewish Life That Most Hungarians Never See." *United Press International*, August 12. https://www.upi.com/Archives/1983/08/12/Photo-exhibit-shows-Jewish-life-that-most-Hungarians-never-see/5715429508800/ (accessed May 20, 2018).

Gruber, Ruth Ellen. 2012. "Young Families Bringing New Life to Budapest Synagogues." Jewish Telegraphic Agency, May 2. http://www.jta.org/2012/05/02/news-opinion/world/young-families-bringing-new-life-to-budapest-synagogues.

Hoare, Liam. 2017. "The Thermometer Interview: Anna Chipczyńska." *Moment*, December 15. https://www.momentmag.com/thermometer-interview-anna-chipczynska/.

Kovács, András, and Aletta Forrás-Biró. 2011. *Jewish Life in Hungary: Achievements, Challenges, and Priorities Since the Collapse of Communism*. London: Institute for Jewish Policy Research.

Liphshiz, Cnaan. 2017. "At Auschwitz, a Jewish Journalist Confronts His Anti-Polish Bias." Jewish Telegraphic Agency, January 25. https://www.jta.org/2017/01/25/lifestyle/at-auschwitz-a-jewish-journalist-confronts-his-anti-polish-bias.

Liphshiz, Cnaan. 2018. "In Kraków, Jews Celebrate Their Community's 'Revival' amid Rising Xenophobia." Jewish Telegraphic Agency, April 23. https://www.jta.org/2018/04/23/news-opinion/krakow-jews-celebrate-communitys-revival-amid-rising-xenophobia.

Pinto, Diana. 1996. *A New Jewish Identity for Post-1989 Europe*. JPR Policy Paper no. 1. London: Institute for Jewish Policy Research.

Pinto, Diana. 2002. "The Jewish Challenges in the New Europe." In *Challenging Ethnic Citizenship: German and Israeli Perspectives on Immigration*, ed. Daniel Levy and Yfaat Weiss, 239–52. New York: Berghahn.

Reszke, Katka. 2013. *Return of the Jew: Identity Narratives of the Third Post-Holocaust Generation of Jews in Poland*. Boston: Academic Studies Press.

Truss, Lynne. 2003. *Eats, Shoots & Leaves: The Zero Tolerance Approach to Punctuation*. London: Profile Books.

Verő Bán, Linda. 2011. *What Does It Mean to Be Jewish?* Budapest: Zsidongo Books.

Wasserstein, Bernard. 1996. *Vanishing Diaspora: The Jews in Europe Since 1945.* Cambridge, MA: Harvard University Press.

II

CONTEXTS

Part II positions the larger conceptual vocabulary of Jewish revival in a historical and ethnographic context. Moving from discourse to practice and from broad observations to concrete case studies, the contributors to this part engage in the spatiality of Jewish life in its diversity and resilience. They flesh out the modus operandi of different revival movements and ask how individual and collective actors act on the various definitions of Jewishness. Moreover, they examine how local state apparatuses and national sentiments regarding the past and future of Jewish peoplehood and Jewish culture engender projects of survival, revival, and renewal.

The six chapters provide a multidisciplinary perspective by following various instantiations of Orthodox and non-Orthodox revival across Europe (Eastern, Central, and Western) and Israel. These cases, each with its own localized context, reveal the various strategies and practices that different social movements, NGOs, informal groups, and individuals take when acting on the urgent demand for revival.

From France to Russia projects of revival led by local ethnic entrepreneurs address a state of emergency in the present and call for the salvage of Jewish heritage and material culture as well as the physical survival of the Jewish people. The first three chapters discuss the predicament of postsocialist Jews in Hungary, Russia, and Poland. Monterescu and Zorandy explore the notion of creativity and improvisation among urban hip community activists in Budapest. Zubrzycki's ethnography describes the backward-looking Jewish revival in Poland in which activists promote acts of salvage, remembrance, and performance and invoke the material creation of Jewish absence. The discovery of Jewish traces and the recovery of Jewish history through museums and modes of storytelling have come to incarnate the loss of multicultural Poland and Hungary. Gitelman surveys the challenges to the creation of public Jewish life in the former USSR and qualifies the festive declarations about the rebirth of an active Jewish community in Ukraine in the transformative decade of the 1990s.

Next, Tzuberi positions Jewish notions of citizenship and inclusion in relation to the German state in the postunification context. The struggles over the borders of the Jewish community and the "gatekeeping" of those borders trap revival politics between philo-Semitic desires and state policies. The two last chapters of this part focus on the Orthodox revival movements in Paris and Israel and highlight the themes of urban space and ethnic identity. As Endelstein shows, in Paris the Orthodox revival realigns Jewish space according to ethnicity and Orthodoxy around the practice of *eruv*. In Israel, however, as Leon illustrates, the Breslov movement expands Jewish visibility by blurring ethnic boundaries and reclaiming secular public space.

4

"Is You a Jew?"

The Jewish Revival Scene in Budapest

Daniel Monterescu and Sara Zorandy

In 1939 there were ten million Jews in Europe. After Hitler there were four million. Today there are under two million. On current projections the Jews will become virtually extinct as a significant element in European society over the course of the twenty-first century.

—Bernard Wasserstein, *Vanishing Diaspora*, vii

We work with non-affiliated Jews who would never go to a synagogue. . . . We try to sneak Judaism into our programming, just to give them a taste and whet their appetite: a klezmer concert here, a Hanukkah candle lighting there.

—Adam Schoenberger, quoted in Liphshiz (2017)

Endogenous Revival: Recovering Identity in Budapest

On a rooftop squat in an apartment building in Budapest, a small group of young men and women gathered to celebrate Sukkot (a major Jewish festival held in the autumn to commemorate the sheltering of the Israelites in the wilderness after they were freed from slavery in Egypt). They did not have a conventional sukkah (a hut constructed for use during the week-long festival) to speak of, but instead they improvised a makeshift tent from a blanket. None of the special ritual artifacts used on this religious occasion were there. No one bothered to bring a prayer book. "Do you know the prayers?" one participant asked. A discussion followed about what they were going to do. Everything was apparently ready, but none of the young men were able to either read or recant the specific prayers. Finally, Anna Bálint picked up the prayer shawl and said, "OK. Never mind, I'll do it." Everyone was relieved. Anna had actually gone to a Jewish school and read Hebrew. The issue of a woman leading the prayer was not even raised. It just seemed normal for the group to celebrate happily, sitting together on the floor in a makeshift tent on a rooftop. Most of them, we learned, were members of Moishe House, a motley crew of second- and third-generation Hungarians with Jewish roots or with partly Jewish roots who were seeking a way of living their Jewish heritage and enjoying their culture and tradition without the stiltedness of the Jewish establishment.

Against a history of communal destruction and alongside demographic projections of assimilation, projects of revival have heralded the "rebirth" and "renaissance" of Jewish communities and Jewish culture throughout Europe and beyond (Finkelstein 1990; Gitelman and Ro'i 2007; Teplinsky 1998). However, more than seventy years after the Holocaust and three decades after the collapse of Europe's communist regimes, scholars remain essentially divided regarding the prospects of restoring active Jewish communities in Europe. Some bemoan the "vanishing Diaspora" (Wasserstein 1996), whereas others celebrate the great "promethean historical moment" (Karády 2006) of the Jewish awakening in Europe (cf. Gruber 2002; Gitelman et al. 2003). How do the Jews who chose to remain in Europe after World War II and 1989 interpret these challenges and define themselves? Is Jewish consciousness, or "Jewishness," perceived in ethnic, cultural, religious, national, or universal terms? Are right-wing extremism and anti-Semitism pushing Jews to regroup, or does fear result in communal disintegration? And finally, under which institutional conditions do cultural entrepreneurs promote what they consider to be a vital Jewish presence in Europe?

Between a projected fear of vanishing and a creative cultural drive, the conundrum of a persistent Jewish presence in post-Holocaust Europe poses a formidable task for the social sciences, one that directly engages the troubled relationship between Europe and its historical alter ego. To address this task, we analyze the emergence in the 1990s and the 2000s of Jewish revival projects in Budapest, home to the largest surviving Jewish community in continental Europe after World War II. We argue that the "vanishing Diaspora" has been repositioning itself in relation to the Hungarian and

European cultural projects in new ways that challenge and redefine national identity and the Jewish condition alike.

Defined here as the practices of transmission, social adaptation, and cultural innovation of religion *qua* "discursive tradition" (cf. Asad 1993), the term *Jewish revival* should be first critically recognized as an emic normative concept often used by political, cultural, and religious actors. By contrast, as a sociological concept the term *Jewish revival* indexes a loose assemblage of social movements and cultural initiatives that make up a transnational field of social action framed as Jewish by its actors. Analytically, therefore, it encompasses a broad range of institutional modalities and individual practices across continents and communities: from Chabad's tactics of global outreach into new religious spaces, through local community-based activities, to alternative cultural initiatives that we can term "Judaism à la carte" (Kovács et al. 2011).[1]

Focusing on the agentive dynamics of contemporary Hungarian Jewish initiatives in concrete urban spaces, we follow the different strategies and practices that Jewish NGOs, informal groups, and individuals use to create and improvise new communal frameworks to define ways of being Jewish. Although the Orthodox institutions promote what they call true Judaism (e.g., Chabad), alternative cultural actors creatively define nondenominational religious modalities: secularized but not assimilated, liberal yet adhering to "tradition" as they see it. Calling to "re-invent tradition," initiatives such as Judapest.org, Marom, and Moishe House are independent of Orthodox, Neolog, or Reform movements, thus promoting a cultural project we identify as lifestyle Judaism.

Whereas scholars of European Jewry argue for "a weakening of collective, communal claims on individual Jews and a concomitant trend toward individualism and making choices about which aspects of Jewish tradition to preserve in one's own life" (Gitelman 2003, 3), we show how, beyond the narrow paradigm of methodological individualism, new associative *bunde* and elective "tribes" emerge to answer the changing needs of Jews in Europe (Schmalenbach 1977; Urry 2000; Maffesoli 1988).

---

1. Under this title, the recent Joint Distribution Committee's (JDC) report (Kovács et al. 2011) analyzes three axes of Jewish identity (anti-Semitism, family environment, and Jewish values) and draws on a statistical analysis of thirteen components of Jewish identity (e.g., birth, family, culture, Shoah memory, anti-Semitism, religion, values, nation) from which individual Jews are selecting within their respective social fields and positions.

Theoretically, to develop the appropriate conceptual vocabulary to describe these processes, we bridge the literature of different disciplines, such as urban anthropology, cultural sociology, European history, religious studies, improvisation, and cultural creativity (Gitelman and Ro'i 2007; Hallam and Ingold 2008; Brauch et al. 2008; Lavie and Narayan 1993). Framed as a form of collective bricolage (understood as the pragmatic re-articulation of available resources to solve new problems),[2] Jewish cultural improvisation is nevertheless bound by a discursive tradition and its rules of interpretation, albeit loosely defined. Moreover, as a patently urban phenomenon, the specific configuration of Jewish claim making should be scrutinized as part of the neoliberal landscape of urban restructuring whereby "Jewish quarters" are turning into spaces of consumption, tourist attractions, and hot spots for gentrification (Gruber 2002).

Hungarian Jewish History: From Strategic Invisibility to Ethnic Consciousness

Modern Hungarian Jewish history displays recurrent attempts at integration and assimilation. Commonly traced back to the Jewish emancipation era in the second half of the nineteenth century, the failed Hungarian revolution of 1849 marks the first promise of full citizenship. Revolutionary progressive nobleman Lajos Kossuth attempted to rid the Magyars of the Habsburg Empire and promised Hungarian Jewry political rights if they sided with the national independence project. Most Jews in the Habsburg Empire who had already chosen to speak German, even among themselves, thus faced a new challenge of linguistic integration. This option emerged again during the political compromise of 1867 as collective assimilation, which Kovács (2010, 35) aptly termed "a singular symbiosis between the Hungarian majority and Jewish minority." In 1867 the laws relating to Jewish emancipation consisted of two paragraphs only: "The country's Israelite residents shall henceforth be entitled to exercise all the civil and political rights enjoyed by

---

2. Anthropologist Claude Lévi-Strauss defines *bricolage* as the process of creating something, not as a matter of a calculated choice and use of whatever materials are technically best adapted to a clearly predetermined purpose, but as a "dialogue with the materials and means of execution" (Levi-Strauss 1966, 29). In such a dialogue, the materials, which are at hand, might "suggest" adaptive courses of action, and the initial aim may be modified. Consequently, such acts of creation are not purely instrumental: "the bricoleur 'speaks' not only with things . . . but also through the medium of things" (21).

Christian residents," and "all laws, customs or decrees to the contrary are hereby abolished."[3] András Gerő notes that because "legislation on religious matters" was missing, "emancipation or assimilation could only take place on the basis of voluntary cultural homogenization" (Gerő 1995, 189). Jews were considered "Hungarians of the Mosaic faith" and were never granted an official minority status (similar to the Roma and unlike national minorities such as Serbs, Germans, and Slovaks). The proposition of Hungarian liberalism in both 1849 and 1867 was framed as a social contract that stipulated the equivalence between Hungarian culture and citizenship. For the sake of this Hungarianness, Jews were required to renounce their own cultural standards and customs in return for full civil acceptance. The Hungarianization project was met with great success, and in the 1890 Hungarian census, 64% of the Jewish population was identified as ethnic Hungarian by their mother tongue against only 33.1% who spoke German.

After World War I and the 1920 Treaty of Trianon, two-thirds of the Hungarian territories were lost but more than half of Hungarian Jewry remained in the "small Hungary." Also after the war, "white terror" fears, the infamous "numerus clausus" (which limited the number of Jewish students in higher education establishments and thereby diminished the Jewish student population to about a fourth of their original number), and a general hope of assimilation accounted for thousands of Jewish converts to Christianity. The same process repeated itself with the Jewish laws of 1938, although most of those conversions took place too late and were easily spotted by fascist administrators looking for Jews during the fateful months of 1944. By 1941, out of roughly 250,000 Jews registered in Budapest, up to 72,000 were Jews by law but did not identify as such religiously. As Hungary was siding with Nazi Germany, Hungarian Jewry was largely left unharmed for the first years of World War II. Once Hungary realized it had betted on the wrong horse once again in its long history and refused further cooperation with the Third Reich, German tanks rolled into Hungary in March 1944. With the crucial support of the Hungarian Arrow Cross Party and their henchmen, Jews were rounded up efficiently.

The first transports to Auschwitz began in early May 1944 and continued until Soviet troops arrived. Based on the thorough analysis by Stark (2000), 500,000–550,000 Hungarian Jews were taken by force, some to labor

---

3. From the Hungarian Statute Book, Laws of 1836–68 (Gerő 1995).

camps and subsequently most to the death camps. According to Stark's calculations, "the number of Jewish survivors in the area of wartime Hungary ranges between 140 thousand to 230 thousand" (Stark 2000, 37).

It should come as no surprise that considering this historical background, after World War II the already assimilated Hungarian Jews attempted once again to leave behind their Jewish identity, which they associated with racism, discrimination, and later horrors. To cope with this traumatic heritage, many survivors chose to Hungarianize their name and raise their children as communist cadre children (Karády 1994), often locking their Jewish roots in the family closet. Holocaust survivors (henceforth the first generation) were so successful at hiding their Jewish origins that often the second generation found out about being Jewish well into their adult lives (Erős et al. 1985). After forty years of authoritarian rule and state-imposed anti-Semitism, the political transformations set in motion in 1989 heralded an unprecedented opening of a cultural field of expression hitherto inaccessible to Jews in Central and Eastern Europe. Thus, in the transition's aftermath, hundreds of NGOs and community organizations emerged in the region—often financed by American, Israeli, and other international agencies. As walls and borders were removed in Europe, questions of collective and individual identity assumed new political meanings. The differences here between Western European Jews and postsocialist Jews are illuminating. While Jews in Central and Eastern Europe were struggling to establish communal institutions and a viable sense of self, Jews in London and Stockholm—"postmodern Jews by choice" (Dencik 2003)—engaged in a search for postdenominational religious distinction. However, we argue that even though in the West the attempt to reappropriate a Jewish culture that was not hierarchical remained marginal (with initiatives such as Limmud and Moishe House) because of the objection of Orthodox centralized national institutions, in postsocialist cities the countercultural became more mainstream by virtue of communal fragmentation and thus served as a crucial force in reshaping the Jewishness of Budapest, Berlin, and Kraków.

Transforming their "latent ethnicity" (Gitelman et al. 2003, 108) to a legitimate and open identity strategy has been a difficult and tortuous process, which is yet to be fully acknowledged by Jews and non-Jews alike. Surveys show that approximately one-fifth of Central and Eastern European Jews have indicated that their Jewishness was concealed from them by their *own* Jewish family. This phenomenon was particularly common in

Poland (36%) and Hungary (29%) (Kovács et al. 2011). Thus, although the reevaluation of Jewish heritage opened a much more public debate than was ever possible under communist censorship, one of the main differences between Eastern and Western Europe is that this publicness cannot be taken for granted in the East. To this day many Jews are still ambivalent about exposing their Jewishness and identifying themselves as such for fear of unknown and grave repercussions. For this reason, after decades of communist oppression, which was internalized by Jewish families, many second-generation Jews still avoid taking part in public Jewish life or do so only hesitantly. The stigma of being Jewish was gradually dismantled only by the third-generation Jews born in the 1970s and 1980s.

The change of political systems in 1989 heralded a national identity-finding period: From the esoteric to the nationalistic, Hungarians were redefining themselves. Many (re)discovered their Jewishness, but Mazsihisz (Magyarországi Zsidó Hitközségek Szövetsége; Federation of Hungarian Jewish Communities) was slow to recognize the new needs of this growing group and was accordingly marginalized and delegitimized. In the 1990s and the 2000s, the growing demand for new institutions and social and communal venues was taken up by young urban "ethnic entrepreneurs" (Gitelman et al. 2003, 106) who were looking for what we call models of revival in Western Europe and the United States. The transnational interaction and exchange of ideas and organizational models between activists from all walks of Jewish life was crucial for establishing both a local Jewish scene and a sense of European Jewishness—diasporic by choice, cosmopolitan yet endowed with a local grassroots agenda. The best known actor among them is Marom, which attracted young urbanites with an interest in their Jewish heritage. Sensitive to the trends seeping in from Berlin, London, and New York, these loosely knit communities are built on the concept of cool-and-happens-to-be-Jewish. Central among these initiatives are Café Sirály, Budapest's "non-official Jewish urban space," until it was forced to close in April 2013 and relocated to the new Auróra; and on a virtual plain Judapest.org ("a wholly homegrown and grass roots online and offline community aiming to uncover the Stimulating, the Relevant and the Cool in the Hungarian Jewish Experience").[4] Judapest, it should be mentioned, was a name devised for Budapest at the end of the nineteenth century

---

4. http://judapest.blogspot.hu (accessed May 28, 2018).

by the anti-Semitic Vienna mayor Karl Lueger; the name was retaken around 2005 for Judapest.org, "an essential source for young Hungarian Jews (re)discovering their identity."

For several years now, organizations such as Limmud (established in London) and Moishe House (established in the United States) have also been active in Hungary. Financially speaking, Mazsihisz is still the organization that receives the bulk of the budget from the state and is accused of corruption. Chabad-Lubavitch is a relatively new phenomenon on the scene; with a pragmatic, hands-on approach it reaches born-again Jews who are looking for an authentic religious definition of their Jewishness but are depressed by the sleepy traditionalism of Neolog congregations. Chabad was highly successful in cultivating special relations with the government and is financed independently of Mazsihisz, though it claims some of the funds of Mazsihisz and frames its activities as heir to the Status Quo Ante community, which was exterminated during World War II.

For most observers the Jewish revival scene in Budapest is often experienced through festivals and cultural events. A lively scene of Jewish culture, which is initiated by Hungarian Jews for a local audience, is evident in various Jewish cultural festivals (Bánkitó, the Jewish Summer Festival, the Jewish Gastro Festival, the Kazinczy Street Ball, the Spinoza Jewish Festival, Pozsonyi Picnic, and the Quarter 6 Quarter 7 Festival); in Jewish theaters (Golem), bars, and restaurants owned and frequented by Jews; and in concerts and shows that somehow relate to Jewish culture (e.g., *Bálint Ház*, the Israeli Cultural Institute, and two film festivals celebrating Israeli movies). As elsewhere in Europe, "culture" becomes an easy gateway to and from Jewish heritage and identity. Commodified to some extent, the experience of Jewish culture through festivals forms a specific form of situational Judaism.

Chabad has also paired up in an unlikely partnership with the Mayer brothers and their friends, a worldly group who saved the Teleki tér *shtiebl* in Budapest's still somewhat dilapidated Eighth District by starting to pray there, to maintain a minyan as original members began to pass away. The community consists of Jewish and Jew-ish people who care about keeping the traditions alive and available. Some are religious and keep kosher, some are atheists, and most are somewhere in-between. Their community is one of identity and togetherness and has become a close-knit group with a solid number of regular members. Chabad assured the rabbi on site, and despite some significant differences in life views, this arrangement works well.

Generational Analysis: The Survivors, the Denied, the Emerging, the Jewish Millennials

During ethnographic fieldwork, conducted between 2011 and 2014, we mostly encountered activists and participants between ages 25 and 45, generally called the third and fourth generation of Hungarian Jewry.[5] We, however, prefer to think of the first generation as those who were born by the time of the Holocaust (the Survivors); the second generation as those born in the 1950s and 1960s (the denied); the third generation as those born in the 1970s and 1980s (the emerging); and the fourth generation as those born after the 1989 transition (the Jewlennials or Jewish millennials). Although Kovács's divide goes back further in time, it does not help to explain vast differences between those born in 1967 or 1980. We think that their differences do not so much depend on how young people were after the Communist thaw but rather on their proximity to the Holocaust.

The first generation of survivors denied their Jewish origins and submerged themselves in a new, Communist identity. Their children grew up not knowing their background and only heard some vague mentions of grandparents killed by "the Fascists" without any further analysis to the why and how. The second generation frequently found out about their Jewish background only by the age of 40 or so and often sought to find this resurfacing identity through religion and tradition. The fall of communism brought a great identity-finding boom to all of Hungary: Buddhism, New Age, feng shui, Protestantism, aromatherapy—all were embraced with a passion. The denied began taking their children to Jewish schools (Anna Frank or Lauder) and Jewish summer camps (Szarvas). The third generation, the emerging, often grew up knowing their Jewish background, learning its traditions as they grew up among other Jews. At the same time, they still had a revolutionary role in transcending their parents' discretion—of "keeping to

5. In the research on European Jewry, András Kovács proposed a different generational divide: "The members of the first generation were born before 1930, who were already adults at the time of the Shoah. The second generational group comprised those who were born between 1930 and 1944, whose life-forming experiences were made during the era of Stalinist Communism. To the third generational group belonged those who were born between 1945 and 1965, i.e. the generation that grew up under consolidated Communist rule and Kadarism. Finally, the fourth group comprised those born after 1966, whose most powerful experiences as a generation may have been the disintegration and collapse of the Communist system" (Kovács 2010, 54).

oneself" and, while honoring one's Judaism, not expressing it pronouncedly and publicly. A good example of the new attitude of openness and confidence is one of our interviewees, Ádám Schönberger, who bluntly expressed his indifference—as opposed to fear—toward anti-Semites and neo-Nazis: "I hate the Nazis, of course, but I would rather punch them than organize programs. They are very annoying people, and that's it." Zsófia Eszter Simon, one of the first inhabitants of Moishe House Budapest, felt that an Israeli expert at a security lecture held by the American Jewish Joint Distribution Committee (commonly known as the Joint or JDC) was "overly freaked out." She explained, "Until now we never had a problem, but of course sometimes I think there might be. What we are doing here—Marom, Sirály, and Moishe House—is all about being open, so this risk comes with it. We're not trying to close ourselves off, like this is just for Jews—quite the opposite, we'd like to do something together."

Personal Trajectories of Key Actors in the Revival Scene

In the 2000s, specific figures led the alternative revival movement in Budapest and carved out new spaces of Jewish relevance. We identify three actors who made a difference by creatively reappropriating Jewishness in the city. The biographies of the people behind three major initiatives—Moishe House, Judapest.org, and Sirály—attest to the incongruence between the existing institutional structure of Jewish life and the aspirations of younger generations. Each of these key actors used the resources and networks they developed in Hungary and abroad. Sharing a constitutive experience outside Hungary (in Israel, the United States, and France), they brought home a positive Jewish experience and could introduce a different model of Jewish identity removed from the common self-victimizing attitude. Bruno Bitter, a new media specialist, created a community for the online generation; Anna Bálint, a project and event coordinator, established Moishe House in Budapest; and finally, Ádám Schönberger founded Sirály, the place to be for young urban Jews.[6]

---

6. Unless otherwise noted, all quotes from Bitter, Bálint, and Schönberger are from interviews conducted in 2013.

Bruno Bitter and Judapest.org

Bruno Bitter (b. 1976) is a new media specialist and creator of Judapest.org: "the wholly homegrown and grass roots *online and offline community* aiming to uncover the Stimulating, the Relevant and the Cool in the Hungarian Jewish Experience. Since 5765." When creating the community in 2004, his main motivation was "to know if it is a personal thing or a phenomenon in my generation, or this situation." Bruno remembers first encountering anything Jewish in a meaningful way when his family moved to the United States in 1987: "In New York we had many Jewish friends, and these Jewish friends were different from the Jewish friends in Hungary as they had a lively, contemporary tradition of being Jewish." He had been aware of being Jewish, but this information was contextless. Once at university, he spent a year in Jerusalem, where he witnessed "a very contemporary culture which is natural and has natural roots and not only in the Bible but in contemporary articulations of pop culture; that was very important and it was a huge contrast seeing the Jewish life in Hungary, which is secret for most of the people: You don't talk about it—you know, it's a whispered term and for many people it's a negative thing, not necessary because they are anti-Semitic but they think, it is a fragile thing, it is a vulnerability to be Jewish because of anti-Semitism, and because of the Holocaust and because of the perceived anti-anything." Because this was a different experience from what he had had in his early teens and early 20s, once blogging took off abroad, Bruno decided to take it to the Hungarian scene: "I see Budapest as a place where lots of Jews live, and they are very active and they are doing all sorts of subversive cultural things, so I will call them Judapest."

When asked why he discontinued Judapest in 2009, he confessed, "Before I had a Jewish family, I probably had to externalize my Jewish identity more. I had to prove it or show it to myself. And now having a Jewish son and a Jewish wife, I have nothing to prove, to myself at least. I think that most Jews have some identity problem. So they always need to reflect on it. They are in the Jewish conflict zone of their identity or many Jews feel that way, at least in Hungary. Once you feel that you are in the identity comfort zone you don't need to do all these external celebrations."

Between 2004 and 2009, Bitter's brainchild, Judapest.org, provided an online community for Jews in a quest for identity. Its importance cannot be stressed enough, as for many urban, internet-using, educated Hungarian

Jews, it was the first time they witnessed a smart, cheerful Jewish identity propagated in a safe space of cultural intimacy (Herzfeld 2004). In one instance, blogger "Tet," Tamás Pásztor, brought out *Zsidó-e vagy?* [Is You a Jew?],[7] which listed Jewish typicalities Pásztor felt would be recognizable by others. The post caused an avalanche of comments, where people freely added new funny typicalities and proudly shared their Jewish ways. To be able to chat and share freely on these oddities of growing up with various forms of hiding and resurfacing was a great source of comfort to many. We present in what follows a few examples from the original post and comments.

> 1.§ A Jew is he/she in whose identity this plays a role.
> Subpoints:
> . . . III. He/she doesn't confuse a micveh for a mikveh
> IV. Is very apt at noticing all Star of David necklaces, *chai* necklaces, menorahs, Jerusalem memorabilia AND is not an antisemite. . . .
> VIII. In the case of boys, the dilemma of to circumcise or not to circumcise was debated even in the Kádár era (independent of outcome). . . .
> XV. Is not religious, doesn't keep kosher, but whenever possible, would rather skip the pork, is all full, thanks. . . .
> XVII. Is learning, used to learn or would like to learn Hebrew. . . .
> XXVI. Had to find out during university seminars and/or at Christian friend's visit that not everyone is used to interrupting each other and having loud discussions. . . .
> XXVIII. Holocaust movie → tears . . .
> XXXII. Can "neither swallow nor spit out" own Jewry, thus just chews-n-chews.

Anna Bálint and Moishe House

Anna Bálint (b. 1983) starts off by invoking her constitutive experience as a young Jew in Budapest.

> My story is at once very typical and very unique. All four of my grandparents' families were touched by the Holocaust, and they stepped

---

7. http://www.judapest.org/zsido-e-vagy-2/ (accessed May 16, 2013).

away from religion after that. Following the initial suppression, something awoke and got stirring in my parents. I was a small child by then and they sent me to Kazinczy street's Jewish kindergarten as early as 1989. That was a pretty big shock, of course, I almost learnt Hebrew earlier than Hungarian. Lauder school for the next twelve years was just a lengthy exit. There, one really gets to feel that horrible herd spirit. Maybe there are some positive values to feeling part of a group, but then for the group to identify itself in a way that is only negative when looking at it from the outside, that's problematic. Although in the very beginning, at the dawn of the system change it was really a sense of liberation, a communal feeling: parents, kids, teachers, everyone was very happy the school had been founded. (Zorándy 2010)

Bálint studied history of art in France and was one of the founding members of Moishe House Budapest and of the alternative prayer group Dor Hadash. Anna herself was raised in a secular family, and her goal was to found an organization to popularize Jewish traditions for Jews and non-Jews alike: "I used to live a more intensive religious life, but had to realize my Jewishness has to come from elsewhere, from the inside" (Czene 2011).

Moishe House Budapest was established in September 2009. Marom activist Eszter Susán wanted to create a "new communal space"[8] after seeing the charm and success of Moishe House London. With Sirály friends Zsófia Eszter Simon and Anna Bálint, they applied for funding on the Moishe House website and were accepted. In general, Moishe House seeks "young adults to connect with their own Jewish identities, their friends, and their wider communities"[9] in exchange for "perks and benefits."[10] Bálint remarks: "The most beautiful thing about Moishe House is to see the youngsters arriving on Friday evening, without any outside pressure, because of their own intentions. Some earlier, some later, some with wine, some without, some by bike, some by car, so as not to forget about the question of keeping the Sabbath. It's good to see how a lot of people, who have either not found their place elsewhere or hadn't even looked for it, because it never occurred to them, can be a part of this Friday evening community. They're here, they

---

8. Sara Zorandy interviewed Moishe House inhabitants for her essay in *Múlt és Jövő* (Zorandy 2010).

9. https://www.moishehouse.org/about-us/our-story/ (accessed March 17, 2022).

10. https://www.moishehouse.org/about-us/join-the-team/ (accessed March 17, 2022).

sing, and feel good. This all has to do with the current Hungarian situation as people need a community especially now" (Zorándy 2010, 128).

Less than five years after it was established, none of Moishe House's original residents were there anymore. Eszter Susán "became too old," Anna Bálint is living with her partner and child in a home of their own, and Zsófia Eszter Simon preferred to move out once she graduated from medical school. All three are still very much involved in Budapest's Jewish community, though. Responding to Wasserstein's fears of a vanishing diaspora, Moishe House seems the ultimate celebration of pluralism: Out of the two dozen resident members, so they say, a quarter have no Jewish roots at all, and half would not be considered Jewish according to the Israeli rabbinate. Ever since, the international Moishe House leadership has implemented stricter rules: At least one parent has to be Jewish if one would like to move in.

Today's Moishe House inhabitants are part of the iGeneration, and growing up Jewish or Jew-ish in Hungary over the last twenty years or so has not been a journey of question marks. Thanks to the Jewish millennials, there are many ways to explore one's Judaism: Early inhabitants of Moishe House meet younger Jews within the framework of Bánkitó Festival or as *madrichs* during a Birthright trip and point them to their activities, from whence new inhabitants come. Being Jewish or Jew-ish is an unproblematic identity element, one of many: One can be a student of art history, a vegan, a Jew, and an animal rights activist. Although previously the question of one's identity was played carefully—What summer camps did you go to? Where do your grandparents live?—and then one felt one's way around the other person's answers, today's young adults can meet up in a Jewsy location and one can say to the other, "Huh, you're Jewish. I didn't know . . ." and the other will go, "You too, eh? Nice."

Ádám Schönberger: Sirály and Auróra

Ádám Schönberger (b. 1980) grew up with another sort of hidden identity. Both of his parents are Jewish, and his father is a Neolog rabbi. His parents divorced when he was 3 years old, and he was raised by his maternal grandparents. He went to a state-run public school and was not sure what his father did, as his family told him his father "is a priest, but not that kind of priest." At the same time, they celebrated Christmas, and whenever

Schönberger had to indicate his father's job in documents, he wrote "priest." After a few years at a regular state school, he continued in the Orthodox Wesselényi school, followed by some years at Anna Frank School, known today as Sándor Scheiber. Not too long after graduating high school, he made aliyah with his then-girlfriend and returned to Hungary a few years later. Ever since, he has been one of the prime players in what has been called the Hungarian Jewish renaissance by some, by way of Marom, Sirály, Bánkitó Festival, and the Quarter 6 Quarter 7 Festival.

Schönberger describes his activities as being in the kitchen of Jewish identity: "We are trying to create this whole thing. We are in a kitchen and can't go to the shop. We have the flour that remains from 40–50 years ago, and we have the new type of flours, which are only barely related. So you have to combine the two: the old flour your grandmother and father used to make bread with the new one. You don't really know how that works, although you've already eaten some new bread. Now if you combine them, you have to measure which one is supposed to be more and less. These kinds of breads are not one or the other, they are always something in between."

An era came to an end when Sirály's location on Király utca 50 was forced to close in April 2013. For seven years, this pub, club, exposition space, café, theater spot, and general hangout was the soul of urban Jewish Budapest. Increasingly intertwined with Marom, Sirály became the place where many urban Jews went so as not to have to be Jewish. After September 2008, when neo-Nazis arrived with buckets of feces to avenge the supposedly "defamed great Hungarian playwright" and actually beat two people, it turned out the community was not afraid: People continued to visit as though the incident had never happened, although at the time everyone was in shock. The Sirály people have since continued in Auróra in the disinvested Eighth District.

Opening its doors in the pre-gentrified Eighth District in 2014, Auróra also became the new home to Marom, Dor Hadash, and a handful of other NGO's.[11] Embracing the principle of *tikkun olam* (repair of the world) beyond Jewish identity, Auróra expanded its activities. Helping Roma children get quality education, temporarily housing Syrian refugees during Hungary's migration crisis (2015), or providing Hungary's LGBTQ community with a

11. https://auroraonline.hu/rolunk/ (accessed April 5, 2021).

Advertisement for the Bánkitó Festival: "It's sexy to be Jewish." Photo by Daniel Monterescu.

safe space—all of this is an integral part of the spirit of Auróra. People from all walks of urban life come to Auróra, whether for a Purim celebration, a retro flea market, or a Bluesbreaker concert.

New Jews vs. Mazsihisz

The Jewish federation Mazsihisz is mostly considered simply out of touch while sitting on the budget, but there are some actual conflicts between the new generation and the official community. In 2007 then-president László Sólyom refused to sign into law a new decree on hate speech, considering it unconstitutional. Following this, Mazsihisz labeled him an anti-Semite and refused to attend the dinner the president was hosting for the heads of the different religious groups. The Judapest.org online community had a lively discussion about Mazsihisz's cancellation,[12] and they eventually decided to send the president a box of kosher *flódni* (a Jewish Hungarian cake) with a letter decrying Mazsihisz's decision and explaining that they did not think it represented Hungary's pluralistic Jews. The president appreciated the *flódni* and actually ate it with the church leaders who did attend the lunch. Mazsihisz did not appreciate the gist of the action and has apparently called Judapest.org "worse than the Hungarian Guard."

Perhaps less dramatic but certainly indicative was Ádám Schönberger's big Hanukkah celebration in the Bethlen tér Synagogue in 2002. Because his father had been a rabbi, Schönberger had the right contacts to approach the Bethlen tér rabbi, yet he shocked the establishment by openly advertising the event on large posters out on the street. Many of the older generation were worried that neo-Nazis would appear. This first event attracted some 800 young Jews. Tensions were already running high during the preparatory phase, though, because Schönberger flatly refused to allow someone from the Mazsihisz offices to sing a song and even denied Gusztáv Zoltai, then the head of Mazishisz, the chance to speak: "It was supposed to be a party, not a clapping congregation," he said. After breaking these unwritten rules, Schönberger and his group were no longer welcome and Bethlen tér Synagogue never again hosted such an event.[13]

---

12. See http://www.judapest.org/?p=1618 and http://www.judapest.org/?p=1618#comments (accessed May 15, 2013).
13. Data partly from Miklósi (2008) and partly from a 2013 interview with Ádám Schönberger by the authors.

Conclusions: Jewsy Futures

The generational dynamics of the Jewish revival in Budapest are striking. While the survivors and the denied coped with the embedded anti-Semitism and forced secularism through what we can term strategic invisibility, the emerging and the Jewish millennials appropriated the general liberties in post-1989 Hungary to create their own mode of cultural distinction—assertive yet situational and flexible. By normalizing Jewish distinction in social and cultural terms rather than in political or religious terms, these "Jewsy" (or Jewish-style) strategies can be seen as a provocative form of improvisation, flirting à la Georg Simmel with doctrinal modalities of Jewish tradition and the authenticity of Orthodox "true Judaism." The available sociological categories of conceptualizing these relational processes of individualization and secularization are limiting because these young urbanites leap across social fields and usurp existing repertoires to their needs.

Is there a Hungarian Jewish renaissance without actors such as Ádám Schönberger and independent of "foreign" funding, such as the Joint Distribution Committee or the Rothschild Foundation? It seems that with the continued denormalization of Hungarian politics, the identity revolution of young Jewry continues on its path. As Chabad continues to secure its special relationship with Prime Minister Orbán and expands its institutional network, new ethnic entrepreneurs are standing out among the millennials and current university students are finding their voice in the urban Jewish landscape, creating multilayered open community spaces at Auróra and in restored synagogues.

The transnational connection is crucial to the viability of the Jewish revival scene. Most of the key players, including Ádám Schönberger, Anna Bálint, and Bruno Bitter, spent their formative years beyond the borders of Hungary in other cities with well-defined Jewish identities: Tel Aviv, Paris, New York. They returned to Budapest with what were, for the locals, novel, cool concepts and models of action, which to them were a means to self-identify as who they are: hip, urban Jews. Today, any Hungarian student can go on an Erasmus scholarship anywhere in Europe, and urban Jews under the age of 40 usually speak English relatively comfortably. Thus they can venture into the United States, backpack around the Far East, and visit Israel without the urge of making aliyah. For many, the blogosphere, social media, and the Jewish global village are key reference points; initiatives from

London, such as Moishe House, are easy to follow and then emulate, and trends are intertwined, linked, and circulating freely. Clearly benefiting from globalization and EU mobility schemes, the young Jewish urban middle class challenges conservative structures as it looks for its place in a postsecular Europe.

References

Asad, Talal. 1993. *Genealogies of Religion: Discipline and Reasons of Power in Christianity and Islam.* Baltimore: Johns Hopkins University Press.

Brauch, Julia, Anna Lipphardt, and Alexandra Nocke, eds. 2008. *Jewish Topographies: Visions of Space, Traditions of Place.* Farnham, UK: Ashgate.

Czene, Gábor. 2011. "Kipa vagy baseballsapka?" [Kippah or baseball cap?]. *Népszabadság,* October 2.

Dencik, Lars. 2003. "'Jewishness' in Postmodernity: The Case of Sweden." In *New Jewish Identities: Contemporary Europe and Beyond,* ed. Zvi Gitelman, Barry Kosmin, and András Kovács, 75–104. Budapest: Central European University Press.

Erős, Ferenc, András Kovács, and Katalin Lévai. 1985. "Comment j'en suis arrivé à apprendre que je suis Juif?" *Actes de la Recherche en Sciences Sociales* 56: 62–68.

Finkelstein, Eitan. 1990. "Jewish Revival in the Baltics: Problems and Perspectives." *Soviet Jewish Affairs* 20(1): 3–13.

Gerő, András. 1995. *Modern Society in the Making: The Unfinished Experience.* Budapest: Central European University Press.

Gitelman, Zvi, Barry Kosmin, and András Kovács. 2003. *New Jewish Identities: Contemporary Europe and Beyond.* Budapest: Central European University Press.

Gitelman, Zvi, and Yaacov Ro'i, eds. 2007. *Revolution, Repression, and Revival: The Soviet Jewish Experience.* Lexington, KY: Rowman & Littlefield.

Gruber, Ruth Ellen. 2002. *Virtually Jewish: Reinventing Jewish Culture in Europe.* Berkeley: University of California Press.

Hallam, Elizabeth, and Tim Ingold. 2008. *Creativity and Cultural Improvisation.* Oxford, UK: Berg.

Herzfeld, Michael. 2004. *Cultural Intimacy.* London: Routledge.

Karády, Victor. 1994. "Traumahatás és Menekülés" [The Effects of Trauma and Escape]. *Múlt és Jövő* 2: 73–91.

Karády, Victor. 2006. "Jewish Identity in Post-Communist East Central Europe." *Monitor ZSA, Ljubljana* 6(1–2): 92–105.

Kovács, András. 2010. "Jews and Jewishness in Postwar Hungary." *Quest: Issues in Contemporary Jewish History* 1: 34–57.

Kovács, András, Barna Ildiko, Sergio DellaPergola, and Barry Kosmin. 2011. *Identity à la Carte: Research on Jewish Identities, Participation, and Affiliation in Five Eastern European Countries*. Oxford, UK: JDC International Center for Community Development.

Lavie, Smadar, and Kirin Narayan. 1993. *Creativity/Anthropology*. Ithaca, NY: Cornell University Press.

Levi-Strauss, Claude. 1966. *The Savage Mind*. Chicago: University of Chicago Press.

Liphshiz, Cnaan. 2017. "In Budapest, Roma and Jews Use Alternative JCC to Fight Right-Wing Populism." Jewish Telegraphic Agency, February 27. https://www .jta.org/2017/02/27/global/in-budapest-roma-and-jews-turn-alternative-jcc -into-anti-government-hub.

Maffesoli, Michel. 1988. *Le temps des tribus: Le declin de l'individualisme dans les societes de masse*. Paris: Meridiens Klincksieck.

Miklósi, Gábor. 2008. "Alternatív zsidó mozgalmak: Önépítkezés" [Alternative Jewish movements—Self-Construction]. *Magyar Narancs*, April 10. https:// magyarnarancs.hu/belpol/alternativ_zsido_mozgalmak_-_onepitkezes-68595.

Schmalenbach, Herman. 1977. *Herman Schmalenbach on Society and Experience*, ed. and trans. Gunther Luschen and Gregory P. Stone. Chicago: University of Chicago Press.

Stark, Tamás. 2000. *Hungarian Jews During the Holocaust and After the Second World War, 1939–1949: A Statistical Review*. Boulder, CO: East European Monographs.

Teplinsky, Sandra. 1998. *Out of the Darkness: The Untold Story of Jewish Revival in the Former Soviet Union*. Jacksonville Beach, FL: HOIM.

Urry, John. 2000. *Sociology Beyond Societies: Mobilities for Twenty-First Century*. London: Routledge.

Wasserstein, Bernard. 1996. *Vanishing Diaspora: The Jews in Europe Since 1945*. Cambridge, MA: Harvard University Press.

Zorándy, Sára. 2010. "Családi Kép" [Family Picture]. *Múlt és Jövő* 21(3): 121–29.

5

Poland's Jewish Turn

Memory, Materiality, and Performance

Geneviève Zubrzycki

Before World War II, Jews constituted 10% (about 3.5 million) of Poland's population. A third of Warsaw's inhabitants were Jewish. After the war Jewish life all but disappeared from Poland, as 90% of Polish Jewry was exterminated in the Holocaust. Many survivors chose to rebuild their lives elsewhere and start over after the war's trauma. Postwar pogroms, personal attacks and intimidation, and the loss of property—often stolen by former neighbors—pushed others to leave (Aleksiun 2003; Gross 2006; Cichopek-Gajraj 2014). Anti-Semitic purges in 1968 forced the emigration of 15,000 more Polish Jews (Stola 2000, 2010). As a result, the number of Jews currently living in Poland is quite small: Only 7,000 Polish residents self-identified as Jewish in the last census (Główny Urząd Statystyczny 2015). Based on that number, Sergio DellaPergola estimates that Poland's "core Jewish population" in 2020 was approximately 4,500 and that 13,000 individuals satisfied the criteria of the Law of Return by having at least one Jewish grandparent or a Jewish spouse (DellaPergola 2020, 311). When asked how many Jews currently live in Poland, however, the chief rabbi of Poland, Michael

Research for this article was funded by grants from the University of Michigan's Office of Research, the Rackham Graduate School, the College of Literature, Science, and the Arts, and the Society for the Scientific Study of Religion as well as by a research leave at the University of Michigan's Frankel Institute for Advanced Judaic Studies (2015–2016). A Guggenheim fellowship in 2021 allowed me to complete the writing. I am grateful to participants of the conference "The Jewish Revival in Europe and North America: Between Lifestyle Judaism and Institutional Renaissance," held at the European University Institute in Florence in June 2013, for their comments on an earlier version of this chapter.

Schudrich, often responds, "How many do you think there are? Take that number and double it. And now add one. There's always one more coming out of the closet."[1]

The small Jewish community of Poland has indeed known a significant renewal thanks to the fall of communism and the lifting of certain taboos; the influx of foreign financial and human resources, which made possible the creation of new Jewish institutions such as schools, student clubs, and community centers; and the coming of age of the third post-Holocaust generation.[2]

Parallel to this renewal is what I call Poland's Jewish turn, characterized by the examination of Poles' role in the Holocaust and the rediscovery of Poland's Jewish past following the publication of Jan Gross's *Neighbors* (2000, 2001) and by a marked interest in all things Jewish. That interest is observable in the forty-odd festivals of Jewish culture celebrated in the four corners of Poland; the popularity of klezmer, Jewish-style restaurants, Jewish folk dances, Jewish mementos, and even clothing; and the growth of Jewish studies programs at top Polish universities and academic production on Jewish-related themes (Gruber 2002; Lehrer 2013; Waligórska 2013; Wodziński 2011; Zubrzycki 2016). It is also visible in the urban landscape, with recent commemorative initiatives meant to render Jewish absence palpable, and in cultural practices meant to resurrect Jewish culture and expand notions of Polish national identity (Zubrzycki 2022). It is on those twin processes that I focus in this chapter.

For many activists involved in acts of salvage remembrance and performance, post–World War II Jewish absence has come to represent the loss of a multicultural Poland (Zubrzycki 2013, 2016). I argue that their activities are meant to *re-member*: not only to recall past Jewish presence on Polish lands but to attach a prosthetic Jewish limb to the Polish national body. If certain Polish social milieus now experience Jewish absence as a form of phantom limb pain, knowledge of the prior existence of the limb is a prerequisite for the pain of amputation to be felt. In other words, for absence to be meaningful and perhaps even felt, an absent presence must be brought

---

1. Personal communication, Warsaw, March 22, 2013.
2. I discuss the renewal of Jewish communal life in Poland in Chapter 6 of my book *Resurrecting the Jew: Nationalism, Philosemitism, and Poland's Jewish Revival* (Zubrzycki 2022). For accounts by its main participants, see Gebert and Datner (2001), Krajewski (2005), Gebert (2008), Penn et al. (2009), and Penn (2014). For numbers in the 1990s, see Gitelman (1990) and Gruber (2000).

back to the surface; erasure itself is being newly refigured. To demonstrate this process of creative historical salvage, I first discuss the material creation of absence. I then focus on the material discovery of Jewish traces and the recovery of Polish Jewish history through museums' material and phenomenological modes of storytelling. I conclude with a discussion of the performance and consumption of Jewishness.

My analysis is based on a varied body of data collected through archival and ethnographic research between the summer of 2010 and the fall of 2019 in several Polish cities, towns, and villages.[3] Ethnographic research included participant and nonparticipant observation in religious events, popular festivals, historical commemorations, political demonstrations, tourist excursions, and museum visits. My data include formal and informal interviews, primary texts (e.g., political speeches, inscriptions on monuments, newspaper editorials), iconographic documents (e.g., photographs, graffiti, ads, pamphlets), audiovisual materials (e.g., films and amateur videos, radio broadcasts, music and soundtracks), and artifacts (e.g., mementos and souvenirs). Although space constraints preclude my referring to all these materials in the present chapter, they do inform my analysis.

Materializing Absence

In Warsaw only the old town and the large avenue leading to it were rebuilt according to past incarnations after the war (Klekot 2012). Other districts, such as the former Jewish quarter, disappeared as socialist districts rose over the rubble. Broad avenues absorbed smaller streets and alleys, and monuments to Polish martyrdom began to pock the urban landscape. In postwar Poland, then, material traces of past Jewish life and death have been mostly erased (Janicka 2011; Chomątowska 2012; Klekot 2015). Across the country Jewish homes that survived the war were taken over by new occupants, and Jewish communal buildings, including synagogues and yeshivas, were either destroyed or repurposed as libraries, cinemas, or cultural centers by the socialist state (Meng 2012; Wilczyk 2009). Cemeteries were abandoned, untended, and left overgrown; even funeral stones were pilfered by local

---

3. I conducted most of my fieldwork in Kraków and Warsaw, where the ongoing Jewish turn is strongest, but I also conducted research in Lublin, Wrocław, Oświęcim, Chmielnik, and Szydłów.

inhabitants for a variety of everyday purposes (Baksik 2013). Except for a few sites and exceptional memorials and monuments, the marks of Jewish life have been nearly erased. And with the loss of living Jews' memories and the transformation of cityscapes, the very memory of Polish Jewish history has been slowly but surely buried.[4]

Warsaw today is therefore so different from its prewar incarnation that the Jewish absence can only be felt by those who knew the former space or with the help of physical markers indicating what was once there. To help conjure the specters of this past, during the past decade the city has been dotted with such historical signposting. The signposting project, however, has not been left to the typical fare of rather banal memorial plaques. Rather, it carefully features significant material markers in ways that engage the senses of passersby. The most prominent initiative is one that traces on the ground the vanished walls of the former ghetto. Twenty-two monuments were also installed along the ghetto's perimeter, each made of concrete and embellished with a bronze map and a Plexiglas plaque that gives its history in Polish and English.[5]

The commemorative path, inscribed in both Polish and English, not only marks the location and extent of the former ghetto but also provides a powerful reminder of the absent walls, whose trace crosses streets and parks and is sometimes interrupted by postwar buildings. By stepping onto the commemorative path, the passerby stumbles onto three realities: that of the past, that of its erasure, and that of its reemergence through new spatial imaginaries in the present. Signposting the former ghetto wall highlights the Polish experience of absence (of Polish Jews) on two levels: It reminds viewers of both the extermination of Jews during the Holocaust and their erasure from memory after the war.

---

4. Since 2002 the Foundation for the Preservation of Jewish Heritage in Poland, established by the Union of Jewish Communities in Poland and the World Jewish Restitution Organization, has been actively working to recover, preserve, and commemorate "surviving sites and monuments of Jewish cultural heritage in Poland." It is the only institution in Poland officially dedicated to that task, which concerns 200 synagogues and 1,200 cemeteries spread over two-thirds of the country (interview with Monika Krawczyk, May 25, 2016; and http://fodz.pl/?d=3&l=en, accessed October 22, 2020).

5. This initiative is akin to that of stumbling stones (*Stolpersteine*) in Germany, as the brick and brass pathway visually and sensorially interrupts the walking surface to tell a story to the casual walker who steps on, over, or beside it. For a list of the monuments' locations, see https://pl.m.wikipedia.org/wiki/Pomniki_granic_getta_w_Warszawie (accessed April 18, 2016).

Commemorative path that marks the emplacement of the vanished Warsaw Ghetto wall. Author's photo, May 17, 2014.

Another form of signposting signals the different experiences and fates of Jewish and non-Jewish Poles during World War II. A street-art piece by the artist Adam X (Adam Jastrzębski) titled *Here Was the Footbridge* in Polish, Hebrew, and Yiddish shows the location of the wooden footbridge that linked the small and the large ghettoes during World War II.[6] It highlights the different experiences of the war for Jews and non-Jews: Packed crowds of Jews are depicted on the stairs and on the bridge crossing Chłodna Street, whereas a few Gentiles appear to walk nonchalantly on the light and airy "Aryan" street.[7]

6. To the (rare) onlooker who can read Hebrew, the inscription in that language (top line) is most interesting, as a mistake in one of the letters in the word *bridge* transforms it into the word *void*. Thus "Here was the bridge" becomes "Here was the void." The mistake was most likely accidental—a diacritic correction has been added underneath the misspelled word—but it acutely captures the meaning of the artwork. My thanks to Efrat Bloom for pointing this out to me.

7. Chłodna Street was excluded from the ghetto because it was an important transport and communication axis.

Here Was the Footbridge, by street artist Adam X. The art piece's title is given in Polish, Hebrew, and Yiddish. Author's photo, May 17, 2014.

The mural was ceremoniously unveiled by Marek Edelman, the last surviving leader of the Warsaw Ghetto Uprising, on April 21, 2007, to commemorate the sixty-fourth anniversary of the event.[8] Meant to be a temporary piece, as street art often is, it eventually led to the establishment in 2012 of a formal, permanent monument to the footbridge in the form of an art installation called *The Footbridge of Memory* (*Kładka pamięci*). The installation, created by Tomasz Lec, consists of two large steel pillars that mark the sites of staircases to the footbridge, linked by wires above the street. At night, the wires are illuminated, creating a virtual bridge. The wires not only represent the platform of the bridge but are also reminiscent of *eruvim*, the wires or cords strung outside ultra-Orthodox Jewish homes that symbolically extend the private domain to allow the residents to carry objects on Shabbat and Yom Kippur, when they are not allowed to perform

8. http://puszka.waw.pl/tam_byla_kladka-projekt-pl-52.html (accessed October 23, 2014). Marek Edelman remained in Poland after the war, became a noted cardiologist, and was an active member of the Solidarity opposition. He died in 2009.

any work. At the foot of the pillars, at eye level, are historical inscriptions and visual materials, including three-dimensional bronze viewers showing photographs of life in the ghetto. The juxtaposition of the monument's contemporaneity and the archival photographs assails the spectator with the (virtual) weight of absence.[9]

Other mnemonic projects also focus on signposting the world that has been lost. The Great Synagogue is a case in point. Opened on Rosh Hashanah in 1878 for Reform Jews, the majestic building could seat 2,400 people, making it at the time the largest synagogue in the world. It was blown up by the Nazis at the end of the Warsaw Ghetto Uprising on May 16, 1943, and the site lay vacant until it was designated as the location for a modern skyscraper. Construction started in the 1970s but was not completed until 1991. On May 16, 2013, the seventieth anniversary of the destruction of the synagogue, the Jewish Historical Institute in Warsaw "brought the synagogue back to remembrance," as it announced several weeks in advance. Part memorial happening and part artistic installation, the event, called "The Great Absentee" (*Wielka nieobecna*), consisted primarily of a 1:10-scale plywood replica of the synagogue situated in a plaza adjacent to the Jewish Historical Institute and the former site of the Great Synagogue. The architect, Jan Strumiłło, also built walls around the replica on which he plastered photographs of prewar façades of the square where the synagogue stood, to give visitors "the feeling of strolling in the authentic square before the war."[10]

Five years later, on the occasion of the seventy-fifth anniversary of the beginning of the Warsaw Ghetto Uprising, on April 19, 2018, another commemoration took place. Open Republic (*Otwarta Rzeczpospolita*), an association fighting against anti-Semitism and xenophobia, and the Jewish Historical Institute organized a ceremonial virtual reconstruction of the Great Synagogue. Conceived by the Kraków-based artist Gabi von Seltmann,

9. This effect is perceived, of course, only to the extent that the passerby stops, looks, and views the photos on the monument; its potential phenomenological effect is necessarily limited by the viewer's ability and desire to engage with the installation in the first place. The installation nevertheless imparts some knowledge of the past presence and current absence even with minimal engagement.

10. https://sztetl.org.pl/en/towns/w/18-warsaw/112-synagogues-houses-of-prayer-and -others/89718-great-synagogue-tlomackie-street-warsaw. More photographs of the replica and the square can be viewed on Strumiłło's webpage, "The Great Absentee," http://janstrumillo.com/the-great-absentee/ (accessed September 21, 2015), and on the website of the design firm that executed the project: www.pracownia-tryktrak.pl/ portfolio/wielka-nieobecna/ (accessed September 21, 2015).

the performance consisted of the digital projection of an image of the Great Synagogue onto the blue skyscraper, accompanied by archival recordings of the synagogue's cantor and readings by the Polish-born Jewish American poet Irena Klepfisz. Lasting approximately 10 minutes, the presentation was repeated in a loop for two hours.[11] The performance was repeated in 2019 and 2020, and the events received coverage in national and international media.

Signposting Ruins

Another strategy of memory activists has been to transform sites of rubble left after the Holocaust and render them visible as distinctively Jewish ruins. In doing so, "empty" things such as bricks and beams are animated; they begin to exert power and act as historical agents. A key case is Próżna Street, the only remaining block of Warsaw's former Jewish district, which had been left to fall into ruins. The street's former apartment buildings were crumbling away, to the degree that metal nets were suspended over the sidewalks to protect pedestrians from falling debris. In 2008, on the occasion of the sixty-fifth anniversary of the Warsaw Ghetto Uprising, memory activists covered the boarded-up windows of the Próżna Street buildings with large prewar portraits and candid photographs of Polish Jews. Photographs were collected through a campaign called "And I Still See Their Faces," initiated in 1994 by the Shalom Foundation and headed by the prominent Polish Jewish actress Gołda Tencer. By the time the exhibit and installation opened on the anniversary of the Warsaw Ghetto Uprising in 2008, more than 9,000 photographs of Polish Jews had been collected.

The giant photographs on Próżna Street transformed the buildings from a faceless, decrepit space into a meaningful, if ephemeral, Jewish place. The street became the heart of Jewish Warsaw and an important site of Polish attempts to remember Jews and celebrate Jewish culture.[12] The material juxtaposition of the large sepia photographs of individuals and the

11. For a description of the event by the main organization sponsoring it, see http://www.otwarta.org/wielka-przywraca-pamiec/ (accessed June 13, 2018). See also the artist's description on her website, https://gabivonseltmann.com/portfolio/the-great-synagogue-restores-memory/ (accessed October 23, 2020). For a YouTube clip of the event, see https://www.youtube.com/watch?v=onlvd6hYz9U (accessed June 13, 2018).
12. Próżna Street and Grzybowski Square are where Warsaw's Jewish festival, Singer's Days (after Isaac Bashevis Singer), is celebrated in August every year since 2004.

dilapidated buildings with giant weeds growing in their gutters created a potent testament to the fate of Polish Jews, long forgotten, and of a new generation of Poles now trying to remember them. It also returned a quality of individual dignity to Jews whose lives and deaths were lost in the anonymity of the Holocaust's mass destruction and its commemoration as the extermination of the 6 million.

Yet unlike the street-art piece *Here Was the Footbridge*, which led to a permanent commemorative installation on Chłodna Street, the Próżna Street project has so far not produced more permanent markers. The tenement houses on the south side of the street have been completely renovated in recent years, transformed from Jewish ruins into office and retail spaces and bourgeois *apartamenty* un-self-consciously called Le Palais. A plaque on the immaculate building at the south corner of Próżna and Grzybowski Square now explains that "this building—a witness to the history of Jewish Warsaw—was renovated and preserved for future generations thanks to support from the Jewish Renaissance Foundation, Mr. Ronald S. Lauder, and Warimpex. TRIUVA, as current owner, contributes to the revitalization process of Próżna St." The buildings on the north side of the street were also renovated, and the large portraits of Jews have been removed.

The situation of Kraków in southern Poland differs sharply from that of Warsaw, because the city was not destroyed during the war. Although its Jewish district, Kazimierz, was left in a pitiful state until it underwent a slow process of gentrification in the 1990s, its seven synagogues, two Jewish cemeteries, and Jewish street names remained.[13] Today, the neighborhood is the stage for the largest festival of Jewish culture in Europe and boasts cafés, hotels, and music clubs where Jewish culture is performed and consumed year-round, as I describe later. Although much material Jewishness in Kazimierz is obvious and evident, there are also hidden traces that remain invisible to the untrained eye. It is precisely that training that designers–*cum*–memory activists Helena Czernek and Aleksander Prugar, founders of Mi Polin ("From Poland" in Hebrew), seek to provide.[14] In their late 30s, they create what they call "tangible Judaism"—modern Judaica design, commemorative objects—and host

13. The gentrification of Kazimierz is related to the filming of *Schindler's List* in the early 1990s, the subsequent development of Holocaust tourism, and the arrival of hipsters moving in because of low rent. See Kugelmass and Orla-Bukowska (2008), Murzyn (2006), and Lehrer (2013).

14. I interviewed Czernek and Prugar on October 26, 2015. See also their website, http://mipolin.pl/.

commemorative and pedagogical design workshops. At one such workshop, sponsored by Kraków's Jewish Community Center (JCC) during the Festival of Jewish Culture in 2014, the designers distributed empty paper frames to participants, giving them the task of roaming through Kazimierz, to find and mark Jewish traces. The exercise was meant to "train the eye"—to change the way one looks at one's surroundings; to look for, to see, and then to render visible the Jewish traces that remain. Absence, in this case, is rendered through the act of noticing past presence. The ultimate goal is not to uncover new Jewish elements in Kazimierz per se but to cultivate a different way of seeing and looking that participants can then take with them to the four corners of Poland. The participants were mostly young adults, some with children, from different regions of Poland. They expressed interest in learning how to discover traces of Jewish presence in their own towns, asking what they should look for and where. Many saw discovering those Jewish traces as an important step in recovering a multicultural Poland. As one young woman told me as we were walking down a street in July 2014, "This [Jewish] culture was taken away from us. First by the Nazis, then by the communists, who transformed old synagogues into storage facilities or neglected to care for cemeteries. Finding some of it again today is a bit like finding pieces of ourselves."

Re-creating the Jewish Past

So far I have discussed small-scale initiatives by individual memory activists, NGOs, and city planners that focused on framing and animating absence, either by signposting what has vanished or by marking anonymous ruins or invisible or ill-defined cultural remains *as* Jewish. In this section I focus on major state-sponsored or state-sanctioned projects, such as museums, which also play an important role in the Jewish turn.

History museums, like schools, play a key role in the creation and maintenance of collective memory and national identity. In post-totalitarian societies they acquire the additional social function of demystification and *re*-education.[15] The current terrain is thus extremely fertile

---

15. That process, however, is not always easy because museums also *objectify* memory and identity, which means that museums in such societies must first *undo*—deconstruct some of what they had previously done—before they can reconstruct. This is sometimes easier said than done, and of course this does not mean that new or revised museums do not engage in a remythologization of another kind. See my analysis of the Auschwitz-Birkenau Museum in Zubrzycki (2006, 98–140).

for history museums, as is evident throughout Eastern Europe: Old museums are being redesigned and their narratives revised. Most obvious in the revised historical narratives of Eastern Europe is the emphasis on the Holocaust, which before 1989 had been mostly effaced or diluted as but one part of a broader history of fascist aggression. In the decades since, new museums are being opened every year, and many more are in the works.[16] Because museums are privileged sites for the transmission of historical narratives and the construction of collective memory—because they are usually legitimized by state authorities—they typically have significant resources that allow them not only to affirm and promote a historical discourse but also to transmit that knowledge with unusually dynamic and technologically sophisticated pedagogical tools. New Holocaust museums increasingly try to impart knowledge not only by relaying information but also by cultivating emotions. Intellectual recognition of a new history is achieved through sensation; in that sense, these newly opened facilities are "phenomenological museums" where the visitor's body directly encounters and engages the recreated history. The goal is to have visitors "feel" and "experience" the past.[17] In the Polish context, Kraków's Schindler's Factory Museum does just that: It plays with visitors' vision and orientation (crossing a narrow, dark passage), hearing (music, archival radio broadcasts), and touch (walking on uneven surfaces), creating bodily sensations in the visitor to generate a multidimensional impression of the historical situation.

Whereas Schindler's Museum focuses on wartime Kraków and thus deals primarily with the Holocaust, Warsaw's Polin Museum of the History of Polish Jews, inaugurated in October 2014, focuses on everyday life,

16. In Poland alone, and specifically on Jewish history and/or the Holocaust, over half a dozen museums have been inaugurated in the past two decades: Kraków's Galicia Jewish Museum was founded in 2003; Schindler's Factory Museum, which focuses on occupation in World War II Kraków, opened in 2010; the Museum of Kraków's Ghetto, The Eagle Pharmacy, opened in 2013; and the Polin Museum of the History of Polish Jews in Warsaw opened its building in April 2013 and its main exhibit in October 2014. Many other smaller museums and educational centers can be found throughout Poland, such as the Świętokrzyski Shtetl in Chmielnik, which opened in 2014.

17. This experiential strategy has been important elsewhere as well. The Holocaust Museum in Washington, DC, presents the visitor with an identification card as she or he enters the premises to foster a temporary virtual identification with a person whose fate the visitor does not know until the end of the tour. The visitor is supposed to live the uncertainty of the war through this historical avatar. This creates a certain emotional investment in the story being told to the visitors, the materials they see, and the facts they learn.

specifically rejecting the tendency to reduce the long and complex history of Polish Jews to their destruction in the Holocaust. The museum stands at the center of Muranów, the former Jewish neighborhood and wartime ghetto, in front of the monument to the heroes of the Warsaw Ghetto Uprising. Financed through public and transnational private cooperation, Polin's core exhibit tells the story of 1,000 years of Jewish life on Polish lands, narrated through a series of multimedia scenarios and interactive props. The core exhibit is exceptionally rich, impressing on the visitor the diversity and complexity of Jewish communities over centuries before the Holocaust. It relies largely on digital magic. Built without a collection and thus with few artifacts, the exhibit relies on strong visual and tactile cues to engage visitors in a specific virtual scene. Its primary mode of communication is storytelling, but always from the perspective of those who lived at a given time, creating an intimate link between a given narrator and visitors, transporting the visitors through sound, sight, and touch to different places and times, from sacred spaces such as a replica of the Gwoździec Synagogue to the shtetl's marketplace, to the city street, the dance hall, and the cinema. By the time visitors enter the Holocaust gallery, they have been trained and equipped to grasp the variety of worlds that were annihilated during World War II and the challenges of rebuilding a many-faceted Jewish life in communist Poland.

By focusing on mundane life, the museum makes two important narrative correctives. One is oriented to foreign visitors, as the exhibit emphasizes that Poland is not only the graveyard of European Jewry but also the place where it grew and where it nourished rich and diverse communities, important religious and secular movements, and historically significant political projects. This emphasis on life before death is important in and of itself but also because it presses guests to fully grasp the tragedy of the Holocaust and its aftermath. After visitors pass through that section of the exhibit, they exit the museum and encounter—not only visually but also aurally and viscerally—the void of Jews and Jewish signs, sounds, and symbols in the streets of Warsaw. The second challenge proffered by the museum is to the dominant mythology of Poland's intrinsic Catholic identity and ethnonational homogeneity. The museum pointedly and irrefutably shows that the current demographic makeup of Poland is the exception instead of the rule in Polish history. Polish visitors therefore learn an important lesson by visiting the museum, namely,

Replica of the seventeenth-century wooden synagogue from Gwoździec (now in Ukraine) in the Polin Museum of the History of Polish Jews. The synagogue was damaged during World War I and destroyed by the Nazis in World War II. It was reconstructed in the exhibit using traditional methods and was hand-painted with natural pigments by artists and volunteers from Poland and the United States. Author's photograph, October 28, 2014.

that Poland was not always the monoethnic and monocultural society it now is.[18]

Kraków's Kazimierz district is a living testament to that diversity, and it is prolifically used as such. Inspired by the ever popular "Museums at Night" events, when museums open their doors free of charge until early morning, the Kraków JCC initiated 7@Nite in 2011, opening Kazimierz's seven synagogues to large crowds of Krakovians eager to learn about the

---

18. The challenge for any museum is that it does not control how its message is received. The specific challenge for the Polin Museum is that it exists within wider physical, cultural, and political environments that emphasize Polish martyrdom and heroism. The message of Polin's core exhibit, then, can be folded into a self-complacent narrative of Polish hospitality that whitewashes anti-Semitism (Zubrzycki 2022: 106–12).

past and present religious landscape of Polish Jews. In the first year of 7@Nite, more than 8,000 people flooded the narrow streets of Kazimierz. The event was such a success that it became a yearly tradition, attracting similar numbers. Each synagogue hosts lectures or workshops, or gives tours during which visitors can meet the local Jewish population, talk to rabbis, and get a feel for places they otherwise would rarely or never enter. In a way similar to that of Kraków's Festival of Jewish Culture, non-Jewish Poles, through events such as 7@Nite, revisit and at least momentarily recover part of Polish history. As Janusz Makuch, the cofounder and director of Kraków's Festival of Jewish Culture, told me in one of our conversations, "Whether people know it or not, it is a *fact* that Jews, for many, many centuries . . . made tremendous contributions to Polish culture. So when we're talking about Polish culture, we're equally talking about Jewish culture. Without the contribution of Jews, true Polish culture couldn't exist. Forget it! What I'm trying to do is to help Poles realize what is theirs."[19] What the Festival of Jewish Culture, the JCC's 7@Nite, and the Polin Museum of the History of Polish Jews are working toward, Makuch explained, is not merely to bring non-Jewish Poles in contact with the past Jewish presence in Poland but to instill an intuitive knowledge in Poles that Jews and Jewish culture are part and parcel of Polish culture and must be recovered and reintegrated as such.

These multifaceted initiatives undertaken by individual artists, NGOs, and state institutions are creating an ideological climate in which Jews, Jewish culture, and Judaism can occupy and even thrive in public space. Since the mid-2000s, for example, a giant outdoor *hanukiah* has been lit in Warsaw on the first night of Hanukkah by Chabad rabbis, accompanied by city and state officials. The chief rabbi of Poland, Michael Schudrich, also lights a *hanukiah* at the presidential palace. Both events are photographed and widely publicized on television and in the press.[20] To give another

---

19. Conversation (in English) with Janusz Makuch, March 1, 2012.
20. Such practices cannot be cynically seen as mere electoral strategies by non-Jewish politicians, because the "Jewish vote" is of little significance, given the small number of Jews in Poland. But they are certainly addressed as much to international audiences as to national constituencies. The Polish state has been keenly aware of the need to rebrand Poland abroad, and there can be little doubt that its support of Jewish-related initiatives is part of that process. A prime example is the recent opening of the Polin Museum of the History of Polish Jews in Warsaw, which the Ministry of Culture advertised and promoted abroad.

example of Jewish traditions carried into public space, in 2012 Warsaw's Joint Distribution Committee invited architectural firms to exhibit their contemporary interpretations of sukkahs, temporary structures built on the occasion of the Jewish holiday of Sukkot, on Grzybowski Square.[21] Half a dozen were built and exhibited in the square, near Próżna Street. The local population was invited to attend, meet members of the Jewish community, and learn about the tradition. I asked a (non-Jewish) commuter walking by what the structures or sculptural installations were; he correctly explained that they were contemporary interpretations of sukkahs, adding that he was happy that the tradition was being revived. "You know," he told me, his eyebrows raised, "Poland is more than the traditional nativity scenes of Kraków."

Jewish markers, whether religious or secular, create visual and material diversity in the cityscape, "monumentally" if modestly diluting Catholicism's sensory dominance. Aneta, a longtime Kraków JCC volunteer who is expressly anticlerical and declares herself an atheist, expanded on this during a Shabbat dinner: "I think it's great to see all of that [Jewish religious activity]. I'm not religious but I think it's good to see that there's something else than what we already know, and frankly speaking, we're sick of . . . processions, pilgrimages here and there, crosses everywhere."

Commemorations and Posthumous Acts of Solidarity

Marek Edelman, the sole survivor of the Warsaw Ghetto Uprising until his death in 2009, used to commemorate the onset of the uprising, on April 19, 1943, with a bouquet of yellow daffodils. After his passing, the tradition was taken up by several of his close friends and members of the Jewish community. And in 2013, on the occasion of the seventieth anniversary of the uprising, designer Helena Czernek created for the Polin Museum a yellow paper daffodil to be worn as a pin. Some 40,000 were made and distributed by volunteers, and the paper daffodil could be seen worn by Poles for weeks after the commemorative events. The memento was effective because it linked the commemoration of the uprising with the memory of Marek Edelman, a much respected figure. It was also semiotically complex. Once

---

21. The event was meant to mark the opening of the Warsaw Jewish Community Center; see https://vimeo.com/55538006.

pinned, the yellow paper flower opened up and looked much like a star.[22] Many affixed the flower/star to their lapels, others to their sleeves, replicating the branding of Jews during the Nazi occupation. Special commemorative marches and bike rides were organized, retracing the now vanished traces of Jewish Warsaw.

The paper daffodil has become a tradition. On April 19, 2016, more than a thousand volunteers distributed 60,000 paper daffodils in Warsaw alone. Eight hundred schools in various regions of Poland made additional daffodils and distributed them in their small towns and villages. In 2019 more than 2,500 volunteers distributed 200,000 paper daffodils.[23] Although the daffodil has come to symbolize, over the years, the memory of the uprising, its paper incarnation that morphs into a yellow star has acquired an additional signification, that of the Holocaust and the fate that separated Jewish from non-Jewish citizens of Poland. Wearing the paper daffodil/star has therefore become a commemorative act as well as a posthumous act of resistance to the distinction made by Nazis (and by many Poles) between Jews and non-Jews.

Although events commemorating the Holocaust in Poland are not new, their scope and frequency have dramatically changed since 1989, to the extent that they are now commonplace. In Kraków, for example, the March of Memory commemorates the liquidation of the Jewish ghetto every year. Participants walk from the Podgórze neighborhood, where Jews were relocated in a ghetto, to the Płaszów concentration camp. The march takes on meaning for its participants as an embodied practice attempting to replicate the forced migration of Jews, as practiced and walked history. These embodied and publicly performed rituals simultaneously allow Polish Jewish history to be phenomenologically internalized by individuals and externalized onto the material cityscape. The material and performative remaking of public space in turn motivates political discourses about citizenship and what

---

22. Czernek told me that she had never intended the daffodil to be a yellow star; that it was a material flaw caused by nothing more than poor glue and problematic execution by the volunteers who had assembled the 40,000 paper flowers. However, it is precisely that additional, accidental signification that made the small paper memento such an impactful one.

23. See www.polin.pl/en/news/2016/04/22/4th-edition-of-the-daffodils-campaign (accessed July 13, 2016); and https://warszawa.wyborcza.pl/warszawa/7,54420,24682689,miasto -cale-w-zonkilach-warszawiacy-upamietniaja-bohaterow.html (accessed December 8, 2020).

constitutes Polishness. Although the march is conducted in silence, speeches are made at the departure and arrival points. In the multiple marches I participated in since the early 2000s, the theme of citizenship has been uniformly prominent, with the emphasis laid squarely on the fact that Jews were Polish. The effect is to not only materially and performatively but also discursively reject a vision of ethnic Polishness narrowly predicated on its association with Catholicism.

Consuming and Performing Jewishness

Many of the practices I have discussed in previous sections are ritual-like (e.g., commemorations, perambulations), educational (e.g., museums, workshops), or festive (e.g., holidays, festivals). Many Poles, however, engage in daily, mundane "Jewish" activities: They listen to Jewish music, from modern klezmer to Israeli hip-hop; they eat in Jewish restaurants and drink kosher vodka (rumored as "purer"); and some even "dress Jewish." What do consumption patterns and individual practices mean to those engaging in them?

A fashionably contemporary clothing label in Warsaw that launched a new "Jewish" line called Risk Oy may offer clues. Initially targeted at young Jews, Risk Oy produces pricey T-shirts and hoodies with slogans such as "Thanks to my Mom" (in English), adorned with a variety of Star of David designs and Hebrew inscriptions. The owner of the brand told the *Times of Israel*, "What we really want . . . is to rebrand Jewish identity. We want to show the modern, positive aspects of it. What we are doing is showing that being Jewish is cool and sexy" (Ghert-Zand 2014). The clothes are not bought and worn by Jews alone, however. One non-Jewish customer quoted in the story, a 40-year-old lawyer living in Warsaw, explained, "Wearing [Risk Oy] is like taking part in a public discussion about Jews in Poland—that Jews live here and that Jews can live here." This is a noteworthy comment on two levels: first, because it emphasizes that public discussion about Jews in Poland is actually one about the very identity of Poland and a critique of the still dominant vision of the nation as ethnically Polish and (nominally) Catholic; and, second, because it indicates that this public discussion is taking place not only in the pages of newspapers and the discourses of public intellectuals but also on the streets among the hoi polloi and in the clothes they wear (or the music they listen to, or the bars they patronize). The NGO Foundation for Freedom several years earlier (2010) had produced "I'm a Jew" T-shirts as part of a campaign that consisted in "spreading . . . slogans signaling the existence of . . . discriminated social groups in Poland," including Jews, atheists, and homosexuals.[24] Hence liberal, leftist youth wore T-shirts and brandished posters in protests against clerical nationalists, subversively claiming that they were "Jews." With this display they mocked anti-Semitic conspiracy theories of the right claiming that Jews rule Poland, but they also called for a different kind of Poland, one in which the right's distinctions between "real Poles," "Jews," and "bad Poles" would have no political traction.

Consuming Jewish food, whether in its Ashkenazi form or in its contemporary Israeli versions, is also a way to acquaint oneself with either the "known" and recognizable (Ashkenazi cuisine, which is quite similar to Polish cuisine, in part because it is constitutive of Polish dishes) or the mysterious and exotic (Israeli cuisine). It is that mix of "ours" and "other," of the familiar and the exotic, that likewise attracts many (non-Jewish) young women who take part in an Israeli dance group. One of the dancers, a young Protestant woman who majored in Judaic studies and art history and is now a museum educator in a Catholic institution, explained to me:

> On one hand, [Jewish culture] is, let's say, "Oriental." But on the other hand, because it developed in Poland, in spite of everything it's somehow very much tied with Poland, yes? It's kind of an exotic element in our environment. It's not something like . . . Swahili somewhere far off in Africa, but [rather] something that is different from Polish culture yet at the same time related to it, inseparable even.

Performing various forms of Jewish dances—Ashkenazi, Sephardic, or contemporary Israeli—brings those young women (and, one presumes, their audiences) closer to a different side of Polish history than the one exalted in Polish national mythology and its sensorium. At the same time, as this woman's explanation suggests, the dances transport them to faraway, exotic, "Oriental" (yet, paradoxically, more "Western" than Poland) places like Israel.

---

24. Other T-shirts that were part of the 2004 campaign included, "I don't go to church," "I don't want to have kids," or "I'm gay." See www.tiszertdlawolnosci.tiszert.com/ (accessed July 22, 2012).

Members of the dance troupe Kachol, rehearsing at the Popper Synagogue in Kraków. Author's photo, March 5, 2012.

Conclusion

As evocative as these endeavors are, we should ask whether they reach large enough audiences to be significant or to constitute a bona fide social movement. Are they merely elite practices by artists and activists that do not quite resonate with the general population? How successful is the mnemonic recovery of material traces of long vanished Jews? From a sociological perspective, it is not yet clear how to define the success of the projects I have analyzed in this chapter. One way to adjudicate or at least gain perspective on the issue is to give close attention to the extent to which Jewish histories are discovered, named, and animated and the extent to which appropriate attunement to their material traces is cultivated, not only among memory activists and cosmopolitan consumers but also in public pedagogy and city planning. By this measure, the Jewish turn is certainly significant, though its effects in transforming Poland's national identity or the manifold ways it may be subjectively internalized remain to be seen.

Moreover, the project of testifying to absence has inevitable limits entailed by the stubborn fact of objective absence. At issue is not the simple commemorative logic of recollection and recovery, reflection, and redress. Rather, at stake is the problem of the phantom itself: How do we represent that which remains lost? How do we reincorporate that which is no longer? What does it mean to rewrite a national history, and imagine its future, when those who have been excised and that which has been erased can never be fully restored? The projects of contemporary Polish artists and activists that I explored here go beyond the conventional ambitions of historical commemoration and engage with a far more elusive and disquieting aspect of history. The Jewish turn in Poland remains primarily a Polish problem, and it may be a problem for Jews insofar as they are construed in these endeavors only as the other through which the national self is constituted.

References

Aleksiun, Natalia. 2003. "Jewish Response to Antisemitism in Poland, 1944–1947." In *Contested Memories: Poles and Jews During the Holocaust and Its Aftermath*, ed. Joshua D. Zimmerman, 249–56. New Brunswick, NJ: Rutgers University Press.

Baksik, Łukasz. 2013. *Macewy codziennego użytku / Matzevot of Everyday Use*. Wołowiec: Wydawnictwo Czarne.

Chomątowska, Beata. 2012. *Stacja Muranów* [Muranów Station]. Sękowa: Wydawnictwo Czarne.

Cichopek-Gajraj, Anna. 2014. *Beyond Violence: Jewish Survivors in Poland and Slovakia, 1944–48*. Cambridge, UK: Cambridge University Press.

DellaPergola, Sergio. 2020. "World Jewish Population, 2019." In *American Jewish Year Book 2020: An Annual Record of the North American Jewish Communities Since 1899*, ed. Arnold Dashefsky and Ira M. Sheskin, 119: 263–353. New York: American Jewish Committee.

Gebert, Konstanty. 2008. *Living in the Land of Ashes*. Kraków: Austeria.

Gebert, Konstanty, and Helena Datner. 2001. *Jewish in Poland: Achievements, Challenges, and Priorities Since the Collapse of Communism*. London: Institute for Jewish Policy Research.

Ghert-Zand, Renee. 2014. "Polish Fashion Entrepreneur Makes Being Jewish Sexy." *Times of Israel*, January 31. www.timesofisrael.com/polish-fashion -entrepreneur-makes-being-jewish-sexy/?utm_source=Newsletter+subscribers &utm_campaign=0c5a586595-JTA_Daily_Briefing_1_31_2014&utm_medium

=email&utm_term=0_2dce5bc6f8-0c5a586595-25416689 (accessed February 1, 2014).

Gitelman, Zvi. 1990. "Eastern European Countries." In *American Jewish Year Book 1990: A Record of Events and Trends in American and World Jewish Life*, ed. David Singer and Ruth R. Seldin, 90: 378–92. New York: American Jewish Committee.

Główny Urząd Statystyczny [Statistics Poland]. 2015. "Struktura narodowo-etniczna, językowa i wyznaniowa ludności Polski" [Ethnonational, Linguistic, and Denominational Structure of Poland's Population]. https://stat.gov.pl/ spisy-powszechne/nsp-2011/nsp-2011-wyniki/struktura-narodowo-etniczna -jezykowa-i-wyznaniowa-ludnosci-polski-nsp-2011,22,1.html.

Gross, Jan. 2000. *Sąsiedzi: Historia zagłady żydowskiego miasteczka*. Sejny, Poland: Pogranicze.

Gross, Jan. 2001. *Neighbors: The Destruction of the Jewish Community in Jedwabne, Poland*. Princeton, NJ: Princeton University Press.

Gross, Jan. 2006. *Fear: Anti-Semitism in Poland After the Holocaust*. New York: Random House.

Gruber, Ruth Ellen. 2000. "East Central Europe." In *American Jewish Year Book 2000: A Record of Events and Trends in American and World Jewish Life*, ed. David Singer and Lawrence Grossman, 100: 373–95. New York: American Jewish Committee.

Gruber, Ruth Ellen. 2002. *Virtually Jewish: Reinventing Jewish Culture in Europe*. Berkeley: University of California Press.

Janicka, Elżbieta. 2011. *Festung Warschau*. Warsaw: Wydawnictwo Krytyki Politycznej.

Klekot, Ewa. 2012. "Constructing a 'Monument of National History and Culture' in Poland: The Case of the Royal Castle in Warsaw." *International Journal of Heritage Studies* 8(5): 459–78.

Klekot, Ewa. 2015. "Memory and Oblivion in the Cityscape: Commemorations in the Warsaw Districts of Muranów and Mirów." *Ethnologia Europaea* 45(1): 58–79.

Krajewski, Stanisław. 2005. *Poland and the Jews: Reflections of a Polish Jew*. Kraków: Austeria.

Kugelmass, Jack, and Anna-Maria Orla-Bukowska. 2008. "If You Build It They Will Come: Recreating a Jewish District in Post-Communist Kraków." *City and Society* 10(1): 315–53.

Lehrer, Erica. 2013. *Jewish Poland Revisited: Heritage Tourism in Unquiet Places*. Bloomington: Indiana University Press.

Meng, Michael. 2012. *Shattered Spaces: Encountering Jewish Ruins in Postwar Germany and Poland*. Cambridge, MA: Harvard University Press.

Murzyn, Monika. 2006. *Kazimierz: The Central European Experience of Urban Regeneration*. Kraków: International Cultural Centre.

Penn, Shana, ed. 2014. *Deep Roots, New Branches: Personal Essays on the Rebirth of Jewish Life in Poland Since 1989*. Warsaw: Taube Foundation for Jewish Life and Culture.

Penn, Shana, Konstanty Gebert, and Anna Goldstein, eds. 2009. *The Fall of the Wall and the Rebirth of Jewish Life in Poland, 1989–2009*. Warsaw: Taube Foundation.

Stola, Dariusz. 2000. *Kampania antysyjonistyczna w Polsce, 1967–1968* [The 1967–68 Anti-Zionist Campaign in Poland]. Warsaw: Instytut Studiów Politycznych Polskiej Akademii Nauk.

Stola, Dariusz. 2010. *Kraj bez wyjścia? Migracje z Polski 1949–1989* [A Country with No Exit? Migrations from Poland, 1949–1989]. Warsaw: Instytut Pamięci Narodowej, Komisja Ścigania Zbrodni przeciwko Narodowi Polskiemu: Instytut Studiów Politycznych PAN.

Waligórska, Magdalena. 2013. *Klezmer's Afterlife: An Ethnography of the Jewish Music Revival in Poland and Germany*. New York: Oxford University Press.

Wilczyk, Wojciech. 2009. *There's No Such Thing as an Innocent Eye*. Kraków: Atlas Sztuki.

Wodziński, Marcin. 2011. "Jewish Studies in Poland." *Journal of Modern Jewish Studies* 10(1): 101–18.

Zubrzycki, Geneviève. 2006. *The Crosses of Auschwitz: Nationalism and Religion in Post-Communist Poland*. Chicago: University of Chicago Press.

Zubrzycki, Geneviève. 2013. "Narrative Shock and (Re)Making Polish Memory in the Twenty-First Century." In *Memory and Postwar Memorials: Confronting the Violence of the Past*, ed. Florence Vatan and Marc Silberman, 95–115. New York: Palgrave.

Zubrzycki, Geneviève. 2016. "Nationalism, 'Philosemitism,' and Symbolic Boundary-Making in Contemporary Poland." *Comparative Studies in Society and History* 58(1): 66–98.

Zubrzycki, Geneviève. 2022. *Resurrecting the Jew: Nationalism, Philosemitism, and Poland's Jewish Revival*. Princeton, NJ: Princeton University Press.

6

Has There Been a "Jewish Revival" in Russia and Ukraine After Communism?

Zvi Gitelman

Communist regimes did not follow a uniform policy toward Judaism and Jewishness. Any "Jewish revival," therefore, would take place against different backgrounds in the postcommunist countries. Communist regimes were antireligious, though they varied in their militancy on this issue. All but one, the USSR, permitted a national religious Jewish organization to exist, though it was carefully controlled by the state. Bulgaria, Poland, and Romania also had secular Jewish organizations, but Czechoslovakia and Hungary did not. Only the USSR officially classified Jews as an ethnic group or "nationality," though there is evidence that in the other Soviet bloc countries security and other state organs kept records of Jews as a distinct entity. The USSR, whose ideologists had rejected Jewish nationhood long before the 1917 revolution, included Jews among the officially recognized nationalities of the federation but never permitted a religious Jewish body to exist beyond the board of twenty that nominally ran a local synagogue. In contrast to the Russian Orthodox church and Muslim institutions, Judaism was never permitted a national or republic-level organization. Jewish religious and linguistic education had ceased in the USSR by 1941, though it existed in the other countries at least until 1950 and in most cases beyond.

The Soviet Union had by far the largest Jewish population in the Soviet bloc, 2,267,814 in 1959, reduced to 1,445,000 by 1989, and today about

350,000 in the former Soviet states. The Jewish population of the Russian Federation, as enumerated in the 2010 census, is 162,409,[1] down from 233,600 in the October 2002 census. In Ukraine the steadily declining Jewish population is estimated to be 46,000 (March 2022), down from 71,000 (2016), which was down from 103,600 in 2001.[2] The 2019 census in Belarus, once part of the Pale of Settlement, enumerated 12,660 Jews, down from 27,202 in 1999.[3] In this essay I focus on Russia and Ukraine, the post-Soviet republics with the largest Jewish populations.

The revival or creation of public Jewish life was made possible by the removal of all restrictions against Jews and organized Jewish communities in every one of the Soviet successor states, a large infusion of funds and personnel dedicated to reviving and reestablishing Jewish life, and a manifest interest in doing so among a significant number of self-identified Jews. On the other hand, "revival" has been vitiated by massive emigration, especially of the young, no traditions of volunteerism and self-organization, widespread ignorance of Judaism and any form of "thick" Jewish culture, and the same forces that militate against intensive involvement with Jewishness in other countries—acculturation, assimilation, low birthrates, and high rates of marriage to non-Jews.

The Consequences of Communism

It is highly likely that before the 1917 revolutions most Jews in Ukraine, most of whom were residing in the Pale of Settlement, lived their lives according to the practices of what we now call Orthodox Judaism. Because the areas now in the Russian Federation were mostly outside the Pale, few Jews lived there. They tended to be more acculturated to Russian culture and more

---

1. The census counted 158,801 "Jews" and 3,608 "Central Asian Jews." *Itogi vserossiskoi perepisi naseleniia 2010 g.*, tom 4, kniga 1: *Natsional'nyi sostav i vladenie iazykam i grazhdanstvo*, pp. 13 and 17 (Moscow: Statistika Rossii, 2012). These are the numbers of people who reported themselves as Jews to the census taker. No documents had to be produced to support their self-identification. It is believed that such people are most likely to have two Jewish parents. Others might have a Jewish mother and are thus Jewish by Jewish law (Halakha) but might consider themselves to be of the nationality of their father, and vice versa.
2. The census scheduled for 2012 was postponed to the fall of 2013, but it was not held then either.
3. *Natsional'nyi sostav naseleniia Respubliki Belarus* (Minsk: Natsional'nyi statisticheskii komitet respubliki Belarus', 2020). Curiously, a 2009 census found 12,611 Jews there.

"liberal" in their religious practices (see Nathans 2002; see also Ginzburg 1944; Kozlov 2007). In both areas, as well as in all the rest of the European USSR, the Soviet government's antireligious drives in 1924–1930s and 1957–1964 closed most of the synagogues and all Jewish religious schools. Only a small minority of Jews continued to practice Judaism. Even in the 1960s–1980s, "the religious movement touched only a small percentage of the adherents of the [Jewish national] movement" (Charny 2012, 333),[4] those who sought to emigrate to Israel.

Although before the revolution Vladimir Lenin and Joseph Stalin had vigorously denied that Jews were a nation, in 1918 the Soviet government classified Jews as a *natsional'nost'*, usually translated as "nationality" but meaning "ethnic group." There were well over 100 such groups in the USSR, and they enjoyed various degrees of cultural services and social-political recognition. Thus, although there were 1,100 state-funded Yiddish schools in the Soviet Union in 1931, that number fell precipitously in the late 1930s and throughout the 1940s. This was because most Jewish parents preferred to send their children to Russian-language schools, which afforded them greater prospects for vocational and social mobility, and because the regime turned away from *korenizatsia*, its policy of encouraging non-Russian cultures. During World War II, 2.5–2.7 million Jews were murdered by the Nazis, their allies, and local collaborators.

By 1950 there was not a single Jewish school of any kind anywhere in the USSR. The creators of the secular, Soviet, Yiddish-based culture that the government had substituted for Hebraic, Judaic, Zionist, or secularist Jewish cultures were murdered, imprisoned, or, at best, forced to curtail their activities. The result was that although Jews were officially identified as such on the fifth line of their obligatory internal passports and were regarded as Jews, often with hostility, by society as a whole, they had no "thick culture" that could be described in any way as Jewish. Several generations of Soviet Jews had no access to any form of Jewish culture at all. Even more generations had no exposure to Judaism (religion). Hebrew was the only language that could not be taught in the USSR (Volvovsky 2012, 334–58), and Yiddish was not taught after 1938 or so.

All Jewish organizations had been closed down; the only Jewish institution that remained was the synagogue, though many cities had no synagogue

---

4. On Judaism in 1941–1964, see Altshuler (2012).

either. Half a century after the Jewish schools had been shut, the first Jewish school opened (1988). Synagogue buildings that had been made into workers' clubs, storehouses, gymnasia, libraries, or other public buildings were sometimes returned to Jewish associations, which had sprung up with amazing rapidity during perestroika (Gitelman 2001).

What "Jewish" Means in Russia and Ukraine

What, then, kept a sense of Jewish identity and consciousness alive among Soviet Jews? Ironically, although Marxism-Leninism had predicted the mutual assimilation (*sliianie*) of all peoples and claimed that it would come with communism, the Soviet system registered all its citizens by "nationality" (ethnicity). Ethnic designation could not be changed, and it could be chosen only if one's parents were of different nationalities, whereupon the citizen could choose one of those, but no other. Because nationality was visible on the "passport," which was displayed often—when applying for a job or higher education, sending a registered letter, purchasing an airplane ticket, etc.—the owner and viewers of the passports were often made aware of one's nationality.

Second, whereas those who grew up in the 1920s and 1930s usually claim that they paid no attention to nationality, because it played no role in social life, by the 1950s Jews came to think of themselves as "invalids of the fifth category," a play on the numerical categorization of disability and the designation of nationality on the *piataia grafa*, the fifth line of the passport. Those who would have liked to think of themselves as Russian were prevented from doing so both by official designation and by social hostility toward Jews. State-imposed ethnicity and anti-Semitism thus became the most common and salient bases for Jewish consciousness. Unsurprisingly, for many this became a pejorative identity.

When, after 1971, a substantial number of Jews began to emigrate from the USSR, it became possible to probe their conceptions of what it meant to be Jewish. Not surprisingly, they did not think about being Jewish in religious terms but as an ethnicity, which led many of them to see themselves as potentially belonging in a Jewish state, the political embodiment of Jewish nationhood, *pace* Lenin. Only after the dissolution of the Soviet system was it possible to inquire about the Jewishness of Jews in the former Soviet Union (FSU) itself. In 1992–1993 two Russian colleagues, Vladimir Shapiro and Valeryi Chervyakov, and I conducted the largest survey ever taken of Jews in the FSU in three cities in Russia (Moscow, St. Petersburg, and Ekaterinburg [formerly Sverdlovsk]) and five cities in Ukraine (Kyiv, Chernivtsi, Kharkiv, Lviv, and Odessa).[5] We repeated the survey in 1997–1998, to see what changes had taken place in the first years after the Soviet collapse.

We found, contrary to outsiders' impressions, that among Russian and Ukrainian Jews, Jewishness is a deeply held identity. But it is *not* connected to religious practice, a Jewish language, or Jewish culture. It is not linked to Hebrew or Yiddish, distinctive dress, special Jewish foods, Jewish holidays, residence, or religious observance. Instead, the feeling that one is Jewish is defined by *boundaries*—the markers of who is in the group and who is out. Thus, who was born a Jew is much more important than what one does as a Jew. Both state and society, including its Jews, were more concerned with establishing who was in and who was out of the group than with what its culture was. For most, being Jewish is based on descent ("blood") and feeling, not culture. To be a Jew, one must be descended from Jews. So, for example, contrary to widespread assumptions among Jews elsewhere, some Russian and Ukrainian Jews did not think that conversion to Judaism necessarily made one a Jew, and some believed that a Jew can be a practicing Christian. Such conceptions conflict with notions of Jewishness prevalent in Israel and the Jewish Diaspora, forcing a reconsideration of the meanings of Jewishness.

When presented with a list of eighteen items that might describe a "good Jew," the most frequently cited attribute of being a "good Jew" was being proud of being Jewish, an emotion or feeling that has no cultural content. This response declined in importance in Russia over the decade, though not in Ukraine. This may tell us that the first reaction of Russian Jews to the fall of communism was to rid themselves of the feeling that being Jewish was something to be ashamed of. The least important attribute of the good Jew was belief in God and observance of Judaism. That remained true for all of the 1990s. Thus, in the 1990s at least, no cultural content was essential to being a good Jew.

This does not mean that post-Soviet Jews are a-religious. We asked our respondents whether they believed in God (Table 6.1). In both 1992 and 1997, between 42% and 48% of Russian Jews averred a belief in God or an

---

5. Details of our method are found in Gitelman (2012, 349–57).

inclination to such belief, and slightly over half did so in Ukraine. This is surprising, in light of decades of Soviet indoctrination. On the other hand, belief in God did not translate into the practice of Judaism. First, when asked which religious doctrine they found most attractive, "no religion" was always preferred to any particular religion. For Jews attracted to any religion, Judaism was chosen over Christianity, the second most attractive religion, by two to two-and-a-half times. Still, 10–15% saw Christianity as most attractive—an astonishing 20% in St. Petersburg in 2004 (Shapiro 2004, 17).[6] The number of those who could not answer the question was quite high, indicating, at least, that Judaism was not a clear choice for them.

Table 6.1: "Do You Believe in God?"

	RUSSIA		UKRAINE	
	1992 (%)	1997 (%)	1992 (%)	1997 (%)
Yes, I believe in God	18.3	22.8	24.2	31.0
I am inclined to such belief	23.9	25.3	29.7	24.4
I am not inclined to such belief	19.1	17.2	18.3	17.1
I do not believe in God	31.1	28.3	23.2	22.1
Don't know, no answer	6.4	7.6	4.8	5.5

Second, it is most striking that though believers who preferred Judaism to other religions claimed substantially higher levels of ritual observance than those who did not believe in God (or who did but preferred a religion other than Judaism), their levels of observance were significantly lower than

---

6. There is no obvious reason for this increase. Perhaps it reflects a presumed greater incidence of interethnic marriage among 2004 respondents than among those of the 1990s. The proportion attracted to Judaism remained the same as in 1997 (28%), although it was higher in 1992 (37%).

among religious Jews in Israel or in the rest of the Jewish Diaspora. Only a minority of those who believed in God and were most attracted to Judaism claimed to observe the Sabbath—and since we did not specify what that entails, it may have meant a minimal symbolic ritual (e.g., lighting candles, reciting Kiddush) rather than adhering to the extensive rituals and laws of Sabbath observance. In 1992, 56% of Russian Jews who said they believed in God *and* preferred Judaism said they "never" observed the Sabbath, as did 27% in Ukraine. By 1997, 31% of those Russian Jews still said they "never" observed the Sabbath. The overall level of "regular" Sabbath observance did increase in both countries over the five-year interval ($p < .01$ in a difference of proportions test). However, self-reported levels of Sabbath observance were still lower than among Orthodox Jews and perhaps Conservative Jews in other countries.[7] This behavior parallels that among Russian Orthodox Christians in Russia. Surveys of religiosity in Russia show that few "believers" actually observe basic practices such as church attendance (Furman and Kaariainen 2003, 25, quoted in Warhola and Lehning 2007, 934). Analysts of Russian Orthodoxy and Islam in the FSU write of "the persistent gap between high levels of belief and negligible levels of religious practice among Russian citizens" (Johnson and Forest 2005, xi).

Jewishness as a "Thin" Ethnicity

Ethnicity is established by cultural content and by borders (Cornell 1996, 2). In the absence of a distinct language, dress, foods, or literature and because of the weakness of Judaism as the nexus of Jewishness, borders rather than "thick" culture bear the weight of Jewish identity. Soviet Jewish ethnicity was based almost exclusively on the boundaries constructed by the state and society to set Jews off from others. Who is a Jew and who is not, who is in the group and who is out, became a crucial issue, not in the sense that it has become in Israel and the West—where it is a matter of religious, social, and political contention—but simply as the definition of Jewishness.

By 1997 Russia and Ukraine had abolished the requirement to register one's nationality on the internal passport. Ethnicity became a matter of choice, though, of course, how others regarded one could not be regulated

---

7. In the United States, only 12% of temple-affiliated Reform Jews, only 15% of affiliated Conservatives, but 60% of affiliated Orthodox defined themselves as *shomer shabbat* (Sabbath observant) (Cohen 2000, 25).

by the state. Our research shows that Jews established informal boundaries that, however, are also becoming less distinct. A defining characteristic of an ethnic group is that members share a sense of solidarity and recognize each other as part of the group. People will generally pick out co-ethnics as friends, at least initially. "Similarity breeds connection" (McPherson et al. 2001, 415), whereas the mere existence of difference arouses suspicion and, often, hostility. This is true of skin color, body shapes, languages, religions, sexual orientations, and ethnicity. Asked to recall the nationality of their three closest friends in the FSU, 55% of emigres in Israel,[8] 89% in Chicago,[9] 58% in Russia (1992), and 71% in Ukraine (1992) mentioned a Jew first. This tendency is somewhat weaker in the youngest cohort (ages 18–29) and weakened overall a bit by 1997 in the FSU, but it was marked. The overwhelming majority of respondents rejected the proposition that "one should choose friends of one's own nationality," but in practice they seemed to do just that. There is an obvious contradiction between principle and practice. Perhaps they wished the principle had governed social relations in the social world the Soviets purportedly constructed, but in "life itself" ethnicity turned out to be thicker than ideology.

However, in both countries and in both surveys, the older one was, the more likely one was to have Jewish friends. Younger Jews were less likely to maintain ethnic boundaries. Indeed, our findings regarding attitudes toward intermarriage bear this out: Younger people were far less likely to condemn marriage of Jews to non-Jews than older respondents, and even among the latter the proportions opposed to marriage of Jews to non-Jews was much lower than it was among British or American Jews, among whom that ethnic boundary line is eroding in any case.

Finally, attitudes toward marriage to non-Jews varied significantly by age. The general tendency was for the oldest to be most opposed and the youngest to be most tolerant. One should bear in mind that there is a generally high tolerance of interethnic marriage among FSU Jews, and our surveys show this clearly.[10] In Russia in 1992, 46% of the 16–29-year-olds

8. From a survey of 808 Soviet immigrants in Israel (Gitelman 1995).
9. From a 1990 survey of some 500 Soviet immigrants in Chicago (Zvi Gitelman, "Becoming American Jews: Resettlement and Acculturation of Soviet Jewish Immigration in Chicago," unpublished manuscript, University of Michigan, 1994).
10. In 1992, only 55% in Russia and 53% in Ukraine agreed that Jews should choose Jewish spouses; in 1997, only 43% in Russia and 37% in Ukraine advocated this (American Jewish Committee 2000, 3).

were *not* opposed to their own children intermarrying, and only 21% *would have* been disturbed; a quarter were indifferent (Table 6.2). Among the oldest people, 43% would have been disturbed. More generally, nearly half of the youngest group said it does not matter if a Jew chooses a non-Jewish spouse, but nearly 60% of the oldest group said Jews should take Jewish partners. By 1997 opposition to intermarriage was even weaker than in 1992 (Table 6.3).

Table 6.2: Reaction to One's Child Marrying a Non-Jew, by Age, Russia, 1997 (%)*

AGE	POSITIVE	INDIFFERENT	NEGATIVE	OTHER	DON'T KNOW
16–29	20.0	40.0	0.0	2.0	20.0
30–39	6.2	60.0	13.8	3.1	16.9
40–49	5.3	57.4	22.3	7.4	7.4
50–59	12.2	58.5	14.6	7.3	7.3
60+	0.0	73.3	20.0	0.0	6.7

*N's are small because only those who have children responded.

Table 6.3: Jews Should Marry Other Jews (%), Russia, 1997

AGE (YEARS)	JEWS	NO DIFFERENCE	OTHERS	DON'T KNOW
16–29	35.3	58.3	2.2	4.3
30–39	37.2	55.8	0.0	7.1
40–49	41.6	52.8	0.5	5.1
50–59	41.3	52.3	1.1	5.3
60+	48.8	48.5	0.2	2.5

The youngest respondents in Russia and Ukraine were more likely to have grown up in ethnically mixed families, to have not been involved with Jewish observances or culture, and to have experienced less discrimination as Jews, because by the time they entered higher education or the workforce, governmental anti-Semitism had disappeared. In the circles in which they mixed, young and educated residents of the largest cities were less likely to encounter anti-Semitism than their (great-)grandparents did when growing up in working-class and less urbanized environments. The young could therefore feel just as comfortable with non-Jews as with their co-ethnics.

Religious and Ethnic "Entrepreneurs"

If the cultural content of Jewish ethnicity was weak or nonexistent and if boundaries were eroding, what was left of Jewish consciousness or identity? Did the "ethnic and religious entrepreneurs" who descended on the USSR in the late 1980s manage to refill ethnic or religious content?

Jewish ethnic and religious entrepreneurs have been virtually unimpeded in their attempts to reach potential adherents.[11] Most prominent among ethnic entrepreneurs have been emissaries of the Jewish Agency for Israel and the Israeli government. Their agenda has been to promote aliyah (immigration to Israel). In the late 1980s and early 1990s they even opposed Jewish cultural revival in the FSU, fearing that would vitiate emigration efforts, though they eventually realized that Jewish culture did not conflict with Zionism. If measured by emigration figures, these ethnic entrepreneurs have been spectacularly successful, though, of course, one should not attribute emigration to their efforts alone. More than 800,000 Jews (and about 300,000 non-Jews) have immigrated to Israel from the FSU. At first glance, this means that the prospects for Jewish revival in the FSU have been radically diminished, not only because the number of Jews has declined so precipitously but also because, first, it is highly likely that the most nationally conscious and religious Jews have gone to Israel, leaving less committed Jews in the FSU; and, second, as is the case in most migrations, the young are overrepresented among the migrants, sapping the energies and initiative that might have been turned to Jewish revival. However, the presence of relatives and friends in Israel surely strengthens the ties to Israel and possibly the cultural interest and knowledge of those remaining in the FSU. On balance, emigration has probably diminished the prospects of Jewish revival in the FSU.

11. From time to time, Russian authorities have denied visas to foreign-born rabbis and clergy of other faiths. At least two Chabad-affiliated rabbis, the sect favored by the governments of Vladimir Putin, have been expelled from Russia for unknown reasons.

The near disappearance of secular expressions of Jewishness in the Diaspora—Yiddishist and Hebraist movements and political parties, secular Jewish schools, Zionist and socialist ideologies—leaves no one to bring their now-forgotten messages to the FSU. Nor are Jews there likely to revive Yiddish-based secularism of the pre-Soviet or Soviet type. They are highly unlikely to develop a culture based on a Jewish language or form Jewish political movements. On the other hand, they have published local Jewish newspapers, student journals, some popular magazines, and "thick journals" and have established a few theaters.[12] All of these, however, have depended to one degree or another on foreign assistance that may not be sustainable. Jewish cultural associations, which first appeared in the heyday of glasnost and perestroika, have blended into Jewish community centers, many of them in former synagogue buildings reclaimed by local communities.

Have religious entrepreneurs created a Jewish revival? By the late 1990s, about 40 full-time Jewish day schools and 120 Sunday schools had been established, many with a religious character. Religious articles, kosher food, matzo, and religious texts are freely available, whereas in the 1960s–1980s they had to be smuggled into the USSR. Successive presidents of Russia and Ukraine have publicly embraced Jewish religious leaders and have appeared at Jewish holiday celebrations and synagogue dedications. The most visible movement—its sophisticated public relations apparatus sees to that—is the Hasidic Chabad-Lubavitch. It has enjoyed great political success, gaining the unremitting patronage of Russian president Vladimir Putin and superseding other Orthodox rabbis and movements. It seems, though, that Chabad has not been nearly as successful in "returning" Jews to religion. Chabad has quietly shifted its agenda from religious proselytization to providing welfare services (thus doing what the American Jewish Joint Distribution Committee has been doing for decades), perhaps as a way of bringing a religious message indirectly to Russian and Ukrainian Jews.

If there is a modest religious revival, it does not come from within but is funded and promoted from without, largely by the "right-wing" Orthodox, especially the Hasidic Chabad and Karlin-Stolin[13] groups, as well as by the

---

12. Publication examples include *Evreiskaya gazeta*, *L'Chaim*, *Tirosh*, *Sefer*, *Vestnik evreiskogo universiteta v Moskve*, *Egupets*, *Shtetl*, and *Mishpoche* (Belarus).

13. Karlin, once an independent community alongside Pinsk in the Polesie region of what is today southern Belarus, was absorbed into Pinsk. Stolin is a town southeast of Pinsk, near the Ukrainian border. The rabbinic Hasidic dynasty of Stolin was established by Asher (1760–1828), son of "Aaron the Great," leader of the Karliner Hasidic dynasty.

Progressive (Reform) movement. Two movements more in the center of the Jewish religious spectrum, modern Orthodox and Conservative/Masorti, are largely absent from the scene. Although it is said that there are seventy-five Reform congregations in the FSU, most are small and few have rabbis.[14] There is no facility in the FSU for training them. A few natives of the FSU have returned after some rabbinic training at Leo Baeck College, a Progressive seminary in London, but in contrast to the Hasidim, as a Reform rabbi put it, "We don't have people that are prepared to go to some God-forsaken [!] place like Siberia."[15]

Nearly all the Orthodox rabbis are from the two Hasidic groups. Many are FSU natives who emigrated and received their rabbinic training in Israel and the United States. Unlike rabbis from other groups, they appear to be willing to stay on in the FSU indefinitely. Chabad[16] has been engaged in "outreach" to Jews all over the world for the last half-century or so. It sees the FSU as its "home grounds," because the movement was founded in the eighteenth century in what is now Belarus, and its last leader, Menachem Mendel Schneerson (1902–1994), was born in Ukraine.[17] Chabad, at least some of whose adherents believe that the last Rebbe Schneerson is the messiah,[18] is active in the FSU but does not enter into larger communal organizations, nor does it cooperate with existing religious communities, a pattern it follows outside the FSU as well.

14. A Moscow woman born in 1922 told an interviewer why she could not take Reform Judaism seriously: "This is not real religion! I heard they can even have a woman rabbi, who can wear pants! This is not real Judaism. My parents would not have approved. No, they are for young people, but not for me" (Shternshis 2007, 285).

15. Rabbi Arnold Hirsch of the UAHC (known as the Union for Reform Judaism since 2003), in *Moment* magazine, quoted in the *Detroit Jewish News*, October 20, 2000. One might have thought that it is precisely to "God-forsaken" places that rabbis would want to go.

16. Lubavitch is the Belarussian town where the founder of the movement, Shneour Zalman, born in the hamlet of Liady, established the movement. "Chabad" is the Hebrew acronym for *khochma, bina, daʾat,* or "wisdom, understanding, knowledge," which the movement adopted as its name.

17. Menachem Mendel Schneerson's father-in-law, Yosef Yitzhak Schneerson, was expelled from the Soviet Union in 1929 but maintained contact with the dwindling number of his followers until his death in 1950. These contacts were expanded by his successor. A hagiographic account of Rabbi Schneerson's emergence from the USSR can be found in Metzger (1999). A rather different account is given by Kuskin (2013, 14).

18. A prominent Jewish historian, himself an Orthodox rabbi, has severely criticized the messianic cult that developed in the late twentieth century around the rebbe, or leader of the group, as being a serious deviation from Orthodox Judaism (Berger 2001).

In December 1989 an "all-union" (national) congress of newly formed local Jewish organizations established the Va'ad (Committee) as a roof organization that would represent all of organized Soviet Jewry. The Va'ad was weakened by the breakup of the Soviet Union and was also heavily dependent on foreign funds. Without independent sources of income, it could not influence the activities of the local organizations. In 1996, when it was clear that an "all-union" organization was not viable, the Russian Jewish Congress was established. Some Jewish entrepreneurs had become wealthy—they were labeled oligarchs[19]—and could support a national Jewish organization. Vladimir Gusinsky, who had gained control of extensive media, was the first president of the congress. When he ran afoul of President Putin, he was replaced by a series of wealthy men, but the congress has not been able to use the wealth of its backers to transform or even guide Russian Jewry. Instead, Chabad made a tacit alliance with Putin, ignored the chief rabbinate of Russia and all other organizations, domestic and foreign, and formed the Federation of Jewish Religious Organizations (FEROR), which quickly gained control of synagogues all over Russia and has engaged in welfare and educational activities as well as religious life. Putin appeared at several Chabad-sponsored ceremonies, embracing Rabbi Berel Lazar, an Italian-born, American-educated Chabad rabbi who was elected by FEROR as chief rabbi of the Russian Federation, though there was a holdover from Soviet times, Adolf Shaevich, who already had that title.

The arrest in 2003 of Mikhail Khodorkovsky, head of the Yukos conglomerate and reputed to be Russia's richest man, and his subsequent sentencing to nine years in prison sent an indirect signal that the Russian Jewish Congress, one of whose presidents, Leonid Nevzlin, had been an important executive in Yukos, was not going to be recognized by the government as a representative of Jewry. Instead, Putin embraced Chabad. This marriage of convenience shielded Putin from any charges of anti-Semitism—Khodorkovsky is half-Jewish, though he was never involved in Jewish affairs, and some other wealthy critics of Putin (e.g., Vladimir Gusinsky and the late Boris Berezovsky) are Jewish. Posing in photos with a bearded, black-hatted rabbi, an "authentic Jew," seemed to make absurd any suspicion that Putin's campaign against the oligarchs was tainted by anti-Semitism. At the same time, Chabad gained the backing of the state and its

19. Marshall Goldman explained the meteoric rise of these Jewish businessmen in "Russian Jews in Business," in Gitelman et al. (2003).

most powerful leader. Ted Friedgut notes that when the Khodorkovsky affair was unfolding, "the Habad newspaper, *Evreiskoe slovo*, was . . . explicitly supportive of the authorities with an editorial headed 'Civilized vs. Uncivilized,' putting forth the thesis that President Putin's authoritarianism was the only alternative to a dictatorship of the anti-Semitic, Communist-led 'Patriotic Front.'"[20]

Chabad was supported mainly by Lev Leviaev, who made his fortune in the diamond and real estate industries. It has been reported that Chabad's annual budget in the FSU was $60 million a year, most of it supplied by Leviaev. The economic crash of 2008 forced Leviaev to cut back his support for Chabad. Before that, there were said to be permanent Chabad rabbis in 105 FSU locales and "circuit-riding" *shlichim* (emissaries) serving another 321 places (Mark 2005). Chabad also claimed to sponsor seventy-one day schools and sixty kindergartens in the CIS (Federation of Jewish Communities 2005).

When American president George W. Bush visited Russia in May 2002, he "compressed a scheduled half-hour of Kremlin sight-seeing into a seven-minute blur" but extended a 20-minute tour of St. Petersburg's Grand Choral Synagogue by more than half an hour. The *New York Times* commented, "The visit was . . . another in a string of honors that Mr. Putin accorded Russia's Lubavitcher Hasidim . . . [who have] all but assumed the mantle of Jewish revival in Mr. Putin's Kremlin" (Wines 2002).[21]

In Ukraine, Yaakov Bleich, an American-born Karlin-Stolin Hasid, was a major force in the revival of Jewish life and in presenting the Jewish community to the broader Ukrainian population. Bleich learned Russian and Ukrainian and made frequent media appearances. He established a large religious comprehensive school in Kiev and oversaw Karlin-Stolin activities in other cities. Predictably, Chabad-Lubavitch installed one of their own in the second large synagogue in Kiev, awarded to them after the building had been a puppet theater for many years. A second chief rabbi of Ukraine, this one affiliated with Chabad, was appointed.

---

20. *Evreiskoe slovo*, 37 (160) (September 2003): 17–23.
21. Earlier, Putin had spent an hour and a half with Lubavitch rabbis from fifteen Russian cities. He thanked them "for their energetic participation in the process of integrating Russia into the international economic space. He particularly singled out Berel Lazar's recent appeal to the US president to repeal the Jackson-Vanik Amendment" (Alekseyeva 2002). The president of the Lubavitch-controlled Federation of Jewish Communities of Russia was Levi Leviaev, born in Uzbekistan.

All this activity has not brought about a religious revival among the Jews of the FSU. In Russia and Ukraine few observe religious practices. Post-Soviet Jews do not use religiosity to express their ethnicity. True, many of those who become observant tend to emigrate, making it inherently difficult to gauge the extent of religious observance and belief at any particular time. Nevertheless, at no point can one see very many people coming to synagogues, adhering to Jewish rituals, or studying religious texts, the norms of traditional Jewish religious behavior. There are some large religious schools, but most children and parents are not observant. Families that do become observant are more likely to emigrate. It is safe to say that the Jews of Russia and Ukraine remain overwhelmingly nonobservant religiously;[22] that is true also of those who have become active in public Jewish life. We learned more about the beliefs and practices of post-Soviet Jews from our two surveys.

Unsurprisingly, few of our Russian and Ukrainian respondents claimed to know much about Judaism; a quarter to a third said they know nothing at all about it. More surprising is that the proportion claiming to know about the basics of Judaism did not increase from 1992–1993 to 1997–1998, despite the activity of religious organizations during that time (though only 9–15% said they were "not at all" familiar with Jewish customs and traditions).

Moving from what these people knew to what they think they should know, slightly over a quarter of respondents (Ukraine, 1993) thought it necessary to know more about the fundamentals of Judaism. The number of people who felt they should know them actually declined over time in both countries. But Russian and Ukrainian Jews are not dismissive of Judaism, because about half or more say it is "desirable," if not "necessary," for them to know about it. Post-Soviet Jews are not fighting against religion, as some Jews did in the 1920s and 1930s. Still, 20–30% said that they felt it "not at all necessary" to know about Judaism. These figures are particularly meaningful when we remember that they report not whether people think they ought to *practice* Judaism in order to be considered genuinely Jewish but simply whether they ought to know about it.

Knowledge of "traditions" is rated as more important than knowledge of Judaism. This may hint at the understanding of Jewishness as an ethnicity

---

22. One estimate, which probably errs on the high side, is that of the 233,439 Jews enumerated in the 2002 Russian census, about 30,000 (about 13%) are "religious" (Filatov and Lunkin 2006, 34).

and not a religion; it is important for members of an ethnic group to know its customs and traditions, for they distinguish it from others. Although over a third think it is not at all necessary to know basic Judaism to be considered a "real Jew," less than 10% said that about traditions. Despite considerable investments of money and manpower, religious organizations established in Russia and Ukraine since the late 1980s seem to have had only a modest influence on the Jewish populations, less so than the nonreligious Jewish organizations. In 1997 in Russia only 14% said the religious institutions had "significant" influence, and in Ukraine 25% said so. But *non*religious organizations were rated as having significant influence by one-quarter of Russian Jews and one-third of Ukrainian Jews.

Along with weak knowledge of traditions, we found clear expressions of positive attitudes toward reestablishing those traditions. Every third respondent in Russia asserted that Jewish traditions are "close" to him or her. Large majorities in Russia and Ukraine considered it "obligatory" or "desirable" to know more about them. But this may be nothing more than lip service, because in Ukraine in 1997, 63% had not attended a single lecture or seminar on Jewish history, religion, or traditions; that was true of over 70% in Russia. Of course, before the late 1980s, just about no one would have been able to attend such an event, so that even modest attendance rates represented a new feature of Russian and Ukrainian Jewish life. Interestingly, the number of those who attended synagogue or a prayer service during the year was higher, ranging from 45% to 66%. No doubt, "attendance" included such communal festivities as Purim and Hanukkah parties and Passover seders that are often celebrated in synagogue buildings. After all, the most direct and chief means of identification with Jewishness is to observe traditions connected with significant dates on the Jewish calendar.

Jewish Revival and Its Prospects

A century ago, Jewishness was for many Jews—religious and secular—an all-encompassing way of life, determining language, friendship and marriage preferences, customs, foods, clothing, and lifestyles. That is true today mostly among the Orthodox. For the rest, Jewishness is a dimension of their lives but not often the largest one. For most post-Soviet Jews, as for most Jews elsewhere, Jewishness is a choice and offers a menu of expressions from which one can choose some courses and ignore others. Ethnicity seems to be more celebratory than obligatory. It does not dictate a way of life. Jewish culture, however expressed, entertains, fascinates, attracts, and engages. It does not determine much behavior or serve as a guide to life.[23] Finally, as the Yiddish expression goes, *vi es kristelt zich, azoy idlt zich* (as with the Christians, so with the Jews). The trajectory of post-Soviet public Jewish life parallels that of political change in Russia and Ukraine since the demise of communism. In the early 1990s in Russia and a few years later in Ukraine there were great hopes for democracy, "civil society," economic prosperity, and cultural renaissance. These hopes have gone mostly unfulfilled. The Jewish populations of these countries, like other nonterritorial minorities, have also gone from great expectations to moderate changes. They are demographically weak but have developed an institutional infrastructure. Their ethnicity is no longer a mark of shame, but neither is it a driving force in their lives. Just as the transition away from communism has not led to a well-established democracy or back to Soviet-style dictatorship, so has the ethnic revival among Jews not led to the extremes: It has not made their Jewish ethnic identity preeminent in their lives, but it has gained cultural content and alternative expressions. The Soviet system did not eliminate ethnicity, but it left its deep imprint on its conception. Post-Soviet Jewish identity is uncertain, not rigidly defined. This may be a source of strength, because it allows easy membership in the Jewish collective, but it may also be a weakness, because it makes the category "Jewish" flaccid and the entity more vulnerable to attrition.

---

23. "A Jewishness based on identity rather than an assumed way of life complicates matters for Jewish survival, but, at the same time, seems to be the only way to achieve Jewish survival in our times. The question remains as to whether even that is enough. First, identity must be built or established and then ways must be developed to translate that identity into concrete and continuing manifestations. . . . Speaking social scientifically, it does not seem likely that it will be a successful project. It requires too much voluntary effort on the part of a population that essentially is becoming more ignorant of what being Jewish all about, generation by generation if not even more quickly. In addition, it must be achieved in the face of horrendous competition which, precisely because it seems so open and welcoming, is so dangerous to the success of the project, imposing its norms and ways on the Jewish people in the name of freedom, choice, and democracy, very real values in their own right. At the same time, however, Jews have confounded social scientists or their predecessors for many centuries. Hence, as long as the effort is made, no final verdict can be registered" (Elazar 1999, 41).

References

Alekseyeva, Oksana. 2002. "Rabbis Come to President for Advice." *Kommersant*, March 20. Translated in *Current Digest of Post-Soviet Press* 54(12), April 17, 2002.

Altshuler, Mordechai. 2012. *Religion and Jewish Identity in the Soviet Union, 1941–1964*. Waltham, MA: Brandeis University Press.

American Jewish Committee. 2000. *Annual Survey of American Jewish Opinion*. New York: American Jewish Committee. https://archive.ciser.cornell.edu/studies/2265/scope-and-methodology.

Berger, David. 2001. *The Rebbe, the Messiah, and the Scandal of Orthodox Indifference*. London: Littman Library.

Charny, Simeon. 2012. "Judaism and the Jewish Movement." In *The Jewish Movement in the Soviet Union*, ed. Yaacov Ro'i, 304–33. Washington, DC: Woodrow Wilson Center; and Baltimore: Johns Hopkins University Press.

Cohen, Steven M. 2000. "Assessing the Vitality of Conservative Judaism in North America." In *Jews in the Center: Conservative Synagogues and Their Members*, ed. Jack Wertheimer, 13–65. New Brunswick, NJ: Rutgers University Press.

Cornell, Stephen. 1996. "The Variable Ties That Bind: Content and Circumstance in Ethnic Processes." *Ethnic and Racial Studies* 19(2): 265–89.

Elazar, Daniel. 1999. "Jewish Religious, Ethnic, and National Identities: Convergences and Conflicts." In *National Variations in Jewish Identity*, ed. Steven M. Cohen and Gabriel Horenczyk, 35–52. Albany: SUNY Press.

Federation of Jewish Communities of the CIS. *Annual Report, 2005*. Moscow: Federation of Jewish Communities of the CIS, 2006.

Filatov, Sergei, and Roman Lunkin. 2006. "Statistics on Religion in Russia: The Reality Behind the Figures." *Religion, State and Society* 34(1): 33–49.

Furman, Dmitri, and Kimmo Kaariainen. 2003. "Religioznaia stabilizatsiia: Otnosheniia k religii v sovremennoi Rossii." *Svobodnaya Mysl* 7(1533).

Ginzburg, Shaul. 1944. *Amolike Peterburg*. New York: Cyco Bikher Ferlag.

Gitelman, Zvi. 1995. *Immigration, Identity, and Israeli Politics: The Resettlement and Impact of Recent Immigrants from the Former USSR*. Los Angeles: Wilstein Institute.

Gitelman, Zvi. 2001. *A Century of Ambivalence: The Jews of Russia and the Soviet Union, 1881 to the Present*. Bloomington: Indiana University Press.

Gitelman, Zvi. 2012. *Jewish Identities in Postcommunist Russia and Ukraine: An Uncertain Ethnicity*. New York: Cambridge University Press.

Gitelman, Zvi, Marshall Goldman, and Musya Glants, eds. 2003. *Jewish Life After the USSR*. Bloomington: Indiana University Press.

Johnson, Juliet, and Benjamin Forest. 2005. *Religion and Identity in Modern Russia*. Aldershot, UK: Ashgate.

Kozlov, S. Ia. 2007. *Moskovskie evrei: realii ėtnokul'turnogo vozrozhdenia (konets XX–nachalo XXI veka)*. Moscow: Institute of Ethnology and Anthropology, Russian Academy of Sciences.

Kuskin, Il'ia. 2013. "Admiral Canaris spasaet rebe." *Shalom* (Chicago) 369 (May).

Mark, Jonathan. 2005. "Chabad's Global Warming." *The Jewish Week*, December 2.

McPherson, Miller, Lynn Smith-Lovin, and James Cook. 2001. "Birds of a Feather: Homophily in Social Networks." *Annual Review of Sociology* 27(1): 415–44.

Metzger, Alter B. 1999. *The Heroic Struggle: The Arrest and Liberation of Rabbi Yosef Y. Schneersohn of Lubavitch in Soviet Russia*. New York: Kehot.

Nathans, Benjamin. 2002. *Beyond the Pale: The Jewish Encounter with Late Imperial Russia*. Berkeley: University of California Press.

Shapiro, Vladimir. 2004. *Jews of St. Petersburg Today and Tomorrow*. Final Report submitted to the American Jewish Joint Distribution Committee. Moscow: Jewish Research Center.

Shternshis, Anna. 2007. "Kaddish in a Church: Perceptions of Orthodox Christianity Among Moscow Elderly Jews in the Early Twenty-First Century." *Russian Review* 66(2): 273–94.

Volvovsky, Ari. 2012. "The Teaching and Study of Hebrew." In *The Jewish Movement in the Soviet Union*, ed. Yaacov Ro'i, 334–58. Washington, DC: Woodrow Wilson Center; and Baltimore: Johns Hopkins University Press.

Warhola, James, and Alex Lehning. 2007. "Political Order, Identity, and Security in Multinational, Multi-Religious Russia." *Nationalities Papers* 35(5): 933–57.

Wines, Michael. 2002. "Visiting Synagogue, Bush Praises Russian Religious Tolerance." *New York Times*, May 27.

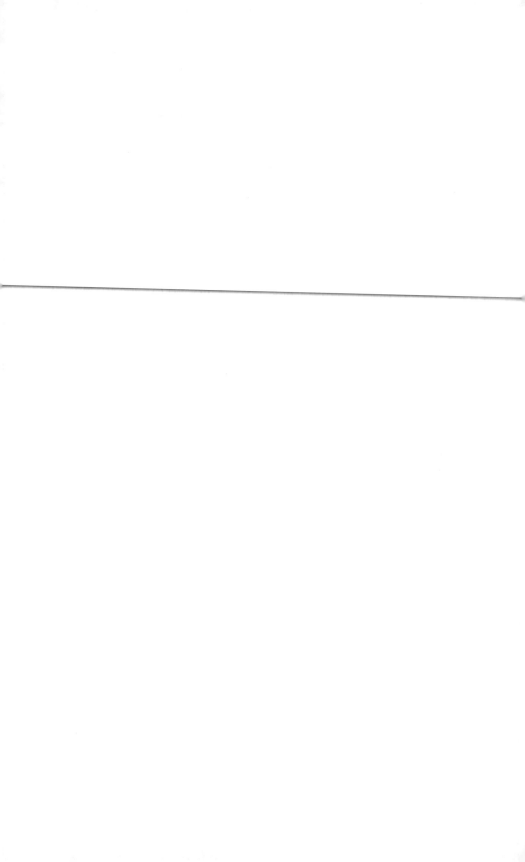

7

Between Boundary Making and Philo-Semitic Yearnings in Contemporary Germany

Hannah Tzuberi

Well, if the Reich had followed Hillel's teaching, there would still be real Jews, and they wouldn't have needed to invent us.
—Harry Turtledove (2011)

In this chapter I consider the recent struggle over the boundaries of the Jewish community in light of an earlier set of struggles over the borders of the Jewish community and the "gatekeeping" of those borders. These different struggles took place at historical moments of German state formation and national unification. The earlier moment pertains to conflicting demarcations of Jewish communal boundaries during the eighteenth and nineteenth centuries. The context of this gatekeeping struggle is the question of Jews' "capability" of becoming full citizens of the emerging German nation-state. For Jews to become citizens of the state, which aspired to be the exclusive site of sovereignty, existing "*personal identities, social formations,* and *normative orderings*" (Brafman 2017, 186; emphasis in original) became permeable and were reconstructed in the image of liberal Protestantism (Batnitzky 2013; Johnston 2017, 317). Far from being a simple liberation of Jews into political equality, emancipation was part of the process of nation building and state building, and even as it liberated some Jews from some restrictions, it

I thank Elli Fischer for his comments and suggestions on drafts of this chapter.

simultaneously subjected them to novel forms of subordination precisely to secure, albeit indirectly, the sovereign self-image of the German state, by facilitating identification with it (Markell 2003, 127). Political modernity thus generated (or necessitated) novel conceptions of Jewishness that challenged and changed the contours of the Jewish collective's pre-emancipatory, prestate boundaries: Jewish tradition became permeable, an object of science, and the boundaries of the Jewish collective as a social-political unit were diffused, so that another collective—the state—could impose new, overriding boundaries within which it could claim allegiance and demand identification. "Self-governing citizens" could not be governed by the laws of another "tribe," that is, of a nonstate political entity (Asad 1993, 127).

The recent gatekeeping struggle, analyzed in the main part of this chapter, takes place in post-1989 Germany. Like the earlier boundary controversy, this one also unfolds in a moment of national unification; yet this moment purports to represent a radical break from earlier, monocultural conceptions of state, which culminated, after all, not in the emergence of a society of equal citizens but in the annihilation of European Jewry. Specifically, since the unification of two German states in 1989, celebration of "Jewish contributions to German culture" and commitment to "reconstruction" of "Jewish life" in Germany became political and medial tropes, aimed at attesting to the state's transformation from an exclusionary, monocultural nationalism to a liberal, tolerant, and democratic ethos of state. In contrast to the first gatekeeping struggle, which emerged in a context that generated questions about Judaism's *survival*, the second struggle thus takes place in a postunification context rife with desires for Jewish *revival*: The decades following reunification have witnessed the rise of an intensive, perpetual discourse of "German Jewish renaissance" accompanied by various state-directed measures to foster this renaissance.

Despite the differences between these two contexts, I do not read contemporary German Jewish revival politics as a radical departure from earlier, monocultural conceptions of a nation-state, nor do I analyze these struggles along a simple "liberal versus traditional" or similar axis. Rather, I argue that in both moments the relation of the state to Jews and Jewish collective existence played a pivotal role for the project of state sovereignty and its legitimation. Whereas one gatekeeping struggle took place at a moment when Jews appealed to the state for recognition *as citizens*, the other takes place at a moment when citizens appeal to the state for recognition *as Jews*;

yet, despite these differences, a yearning for national unity, integrity, and sovereignty animates both. Viewed in this light, the context that generated the question of Judaism's *survival* does not appear to have been "overcome," as the narrative of a radical post-1945 break suggests, because the project of state sovereignty *continues* to animate the question of what kind of relation between Jews and Judaism (and, in a broader sense, between the self and culture) can survive within conditions of state sovereignty. As I will demonstrate, both gatekeeping struggles involve state interpolation of native modes of boundary making, so that the gates and gatekeepers of nonstate, nonindividualized collectivities *remain* illegible and/or problematic. By analyzing two historically distinct gatekeeping struggles through the lens of state sovereignty, I thus argue that revival politics takes place very much *within*, and not apart from, the political-epistemological conditions of *survival*.

Because my analysis is framed by the notion of state sovereignty as a project that animates past and contemporary exchanges of recognition between Jews and the state, I preface it by outlining my understanding of this relation between state sovereignty and state recognition. I take my cues here primarily from the work of anthropologists Talal Asad and Saba Mahmood, who have analyzed the secular state's effects specifically on "religious" collectives, cast as "religious minorities" within the context of political secularism (Asad 2003, 2018; Mahmood 2015).

State Sovereignty and the Politics of Recognition

In line with Asad, secularism creates a political-epistemic framework in which subjects, relationships, sensitivities, and practices are reordered and categorized as either modern and "in time" or traditional and "out of time," free or oppressed, traditional or modern, religious or nonreligious, and so forth. Thus the secular is an epistemic category that prioritizes the mundane and situates it within a notion of temporal progress (Raz-Krakotzkin 2015). Relatedly, political secularism can be described as a political doctrine that did not effect a neat separation of the political from the religious but generated a new relationship between the political and the religious, one based on the state's prerogative to define religion and demarcate the realms of action and authority that religious institutions and figures can claim. Rather than being banished from the public or separated from the state, in secular-liberal political orders, the secular and the religious are rearranged and reset in an unequal relation.

Political secularism is thus a form of government that not only regulates religion but also mobilizes a rearticulation of religion, a rearticulation that co-structures the secular. A secular state is neither neutral with respect to the religions it governs nor completely separate from these institutions and the sphere of the religious: In a secular order the religious is not simply banished to the private sphere, thereby becoming invisible. Rather, certain phenomena are *understood as religious*, are negotiated and constructed as religious, and, as such, become subject to governmental discipline, control, and domestication. As a result, in the exchange of recognition between a "religious minority" and the state, the state does not grant retroactive recognition to something preexisting; rather, the act of recognition itself constitutes, *calls into being*, both the state as sovereign *and* the minority (in this case, Jewish) collective as, for example, a "religion."

Political theorist Patchen Markell describes processes of religionization in the course of Jewish emancipation as a result of this recognition exchange, animated by the project of state sovereignty: "Emancipation was not exactly a device of assimilation; nor was it a device of differentiation, but a contradictory combination of the two, whose structure reflected its role in the pursuit of an attractive but impossible project of sovereignty" (Markell 2003, 153). Understanding the pursuit of sovereignty as a secular state practice, Markell argues that the state paradoxically needed to see perpetually that "Jews have ceased to be Jews," to reassure itself constantly that it is, indeed, sovereign: "On the one hand, Jewishness (otherness) must be eradicated, in this case through a peaceful act of inclusion; on the other hand, in order for the consequent recognition of sovereignty of the state to be more than momentary and ephemeral, the institutions of the state must maintain a vigilant surveillance of the Jews to be sure that they are conforming to the terms of their emancipation—and such a surveillance requires that Jews be recognizable" (146). An exchange of recognition between the state and a religious minority thus establishes and sustains, however incompletely, the state as sovereign and *creates* rather than merely represents "new relations of political identification and allegiance and displac[es] or demot[es] competing ones" (26–27).

The creation of new relations of political identification and allegiance and the displacement of competing ones are what characterize processes of religionization of Judaism. As has been demonstrated by, among others, Leora F. Batnitzky, "Judaism became a religion" in the context of eighteenth and nineteenth German state formation when Jewish thinkers with vastly different outlooks premised their views of Judaism on the notion of Judaism as an essentially private, nonpolitical entity that did not compete with the modern state's claim as the sole site of the political (Batnitzky 2013; Masuzawa 2005, 295–307). Thus religionization not only was a condition of national belonging erected from above but was also internalized by subalterns themselves and provided a framework through which agency and self-affirmation could be sought.

An important part of this internalized religionization relates to the realm of aesthetics, that is, the cultivation of sensibilities and affects that realign the material texture of Jewish life on a temporal scale, with the "modern" being perceived of as more aesthetically pleasing than the sounds and looks of the "old."[1] Apart and beyond the reform of aesthetics that would synchronize Jews with modernity in terms of sensibilities and affects, it was in particular the status of the Jewish legal tradition that was perceived as a hindrance to emancipation. This subject is of immense scope, however; for the purpose of this chapter it is important to note that eventually at stake here was the status of Jewish law *as law*, that is, the question of the law in a moment when said law could be conceptualized as a product of history, the adherence to which was essentially voluntary, and ceased to be a self-evident, nonnegotiable plausibility structure that hitherto constituted Jewish communities as social-political collectives.[2] For instance, for radical reformers such as Samuel Holdheim, communal halakhic boundaries became inconsequential: Holdheim was willing to lend rabbinic sanction to wedding ceremonies between Jews and non-Jews, justifying this position by arguing that the prohibition of intermarriage refers to "foreign people, not religions" (Meyer 1988, 82). As Meyer expounds, the differences between "an undogmatic Christianity and a Judaism purified of its legal component" thereby vanished, so that "what is Jewish is what has passed into the religious consciousness of the individual Jew" (82), or as Holdheim himself had put it, "The holy God and Father of humanity [substitutes] for the

---

1. An exemplary case in point may be the marriage choreography that was worked out by rabbis officiating under the consistory in Westphalia; see Meyer (1988, 35). On the role and importance of aesthetics, see also Efron (2015).
2. On nonprivatized notions of Judaism, cf. Brafman (2017) and Stern (2016).

holy God of Israel, the holy human race for the holy people, the covenant between God and humankind for the covenant between God and Israel" (82). According to Holdheim, Jewish *law*—conceptualized as different and separable from Jewish *religion*—categorically has to give way before the laws of the state (84). Consequently, Holdheim also considered rites such as circumcision to encourage a "fictive theocratic-national impulse," bolstering Jewish sovereignty by encouraging Jewish communities to punish the fathers who abdicated the rite and enforce the ritual against parental wishes: It is not Jewish communities but the state apparatus that is the locus of legitimate violence.[3]

As emphasized by Leora Batnitzky, religionization was by no means a feature only of reformers but characterized also the thought of, for instance, Samson Raphael Hirsch. The conversion of Jews into modern subjects and citizens of the German state thus may not necessarily be described as a story in the course of which "religion" was gradually questioned, remodeled, or abandoned but rather as a story by which the very notion of a Jewish religion came into being, as put by Patchen Markell: "The notion of Judaism as a mode of belief or as one faith among others—interchangeable, in that sense, with Christianity and equally representative of 'religion in general'—was itself in important ways a product of the initial work of political emancipation, which did not just entrench Jewish religious consciousness by privatizing it, but *transformed the meaning of Jewishness itself, working to convert it into a matter of religious consciousness and doing so in the service of the project of nation-state sovereignty*" (Markell 2003, 136; emphasis mine).

With this brief background in mind I now turn to a contemporary boundary struggle that equally takes place at a moment of German nation-state formation and in which the boundaries of Jewish collectivity are negotiated by various Jewish and non-Jewish actors.

Setting the Stage

In early 2003 German newspapers started reporting on an imminent split of German Jewry. A fierce struggle between representatives of different German Jewish umbrella organizations had developed, triggered by the ratification of a state contract that was signed on January 27, 2003, by Paul Spiegel

---

3. For an analysis of the contestation of other Jewish practices, see Judd (2007).

(then head of the Central Council of Jews in Germany) and German Chancellor Gerhard Schröder,[4] institutionalizing state support for German Jewry through the transfer of a specific sum—€3 million at the time—to the Central Council.[5] According to the signatory parties, this sum was supposed to benefit "all Jews," and the Central Council, founded in 1950 in Frankfurt as an umbrella organization and political representative of the 100,000 Jews (in 2015) registered in Jewish communities in Germany, regarded itself as the legislative representative of "all Jews." However, against the claim of the Central Council, the Union of Progressive Jews in Germany, founded in 1997 in Munich, argued that the Central Council neither represented liberal Jews nor endowed them with state funds. The Union represented liberal communities that had emerged mostly after the unification of the two German states in 1989 and that were not part of either the *Einheitsgemeinden* (unified communities)[6] or the federal states' *Landesverbände* (state associations, which function as an umbrella of *Einheitsgemeinden* at the level of the federal states). When the contract was signed, the Union had about 2,000 members.[7] Excluded from the Central Council's representational and administrative scope, the funds, which the contract had envisioned as benefiting all Jews, were not conveyed to members and communities of the Union. On the face of it, the struggle between the Central Council and the Union thus revolved around the just distribution of state funds. Yet, as I will show, its undercurrents went much deeper than finances—to divergent memories of the past and the resulting divergent perceptions of Jewishness in relation to the German state in the present.

4. The text is retrievable at the homepage of the Federal Ministry of Justice and Consumer Protection (Bundesministerium für Justiz und für Verbraucherschutz, 2003).
5. For an overview of state contracts established between the German federal states and their respective Jewish communities, see Lutz-Bachmann (2016).
6. An *Einheitsgemeinde* is the default structure of Jewish communities in Germany. Its roots are a Prussian law issued on July 23, 1847, that allowed Jews to maintain only one community per municipality and obligated them to register in this community. The structure of the *Einheitsgemeinde* is largely maintained up to the present day. In practical terms it means that if in a specific locality different denominational Jewish communities develop, these "branches" nonetheless remain within the administrative and representative superstructure of the *Einheitsgemeinde*.
7. "Die jüdische Gretchenfrage," *Süddeutsche Zeitung*, November 18, 2004. Reliable statistics on the number of Jews represented by the Union are not publicly accessible. Media reports mention between 1,000 and 2,500 members between 2000 and 2003.

An Inter- or an Intracommunal Conflict?

Legal scholar Julia Lutz-Bachmann, in an analysis of state contracts between religious minorities and the German state, subsumes the conflict as follows:

> The state as contract partner let the Central Council of Jews develop the criteria and modalities of inclusion into the circle of beneficiaries independently. The formulation of Article 1 of the state contract thus entails a tautology: It is the Central Council that determines who represents a "stream of Judaism" to whom it wants to be open. The formulation focuses on the self-concept of the Central Council, so that the state cannot demand [from the Central Council] that it support all those whom the state itself—without explicitly mentioning so—wants to see included in the Jewish community. (Lutz-Bachmann 2016, 231; my translation)

"It is unclear," in the jurist's dry parlance, "on whose definition of Judaism the further transfer [of state funds to communities] is to be based: that of the state or that of the religious community to whom the transfer is delegated [here, the Central Council]" (Lutz-Bachmann 2016, 439; see also Lutz-Bachmann 2016, 248, 251–53, 327–28). The state, in the moment it became a contracting partner with respect to the Jews, thus became a broker of recognition: It had to determine whether a specific collective was eligible to receive state funds earmarked for "Jews." And determine it did: In numerous parliamentary debates both before and after the contract's ratification, German politicians explicitly articulated that they expected the Central Council to include the communities represented by the Union. The state unambiguously favored a redefinition of the Central Council's definition of "all Jews" (German Parliament 2003a, 2003b, 2003c; Lutz-Bachmann 2016, 231–32; Schwarz 2005, 124).

This expectation was perceived and presented as a concern for nondiscrimination. The state, when setting up a state contract with "Jews in Germany," identified the Central Council as its representative of Judaism and thereby—without necessarily intending to do so—recognized the contracting partner's self-conception of Judaism. Yet because the state cannot discriminate against or privilege any specific self-perception among those who call themselves Jews, it cannot confer exclusive legitimacy to its contracting partner's definition of Judaism and shun the competitor's claim to represent Jews too: As a neutral state, it has to address "all Jews" equally.

According to state actors, then, the conflict between the Central Council and the Union was an *intra*religious conflict, a struggle of "Jews versus Jews," and the state's support of the Union was considered a matter simply related to the just distribution of funds among "all Jews." However, by framing the conflict as one of "Jews versus Jews," the state had done much *more* than safeguard the just distribution of funds. As becomes abundantly clear from media reports accompanying the conflict, representatives of the Central Council did not perceive said conflict as a debate between different kinds of Jews, a struggle among representatives of different denominations; rather, they perceived it as an appropriation of representational power by "new Jews," who represented a Jewish movement that had developed *beyond* the purview of the Central Council or the established communal structures.[8] The struggle thus coalesced at a point where the stakes were Jewry's communal boundaries, the identity of their gatekeepers, and, ultimately, the content of the space that those boundaries were supposed to protect.

To better substantiate this undercurrent of the struggle, I briefly recapitulate the genealogies and constitutions of the respective parties.

Before the onset of migration from the former Soviet Union, German Jewry was made up primarily of Holocaust survivors and their descendants, who had been in displaced persons camps and eventually settled in Germany after World War II.[9] Reflecting this overall makeup of postwar Jewry in Germany, the Central Council represented the communal structures as they had emerged in the first decades after the war. As an institution, the Central Council explicitly did not define itself as an "Orthodox organization" and regarded its *Einheitsgemeinden* as structures that could harbor communities of all denominations (Riebsamen 2004). Nevertheless, the Central Council did not represent, either in terms of "personnel" or ideology, a continuation of the highly acculturated, liberal strands of prewar German Jewry. Quite the contrary, its representatives initially explicitly defined themselves as "Jews in Germany," not as "German Jews," thereby consciously affirming

---

8. It appears that a sense of "intrusion" regarding the rising number of converts and their claims for leadership crosses denominational divides. See, for example, Lehming (2000) and Steiner (2015, 46, 267–73).

9. For a more detailed account of the situation of Jews in displaced persons camps in the immediate postwar years, see Diner (2012).

an exterior relationship of nonbelonging to the Germanness of the nation-state. The renewed propagation of liberal "made-in-Germany" Judaism was not something that Jews in Germany deemed desirable, appropriate, or even possible. In Berlin, for example, Heinz Galinski (1912–1992), then head of the Central Council and of the Jewish Community of Berlin, wrote, in an open letter in 1950:

> The dream of emancipation . . . has turned out to have been an illusion, a seductive chimera and lastly a moral falsehood. We wanted to be Europeans and maintain our Jewishness only insofar as it was reconcilable with this Europeanness. Europe, however, has cruelly expelled us. Today therefore we are only Jews and we are therefore also no longer interested to make our synagogue service palatable to the German environment. We want to fashion it only according to the traditions of our people. (*Allgemeine Jüdische Wochenzeitung*, February 17, 1950, quoted in Bodemann 1996a, 27)

The fact that most Jews—among them the families of those who established the communal structures of postgenocide Jewry in Germany—did not survive their encounter with German nationalism thus fostered an understanding of emancipation as not *only* but *also* a process of loss, injury, and subjugation.[10] Of course, as time passed, Jews' assessment of their contemporary situation in Germany underwent changes. Jews in Germany gradually started to consider Germany a place they would not only pass through but also live in. Still, they did not "return" to assimilated German prewar Judaism. Salomon Korn, vice-president of the Central Council from 2003 to 2014, echoed Heinz Galinski when writing in 2003 that

> in my impression, non-Jewish Germans who are dealing with Jewish culture in Germany still have that ideal of a "German-Jewish" culture in the sense of a glorified "German-Jewish symbiosis" in mind. This is probably linked to the wish to find a lost part of one's own tradition in

10. The first German postwar Liberal communities were founded by Americans who had settled in Germany after having been stationed there as members of the Allied troops. See, for example, the history of the Liberal community Beth Shalom in Munich: Beth Shalom, Liberale Jüdische Gemeinde München, "Gemeindechronik," https://beth-shalom.de/gemeinde/gemeindechronik/ (accessed March 3, 2021).

the big pot of a revitalized "German-Jewish" culture. . . . From a Jewish perspective, however, the history of a Jewish culture in Germany,
and especially of a "German-Jewish" culture, remains one of futile
bloodletting of Jewish substance, an ongoing self-alienation without
sustainable societal compensation. So why should one, from a Jewish
perspective, revitalize such a chapter? (Korn 2003, 114–15)

The revitalization of this chapter was gradually taken up by German
non-Jews. As has been documented by sociologist Michal Bodemann, Holocaust commemoration has become increasingly infused with moments that
entail a German part in acts of merging, incorporation, and interchange-
ability with Jews: "In order to accomplish national redemption, they [i.e.,
German non-Jews] had to become, in their own consciousness, Jews themselves" (Bodemann 1996b, 212; see also Schmidt 2018). It was not difference
between Jews and non-Jews that dominated German commemoration but
rather a notion of proximity and familiarity that marked German citizens
as standing "on the good side" (Gruber 2002, 10). The decade following the
German states' unification—that is, when democratic principles required
demonstration—witnessed a massive boom in the popularity of things Jewish within a specific sociocultural milieu: liberal, left-leaning theologians,
artists, teachers, and academics—the participative carriers of the new Germany's self-image. Largely unrelated to institutional commemoration, the
joint efforts of these engaged citizens contributed to the popularization of
Judaism in Germany and initiated what Bodemann calls a "proliferation
of the Jewish fringe" or "Judaizing milieus" (Bodemann 2006, 174), also
known as Diana Pinto's "Jewish spaces" (Pinto 2006), Ruth Ellen Gruber's
more ambiguous "virtual Jewishness" (Gruber 2002), and Michael Brenner's
"non-Jewish Jewish cultures" (Brenner 2002, 58).

Approaches and valuations of these "non-Jewish Jewish cultures" vary.
Diana Pinto interprets the phenomenon positively, as a cross-fertilizing
meeting ground between noncommitted Jews and non-Jews, and proposes
"an adaption of Jewry to the overarching standards of civil society; a shift
from Judaism as a coherent religious definition, to a weaker, less easily cir-
cumscribed entity: Jewish culture" (Leveson 2004, 2). Others take a more
ambivalent stance. Bodemann characterizes the Jewish fringe as a "meeting ground of Jews and non-Jewish Germans from 'Judaizing milieus'"
and concludes, "At these fringes—and at these fringes alone—the cultural

expressions and the thinking of Jews and non-Jews about Jewish matters are sometimes 'virtually' identical" (Bodemann 2006, 175). Ian Leveson argues that "Jewish spaces" engage their participants not only as consumers of various kinds of Jewishly inflected cultural items but, potentially at least, as participative Jewish subjects themselves (Leveson 2004). Precisely because of their permeability, Jewish spaces offered to Germans, who had become (as Bodemann had put it) "in their own consciousness Jews," the opportunity to *perform* this consciousness. Along this argument, Jewish spaces served not only as "cross-cultural meeting grounds" between Jews and non-Jews but also as bridges for non-Jews *into* Judaism.[11]

Leveson's analysis seems to be corroborated by Barbara Steiner, who, in her research about motivations of German converts to Judaism in postwar Germany, concludes:

> In the future, Jewish communities in Germany will be religiously shaped mainly by two groups: on the one hand, by Russian migrants, and on the other hand, by German converts. . . . It seems to become apparent . . . that Orthodoxy, shaped by Israeli and American guest-rabbis, will be formed primarily by young rabbis of Russian descent. . . . On the other hand, a new liberal Judaism, which was made popular mainly by former non-Jews, will be further established. According to the interviewed rabbis, part of a German peculiarity is that this new liberal Judaism is, to a large extent, formed by converts who grew up as Christians and converted of their own accord. (Steiner 2015, 270)[12]

Without converts, as noted by Walther Rothschild (a Liberal rabbi serving in Germany), the General Rabbinical Assembly would not have been founded (Steiner 2015, 78), nor would have the Union of Progressive Jews in Germany, as Steiner adds (14). The conversion of Germans to Liberal Judaism thus can be described as a *collective* movement: Individuals pass

---

11. This is also noted by Barbara Steiner, who begins her research into the motives of German converts with a description of "Jewish spaces." See Steiner (2015, 11).
12. According to Steiner (2015, 12), between 2009 and 2013, 95 German citizens converted by means of the Orthodox Rabbinical Conference of Germany and 405 converted by means of the General Rabbinical Assembly, which includes whoever is not in the Orthodox Rabbinical Conference.

into a community consisting primarily of those who had previously made just that same passage. As Steiner notes further:

> Among German non-Jews, Judaism enjoys popularity to such an extent that not all those who want to convert can be absorbed. Converts today constitute, at least within liberal Judaism, a significant part, a fact that attracts other conversion-candidates. As experts for a conversion to Judaism, they are contact-persons for those who also want to become Jewish. Within Orthodoxy, this phenomenon does not exist in comparable measure. A person who wants to engage him/herself on behalf of the Jewish community will obviously choose the route into liberal Judaism. (Steiner 2015, 268)[13]

This does not mean that nonconverted Jews did *not* participate in the "revival" of Liberal Judaism. It means, however, that beginning in the 1990s, German citizens created—independently from existing Jewish communities in Germany—their "own" Judaism, which was, as opposed to most Jewish communities in Germany, Liberal. The emergence of Liberal Judaism in postunification Germany thus has to be situated *within* the context of German postwar memory culture and revival politics and can be read as an expression, or materialization, of the intrinsic undercurrents of Germany's coming to terms with the past.

The German state, in framing the conflict between the Union of Progressive Judaism and the Central Council as an *intra*religious conflict of "Jews versus Jews," rendered the Central Council's perception of the conflict legally and politically irrelevant. This is not to vindicate the Central Council's perception of the conflict but to highlight two interrelated points: First, "Jewish spaces" responded to the political desire of "Jewish life in Germany" and constituted, both in terms of personnel and ideology, a breeding ground for the emergence of a new, quasi-homemade, German Liberal Judaism. And second, when the founders and organizers of new German Liberal Judaism demanded representational power, it was indeed *the state* that granted this demand momentum.

---

13. A sense of one's own precariousness and marginality is aptly reflected, for instance, in the "conversion policy" of the website of the Liberal community Gescher laMassoret in Cologne. See Gescher laMassoret, "Geschichte," https://www.jlgk.de/seite/475820/geschichte.html (accessed May 24, 2018).

Clashing Memories

The conflict between the Central Council and the Union alludes to a tension inherent in a contract that conveys benefits to a group on the basis of this group's recognizability as the carrier of a specific identity, a tension that necessarily turns into a full-fledged conflict when those who *convey* the benefit and those who *receive* it have divergent assumptions about what, exactly, makes one a carrier of this specific identity. The state administers Jews as a religion, a category historically and epistemologically linked to Protestant Christianity, that acquires its meaning by being connoted with beliefs in the transcendent or supernatural and that is assessed qualitatively, with levels of sincerity and interior conviction being the yardstick for measuring religiosity. Accordingly, whether or not a person is treated as a carrier of a specific "religion" is deemed primarily a matter of voluntary confession rather than an ethnolegal and substantively involuntary fact (conveyed by birth). The state's policy of nondiscrimination thus presumes a particular notion of religion and then normalizes and neutralizes *this* notion, which means, however, that nondiscrimination here does not protect communal boundaries that are not legible as "religious" (as is the case with respect to Jews who settled in Germany after the war) and indeed *cannot* protect boundaries that it—by virtue of its particular notion of what a religion *is*—does not recognize as binding or in need of protection.[14]

Moreover, there were other, more subtle ways in which the German state was no mere passive, neutral player. The conflict surrounding the state contract erupted in the midst of an ambitious state-fostered revival project, namely, the directed migration of Jews from the former Soviet Union after the fall of the Berlin Wall. Jews of the former Soviet Union were supposed to foster the visible "renaissance" of German Jewry (Laurence 2001, 22), yet already in 1996 it had become clear that the "import" of Jewish migrants did not *automatically* lead to such a renaissance. Reports of large numbers of unreliable documents reached Parliament, and surveys conducted among migrants led to

---

14. Saba Mahmood analyzes the "generative contradiction" of secular state sovereignty, which consists in the promise of indifference to religious affiliation, that positions the secular state time and again as an arbiter of religious difference (Mahmood 2015, 3). The definition of religion of the German state can be contrasted with that of the Israeli state, which equally aimed to turn migrants from the former Soviet Union into (halakhic) Jews but sustained the set-up of state-directed conversion programs for migrants in national terms and emphasized, for example, migrants' identification with the national collective through army service or the Hebrew language.

the unsettling realization that the move to Germany was apparently motivated by economic considerations and not (or not only) by a wish to be the bearers of the future of German Jewry.[15] To add fuel to the fire, politicians noticed a discrepancy between their migration policies and the German Jewish communities' definitions of Jewishness, that is, between the Soviet registration of Jews and the matrilineal registration of Jews commonplace in German Jewish communities. Ignatz Bubis (1927–1999), head of the Central Council, sparked a parliamentary debate that led to a restriction of Russian Jewish migration when explaining, in an interview with *Der Spiegel*, that a large number of those who migrated as Jews "are not Jews"; that even among those who are, not all register in local Jewish communities; and that among those who do, most do so to gain administrative or financial aid rather than to revive German Judaism.[16]

It thus became clear that "the Russians" would have to be *made* into Jews—integrated into a Jewish community or otherwise induced to perform something identifiably Jewish. Within this context of a state seeking to turn Russian migrants into the bearers of flourishing Jewish life, the Union presented Liberal Judaism as a denomination to which unaffiliated Russian Jews would be naturally attracted: With its greater emphasis on autonomous self-definition and general "openness," for example, it was thought that Liberal communities would attract those who identified as Jews but were not recognized as such by Orthodox institutions. Practically speaking, most Russian Jews were not attracted to Liberal Judaism, yet the Union's promise of transforming the broadest possible array of Russians into Jews converged with the state's "reforestation" aims, and the state accordingly deemed the Union supportable (see, e.g., Simon 2015).

Most crucially, political support for the Union was inherent in the framing of the state contract as an act of restitution,[17] as was the particular

---

15. Migration policy was gradually restricted between the end of 1995 and 2006. Restrictions were pushed forward largely "behind the scenes" and discussed in Parliament only after the fact. In 2006 migration was made dependent on a migrant's "prognosis of integration," whereby an applicant could attain "credit points" for age, profession, education, language skills, and Jewishness. See "Dilemma für Schily" (*Der Spiegel*, March 7, 2005), von Hardenberg (2006), and "Punktekatalog für Juden" (*Der Spiegel*, July 24, 2006).

16. "Eine gewisse Unsicherheit," *Der Spiegel*, June 11, 1996.

17. In its first clause, the contract's purpose—"the cultivation of the German Jewish cultural heritage, the construction of Jewish communities, and support of the Central Council's integrational-political and social tasks"—is accordingly described as a result of Germany's "special historical responsibility." The reinstallation of German Jewry became, as expressed by MP Wolfgang Bosbach (Christian Democrat), a project "of importance for our country as a whole, for the entire society" (see German Parliament, 2003c, 4120).

character this restitution was imagined to have: The idea of a "revitalization" of Judaism in Germany was linked to the memory of a time when Jews made contributions to all those spheres that politicians identified as positive German achievements. The aim was the restoration of *this era*. In parliamentary debates about the migration of Soviet Jews, for instance, German politicians imagined (or tacitly presented) their support for the migration of Jews as support for a people whose "true essence" is historically German. The commissioner of integration and migration (formerly the commissioner of foreigner affairs) of the Berlin Senate thus reasoned: "The cultural legacy of German Jewry is German! It is not Turkish or Rumanian or anything else!" (Laurence 2001, 41). The secretary of the Ministry of Interior Affairs likewise declared:

> Immigration of Jews and the strengthening of Jewish communities will lead—and I want to emphasize this emphatically as a positive thing—also to a revitalization of the Jewish element in German cultural and spiritual life, which has played such an important role in the past. I may just remind of the many Nobel laureates, musicians and literates, which testify to the importance of the Jewish element for German science and culture. This is also something to be aware of when Jews from Eastern Europe today desire entry. I am referring also to the accomplishments of many, nameless citizens of Jewish descent, who made Germans Jews, before the advent of the evil NS-regime, a widely respected part of German history [*sic*]. (German Parliament, 1990)[18]

The institutional embrace of Jews in the present is thus quite literally the embrace of an imagined "Jewish element in German cultural and spiritual life," an embrace predicated on Jews' essential belonging within Germanness.[19] Conceptualized as a migration of *Germans*, Jewish migration was not thought to contradict Germany's citizenship law, which was, up to its first reform in 2000, based on *ius sanguinis* (i.e., on ethnic German

---

18. On Jews as valuable and patriotic German citizens, cf. also German Parliament (2003a).
19. In line with this understanding, politicians and countless media reports described Germany's new Jews as highly educated professionals, lawyers, doctors, artists, Nobel laureates, writers, and academics. About Jewish migrants as ideal refugees, see also Körber (2005, 65).

ancestry), nor did it intersect with concurrent debates about a restriction of asylum policies. Jonathan Laurence, who has researched the differential treatment of Turkish Muslim migrants in relation to Russian Jewish migrants, thus concludes, "The strongly divergent bureaucratic treatment of two 'transnational' immigration groups . . . has not been influenced by overarching human rights discussions or international institutions. The outcomes are rather the resulting national debates over historical responsibility and the assimilability of immigrants in German society," an assimilability that results from "the projection of 'German traits' onto non-German Jews" (Laurence 2001, 25). In parliamentary debates about the struggle surrounding the state contract, too, an explicit call was made time and again to "those who today are a minority in our country but were, in the past, the majority of German Jews, namely, the liberal Jewish communities. . . . Liberal Judaism has a long tradition and deep roots in Germany," as MP Volker Beck (Green Party) stated (German Parliament 2003a, 4121; Lutz-Bachmann 2016, 293). Restitution was premised on the incorporation of Jews (or an image of Jews) as part of an injured *German* collective in which the Holocaust could be metaphorized as a physical injury (*Aderlass*, according to MP Sebastian Edathy [Social Democrat]; or *Selbstauslegung*, according to MP Maik Reichel [Social Democrat]) (German Parliament 2003a, 4123; German Parliament 2008, 19,562).

The Central Council was thus in and of itself fundamentally out of sync with the very nature of the German restorative project: The image of the Jew that dominated German memory and reforestation politics *differed* from the self-image of the majority of Jews who lived in Germany. As an institution, the Central Council represented the pragmatic necessities of postwar Germany rather than prewar German Jews, which the German state's Jewish reforestation politics aimed to reconstruct in the present. If Heinz Galinski expressed in 1950 that "the dream of emancipation . . . has turned out to have been an illusion, a seductive chimera. . . . We wanted to be Europeans and maintain our Jewishness only insofar as it was reconcilable with this Europeanness," then the contemporary project was to shift and undo precisely this sentiment: It entailed the *affirmative* return to a pregenocidal German Jewry where Jewishness was maintained "insofar as it was reconcilable with this Europeanness" and where the state's claim to supreme sovereign authority demanded, or necessitated, the transformation of Judaism into a privatized religion or its nationalization as Zionism (Batnitzky 2013).

Responding to this particular character of reforestation, Walter Homolka, a central figure for Liberal Judaism's institutionalization, for instance, referred to contemporary German Jews as educators of not-yet-liberalized Muslims: Muslims today may learn from Jews how to cope with modernity, according to Homolka, by subjugating their law to state law (Main 2017). Muslims are capable of being integrated as citizens, provided that they confessionalize Islam, as the Jews did with Judaism.

In the context of postunification revival politics, as before, in what I have termed survival politics, the nation-state's claim to sovereignty is thus set as a universally valid and ahistorical norm and as the natural, ahistorical, and desired site of the political. "Religion" here exists as an apolitical device of personal meaning making that does not compete with the citizen's normative loyalties and desires: In the struggle surrounding the state contract, the state played a crucial role in the constitution and consolidation of those conceptions of Jewishness that *affirm* secular state sovereignty, a liberal self, and privatized-individualized accounts of religion. The injuries inflicted, both in the past and today, as part of the state's quest for sovereignty remain illegible as injuries, and the fact that political modernity (the organization of the world in sovereign nation-states) ended in the annihilation of European Jewry seems not to have shaken confidence in the fundamental desirability of this organization. Violence is viewed as an unfortunate *misapplication* of state power, an exaggeration, an ill-fated accumulation of circumstances, rather than as a constitutive practice of state sovereignty that sets populations in relation to the state and subjects them to different degrees of vulnerability.

Revival politics was, in this sense, the consummation of an image that Helmut Kohl painted on his visit to Yad Vashem in 1984, when he referred to the prewar "German-Jewish symbiosis" as an "Überwölbung von Auschwitz," literally a bridge or bulge above Auschwitz. Auschwitz, indeed, was "bridged," inasmuch as the questions that emerged in its wake (and partly, the Jews, who posed those questions) were not assimilable to the undercurrents of postunification nation building. Paradoxically, the political will to establish "Jewish life flourishing" thus resulted in a struggle of the German state *against* those Jews whose memories and definitions of Jewishness were less compatible with postunification revival politics. The narrative of a Jewish revival, I suggest, is attractive not only precisely because it offers a sense of relief to a liberal society marked by a heightened sensitivity to its own history but also because it does unacknowledged work for the continuing project of national unification and sovereignty, shunning those conceptions of culture and cultural identity that potentially destabilize state power.

References

Asad, Talal. 1993. *Genealogies of Religion: Discipline and Reasons of Power in Christianity and Islam*. Baltimore: Johns Hopkins University Press.

Asad, Talal. 2003. *Formations of the Secular: Christianity, Islam, Modernity*. Palo Alto: Stanford University Press.

Asad, Talal. 2018. *Secular Translations: Nation-State, Modern Self, and Calculative Reason*. New York: Columbia University Press.

Batnitzky, Leora F. 2013. *How Judaism Became a Religion: An Introduction to Modern Jewish Thought*. Princeton, NJ: Princeton University Press.

Bodemann, Michal. 1996a. "'How Can One Stand to Live There as a Jew . . .': Paradoxes of Jewish Existence in Germany." In *Jews, Germans, Memory: Reconstructions of Jewish Life in Germany*, ed. Michal Bodemann, 19–46. Ann Arbor: University of Michigan Press.

Bodemann, Michal. 1996b. "Reconstructions of History: From Jewish Memory to Nationalized Commemoration of Kristallnacht in Germany." In *Jews, Germans, Memory: Reconstructions of Jewish Life in Germany*, ed. Michal Bodemann, 179–223. Ann Arbor: University of Michigan Press.

Bodemann, Michal. 2006. "A Jewish Cultural Renaissance in Germany?" In *Turning the Kaleidoscope: Perspectives on European Jewry*, ed. Ian Leveson and Sandra Lustig, 164–75. New York: Berghahn.

Brafman, Yonatan Y. 2017. "Towards a Neo-Ḥaredi Political Theory." *Journal of Religion and Violence* 5(2): 185–204.

Brenner, Michael. 2002. "The Transformation of the German-Jewish Community." In *Unlikely History: The Changing German-Jewish Symbiosis*, ed. Leslie Morris and Jack Zipes, 49–61. New York: Palgrave.

Bundesministerium der Justiz und für Verbraucherschutz, Bundesamt für Justiz. 2003. "Vertrag zwischen der Bundesrepublik Deutschland, vertreten durch den Bundeskanzler, und dem Zentralrat der Juden in Deutschland—Körperschaft des öffentlichen Rechts—vertreten durch den Präsidenten und die Vizepräsidenten." January 27. https://www.gesetze-im-internet.de/zjdvtr/BJNR159800003.html (accessed March 3, 2021).

Diner, Dan. 2012. "Im Zeichen des Banns." In *Geschichte der Juden in Deutschland von 1945 bis zur Gegenwart: Politik, Kultur und Gesellschaft*, ed. Michael Brenner, 15–44. Munich: C. H. Beck.

Efron, John M. 2015. *German Jewry and the Allure of the Sephardic*. Princeton, NJ: Princeton University Press.

German Parliament. 1990. Plenary protocol 11/231, October 25, 1990. Agenda item 8, "Aktuelle Stunde betr. Einreise für Juden aus Osteuropa." http://dipbt.bundestag.de/doc/btp/11/11231.pdf (accessed March 3, 2021).

German Parliament. 2003a. Plenary protocol 15/49, June 6, 2003. Agenda item 18, "Gesetz zum Vertrag vom 27. Januar 2003 zwischen der Bundesrepublik Deutschland und dem Zentralrat der Juden in Deutschland—Körperschaft des öffentlichen Rechts." http://dipbt.bundestag.de/doc/btp/15/15049.pdf (accessed March 3, 2021).

German Parliament. 2003b. Printed matter 15/347, January 24, 2003, "Schriftliche Fragen mit den in der Woche vom 20. Januar 2003 eingegangenen Antworten der Bundesregierung," inquiry no. 14. http://dipbt.bundestag.de/doc/btd/15/003/1500347.pdf (accessed March 3, 2021).

German Parliament. 2003c. Printed matter 15/1612, "Schriftliche Fragen mit den in der Woche vom 22. September 2003 eingegangenen Antworten der Bundesregierung, Sept. 26, 2003," inquiry no. 10. http://dipbt.bundestag.de/doc/btd/15/016/1501612.pdf (accessed March 3, 2021).

German Parliament. 2008. Plenary protocol 16/183, October 16, 2008. Agenda item 27, "Zweite Beratung und Schlussabstimmung des von der Bundesregierung eingebrachten Entwurfs eines Gesetzes zu dem Vertrag vom 3. März 2008 zwischen der Bundesrepublik Deutschland und dem Zentralrat der Juden in Deutschland—Körperschaft des öffentlichen Rechts." http://dipbt.bundestag.de/doc/btp/16/16183.pdf (accessed March 3, 2021).

Gruber, Ruth Ellen. 2002. *Virtually Jewish: Reinventing Jewish Culture in Europe*. Berkeley: University of California Press.

Johnston, Elizabeth Eva. 2017. "Semitic Philology and the Wissenschaft des Judentums: Revisiting Leopold Zunz's *Etwas über die rabbinische Litteratur* (1818)." *Philological Encounters* 23(4): 296–320.

Judd, Robin. 2007. *Contested Rituals: Circumcision, Kosher Butchering, and Jewish Political Life in Germany, 1843–1933*. Ithaca, NY: Cornell University Press.

Körber, Karen. 2005. *Juden, Russen, Emigranten: Identitätskonflikte jüdischer Einwanderer in einer ostdeutschen Stadt*. Frankfurt: Campus.

Korn, Salomon. 2003. *Die fragile Grundlage: Auf der Suche nach der deutsch-jüdischen "Normalität."* Berlin: Philo Verlag.

Laurence, Jonathan. 2001. "(Re)Constructing Community in Berlin: Turks, Jews, and German Responsibility." *German Politics and Society* 19(2): 22–61.

Lehming, Malte. 2000. "Walter Homolka, der ehrgeizige Öko-Rabbiner, wird Kulturchef der Deutschen Bank." *Tagesspiegel*, January 12.

Leveson, Ian. 2004. "Jewish Space—No Medium for Yiddishkeit?—and Its Possible Effects on Judaism, Jewish Culture, and Jewry." Seedingsparks (blog). http://bit.ly/2IgbleN (accessed March 3, 2021).

Lutz-Bachmann, Julia. 2016. *Mater Rixarum? Verträge des Staates mit jüdischen und muslimischen Religionsgemeinschaften.* Tübingen: Mohr Siebeck.

Mahmood, Saba. 2015. *Religious Difference in a Secular Age: A Minority Report.* Princeton, NJ: Princeton University Press.

Main, Andreas. 2017. "Juden haben Erfahrungen gemacht wie Muslime heute." *Deutschlandfunk*, October 30. http://bit.ly/2V2OkgU (accessed May 24, 2018).

Markell, Patchen. 2003. *Bound by Recognition.* Princeton, NJ: Princeton University Press.

Masuzawa, Tomoko. 2005. *The Invention of World Religions, or, How European Universalism Was Preserved in the Language of Pluralism.* Chicago: University of Chicago Press.

Meyer, Michael A. 1988. *Response to Modernity: A History of the Reform Movement in Judaism.* New York: Oxford University Press.

Pinto, Diana. 2006. "The Jewish Space in Europa." In *Turning the Kaleidoscope: Perspectives on European Jewry*, ed. Ian Leveson and Sandra Lustig, 179–86. New York: Berghahn.

Raz-Krakotzkin, Amnon. 2015. "Secularism, the Christian Ambivalence Toward the Jews, and the Notion of Exile." In *Secularism in Question: Jews and Judaism in Modern Times*, ed. Ari Joskowicz and Ethan B. Katz, 276–98. Philadelphia: University of Pennsylvania Press.

Riebsamen, Hans. 2004. "Spaltet sich das deutsche Judentum?" *Frankfurter Allgemeine Zeitung*, April 4.

Schmidt, Christoph. 2018. *Israel und die Geister von '68: Eine Phänomenologie.* Göttingen: Vandenhoeck & Ruprecht.

Schwarz, Kyrill-Alexander. 2005. "Die Verteilung der Finanzmittel aus dem zwischen der Bundesrepublik Deutschland und dem Zentralrat der Juden in Deutschland geschlossenen Staatsvertrag." *Religion—Staat—Gesellschaft* 6: 123–64.

Simon, Anne-Catherine. 2015. "Homolka: 'Das würde Hitlers Rassenwahn fortsetzen.'" *Die Presse*, April 9. https://diepresse.com/home/panorama/religion/4704821/Homolka_Das-wuerde-Hitlers-Rassenwahn-fortsetzen.

Steiner, Barbara. 2015. *Inszenierung des Jüdischen: Konversionen von Deutschen zum Judentum nach 1945*. Göttingen: Wallstein Verlag.

Stern, Eliyahu. 2016. "Catholic Judaism: The Political Theology of the Nineteenth-Century Russian Jewish Enlightenment." *Harvard Theological Review* 109(4): 483–511.

Turtledove, Harry. 2011. "Shtetl Days." Tor.com, April 14. https://www.tor.com/2011/04/14/shtetl-days/ (accessed March 3, 2021).

von Hardenberg, Nina. 2006. "Punktesystem für Einwanderer." *Süddeutsche Zeitung*, July 25.

8

Ultra-Orthodox Judaism, Place Making, and Urban Boundaries in Paris

Lucine Endelstein

Although shtetls, *juderías*, and *mellah*s are now only vestiges evoking an ancient Jewish past in old centers of the Jewish world, Jewish neighborhoods have reappeared in the last decades in a large number of cities around the world. These places have emerged as a result of religious revival, especially Orthodox forms of Jewish revival (Gutwirth 2004). Indeed, the strict observance of Jewish law implies particular uses of space, such as the obligation to walk to the synagogue on Shabbat, Orthodox schooling, and kosher food supply. Along with those specific practices, the intense religious life makes the geographic proximity of the community and its leaders a crucial criterion for observant Jews' residential choices.

The success of ultra-Orthodox movements since the 1980s is one of the most visible aspects of Jewish revival in France, which is part of the international rise of ultra-Orthodox Judaism. Nevertheless, other religious movements, such as Liberal and Conservative Judaism,[1] participate in the transformations of French Judaism. These trends are still minor, however, and their impact on urban change is negligible. In France the demographic boom of ultra-Orthodox movements is mostly due to their success among

---

1. Liberal and Conservative Judaism are denominations that defend a critical understanding of sacred texts and the evolving nature of Judaism across history, incorporating progressive values and providing women's active participation in the ritual (Azria 2010).

the Sephardic population. In fact, since the end of World War II and a period of demographic and religious decline, the French Jewish population has been deeply transformed: first, by the immigration of 200,000 Jews from North Africa between 1950 and 1970 (Bensimon 1971); and, second, by the success of Orthodox and ultra-Orthodox movements in the context of globalization of religion, which made some Sephardic Jews adopt religious practices from Eastern Europe (Podselver 2010). The demographic rise of these movements is explained by the high fertility rate of ultra-Orthodox women and their early marriage.[2]

This chapter is based on a bottom-up analysis of Orthodox forms of Jewish revival and the internal transformations of Judaism linked to this phenomenon.[3] By taking the example of the urban insertion of Orthodox and ultra-Orthodox movements in northeast Paris, I explore the articulation between religious revival, place making in the city, and "boundary making" (Wimmer 2008) inside the Jewish communities. First, urban space and the convergence of ultra-Orthodox movements expose the links between migration, transnational circulation, and religious revival. Second, new boundaries inside ultra-Orthodoxy have emerged, based on the competition between religious leaders for the definition of religious norms. This phenomenon is observed through a specific religious system called *eruv*, a rabbinic system that symbolically transforms a city, a closed neighborhood, or a building into private space where it is possible to carry objects on the Sabbath.[4] By observing the uses of *eruv* established in high-rise buildings in Paris, this ritual system reveals the new boundaries emerging in ultra-Orthodox movements as a driving force of religious revival.

Although Orthodox forms of religious revival are perceived by their protagonists as a form of continuity with the Jewish past, these examples shed light on the transformations produced by religious revival that change

---

2. No statistical data on ultra-Orthodox demographics are available in France because the national census does not provide ethnic and religious data. Through years of fieldwork I have observed large to very large families (5 to 12 children) in the core of ultra-Orthodox movements. In Israel the birthrate of ultra-Orthodox women is higher than the national average and provides a rapid demographic increase to this population; nevertheless, this rate is slowly decreasing.
3. This chapter contains the findings of several years of fieldwork conducted in the 2000s (Endelstein 2009) and in the 2010s (Endelstein 2013, 2019).
4. Carrying objects from the private to the public space is one of the thirty-nine sabbatical prohibitions.

the processes of identification with Judaism, blurring ancient cultural boundaries and creating new religious divisions.

Jewish Revival and "Soft Ultra-Orthodoxy" in France

After World War II and a period of demographic decline of Orthodox Judaism in Europe and in France, some ultra-Orthodox movements experienced a renaissance, beginning in the 1980s. This revival is geographically tangible and is characterized by the creation of a large number of places of worship, yeshivas (institutions for young men that focus on the study of the traditional religious texts), *kollel*s (a type of yeshiva but for married men), and Jewish schools.

The term *ultra-Orthodoxy* in France is generally applied to the most conservative and pious denominations of Judaism, designated as Haredi Judaism in Israel. Members of ultra-Orthodox communities define themselves as Orthodox and claim an authentic interpretation of Jewish law that has been increasingly competing with the Consistoire, the official representative institution of Judaism in France, created by Napoleon in 1808. Broadly, the Judaism of the Consistoire can be defined as modern Orthodox, generally applied to denominations aspiring to full participation in secular society (Heilman and Cohen 1989). In contrast, the so-called ultra-Orthodox movements operate as enclavist movements and view non-Jewish society as incompatible with their religious aspirations and the preservation of their group.

Nevertheless, this common distinction between modern Orthodox and ultra-Orthodox movements does not capture the relations between the Judaism of the Consistoire and the religious actors who claim a more radical application of Jewish law. First, the boundaries between these denominations are not clear-cut. Because the Consistoire is competing with the rise of ultra-Orthodox movements, it is more and more influenced by ultra-Orthodoxy, including some Lubavitch[5] rabbis in its *beth din* (rabbinic tribunal). This evolution resonates with the "slide to the right" in the Jewish world in the United States, described by Heilman (2006). Second, this slide to the right, which affects many centers of Jewish life, is not a linear evolution to

---

5. The Lubavitch movement is a Hasidic sect that emerged in Eastern Europe in the eighteenth century. The movement actively seeks to interact with non-Orthodox Jews to bring them back into the fold—that is, to a strict observance of Jewish law.

an enclavist ultra-Orthodox model. On the contrary, several recent studies have described the rise of a "moderate ultra-Orthodoxy" (Krakowski 2012), highlighting the involvement of ultra-Orthodox Jews in many aspects of modern life: taking jobs in secular workplaces, attending universities, reading newspapers and nonreligious literature, or engaging with secular society (Stadler et al. 2005; Stadler and Taragin-Zeller 2017).

As Leon (2016) has observed in Israel, the rise of a Sephardic ultra-Orthodoxy transformed ultra-Orthodox Judaism into a "soft ultra-Orthodoxy." Several phenomena explain this evolution. First, Sephardic ultra-Orthodox Jews, with their extended family and community ties, interact on a daily basis with the nonreligious society. As Leon argues, the multiple belongings of Sephardic ultra-Orthodox Jews "serves as a rough surface that halts 'the slide to the right,' or at least slows and moderates the process" (Leon 2016, 156). Second, unlike Israeli, American, or British ultra-Orthodox neighborhoods, in France there is no urban insularity. Moreover, unlike some specific Ashkenazi ultra-Orthodox groups in Israel or the United States who use Yiddish in their daily life, French ultra-Orthodox Jews speak French and their daily interactions are not based on isolation. Third, in the context of religious renewal activity of the Lubavitch movement, the ultra-Orthodox leadership and the non-ultra-Orthodox public have continuous interactions. This singular combination led to the emergence of a moderate Jewish ultra-Orthodoxy in France.

Ultra-Orthodox Judaism in France is a constellation of independent groups that fall into three categories: Lithuanians (members of the Lithuanian yeshivas, emphasizing rigorous study of the Talmud), Hasids (the Hasidic movement emerged in Central Europe in the eighteenth century in opposition to Lithuanian Judaism and favored mysticism and joy in the practice against yeshiva elitism), and Sephardim (Jews from Islamic countries who adopted Lithuanian or Hasidic models).[6] In France the Lubavitch Hasidic movement is undoubtedly the largest ultra-Orthodox group, and their success is connected to their transnational missionary action. Other Hasidic groups are not represented in France, except for a small Breslov community. The Lithuanian Haredi community is a small but active minority that includes some charismatic rabbis and some attractive yeshivas in Paris and in provincial cities (e.g., the yeshiva in Aix les Bains, which has received Sephardic students since the 1950s). Indeed, in

---

6. For more detailed information on Orthodox forms of Judaism in France, see Endelstein (2019).

the 1950s Lithuanian yeshivas recruited Sephardic Jews or created separate institutions for the newcomers. Around 4,000 Jewish children from Morocco studied in Ashkenazi yeshivas in Western Europe and the United States (Lupo 2004). This early recruitment played a key role in the adoption of ultra-Orthodox Judaism by future Sephardic religious leaders and in the diffusion of ultra-Orthodox culture among a wider public. Today, the specificity of the French ultra-Orthodox world lies in the predominance of Sephardic Jews among the public.

Since the 1980s, a new Sephardic leadership has emerged, formed in yeshivas in France and in other countries before establishing their own places of worship and education, which disseminated a Lithuanian culture among a Sephardic public. Thus Ashkenazi Judaism has gradually imposed its model on some Sephardic Jews, who now pray and dress as Ashkenazim and sometimes even learn Yiddish. However, as in Israel, some of the ultra-Orthodox Sephardic Jews defend and promote Sephardic traditions and culture (Leon 2016).

In France ultra-Orthodox communities are essentially installed in the Greater Paris region and in some provincial cities (Lyon, Marseille, Nice, Toulouse, Aix les Bains). A large number of schools, places of worship, and some yeshivas have been created in the Paris suburbs since the 1960s; suburbs such as Fublaines, Armantières, Epinay-sur-Seine, Bussières, and Gagny have become popular among the French ultra-Orthodox. Inside Paris most ultra-Orthodox places are concentrated in the northeastern districts, which are also the most popular areas in the capital. Their specific clothing habits (*kippot*, dark overclothes) create a strong impact on religious visibility in urban space. Nevertheless, ultra-Orthodox groups still remain a minority in their districts of settlement, and the so-called Jewish neighborhoods in France are not comparable with ultra-Orthodox neighborhoods or localities in other urban contexts, such as Bnei Brak in Israel, Stamford Hill in London, and Williamsburg or Kiryas Joel in the United States.

Orthodox Forms of Judaism and Place Making in Eastern Paris

The urban history of the Jewish population in Greater Paris combines migratory and religious processes. Some neighborhoods in Paris (Le Marais, Belleville) and some suburbs (Sarcelles, Créteil) were historical places of

Jewish immigration revived by the rise of Orthodox and ultra-Orthodox movements in the 1990s. At the same time, because of religious revival, a large number of new Jewish centers have emerged inside and outside Paris, producing a dispersion of small Jewish concentrations in the metropolis. Among these new concentrations, the 19th arrondissement in northeast Paris has become a major place for French Orthodox Jews. This district is still inhabited by families on a modest income, thanks to a high rate of social housing (42% of the housing in 2019),[7] but it is quickly gentrifying, and it has been largely rebuilt since deindustrialization in the 1970s. It has a high density of immigrants, including North African Jews and Muslims.[8] Urban renewal brought together different migratory and religious Jewish networks, because of the characteristics of the housing in this area: availability of large apartments for large families, affordable rent compared with other Paris districts, and social housing. At the same time, the deindustrialization of these eastern neighborhoods reconstituted former industrial spaces as new places of worship.

The history and geography of the places of worship reflect the links between the gradual establishment of Jewish migratory networks and the revival of Orthodox Judaism. There are about twenty-five synagogues in the 19th arrondissement, but only a few were founded by Jews from Eastern Europe and North Africa. Instead, many were founded as a result of the rise of Lubavitch and other ultra-Orthodox movements. Northeast Paris is where the Lubavitch movement started to develop in the 1980s, with the expansion of a large school network. Alongside the Lubavitch movement, the number of Orthodox places of worship multiplied, showing the dispersion of Orthodox Judaism.

Northeast Paris provides a case study for ultra-Orthodox Judaism in France and its complex internal composition and evolution. The development of places of worship connect different scales of religious mobility: the continuum between migration and religious revival; the links between transnational circulations of religious leadership and the appearance of new religious places; and the local circulations of followers between different places of worship that contribute to the boundary making between

---

7. Atelier Parisien d'Urbanisme, *Cartographie du logement social à Paris*, May 2021.
8. On Jewish-Muslim interactions and relations in Paris, see Arkin (2014) and Everett (2020).

Sephardim and Ashkenazim and to the porosity of boundaries between religious movements.

Two representative places of worship shed light on the gradual rise of ultra-Orthodoxy among Ashkenazi and Sephardic migrants and their descendants. The first is an Ashkenazi synagogue that was founded in an apartment at the end of the nineteenth century by Jews coming from Alsace, joined by Eastern European Jewish migrants. The second appeared with the arrival of Jews from North Africa. Until the 1990s these two places of worship were hosted by the Lucien de Hirsch school (the oldest Jewish school in France, founded in 1901).

The fact that each community could create a synagogue in a building in the district expresses the religious dynamism experienced in the 1990s when both communities became more Orthodox. Whereas the Ashkenazi synagogue became closer to the Ashkenazi ultra-Orthodox world, the Sephardic place of worship became a hot spot of the French Sephardic ultra-Orthodoxy, hosting a yeshiva and a *kollel*. The religious evolution of these synagogues shows that both Sephardic and Ashkenazi Jews have taken part in the rise of ultra-Orthodoxy, even if Sephardic Jews are the majority today in France.[9] These two synagogues are connected to transnational religious networks, receiving spiritual leaders from different countries and Israeli hazans for Yom Kippur and sending some young boys to yeshivas in Israel and some young girls to religious seminaries. They exemplify the influence of the world of yeshivas on a part of French Judaism.

The three main ultra-Orthodox movements are represented in northeast Paris: Hasidic (Lubavitch), Lithuanian, and Sephardic. However, these three movements are not separated by strong boundaries. Many Jews move between different places of worship. The local grouping of synagogues favors informal relations between Orthodox movements and regular interactions between the Ashkenazi and Sephardic followers of those places of worship. Jewish schools play a key role in these local dynamics between ultra-Orthodox movements, partly because some places of worship are hosted by schools and partly because these schools have become an important center of local sociability. Moreover, because most of these schools cater to Sephardic children, they contribute to a mingling of Ashkenazi and Sephardic

---

9. In one of the last surveys on Judaism in France, 53.5% of Sephardic and 39% of Ashkenazi interviewees declared that their religious practices were "strong" (Schnapper et al. 2009).

cultures, with the result that some Ashkenazi traditions and elements of culture are adopted by Sephardim (such as clothing habits, music, or Yiddish), which reduces the importance of cultural belonging as a principle of religious organization.

Seen from outside, the gathering of Jewish schools and places of worship can be perceived as a single unified ultra-Orthodox community. But the local development of places of worship is linked to a complex articulation of urban dynamics, internal diversification of Jewish Orthodoxy, and transnational circulation in a context of religious revival. If the geographic proximity favors daily interactions and informal boundary blurring between different groups, the uses of urban space shed light on the internal social distance produced by the revival of ultra-Orthodox Judaism.

The *Eruv*: Residential Territory and Ritualized Community

Despite their geographic and denominational differences, observant Jews share a practice that highly affects their weekly uses of urban space in all major cities around the world: the prohibition to carry objects between the private and the public sphere on the Sabbath. This rule dictates that they cannot carry food, medicine, umbrellas, or even their babies in their arms on the street, nor can they use strollers. The *eruv*, meaning "mixing" in Hebrew, is a rabbinic system established in Talmudic times to redefine the limits between public and private space during Shabbat. The *eruv* allows the carrying of objects in a physically marked public space that is temporarily defined as private. In other words, the *eruv* is a ritual system of temporary and symbolic shifting of public and private boundaries. There are several types of *eruvim*. The *eruv hatserot*, or "fusion of courtyards," is a small *eruv* that assembles several dwellings inside a building or an enclosed space separated by walls, doors, and grids. The *eruv rashuyot*, or "fusion of areas," brings together a neighborhood or a whole city, when the area is enclosed with natural or urban elements: walls, rivers, railway. These large *eruvim* often require poles and wires to mark the symbolic enclosure of the area. Inside these materially closed areas, this system is created by a symbolic sharing of food,[10] which defines an *eruv* community. Food symbolizes the fact that all the inhabitants living inside the *eruv*'s limits are owners

---

10. A food that can be preserved for a long time (often a box of matzo) is usually deposited in a safe place, and a benediction is pronounced by those responsible for the *eruv*.

of the food and live "in the same house," as though the boundaries between the dwellings were blurred by this process (Fonrobert 2005). Talmudic law stipulates that to be valid, this system needs to be negotiated with neighbors whose houses are included in the process of symbolic fusion of spaces. This written agreement specifies that during the sacred time, the *eruv* area is one single private space, owned by the Jews.

Even if the ownership of the space of the *eruv* is fictive and temporary, it poses sensitive questions, such as the public status of religion and the ethnic demographic mapping of the city. Moreover, the construction of symbolic markers such as poles and wires can be perceived as a materialization of a communal territory and, as such, an intrusion of religion into public space. For these reasons the negotiations around *eruvim* often give rise to controversy. Its opponents compare the *eruvim* to ghettos, whereas its defenders highlight its practical dimension, for example, allowing the elderly and disabled individuals to go out with canes and wheelchairs and young parents to go out with their babies.

The *eruvim* that enclose neighborhoods or cities have multiplied since the 1990s in tandem with the rise of ultra-Orthodoxy, especially in Anglo-Saxon countries (Cooper 1996; Stoker 2003). In France there are only two established *eruvim*, in Strasbourg and Metz. In these former German territories the public status of religion is not regulated by the 1905 law of separation between state and church but by the Concordat, a state rule that regulates the organization of churches. In other parts of France, large *eruvim* may be perceived as antithetical to quintessential national values such as *laïcité* (secularism) and urban *mixité* (mixing). Nevertheless, small *eruvim* established in buildings are quite common in Jewish residential areas.

Religious Revival and Internal Boundary Making

In northeast Paris some *eruvim* were created in high-rise buildings where Jewish families are a substantial minority (between 10% and 30% of the apartments, when the Jewish population in France is less than 1% of the total population).[11] These high-rise complexes include several thousand inhabitants. They were built in the late 1970s and 1980s and were bought by private institutions that rented out the apartments, offering opportunities for

---

11. I made these estimates in the 2000s with the inhabitants of these buildings, counting the Jewish names on the mailboxes.

several Jewish migratory and religious networks to gradually come together. In the 1990s the privatization of these complexes (with grids, digital access codes, and intercoms) made possible the setting up of *eruvim*.

Considered from a theoretical point of view, the *eruv* seems to be a ritualization of territorial marking by a community. It can also be considered a boundary-making system, creating a community and excluding outsiders. But the *eruv* has also been described as a ritual system of acknowledgment of the presence of the other: The Jewish *eruv* community needs the agreement of the neighbors. By giving this agreement, the non-Jewish neighbors recognize the presence of observant Jews in their residential environment. Thus this system does not imply a sociability but a symbolic interaction and mutual recognition (Fonrobert 2009, 28).

However, the *eruv* is not only a ritual and symbolic system but also a space of living. Looking at the uses of space at the local level, what are the implications of the *eruv* on the local everyday experience and boundary making? My fieldwork shows that this rabbinic system is more an internal boundary-making system than an external one.

First, among the thousands of inhabitants (between 2,000 to 5,000) of these complexes, only a small number of people who took part in the negotiations around the *eruv* many years ago are aware of the existence of this invisible boundary coded on the walls and fences of the neighborhood. Moreover, *eruvim* are not forms of sacralization of space. Rather, they allow for secular uses of space (carrying food, taking books or balls into the courtyards, or carrying a child) that are perceivable only to those who are familiar enough with Judaism to realize that observant Jews, wearing *kippot* or Orthodox clothing, are circumventing a halakhic rule. These temporary and invisible boundaries exist only for those who use it. Therefore their most important function is *not* to highlight a religious practice but to facilitate local Jewish sociability. In fact, on the Shabbat the communal areas of those residences become meeting places for Jewish adults and playgrounds for Jewish children. Nevertheless, even if this system is perceived as the ritualization of a unified local Jewish community, looking closely at the way it is created and used also reveals the formation of internal religious boundaries.

In fact, this complex Talmudic system—detailed over 200 pages in the Talmud—is an object of contention between rabbis and religious orientations. Some ultra-Orthodox groups refuse to use such systems that circumvent a Shabbat prohibition and therefore oppose the creation of an *eruv* in their city, neighborhood, or building. Others used to accept the *eruvim*. However, in the context of religious revival and strict adherence to religious norms, this rabbinic system is suspected of not conforming to Halakha. Are the physical characteristics of the *eruv* limits done in accordance with halakhic rule? Is the *eruv* kosher? *Eruvim* are objects of increasing competition between Orthodox and ultra-Orthodox movements, whose followers are solicitous about their compliance to religious law.

For this reason, as has been described in other contexts (Cooper 1996; von Busekist 2016), northeast Paris *eruvim* do not unify all the Jewish observant inhabitants living in the same high-rise building complex. Some of them refuse to use the *eruv*, because their rabbi disagrees with the principle of making an *eruv*, and they observe the prohibition on carrying objects out of their dwellings. Others refuse to use the *eruv* because they follow a rabbi who contests the religious legitimacy of the creator of the *eruv*. Thus the existence of *eruvim* can reveal boundaries inside ultra-Orthodox communities; when created by members of the Lubavitch movements, the *eruv* is criticized by non-Hasidic ultra-Orthodox leaders. As observed in the kosher food sector, the growth of ultra-Orthodox Judaism has also multiplied rabbinic certifications. Confidence or distrust in the leader who certifies the conformity to Halakha is a key point in understanding the competition between Orthodox movements and the expansion of religious practices.

Not only can observant Jews refuse to use an *eruv*, but several *eruvim* can be superimposed in the same place, made by rabbis from different movements living in the same complex. In other urban contexts (New York, Jerusalem), several *eruvim* coexist in the same area, also pointing to the boundaries and the competition between Orthodox or ultra-Orthodox groups. Surprisingly, in Paris, Jews are likely to use an *eruv* without being aware of the actual creation of this system. In other places *eruvim* can appear without consultation among the observant Jews. In one building, at the time of my fieldwork, two *eruvim* coexisted, organized spontaneously by two different individuals without prior coordination.[12] The superposition of *eruvim* and the fact that most observant Jews living in the same place are not necessarily aware of them contradict the image of a unified community symbolized by the *eruv*. In other words, *eruvim* do not unite local

---

12. It is not necessary to be a rabbi to establish an *eruv*.

Jewish communities. On the contrary, they point to the limits of sociability among observant Jews and the competition between Orthodox movements.

Although the pragmatics of *eruvim* give rise to suspicions on the part of observant Jews and to disputes between religious leaders, these rabbinic systems are ignored by the non-Jewish neighbors. In ultra-Orthodox communities in the United States and in Israel, *eruvim* can be considered an expression of a religious spatial power. But in the Parisian cases the *eruv* appears as an internal boundary-making process, separating ultra-Orthodox leaders and followers. High-rise buildings are mixed territories where Jews are a minority and have neither authority nor power. *Eruvim* are objects of avoidance or discord inside the Jewish world; their multiplication echoes the rise of religious norms and practices and the division of ultra-Orthodox Judaism.

Conclusion

In this chapter I have approached the study of Jewish revival through the urban perspective by exploring the cohabitation of ultra-Orthodox movements and their internal diversification. Seen from the outside, the so-called Jewish neighborhoods are often perceived as unified communities, but in practice the communal use of space redefines the cultural and religious boundaries inside Orthodox and ultra-Orthodox movements.

In the context of globalization of religion and religious renewal, the *eruv* shows how the different scales of religious mobilities play an active role in the making, redefining, or blurring of ethnic boundaries. The global success of Ashkenazi ultra-Orthodox movements (Hasidic or Lithuanian) and the recruitment of Sephardic Jews are key factors in the "slide to the right" movement of part of North African Jewry in France. On the local scale the circulation of individuals between places of worship of different religious groups and Sephardic children's attendance at Ashkenazi Lithuanian or Lubavitch schools contribute to a blurring of cultural boundaries. This development does not mean that the processes of identification as Sephardic or Ashkenazi have disappeared but that they are partly redefined into a complex blending of traditional and religious practices. More detailed research is needed to fully understand to what extent cultural identification as Ashkenazi or Sephardic remains a principle of classification and social organization inside these movements in a context where the Sephardic public is now a majority and the impact of its leadership is growing.

Although religious Orthodox revival is proclaimed as a continuity with the past, it also produces new religious identifications and new internal boundaries within Judaism, both globally and locally. The example of the *eruv*, a "Shabbat territory" (Fonrobert 2005), which ritualizes the link between faith and space, highlights the limits between geographic proximity and communal unity and the increasing competition between religious leaders. Redefining cultural forms of identification, ultra-Orthodox revival is creating new religious divisions inside the Jewish world and new identifications that straddle geographic origins.

The Jewish residential complexes that have emerged in Greater Paris over the last two decades can be considered a geographic aspect of religious revival among the French Jewish population. Nevertheless, this geographic dispersion stands in opposition to the urban insularity of ultra-Orthodox movements in other geographic contexts and shows that the "slide to the right" process is also giving birth to an ethnically mixed soft ultra-Orthodoxy.

References

Arkin, Kimberly. 2014. *Rhinestones, Religion, and the Republic: Fashioning Jewishness in France*. Stanford, CA: Stanford University Press.

Azria, Régine. 2010. *Le judaïsme*. Paris: La Découverte.

Bensimon, Doris. 1971. *L'intégration des Juifs nord-africains en France*. Université de Nice, Publications de l'Institut d'études et de recherches interethniques et interculturelles 1. Paris La Haye: Mouton.

Cooper, Davina. 1996. "Talmudic Territory? Space, Law, and Modernist Discourse." *Journal of Law and Society* 23(4): 529–48.

Endelstein, Lucine. 2009. "Les lieux de revitalisation du judaïsme aujourd'hui: Vers un brouillage des frontières entre Ashkénazes et Séfarades?" *Archives Juives* 42(2): 98–111.

Endelstein, Lucine. 2013. "L'erouv, une frontière dans la ville?" *Ethnologie Française* 43(4): 641–49.

Endelstein, Lucine. 2019. "Le judaïsme orthodoxe non consistorial." In *Les minorités religieuses en France*, ed. Anne-Laure Zwilling, 776–95. Paris: Bayard.

Everett, Samuel. 2020. "Une Ambiance Diaspora: Continuity and Change in Parisian Maghrebi Imaginaries." *Comparative Studies in Society and History* 62(1): 135–55.

Fonrobert, Charlotte Elisheva. 2005. "The Political Symbolism of the Eruv." *Jewish Social Studies* 11(3): 9–35.

Fonrobert, Charlotte Elisheva. 2009. "Une cartographie symbolique: l'eruv en Diaspora." *Les Cahiers du Judaïsme* 25: 5–21.

Gutwirth, Jacques. 2004. *La renaissance du hassidisme: de 1945 à nos jours*. Paris: O. Jacob.

Heilman, Samuel C. 2006. *Sliding to the Right: The Contest for the Future of American Jewish Orthodoxy*. Berkeley: University of California Press.

Heilman, Samuel C., and Steven M. Cohen. 1989. *Cosmopolitan and Parochials: Modern Orthodox Jews in America*. Chicago: University of Chicago Press.

Krakowski, Moshe. 2012. "Moderate Ultra-Orthodoxy: Complexity and Nuance in American Ultra-Orthodox Judaism." *Religion and Education* 39(3): 257–83.

Leon, Nissim. 2016. "The Ethnic Structuring of 'Sephardim' in Haredi Society in Israel." *Jewish Social Studies* 22(1): 130–60.

Lupo, Yaacov. 2004. *Métamorphose ultra-orthodoxe chez les juifs du Maroc: Comment des séfarades sont devenus ashkénazes*. Paris: L'Harmattan.

Podselver, Laurence. 2010. *Retour au judaïsme? Les loubavitch en France*. Paris: O. Jacob.

Schnapper, Dominique, Chantal Bordes-Benayoun, and Freddy Raphaël. 2009. *La condition juive en France: La tentation de l'entre-soi*. Paris: Presses Universitaires de France.

Stadler, Nurit, and Lea Taragin-Zeller. 2017. "Like a Snake in Paradise: Fundamentalism, Gender, and Taboos in the Haredi Community." *Archives de Sciences Sociales des Religions* 62(177): 133–56.

Stadler, Nurit, Eyal Ben-Ari, and Einat Mesterman. 2005. "Terror, Aid, and Organization: The Haredi Disaster Victim Identification Teams (ZAKA) in Israel." *Anthropological Quarterly* 78(3): 619–51.

Stoker, Valerie. 2003. "Drawing the Line: Hasidic Jews, Eruvim, and the Public Space of Outremont, Québec." *History of Religions* 43(1): 18–49.

Von Busekist, Astrid. 2016. *Portes et murs: des frontières en démocratie*. Paris: Albin Michel.

Wimmer, Andreas. 2008. "Elementary Strategies of Ethnic Boundary Making." *Ethnic and Racial Studies* 31(6): 1025–55.

9

Breslov Hasidic Social Renewal and the Mizrahi Haredi *Teshuva* Movement

Nissim Leon

Although Breslov Hasidism traces its roots back to the early stages of the Hasidic movement, this group is distinctive not only in its religious approach but also in the fact that, since the death of its founder, Rabbi Nachman, no one has taken the helm as officially designated *admor*. Over the years communities have developed around the teachings of Breslov Hasidism—some direct descendants of early Breslov Hasidim but others of more contemporary origin. Over the years the survival of Breslov Hasidism, its unique teachings, and the life and legacy of its enigmatic founder have been the focus of extensive research (Piekarz 1972; Green 1979; Weiss 1985; Mark 2011). Many scholars have addressed the religious and theological aspects of the renewal wrought by Breslov Hasidism, with a focus on its textual world. Less attention has been given to the social renewal that Breslov Hasidism has brought about in recent decades among newly religious Jews (or those in the process of committing themselves to a religious lifestyle), for whom the conceptual and experiential world of Breslov Hasidism is a new and meaningful axis for their lives.

As Eliezer Baumgarten (2012) explains in his pioneering article on this subject, newly religious youth whose families originated in Islamic countries—"Mizrahim" in the terminology of Israeli sociology—feature disproportionately in Breslov religious renewal circles in Israel. Of course, the decision to commit oneself, whether gradually or wholly, to a religious lifestyle is a matter of personal circumstances and context; it can serve as a solution or response to a personal problem or as a quest for a spiritual approach to the challenges of the era, molded by the individual personality and the tools relevant to the times (Beit-Hallahmi 1987). Nevertheless, the choice is made from within a field of interpretive and social possibilities that is narrower than it may seem. In addition, it is guided not only by personal experience but also by collective experience—what sociologists such as Pierre Bourdieu (2008) and Laurence Iannaccone (1990) might refer to as socioeconomic, cultural, and religious capital. It speaks to the cultural and religious place and environment from which the quest for a return to religion emerges (El-Or 2006). For this reason, the prominent presence of Mizrahi youth among newer Breslov circles in Israel presents a sociological riddle.

In this essay I attempt to offer a possible answer, set in the somewhat complex story of the Mizrahi Haredi *teshuva* movement in Israel. This movement, whose significance I discuss later, has brought renewal to the religious infrastructure of Mizrahim in Israel, including their religious leadership, theological emphases, ceremonies and liturgy, and the world of the local synagogue. In the early stages of the Mizrahi Haredi *teshuva* movement the influence of the Ashkenazi Lithuanian Haredi element was dominant, because many of the movement's leaders had been nurtured in Lithuanian-style yeshivas. The worldview that nourished the *teshuva* movement likewise flowed from the Lithuanian Haredi ideal of the scholar society. But over the 2010s Breslov Hasidism has become an increasingly dominant presence, and a great many Israeli Jews of Mizrahi descent, mostly youth, have found room for their personal religious growth in the message of *teshuva* (repentance) according to Breslov Hasidism. In this chapter I discuss three factors that have played a role in advancing Breslov's popularity and prominence in the Mizrahi Haredi *teshuva* movement: (1) the blurring of ethnicity in Breslov Hasidism, (2) the desire for rejuvenation of the fire of the *teshuva* movement, and (3) the problems associated with the reality of "soft" Mizrahi Haredism.

The Mizrahi Haredi *Teshuva* Movement and Its Local Communal Activism

The idea of *teshuva* (literally, "return" but often translated as "repentance") is integral to the traditional Jewish worldview and is anchored in a set of holy days, prayers, customs, and ceremonies. Indeed, this deeply rooted concept and aspiration has prompted some influential initiatives in Jewish history, which I do not elaborate on here. With regard to modern Israel, the term *teshuva movement* is identified in the research with informational and outreach activity by the Orthodox stream. In essence, this activity seeks to persuade Jews who are considered secular or nonobservant in Orthodox eyes that a lifestyle that adheres strictly and consistently to Halakha (Jewish law) is the proper Jewish way (Aviad 1983). Similar efforts to counter the trend toward secularism in the public and private sphere are also found in Islam and Christianity in the form of activist, creative, and charismatic approaches to religion that seek to redirect history back onto its religious tracks—or that even adopt an eschatological endeavor to propel its teachings in the direction of the prophecies concerning the End of Days (Harding 2000; Zeidan 2003). These efforts are the background for the appearance of trends of religious awakening and revival that seek to remodel the social, religious, and communal landscape in the image of a new and energized religio-conservative order (Ammerman 1997).

The research literature traces the background and growth of the *teshuva* movement in Israel to the attenuation of various axioms that had accompanied the system of ideology, identity, and culture on which modern Jewish society in Israel was based in the late 1960s and early 1970s (Caplan 2001). The call for a return to Jewish tradition as a possible solution to problems of identity crossed ideological and sectorial boundaries, finding a receptive audience in the secular kibbutz movement, religious Zionism, and Haredi (ultra-Orthodox) society alike. Admittedly, a great distance separated the message of Jewish renewal proclaimed by the Shadmot group, for instance, in the kibbutz movement, and the religious renewal of the Haredi *teshuva* movement, but both emerged, to some extent, from a platform of questions of identity and purpose that young people in Israel were asking in their quest to discover the meaning of the "Jewish" component of the "new Jew." Over the course of the 1970s, traditional Judaism, as a system of religious belonging, identity, and culture, gradually emerged from its defensive stance to become a hub of religious activism.

In the religious Zionist sector the call for *teshuva* activism as a movement of national repair was sidelined by the settlement movement in Judea, Samaria, and Gaza, which became the leading religious Zionist channel for social change and the molding of Israeli history. On the other hand, for

Haredi society the *teshuva* movement was a means of penetrating Zionist history not as a remnant of the past or as a sector trying to survive in the present but rather as a group seeking, like others, to play an active role in molding the future of the nation. The 1970s witnessed three relatively organized channels of a Haredi *teshuva* movement. One channel focused on providing a response to questions of identity and faith that arose among young Jews in developed countries and among elite groups in Israel, including artists and performers, senior military personnel, and kibbutz members. A second channel focused on convincing older students at religious Zionist high schools of the truth and rightness of Haredi ideology before their enlistment in the Israel Defense Forces (IDF). Neither of these channels succeeded in attracting a significant following.

The *teshuva* phenomenon as a mass movement began to appear only in the early 1980s, with a shift from local outreach activity to a large-scale movement of religious revival in low-income neighborhoods, development towns, and moshavim—all areas where Mizrahim represented a large percentage of the population (Leon 2010, 147–56). We might call this third channel the Mizrahi Haredi *teshuva* movement. The Haredi component of this title reflects the fact that the great majority of the movement's main spokespeople, preachers, and activists have been educated in Haredi institutions and view themselves as belonging to Haredi society. The rabbinic leadership with which they consulted, and which they viewed as authoritative, was Haredi, and the movement directed its adherents, whether directly or indirectly, to view integration into the Haredi scholar society as a worthy and proper model. The Mizrahi component of the title signifies the ethnic identification of these activists and preachers with the culture and life story of the Mizrahi public. Many of them had been born to religious or traditional Mizrahi families that, for various reasons, sent their children to Haredi educational institutions during Israel's early decades.

Tamar El-Or (2006) describes these local projects and their respective social, cultural, and religious capital using the term *teshuva locales*. In *teshuva* locales a new style and new standards of Mizrahi religiosity were established, characterized inter alia by an assertive and activist religious stance; preference for the written word over living tradition; the inculcation of Haredi society's worldview, mythos, and political behavior and organization; and a sometimes eclectic merging of styles and principles originating in mutually incompatible Haredi streams (Leon 2010).

The wave of religious and ethnic renewal spurred by the Mizrahi Haredi *teshuva* movement, as expressed in the popularity of the Shas Party (Lehmann and Siebzehner 2006), brought some challenges in its wake. First and foremost among these was the question of ethnic identity—that is, the Sephardic identity of the outreach activists and their target audience. On one hand, this identity was bound up with the world of religious law and customs associated with the ethnic environment in which Mizrahim had grown up and that they liked to envision as having its origins in the ancient traditions of the Jews of Spain. At the same time, their designation as Sephardic was inextricably linked with the modern ethnic and socioeconomic separation between Ashkenazi and Mizrahi Haredi communities. Although this separation mirrors the Ashkenazi-Mizrahi ethnic tension in Israeli society in general, in the Haredi context the division rests on the notion that the Haredi identity of Mizrahim is not authentic, and the Mizrahim's apparent commitment to the Haredi lifestyle is always suspect. This results in a system of discrimination against Mizrahi families even after a generation or two of immersion in Haredi society, finding expression in such areas as acceptance into educational institutions, matchmaking, and so on.

A second challenge concerned the question of institutionalization versus renewal within the *teshuva* message and movement itself. Many local initiatives were transformed over the years into institutions that followed a religious and communal routine, and the question of how to maintain the burning intensity of the *teshuva* ideal thus needed to be addressed. A third problem pertained to the profound sociological difference between Mizrahi Haredi *teshuva* communities and established Ashkenazi Haredi communities. Whereas the Mizrahi communities maintained a heterogeneous environment full of religious tensions and paradoxes, the Ashkenazi communities maintained a homogeneous environment aimed at distancing and secluding members from friction with the outside world and its confusing influences. These problems were the gateway through which the Breslov option entered and took up a prominent place in the Mizrahi Haredi *teshuva* movement, as we shall see.

Blurred Ethnicity

The origins of Breslov Hasidism in Mizrahi Haredi circles took the form of two major projects. The first was the long-standing textual and community initiative of Rabbi Eliezer Shlomo Schick. The second was the Shuvu Banim yeshiva for newly religious men, established by Rabbi Eliezer Berland in the late 1970s.

Schick was born in Palestine in 1940 and in 1954 moved with his family to the United States, where he studied in "Lithuanian" yeshivas. His path to Breslov Hasidism consisted of self-study of its texts, after which he worked to disseminate the writings of Rabbi Nachman. In the early 1980s Schick began operating in Israel too. He settled in the northern village of Yavne'el, in the lower Galilee region—a move that caused considerable local controversy, owing to the opposition of the village's veteran members, in the face of Schick's followers' perception of the move as a matter of principle and an undertaking filled with profound mystical and messianic significance (Katz 2007; Sobel 1993).

A community of newly religious men and women, many of them from Mizrahi backgrounds, developed around Rabbi Schick, and they viewed him as their religious leader and authority. The unusual rules that he set down for members of his community (e.g., his encouragement to marry at a young age) led to frequent confrontations with the law. Schick became well-known in *teshuva* circles inter alia by virtue of short booklets that he wrote on various aspects of faith in Breslov style. By the 1980s these booklets were already being disseminated in hundreds of synagogues, at central bus stations, and at IDF bases. They were easily recognizable by the vocalized Hebrew text written in personal and somewhat archaic style and by the distinctive Breslov crown on the cover. The booklets became a prominent hallmark of Breslov popular *teshuva* discourse. It was easy to dismiss them as disconnected from reality, or to heap scorn on their archaic language and seemingly simplistic messages. However, there is considerable evidence that at specific times, at particular junctions in life, and in underprivileged environments, the simple, personal style caught the attention of young people and provided them, whether momentarily or in the longer term, with firm ground to stand on and the meaning and purpose they were looking for. For some, the transient encounter inspired the choice of Breslov Hasidism as a way of life, whether on the personal level or through joining a communal framework. For others, the booklets made Breslov Hasidism (or, at least, Schick's version of it) into a personal tool in personal identity work, independent of any communal or social organization. Either way, Schick's effectiveness as an easily recognizable figure in the *teshuva* movement, by virtue of his interpretation of the teachings of Breslov Hasidism, was not lost on the chief beneficiary of the Mizrahi Haredi *teshuva* movement, the Shas Party. Schick was introduced into the circle of close associates of Rabbi Ovadia Yosef, and his public call to vote for Shas was included in the party's propaganda cassettes in the late 1990s. Schick passed away in 2015, leaving a large community of followers plagued by internal disputes and competition over succession.

The second Breslov initiative of note was the Shuvu Banim yeshiva associated with Rabbi Eliezer Berland and his followers. Berland was born in 1937 to a religious Zionist family in Haifa, and as a teenager he was drawn to the path and teachings of Breslov Hasidism. In the late 1960s Berland drew a group of students from Lithuanian yeshivas with him in the direction of old-style Breslov Hasidism. In 1978 he was appointed *rosh yeshiva* of the Shuvu Banim Breslov yeshiva (Yifrah 2016). At first the yeshiva was located in Bnei Brak; later it moved to East Jerusalem. Berland and his yeshiva stood out in the landscape of religious society in the capital. A few years after its founding, a journalist for the *Maariv* newspaper described the students of Shuvu Banim as "considered exceptions to all the yeshivot for newly religious students in Jerusalem. The 120 students are distinctive for their unique prayer customs and their shabby appearance, emphasizing man's insignificance. They jump and sway energetically, with great concentration. They sing gustily and pray loudly" (Bender 1986). The yeshiva was a magnet for youngsters from Mizrahi families in low-income neighborhoods of Jerusalem who were looking to strengthen their religious identity and take on a religious lifestyle. Berland and his teachings offered what they were looking for.

In both of these yeshiva communities, two complementary social dynamics developed. One was a lack of any separation or distinction between Ashkenazim and Mizrahim; the second was the possibility of maintaining the Sephardic-Mizrahi tradition within the Ashkenazi framework, sometimes even combining them. With regard to the lack of separation, the Breslov world of *teshuva* allowed for an ethnically mixed community of equals that was unknown in other yeshivas for newly religious students. In *teshuva* movement circles, there was no separation or hierarchy between Ashkenazi and Mizrahi Breslov Hasidim, a notable and unusual phenomenon in an environment where ethnic separation was the norm. Breslov frameworks offered an "Israeli," "sabra" environment in which former IDF soldiers and children of well-known Israeli personalities mixed with youngsters from anonymous working-class Mizrahi families in a melting pot fired by the charismatic Berland and his interpretation of Breslov teachings. With regard to observance of Sephardic-Mizrahi customs within the Ashkenazi framework, it seems that the Breslov approach—at least, as Berland and Schick practiced it—facilitated and even encouraged dialogue and coexistence between the Eastern European Breslov identity and the Mizrahi ethnic identity. Moreover, initial findings of research by linguist Dalit Assouline (2017) indicate the use of "ethnolect" (ethnic dialect) among Breslov *teshuva* circles, with emphasis on the pronunciation of guttural Hebrew letters and use of Arabic slang, all serving to connect the speakers with all that is associated in Israeli discourse with the term *Mizrahi*. Eliezer Baumgarten (2012) showed that Rabbi Schick's community published Breslov prayer books and *selichot* (penitential prayers) booklets adhering completely to the "Sephardic and Oriental" prayer traditions. The "Breslov" element of these prayer books finds expression in the insertion of Schick's interpretations of the prayer text and thoughts on *teshuva* and religious life.

In this respect, Mizrahi Breslov Hasidism differed from other Mizrahi Haredi *teshuva* environments. Its distinctiveness was established from the outset by a difference of worldview and not by differences originating in ethnic divisions. This new merging challenged the fraught ethnic divisions in Haredi society: The presence and acceptance of Mizrahim in Breslov Hasidism meant assimilation within Ashkenazi Hasidic culture without forgoing ethnic traditions. With regard to ethnic signifiers, on the one hand the Breslov reality allowed unfettered access to and "passing as" throughout its frameworks; on the other hand, it allowed the ethnic traditions and ethnic background to be a vital presence in the song, sound, and discourse of religious experience. In other words, if a newly religious individual of Mizrahi descent wanted to hold a Haredi identity that considered itself authentic and yet entailed no ethnic discrimination, even if that person chose to maintain some Mizrahi customs, then Breslov Hasidism was a good option.

Over the years, the Breslov *teshuva* message, as molded by Rabbis Schick, Berland, and others who joined their activist trend, expanded outward from the newly religious communities in Jerusalem, Bnei Brak, Yavne'el, and Safed to the Mizrahi Haredi *teshuva* circles in medium-size Israeli cities, such as Holon, Bat Yam, Netanya, Ashdod, Ashkelon, Yehud, and Or Yehuda, as well as in development towns and moshavim in the country's periphery. Small local study halls and Breslov-style prayer congregations began to pop up in these locations. From a phenomenon on the fringes of the Mizrahi Haredi *teshuva* movement, Breslov Hasidism became a highly visible social phe-nomenon; in some places, such as Safed, it became a significant and popular stream within the Mizrahi Haredi *teshuva* movement.

Renewal of the *Teshuva* Message

Another factor in the background to the Breslov *teshuva* movement in Miz-rahi Haredi *teshuva* circles pertains to the search for renewal among the newly religious and those in the process of transitioning to a religious life-style, in view of the institutionalization of older local *teshuva* initiatives. In the 1970s and 1980s the Mizrahi Haredi *teshuva* movement was active in old, neglected, temporary local venues, lending an air of the underground, innovation, and even revolution. In contrast, by the first decade of the new millennium, the local *teshuva* initiatives that had survived had grown stronger, acquired local prestige, and turned into institutional systems—in many cases, housed in impressive quarters. The *teshuva* preachers who had established communities were transformed from a charismatic leadership fueled by a fiery message into an elite group that operated as part of the state bureaucracy or by dint of the local dynasties that it created. Although the first generation of leaders of the Mizrahi Haredi *teshuva* movement had been characterized by an entrepreneurial approach powered by personal charisma and a spirit of religious renewal, later a more institutionalized approach arose that sought to establish local rabbinic dynasties that used the power of symbolic assets and local prestige that they had accumulated to acquire and maintain local institutional assets, including jobs as neigh-borhood or city rabbis. Some figures were transformed from local *teshuva* preachers into widely known rabbinic authorities, and their students con-tinued their teachers' path and adopted their style, building branches of the original community. Amid the institutionalization of the Mizrahi Haredi *teshuva* message, Breslov Hasidism became a source of religious renewal. A prominent example of a messenger of Breslov's *teshuva* discourse was (and remains) Rabbi Shalom Arush.

The late 1990s witnessed the appearance of Arush's audiocassettes among Mizrahi Haredi *teshuva* circles. Arush was born in Morocco in 1952 and moved to Israel with his family in 1965. Following his military service and during his studies at university, he became religious and was drawn to Breslov Hasidism by way of Shuvu Banim yeshiva. In the mid-1980s he embarked on his own path and established religious institutions under the name Hut shel Hesed (thread of kindness), which aimed to disseminate a Breslov-style *teshuva* message. Like many *teshuva* preachers, Arush traveled from place to place, from city to city, from one synagogue or study hall to the next. Some of his sermons, which in the beginning would sometimes be delivered to exceedingly small audiences, were recorded by students and followers who had started to attach themselves to him, and these were disseminated among the public. Arush's presentation of Breslov teachings was a new, outwardly oriented exposition of old-style Breslov Hasidism, now harnessed in the name of the *teshuva* movement. Arush's approach was a far cry from the vehement polemical style that characterized preachers of the Mizrahi Haredi *teshuva* movement such as Amnon Yitzhak or Daniel Zer. Arush made no attempt to present sophisticated or logical "proofs" for God's existence (Caplan 1997), nor did he turn his sermons into an arena for bashing secular society. Arush brought something new to the propaganda of the *teshuva* movement: a new, more personal, more everyday language that was less zealous and political. He spoke about everyday issues, about relationships between spouses, between children and their parents, between newly religious Jews and the people around them. In Haredi *teshuva* circles, where poverty and marginalization were perennial issues that seemed to intensify with the decision to adopt a Haredi lifestyle, the Breslov *teshuva* message as formulated by Arush was presented as a repair of the individual not through a revival and empowerment of the person's collective identity but rather through connecting to their life's conditions and turning those very conditions into a religious message. Over the years, Arush's followers became an increasingly heterogeneous group. His messages were a source of strength and religious meaning not only for the newly religious but also for many individuals—men, women, and youth—who belonged to religious and Haredi communities.

The Breslov *teshuva* movement took root in places where poverty, deficiency, and marginality were integral to the everyday lives of Israelis of Mizrahi origin. This setting provided fertile ground for a kabbalistic-Hasidic theology about repair of place and of humanity (Katz 2007). The life of Rabbi Nachman, with all its challenges, the profound faith that he sought, the solitary meditation, the marginalized existence, and the persecution of himself and his followers—all this was invoked by Breslov preachers in their weaving of the connection between the stereotypical Mizrahi life story and the personal life story on the economically underprivileged margins to which Mizrahim in Israel had been relegated. However, from the perspective of these preachers, poverty was a divine decree that should be consciously imbued with religious purpose in this world. Poverty was presented as inseparable not only from humanity's repair in the world but also from the world's repair through individuals. Poverty-stricken individuals have a role in the world: They offer an opportunity for others to practice charity; they live simply, always on the brink, with next to nothing on the material level, and for this reason they are in close touch with themselves on the existential-spiritual level. Their existence represents an ongoing divine miracle, reminding them of God's divine providence. This idea is given most eloquent expression in the film *Ushpizin*, directed by Shuli Rand, a Breslov returnee to Haredi Judaism and a follower of Rabbi Arush. The film tells the story of Moshe and Mali Balanga, a childless Breslov couple of Mizrahi origin. They live in abject poverty in one of Jerusalem's Haredi neighborhoods. Moshe, a former criminal, finds his religious studies difficult and is preoccupied with the problem of how to obtain money to buy the four species required by religious law for the Sukkot festival. When through a miraculous chain of events the couple receives $1,000 just before the festival, Moshe decides to use the money to buy an especially fine *etrog* (citron). Although the fruit will be of ritual value only for seven days, the opportunity to fulfill the commandment in such superior style is precious to him. During the festival, two friends from Moshe's distant past arrive and stay over. The two men, who have just been released from jail, are suspicious of the new path that their friend has chosen for himself. They exploit his goodwill and accidentally chop up his expensive *etrog* into their salad. Despair gnaws at Moshe and Mali, who have now lost both the *etrog* and the money. The situation becomes a spiritual test. Their unwavering commitment to the commandments of hospitality and the holiday earns them a divine reward, in the form of Mali's pregnancy and the reconciliation of the two guests with the change that has come over Moshe. The film reflects the socioeconomic reality of many Breslov Hasidim of Mizrahi origin. It invokes the vacillation characterizing the way of life of newly religious Jews to focus on the ongoing and intense contest between the material and the spiritual. In the film, obviously, it is the spiritual that emerges victorious. From this perspective, the Breslov *teshuva* message functions as a "beggars' entrance," as it were, to the Protestant ethic that the Israeli middle class began to embrace more strongly in the first decade of the new millennium, with the consolidation of a neoliberal economy whose leaders sought to distance themselves from the welfare state model.

Problems of "Soft" Haredism

The Breslov *teshuva* message also offered a response of sorts to the question of personal salvation in the realm of soft Mizrahi Haredism. I proposed the term *soft Haredism* some years ago to describe the broad margins of the brand of Haredism that developed in Mizrahi Haredi *teshuva* circles (Leon 2010). The softness that I attributed to this environment refers not to the pragmatic approach that is attributed to Mizrahi religiosity (Shokeid 1995) but rather to the range of religious (or "becoming religious") identities that gather under the Mizrahi Haredi umbrella. This type of situation invites tension. It is full of paradoxes, contradictions, and questions relating to the connection between *teshuva* as a culture and Haredism as an ideological framework. Taking up a position on the broad margins of soft Haredism allows for, on the one hand, the structuring of fervent, demonstrative, puritanical, and radical Haredism along with, on the other hand, constant deconstruction and reconstruction—in other words, constant movement out of and into Haredi frameworks. Sometimes these are not two separate vectors but rather two interrelated and concurrent realities. Against this background, the question of personal salvation is always in the air: What ensures my salvation and that of my family and loved ones? What guarantees this salvation despite the distance that still separates my lifestyle from full observance of the commandments? What ensures this salvation in view of my awareness of myself as a sinner? This constantly liminal existence creates a need for communal experiences or gatherings in the *communitas* style described by Victor Turner (1969), including mass pilgrimages to sites considered sacred and the spiritual deals effected there. In the context of the Breslov *teshuva* movement, a prominent example is the pilgrimage to the grave of Rabbi Nachman in the Ukrainian town of Uman.

The collapse of the communist regimes in Eastern Europe in the early 1990s made it much easier to visit the final resting places of central figures in the Hasidic movement, including the Ba'al Shem Tov, Rabbi Elimelekh of Lizhensk, and Rabbi Nachman. This trend exposed the deep roots of contemporary popular traditional Judaism. Whereas the practice of visiting the graves of the righteous had previously been viewed in Israel as highlighting the role of Jews of North African descent in developing popular religion (Bilu 1992), the resumption of pilgrimages to the graves of Hasidic leaders lent a global perspective and exposed the significant and early role of Hasidism in the development of this style of traditional Judaism. Research on the development of popular religion in Israel points to the diverse ethnic, religious, and socioeconomic profile of participants in such mass gatherings in recent decades (Deshen 1979; Bilu 2001; Levy 2015, 174–96). With regard to pilgrimages to the grave of Rabbi Nachman, it is clear that the crowd comprises diverse groups, each with its own world of imagery as to what it seeks in Uman. A considerable portion of those visiting the grave are Breslov Hasidim, who view the pilgrimage as a fundamental expression of their faith. Others come to Rabbi Nachman's grave seeking to enrich their spiritual experience, out of religious curiosity, to accompany a friend, out of some personal need, or for other reasons. Breslov preachers tell their audiences that Rabbi Nachman promised before he died that anyone who visited his grave on Rosh Hashanah would receive his personal help and intervention.

What is required of the pilgrims? They are encouraged to take some obligation upon themselves, indicating an intensification of their observance of the commandments or a return to observance. However, the fact that they have taken the trouble to travel to Rabbi Nachman's grave, the fact that they utter a prayer there, the fact that this holy site is not left abandoned, is regarded as a great atonement and source of salvation. This promise is critical in the reality of soft Mizrahi Haredism.

An ethnographic essay about the journey to Uman explains that the Mizrahi traditional public "visits R. Nahman just as it visits the grave of R. Yaakov Hatzeira in Egypt, or to the grave of the Baba Sali" (Weinstock 2011, 356)—that is, the visits are prompted by tradition and a traditional belief in the spiritual powers of the righteous. However, attention should also be paid to an important element that has developed in the Mizrahi Haredi *teshuva* movement: the spiritual transaction. Sociologists Asaf Sharabi and Shlomo Guzmen-Carmeli have published a series of articles about the important role of the spiritual transactions that take place at local and mass gatherings among Mizrahi Haredi *teshuva* circles (Sharabi and Guzmen-Carmeli 2013). The transactions are accompanied by a sort of dialogue or negotiation between the preacher and someone in the audience—an individual seeking help for some problem that he or she discloses in public. The preacher offers a deal: the fulfillment of some commandment, indicating a process of *teshuva*, in return for a blessing from himself and the audience. A gesture of *teshuva* in exchange for great salvation. Such spiritual transactions take place at the grave of Rabbi Nachman in Uman. The pilgrimage is the atonement required for *teshuva*; it is the gateway to a cleansing—if not a turnaround—of the heart. On the broad margins of soft Haredism, the Breslov message of salvation and the spiritual deal that it offers play an important role in easing the demanding religious standards and consciousness that accompany the choice to adopt a Haredi religious identity.

The reality of soft Haredism in Mizrahi Haredi circles brought to the fore another problem for which Breslov discourse offered a response. The problem relates to one of the ramifications of the processes of Haredization among Mizrahi returnees to religious observance. Beyond a change in dress code or joining a Haredi community, becoming Haredi also meant integrating into the world of Lithuanian yeshivas—or, at least, exposure to the scholar society culture. This is a world of service of the text, revolving around the Babylonian Talmud, a text that is written largely in Aramaic and follows its own set of rules of logic. The Talmud is awarded enormous importance and status among the Haredi scholar society, and proficiency in it and in the basic skills required for its study are the gateway to an intellectual fraternity. This translates into many hours of learning, which, in most cases, rests on a solid foundation of years spent developing this skill. To borrow Pierre Bourdieu's term, we might refer to this foundation of learning as intra-Haredi cultural capital. This does not mean that Talmud study is impossible for those lacking the background and training, but it is a most difficult task. In view of the great array of external temptations that remain in the memory of the newly religious scholar situated in the broad margins of soft Haredism, the challenge may well seem overwhelming. A possible and popular alternative is to invest one's efforts in the study of books of practical Halakha (Jewish law), such as the *Yalkut Yosef* compendium authored by Rabbi Yitzhak Yosef. Study of Halakha is vital for punctilious day-to-day observance of the commandments. Through strict adherence to Halakha one is able to refine the customs of piety, but study of the central text—the Talmud—remains the foundation on which the entire edifice of halakhic logic and halakhic practice rests.

From this perspective, the energetic Breslov *teshuva* message was not only a source of religious renewal but also the basis for service of a text that was more easily accessible: the Hasidic corpus, written in Hebrew. Although the language of the Hasidic works is somewhat archaic, the exegetical work surrounding them serves not only to clarify their meaning but also to transform them into a way of thinking and practical guidance. The content, too, is more immediately associated with everyday life. Hasidic literature talks about the challenges of divine service, individuals' purpose in God's world, and the actions and thoughts required of the believer. The minute attention to the Talmud is replaced with minute study of the teachings of the tzaddik—in the case of Breslov Hasidism, Rabbi Nachman. In Mizrahi Haredi *teshuva* circles, there is great demand for Breslov discourse, study, and text, because it bridges the perennial gap between elite scholarly culture and popular religious culture. Although the study of the Talmud focuses on questions pertaining to legal forms that have implications for collective halakhic behavior, the Breslov teachings offer their own canonical literature, focusing on questions that pertain to the individual seeking his or her way back to religious observance. Even if they relate to a collective redemptive principle, these works are usually interpreted in the personal context.

Conclusion

Over the last third of the twentieth century, Breslov Hasidism was transformed from a small group barely surviving and appealing mainly to Jewish intellectuals into a social and cultural phenomenon with a strong presence on the Israeli street. An important element in this process was the growth of Breslov Hasidism's popularity among Mizrahi Haredi *teshuva* circles. Analysis of this trend shows that it rests on a number of factors. First was the spread of *teshuva* activity and assertive religious outreach on the part of Breslov rabbis and the building of communities of newly religious Jews in the Breslov style, offering a sense of belonging and an ideological approach that ignores the ethnic division in Haredi society while recognizing differences in custom and ritual. Second, in the latter part of the twentieth century and even more so since the turn of the twenty-first century, Breslov Hasidism has been a source of renewal of the religious fervor accompanying the Haredi *teshuva* movement in general, including the Mizrahi Haredi sector. Breslov Hasidism has presented itself as rebelling against the existing order and as a personal and collective alternative to the social reality, including its ethnic aspect. *Teshuva* communities that situated themselves within the organized and institutionalized yeshiva world experienced an ebbing of religious fervor. The Breslov teachings and practices, including meditation, pilgrimage to Uman, and gathering around charismatic rabbinic figures, served as a significant alternative to the institutionalized path of *teshuva*. Third, Breslov Hasidism in the popular perception is far removed from the demanding scholarship of the world of Talmud, leaning instead toward religious practice and study of Hasidic works. This approach provided a more relaxed *teshuva* space, especially among those whose religious cultural capital emphasizes custom and ceremonial observance as opposed to theoretical scholarship. As such, Breslov Hasidism drew in those seeking to position themselves within Haredi society while neutralizing, as far as possible, their ethnic markers; those wanting to maintain religious fervor in their quest for personal salvation; and those seeking to bring national redemption and repair the world not through intellectual study but rather through personal and *communitas* activity.

These factors combined with subjective, personal elements to make Breslov an important force in the renewal of the Mizrahi Haredi *teshuva* movement and in the transformation of Breslov Hasidism over recent decades from a small Hasidic group fighting for the survival of its groups of adherents in Jerusalem, Bnei Brak, and Safed into a vibrant Hasidic movement and a wellspring of religious strengthening, with the establishment of a range of new Hasidic Haredi communities that associate themselves with its teachings.

Although this new reality turned Breslov Hasidism into a highly visible force in Mizrahi *teshuva* movement circles, it also aroused competition, criticism, and fierce opposition within these same circles. This response deserves a discussion all on its own.

References

Ammerman, Nancy. 1997. "Organized Religion in Voluntaristic Society." *Sociology of Religion* 58(3): 203–16.

Assouline, Dalit. 2017. "Sidna Rabbi Nahman: The Language of Mizrahi Preachers in Breslov Hasidism." Lecture at the Center for the Study of Jewish Languages and Literatures, Hebrew University of Jerusalem, May 8. [Hebrew]

Aviad, Janet. 1983. *Return to Judaism: Religious Renewal in Israel*. Chicago: University of Chicago Press.

Baumgarten, Eliezer. 2012. "Morocco vs. Uman: Ethnic Identities in Breslov Hasidisms." *Pe'amim* 131: 147–78. [Hebrew]

Beit-Hallahmi, Benjamin. 1987. "'Born Again' Jews in Israel: The Dynamics of an Identity Change." *International Journal of Psychology* 22(1): 75–81.

Bender, Aryeh. 1986. "Elijah Would Be Torn to Shreds." *Maariv*, November 16. [Hebrew]

Bilu, Yoram. 1992. "The Making of Modern Saints: Manufactured Charisma and the Abu-Hatseiras of Israel." *American Ethnologist* 19(4): 672–87.

Bilu, Yoram. 2001. "Moroccan Jews and the Shaping of Israel's Sacred Geography." In *Divergent Jewish Culture: Israel and America*, ed. Deborah Dash Moore and S. Ilan Toren, 195–211. New Haven, CT: Yale University Press.

Bourdieu, Pierre. 2008. *Sketch for a Self-Analysis*, trans. Richard Nice. Chicago: University of Chicago Press.

Caplan, Kimmy. 1997. "God's Voice: Audiotaped Sermons in Israeli 'Haredi' Society." *Modern Judaism* 17(3): 253–79.

Caplan, Kimmy. 2001. "Israeli Haredi Society and the Repentance ('Hazarah Biteshuvah') Phenomenon." *Jewish Studies Quarterly* 8(4): 369–98.

Deshen, Shlomo. 1979. "The Judaism of Middle Eastern Immigrants." *Jerusalem Quarterly* 13: 98–110.

El-Or, Tamar. 2006. *Reserved Seats: Gender in Ethnicity in Religious and Newly-Religious Circles*. Tel Aviv: Am Oved.

Green, Arthur. 1979. *Tormented Master: A Life of Rabbi Nahman of Bratslav*. Tuscaloosa: University of Alabama Press.

Harding, Susan. 2000. *The Book of Jerry Falwell: Fundamentalist Language and Politics*. Princeton, NJ: Princeton University Press.

Iannaccone, Laurence. 1990. "Religious Practice and Human Capital Approach." *Journal for the Scientific Study of Religion* 29(3): 297–314.

Katz, Yossi. 2007. "Yavne'el, Breslov City: R. Eliezer Shlomo Schick (Mohorosh) and the Sanctification of Yavne'el in the Galilee." *Daat: A Journal of Jewish Philosophy and Kabbalah* 82: 347–77.

Lehmann, David, and Batia B. Siebzehner. 2006. *Remaking Israeli Judaism: The Challenge of Shas*. London: Hurst.

Leon, Nissim. 2010. *Soft Ultra-Orthodoxy: Religious Renewal in Oriental Jewry in Israel*. Jerusalem: Yad Izhak Ben-Zvi. [Hebrew]

Levy, Andre. 2015. *Return to Casablanca: Jews, Muslims, and an Israeli Anthropologist*. Chicago: University of Chicago Press.

Mark, Zvi. 2011. "The Contemporary Renaissance of Braslav Hasidism: Ritual, 'Tiqqun' and Messianism." In *Kabbalah and Contemporary Spiritual Revival*, ed. Boaz Huss, 101–16. Beer-Sheva: Ben-Gurion University.

Piekarz, Mendel. 1972. *Studies in Braslav Hasidim*. Jerusalem: Bialik Institute. [Hebrew]

Sharabi, Asaf, and Shlomo Guzmen-Carmeli. 2013. "The Teshuva Bargain: Ritual Healing Performances of Rabbi Yitzchak's Rallies." *Journal of Ritual Studies* 27(2): 97–110.

Shokeid, Moshe. 1995. "The Religiosity of Middle Eastern Jews." In *Israeli Judaism: The Sociology of Religion in Israel*, ed. Shlomo Deshen, Charles S. Liebman, and Moshe Shokeid, 312–39. New Brunswick, NJ: Transaction.

Sobel, Zvi. 1993. *A Small Place in Galilee: Religion and Social Conflict in an Israeli Village*. New York: Holmes & Meier.

Turner, Victor. 1969. *The Ritual Process: Structure and Anti-Structure*. London: Routledge & Kegan Paul.

Weinstock, Moshe. 2011. *Uman: The Israeli Journey to the Grave of Rebbe Nachman of Breslov*. Tel Aviv: Miskal.

Weiss, Joseph. 1985. *Studies in Eastern European Jewish Mysticism*. Oxford, UK: Oxford University Press.

Yifrah, Yehuda. 2016. "The Berland Riddle." *Makor Rishon*, August 18.

Zeidan, David. 2003. *The Resurgence of Religion: A Comparative Study of Selected Themes in Christian and Islamic Fundamentalism Discourses*. Leiden: Brill.

III

BODIES

Part III shifts from Orthodox and European-based communal projects to the intersection between future-oriented renewal endeavors, performativity, and New Age spirituality in Israel and the United States. Rejecting both the state-sponsored Jewish establishment and institutionalized Jewish organizations, these movements call to retain individual autonomy and expressive freedom, bringing the interpretation of Jewish traditions into conversation with contemporary trends—feminism, shamanism, esotericism, or the therapeutic discourse.

The three ethnographic chapters document the creative frontiers of Jewish expressivity in which the past provides an adaptable inspiration source amenable to radical alterations. Describing the new configurations of Jewish spirituality in Israel and the United States, Werczberger and Rock-Singer's chapters explore the intersection of Jewish renewal with the body and the self. Guzmen-Carmeli's ethnography presents the interpretations, adaptations, and negotiations of the students in the BINA secular yeshiva over canonical Jewish and Zionist texts.

Marking the individualization of Jewish tradition, Part III points to the ways in which the turn to the past in service of the present engenders new Jewish authenticities that align with consumer capitalism and postmodern ideologies. The global currency of concepts such as hybridity, ritual, and introspection highlights the fruitful exchange between "secular" public culture and renewed Jewish identities.

10

Healing the Self, Renewing Tradition

The Hybrid Discourse of Authenticity of New Age Judaism in Israel

Rachel Werczberger

Judaism is sick. It is worth saying this without mincing words. And I am not motivated by some kind of self-hatred. On the contrary—it is because of my great love for the Torah that I am saying this. Judaism lies before (or within) us in critical condition, and no one will invent a cure for it except for us, our very own selves, for if we do not [find a remedy] it will die in our midst.
—Ezrahi (2004, 32)

The epigraph is taken from a text titled "Healing Judaism," written by Rabbi Ohad Ezrahi, the founder and leader of the Hamakom community, a Jewish New Age community that was active in Israel at the beginning of the millennium. In typical New Age rhetoric, Ezrahi predicates his ideas of Jewish renewal on the concept of healing. At the same time, he chooses to use distinct Jewish language to describe the current condition of Judaism as "the state of being in exile" (Ezrahi 2004, 32). According to Ezrahi, to heal Judaism and return it to its authentic, pre-exilic state, it must be renewed. This will be achieved by fusing Jewish tradition, especially its mystical traditions (i.e., Kabbalah and Hasidism), with New Age practices and rituals.

Importantly, Ezrahi's call for Jewish renewal was entwined with his quest for Jewish spirituality. It was the search for these sorts of experiences that led him on a circuitous spiritual quest, a quest that propelled him first to an ultra-Orthodox community, then to radical political religious Zionism, and finally to the establishment of the Hamakom community. This type of spiritual search is also emblematic of other Israeli Jewish New Agers I met in the field, who like Ezrahi, searched for authentic Jewish spiritual experiences: direct, unmediated, often embodied experiences of the sacred.

Focusing on the intersection between the desire for Jewish renewal and the search for personal authenticity, in this essay I offer an ethnographic view of two New Age Jewish communities, Hamakom and Bait Chadash, that were active in Israel from 2000 to 2006. Emerging from the flourishing local New Age scene, New Age Judaism (NAJ) is a collective, partly organized phenomenon that evolved in Israel in the late 1990s. I use the term *New Age Judaism* here to refer to various projects and initiatives, such as the Jewish Renewal movement in North America; hybrid mind-body techniques such as Torah yoga, Jewish healing, and Hebrew shamanism; and several Jewish New Age communities in Israel, including the two that are the focus of this chapter (Rothenberg 2006a, 2006b; Weissler 2006; Werczberger 2016). These cultural-religious configurations are critical of institutionalized Jewish denominations and, in turn, attempt to spiritually renew Jewish life by means of hybridity and cultural creativity.

Like other contemporary modalities of religious renewal, from fundamentalist forms of Islam through New Age spiritualities, the NAJ project of renewal articulated its mission using the discourse of authenticity. Often, adherents and leaders claimed to revive Judaism through the return to earlier, allegedly more authentic modes of Jewish devotion and practice (Persico 2014; Weissler 2006). At the same time, New Age Jews, like other New Age adherents, aspire to self-realization by discovering their true self (Heelas 1996). They believe that deep within the self lies a genuine and sacred core that has yet to be polluted by society, culture, or history. By engaging in Jewish spirituality, they hope to discover and realize their authentic self.

In this chapter I focus on the discourse of authenticity of the two New Age Jewish communities. Drawing on Stuart Charmé's work, I argue that this discourse is a "hybrid discourse" (Charmé 2000, 134). My ethnography reveals that the communities and their members fused the personal and highly subjective search for the authentic-expressive self with the quest for an authentic form of Judaism and Jewish spirituality. This hybrid discourse of authenticity unveils the complex relations between the individualized search for personal authenticity that is typical of modern subjects (Illouz

2008) and the need to frame this search within existing religious tradition and communal belonging. In NAJ the subjective turn inward and the ambition to be true to one's self were entwined with a desire to be true to one's origin, thus creating a new Jewish mode of sociality that drew on Jewish tradition and simultaneously accommodated and transformed it.

This chapter is based on anthropological fieldwork that I undertook in 2004–2006 in two Israeli NAJ communities: Hamakom and Bait Chadash. During these years I observed and participated in the activities of the two communities: weekend workshops, prayer services, study sessions, and the like. In addition, I carried out formal and informal interviews with community members and the leaders of each community and analyzed online texts and published materials written by the communities' leaders and members.

The Age of Authenticity and New Age Spiritualities

Scholars of society and culture posit that the modern ethos of authenticity has become a key criterion for the value of the human experience, both private and collective (Lindholm 2008). It has become a salient cultural construct that affects the way contemporary individuals understand their moral frameworks and their very selves and influences the way they choose to live their lives. In his seminal work, *A Secular Age* (2007), Canadian philosopher Charles Taylor suggests that the present era can be perceived as the "age of authenticity." According to Taylor, being a full person in this day and age is linked to the imperative of listening to one's self and following one's unique path, both of which are to be individually discovered (Taylor 2007). The modern ideas of expressivity, personal creativity, and genuineness, argues Taylor, are part and parcel of this generation's intensive search for authenticity. These elements are perceived as running counter to and even undermining established social norms: "I am called upon to live my life in this way, and not in imitation of anyone else's. . . . This gives a new importance to being true to myself. If I am not, I miss the point of my life; I miss what being human is for me" (Taylor 1992, 29).

Although the concept of authenticity encompasses diverse sets of meaning that range from genuineness and originality to accuracy and truthfulness (Handler 1986; Lindholm 2008), one aspect of authenticity, in the form of "being thyself," has come to serve as a prevalent trope for transcendence in the Western world. Individuals feel spiritually authentic if they believe that they are true to their heritage and if their life is a direct and immediate expression of their essential being, that is, if "I am true to myself" (Lindholm 2013).

Taylor rightfully recognized that the rise of the ethics of personal authenticity is intimately bound up with another cultural phenomenon: the postwar growth and entrenchment of a therapeutic ethos (Foster 2016). According to Eva Illouz, the extraordinary success of psychoanalysis and the therapeutic can be explained by the way in which it "seamlessly combined, and in this way reconciled, two central and contradictory aspects of modern selfhood. First, the self was now turned inward, in search of its authenticity and unique individuality within the confines of private life. Second, the self was summoned by the culture and institutions of modernity to be rational" (Illouz 2008, 50). Following Freud, therapy has become the privileged site for the expression of the inner self as well as a site that encourages introspection, a focus on feelings, and, most of all, a search for the lost and true self (50).

It is under late capitalism that the psychological focus shifted to the realization of self-engendered new forms of spirituality that fuse the religious with the therapeutic (Altglas 2014; Rudnyckyj 2009). This fusion is especially evident in contemporary spiritualities that tend to use therapeutic language to emphasize that spiritual development is attained through self-improvement, autonomy, and accountability (Simchai and Shoshana 2018; Tucker 2002). Consequently, under the sway of late capitalism, the idea of the spiritual authentic self has become tantamount to the focus on the individual, the inner self, and the formation of a selfhood that should be constantly realized and transformed (Simchai and Shoshana 2018). Furthermore, consumer culture, which redefines life and society as arenas of choice, reshaped religion in a context of cultural deregulation by opening up a vast range of new possibilities—for new religious knowledge, practices, leaders, organizations, and forms of political action (Gauthier et al. 2013; Possamai 2017).

The synthesis of the search for authenticity, therapy, and religion is evident in New Age spiritual activities that have become popular since the mid-1980s (Heelas 1996). New Age spiritualities underscore the approach according to which everyone can consume anything and everything that is deemed to be of worth, no matter from which religion or philosophy it derives (Possamai 2017, 22). In New Age culture, therapeutic practices have evolved into acts of worship aimed at enhancing spiritual development.

Psychological concepts such as self-realization, self-fulfillment, and self-growth as well as psychological techniques such as self-reflection, group-sharing, and guided imagery serve as methods for discovering one's authentic self and spiritual development and well-being (Tucker 2002).

The Jewish New Age, a specific subculture within the wider New Age culture, embraces these features and simultaneously adapts them to its needs. As such, NAJ is a radical illustration of a wider inward subjective turn of contemporary Jewish life that has brought about the rejection of external authority (rabbinic, halakhic, etc.) and, with it, the turn toward the self (Cohen and Eisen 2000; Illman 2019). The current scholarship on Jewish identity and religion and Jewish spirituality underscores the turn to individualized modes of Jewish worship that allow each Jew to interpret and mold their own Judaism to suit their personal needs (Cadge and Davidman 2006; Kelman et al. 2017; Cohen and Eisen 2000). According to Steven Cohen and Arnold Eisen, even mainstream Jews today adopt a pick-and-choose approach whereby "the only criterion governing the selection is what is meaningful to the self" (Cohen and Eisen 2000, 193). This attitude is especially prominent in the New Age forms of Judaism, such as the Jewish Renewal movement in North America and the Israeli NAJ communities under discussion here (Weissler 2006; Werczberger 2016).

Importantly, the efforts at Jewish renewal such as those of NAJ also involve a "turn to tradition" (Illman 2019). As Danièle Hervieu-Léger insightfully notes, it is the "chain of memory" that makes the individual believer a member of the community, and it is the tradition that becomes the basis of legitimation for this religious belief (Hervieu-Léger 2000). The turn to tradition of contemporary Jews takes place on both the discursive level and the practical level. For instance, Kelman et al.'s (2017) study of post-baby-boomer Jews showed that more than half of the interviewees formulated their engagement with Judaism and understood their Jewishness using the language of tradition, instead of the language of religion or ethnicity. This is even stronger in cases of renewal and invention of tradition, in which the turn to the past evokes "certainty, security, and imagined community" (Ochs 2010, 6). By emphasizing the Jewish origin of emerging rituals, a sense of familiarity is created, and new practices can feel "genuine" even when tried out for the first time. Thus the retraditionalization of Jewish life is interweaved with the discursive emphasis on the authenticity of these efforts (Illman 2019).

Authenticating Judaism, Authenticating the Self

According to Stuart Charmé, the Jewish discourse of authenticity is a "hybrid discourse" (Charmé 2000, 134) composed of three different levels, or claims, for Jewish authenticity: descriptive-essentialist, prescriptive, and existential. In the first type of claim, authenticity is invoked in reference to specific Jewish content in a person's life, usually based on an essentialist assertion of a continuation of particular traditions from the past, which are regarded as a source of authority in the present. The prevalent example of this type of argumentation is the ubiquitous claim that Orthodox Judaism is the true and authentic form of Judaism, whereas liberal forms of Judaism are diluted, if not spurious, imitations of the "real thing." Related to the essentialist claims are the prescriptive statements. These assertions, which are about the superiority of one form of Jewish life over another, indicate a belief in the primacy of a certain form of Jewishness and Jewish practice over other forms of Judaism, for instance, of Orthodox observance of the Jewish law over a liberal nonhalakhic lifestyle.

Existential claims, the third type of assertion, are of a slightly different kind. These assertions are oriented toward the self and involve one's deepest values and sense of self as a person and as a Jew. Charmé (2000) suggests that existential claims for an authentic Jewish identity are engendered by a critical new ingredient in the identity of the twentieth-century postemancipation, post-Enlightenment, non-Orthodox Jew: the enormous freedom to decide the content and meaning of being Jewish. Thus the term *authentic* has become an important qualifier of Jewish identity, tradition, culture, and religion, not only for Orthodox proselytizing attempts but also for postmodern reconstructions and renewals of Jewish identity (Charmé 2000, 133–35).

In the NAJ communities I studied, the idea of authenticity, both of the descriptive-essentialist type and the existential-expressive type, was embraced in various ways: first, in the way community members articulated the need for Jewish renewal by referring to the Jewish past; second, in their reinvention of Jewish ritual as a spiritual experience geared toward the uncovering of the authentic self; and, third, by framing their Jewish spiritual identity in terms of an authentic choice.

Re-Turning to the Authentic Past

The return to an authentic form of Judaism was first and foremost apparent in the declared intention of the two communities to spiritually renew the Jewish tradition. Institutionalized Judaism was conceived as "sick," unspiritual, and irrelevant to contemporary Jews. By re-turning to Jewish mystical traditions and fusing them with New Age practices and rituals, Judaism would be revived and renewed.

Like other cultural, ethnic, and religious projects of identity construction, this kind of notion of transformation and renewal was accompanied by the claim of a return to the true and authentic tradition. Concurrently, NAJ drew on an idealized Jewish past as a means of resisting the alienating effects of rabbinic Judaism, focusing on two specific historical time periods that were conceived as eras of authentic Jewish spirituality. The first is Hebrew antiquity and the second is the late-eighteenth-century Hasidic movement.

According to Ezrahi, the current condition of Judaism is rooted in Jewish history, namely, in antiquity, when following the destruction of the Second Temple in 70 CE, the Jews were exiled from the Land of Israel. The exile, which severed the Jewish people from the land, brought about the extrication from the direct, unmediated, and embodied experience of the sacred (Werczberger 2011a). Rabbinic Judaism, which evolved in the centuries that followed, left Jewish practice "dry" and empty.

Here is how Ezrahi describes this period.

> Before it [Judaism] became a religion of rabbis with hats and modest women covering every inch of their body, a religion of books blending erudition and Sabbath *cholent*, Judaism was a tribal culture of warriors and poets, such as King David, of women bathing naked on the rooftops, like Bathsheba, the wife of Uria the Hittite. Judaism was a religion of peasants who lived on their ancestors' land, like Naboth the Jezreelite; of farmers sleeping on the threshing floor, like Boaz; who celebrated the vintage with love rituals of Tu-B'ev, like the daughters of Shilo, who danced in the vineyard in the light of the full moon. It was a religion of shepherds who sometimes met angels in the field, like Samson's parents, and saw colorful visions of God, like Ezekiel. (Ezrahi 2007, 43)

In this romantic description Ezrahi portrays Hebrew antiquity as a spiritual era, a period distinguished by noninstitutionalized forms of religious life, pagan and nature worship, and direct divine revelation. This imaginative reconstruction provides the basis for the call to renew Jewish tradition and return it to its original spiritual state.

Beyond Jewish antiquity, NAJ points to another historical moment in which allegedly authentic Jewish spirituality existed: the late eighteenth century and the Eastern European Hasidic movement. Hasidism has long been regarded as a source of inspiration for Jewish spiritual renewal. By internalizing and psychologizing kabbalistic-mystical concepts, stressing inner psychological awareness, and emphasizing personal ecstatic modes of devotion, Hasidism provides a good fit for NAJ's spiritual aspirations (Margolin 2010). NAJ depicts Hasidism as a Jewish spiritual path and the Hasidic rabbis as spiritual masters searching for deeper spiritual truths.

For example, in Ezrahi's retelling of the Ba'al Shem Tov's ascent of the soul, the founder of the Hasidic movement is portrayed as a shaman on a shamanic journey. According to Ezrahi, *aliyat neshama* "is a spiritual technique very similar to the renowned shamanic journeys of the Earth Cultures, where the shaman leaves his body lying on the ground in order to travel in the upper world, meet spirit entities, ask them questions, receive answers, and sometimes saves his own community or the whole world" (Ezrahi 2008). By associating the Jewish mystical practice of soul ascent with shamanic practice, early Hasidism is conceived as an authentic form of Jewish spirituality and as an appropriate model for Jewish renewal.

Authenticizing Devotion

Inspired by Hasidic modes of devotion, the two communities I studied attempted to spiritually revive and renew Jewish ritual. These rituals were intentional creations of cultural invention and revision and involved embodied, emotionally ecstatic performances that incorporated New Age elements gleaned from various geographic areas and cultures. At the same time, they drew on Jewish sources, especially kabbalistic texts and Hasidic tales and tunes. In this sense, both Judaism and New Age culture served as a cultural tool kit (Ochs 2010; Swidler 1986). By heightening the experiential aspects of the rite and placing the self at its focus, these hybrid rituals were meant to offer a spiritual alternative to mainstream Jewish rituals.

These sorts of experiences were provided in two ways. First, rituals, and especially prayer services, were designed to generate an intense, immersive experience in which the conventions of Jewish worship were loosened and supplanted with spontaneity and expressivity. Unusually long (lasting over three hours sometimes), the prayer service was recreated as a multisensory event that enraptured participants with music and bodily motion, thereby stimulating synesthesia, an all-encompassing, unified, and overflowing sensory experience (Sullivan 1986), and the experience of flow and *communitas*, that is, the sense of equality, intimacy, and brotherly love shared by the participants (Turner 1979). Whereas traditional prayers normally take place in synagogues, these prayers usually took place in simple makeshift and improvised structures, such as classrooms, tents, and shacks, or even in outdoor settings. Mattresses and cushions replaced chairs. The walls, if there were any, were adorned with colorful pictures and posters. When participants were seated in a circle, objects such as burning incense or crystals were placed at the center. The traditional Jewish liturgy based on long paragraphs in Hebrew and Aramaic was replaced with Sufi and Hindu styles of devotional chanting. The chants typically consisted of a single verse taken from the *siddur* (prayer book) or the scripture and were sung repetitively, mantra-like. The tunes for these chants were inspired by Eastern and Middle Eastern music styles, which were played on Oriental musical instruments. The melodies of the chants were especially important, as they set the bodily and emotive responses of those who were praying. Slow, melodious, quiet melodies evoked a contemplative mood, with the worshipers sitting quietly, their eyes closed, meditating; at times this position was supplemented with a rocking movement of the upper body, with a hand resting on the chest. Livelier music, accompanied by rhythmic beating on Eastern drums, created an atmosphere for dancing. Often the participants in the service joyfully sang and danced for hours. Thus, although NAJ services preserved some of the basic indexes of Jewish traditional prayer, the overall form, content, and ambience of the ritual resembled New Age festivals and mass gatherings that celebrate self-transformation and universal human connectedness (Gauthier 2014).

When I asked some of the members about these events, Danya, a Conservative rabbinic student and Hamakom member told me that "a ceremony is not something that happens outside. [It] is . . . supposed to convey something to you. . . . A ceremony is a tool for personal development. . . . And the ceremony is [the] tool through which it is done." Meirav, another member of Hamakom, told me that "there are more diverse ways [to pray] than to stand with a *siddur* [the Jewish prayer book] in a synagogue and pray. I can sing, I can shout, I can dance. . . . [For me] to create a prayer is to find my own words." According to my interlocuters, then, prayers, and rituals more generally, are rendered spiritually authentic by their subjectification—an introspective experience that is predicated on embodied sensual and physical elements. These types of experiences of embodied authenticity (Meintel 2014) facilitate self-discovery and personal and spiritual growth.

Second, NAJ rituals incorporated manifestly therapeutic elements that are considered conducive to emotional healing and self-realization. This was evident in the workshops that took place during the Jewish festivals. These workshops were based on a succession of sessions in which intersubjective interactions were facilitated in the form of group sharing and support. The sessions allowed the participants to identify, discuss, and consequently "heal" their authentic selves. For instance, during a celebration of Yom Kippur (Day of Atonement), Ezrahi suggested a new ritual, which he dubbed "Vow Annulment Workshop," as an alternative to the traditional Kol Nidrei prayer. I observed the ritual one year and provide a brief ethnographic description of it in what follows.

After the lesson, Ezrahi asked the participants to take part in a brief vow annulment ceremony based on the annulment of vows prayer traditionally recited before Rosh Hashanah and Yom Kippur. Before splitting up into teams of four, he explained that vows are "recurrent patterns of behavior or personal or interpersonal feelings" that keep individuals from liberating themselves and becoming "whole." Every member of the group was asked to describe three patterns that he or she wished to discard. Using a formula created by Ezrahi, each participant asked their three colleagues, who assumed the role of a rabbinic court, to rescind the vows. The participants diligently carried out Ezrahi's instructions, rotating between the roles of supplicant and judge. From every corner of the room, it was possible to hear declarations of "All is annulled for you; all is forgiven for you." Most people, so it seemed, wished to break emotional patterns or personal habits involving relationships with others. Some brought up emotional issues, such as self-criticism, stress, and anxiety. Others, usually women, wished to extricate themselves from recurrent patterns that plagued their relationships with their mothers. The entire activity lasted about twenty minutes, whereupon the entire group reconvened for the traditional Kol Nidre service.

Ezrahi's ritual directed the concept of the vow onto the self and reconceived it as habits, or emotional patterns, that prevent the individual from realizing his or her true and authentic self. In a dramatic role play the participants confessed their "vows" before a mock court. In a performative utterance (Austin 1975)—"All is annulled for you; all is forgiven for you"— the group granted the petitioner's pardon. The final outcome was a ritual featuring a personal confession turned into an embodied performance of a therapeutic narrative of personal change and self-transformation. Similar to commodified support groups such as the Forum, the reflection about and the public acknowledgment of psychological hardships and challenging social issues was meant to advance self-awareness (Illouz 2008). The participants understood this ritual as a healing ritual, in that it liberated their selves and elevated them to their authentic state (Werczberger 2011b).

In sum, NAJ recreated Jewish rituals as an authentic spiritual experience in two disparate social forms: mass gatherings and intimate circles (Gauthier 2014). The mass prayer services, with their sensuous, embodied, and emotional arousal aspects, are an example of the first. The Kol Nidre healing ritual, with its psychological overtones and support group ambience, is an example of the second. In both, the stimulation of powerful emotions through embodied or discursive performance in tandem with the psychologization of Jewish symbols and practices confirmed their authenticity as truly *Jewish* spiritual experiences.

Choosing to Be Jewish

I have described how, in order to authenticate NAJ as truly Jewish, the participants draw on specific Jewish sources, such as traditional Jewish ritual or historical traditions such as Hasidism. Yet expressive authenticity pertains, first and foremost, to the self and the imperative of listening to one's self and following one's unique path. In the context of Jewish renewal and NAJ, this aspiration propels a turn inward, not only in terms of an inward expressive spirituality but also in terms of justifications regarding the *choice* of NAJ. For the NAJ participants I met, "the religious life or practice that [they] became a part of must not only be [their] choice, but it must speak to [them]. It must make sense in terms of [their] spiritual development as [they] understand this" (Taylor 2007, 486).

Israeli New Age Jews are active participants in the local Jewish and non-Jewish spiritual marketplace (Roof 1999). They are surrounded by numerous options of non-Jewish spiritual practices as well as more traditional Orthodox options (Werczberger and Huss 2014). Yet they deliberately and consciously choose to engage in a Jewish form of New Age culture. My study shows that they frame this choice primarily through the language of authenticity. This is how Nadav, a Hamakom community member, explains his choice.

> I am a Jew; as such I was born. I am a son of this ancient tribe. My language is Hebrew and my citizenship is Israeli. I live in a state in which my people are the sovereign; I absorbed a legacy and way of life. And in this fashion, I formulate my spiritual path. . . . From my personal standpoint, it is wrong and inauthentic to formulate my path other than through my own heritage. . . . This [Jewish] culture is an infinite resource for finding my own unique, personal road.

Several elements stand out in this quote. First, Nadav's perception of his autonomous choice of a Jewish spiritual identity reflects contemporary notions of identity construction and the freedom of choice this involves (Cadge and Davidman 2006; Roof 1999). Living in Israel, the options for religious expression are not infinite, and the range of choice is constrained by family, culture, and ethnonational sentiments and affiliations. Moreover, as previous scholars have argued, this allegedly free choice is determined by social factors and power relations based on class, race, or gender (Altglas 2014; Kaplan and Werczberger 2017). Yet Nadav and the other community members I met conceived their engagement with their Jewish identity in terms of a free choice.

Moreover, more than an autonomous rational choice from an assortment of possibilities, the choice was above all a decision guided by an emotional and subjective experience. Their explanations pointed to their emotional affinity with their ethnonational group and to their cultural and religious heritage. "In Judaism," said Meirav, "I feel at home. . . . My soul really rests . . . and is content there." And in the same online text quoted earlier, Nadav said, "Traveling on the Jewish road causes me to listen to the melodies of the heart . . . for the purpose of finding a path and rectifying the heart." Furthermore, according to Nadav, choosing Jewishness—which he sees as his cultural and religious legacy—allows him to realize his authentic self and at the same time to remain attached to the Jewish community and identity.

Conclusion

I have described the hybrid discourse of authenticity of New Age Judaism. This discourse intermingles essentialist claims of a true and authentic form of Judaism with the search for an authentic and expressive Jewish self. The members of the communities described here searched for an authentic Jewish spirituality—a direct, unmediated, and embodied experience of the sacred. They did so by revising Jewish rituals into what they conceived as spiritually uplifting and self-transformative experiences, by framing their choice of NAJ in terms of authentic and expressive choices and by pointing to specific, allegedly spiritual moments in Jewish history.

Their claim of an authentic Jewish spirituality was based on an assertion of a continuation of a particular tradition from the past, namely, of two time periods in Jewish history: the Hasidic movement of the late eighteenth century and the Hebrew pre-exilic antiquity. Both were understood as the collective expression of a Jewish essence, or *volksgeist*—authentic forms of "true" Judaism to which New Age Jews wish to return. This unique amalgam of an individual search for self-transformation and the attempt to ground this search in a specific collective tradition points to the thin line that separates "the desire for individual authenticity and the calling to convince others of the correctness of [a] particular rendering or localizing of the authentic" (Bendix 2009, 20).

Allegedly, NAJ, like other New Age spiritual modalities, is a highly personalized, deinstitutionalized form of religiosity. Yet its adherents do not distance themselves from their collective religious tradition or disengage from communal Jewish life. Unlike the participants of New Age configurations such as the Kabbalah Center (Altglas 2014; Huss 2007), NAJ draws on Jewish mysticism not only as a universal technique for self-therapy and self-realization but also as a powerful catalyst for modifying and reviving Judaism, thus fusing the personal and the communal.

The New Age Jews described in this chapter yearn for their authentic self and an authentic Jewish spiritual identity and realize their search through their engagement with the NAJ communities. Through the hybrid discourse of authenticity, they establish a sense of self and a sense of communal belonging to their particular communities and to their wider tribe, the Jewish people. Thus the case of NAJ demonstrates that even highly individualized and subjective forms of religion may still be embedded in age-old traditions and that the personal search for self-transformation does not necessarily negate the wish to belong to a religious or ethnic collective. In NAJ the desire to be true to one's self and to one's origin resulted in the creation of spiritual communities—a "new mode of sociality" (quoted in Meintel 2014, 199) in which the ad hoc engagement with alternative communities replaced lifelong commitment to established Jewish denominations and institutional synagogues. Although small, heterogeneous, and ephemeral, these communities uncover the ways in which religious sociality continues to be indispensable, even for those who have fully adopted an inward turn and the ethos of authenticity.

References

Altglas, Véronique. 2014. *From Yoga to Kabbalah: Religious Exoticism and the Logics of Bricolage*. Oxford, UK: Oxford University Press.

Austin, John Langshaw. 1975. *How to Do Things with Words*. Oxford, UK: Oxford University Press.

Bendix, Regina. 2009. *In Search of Authenticity: The Formation of Folklore Studies*. Madison: University of Wisconsin Press.

Cadge, Wendy, and Lynn Davidman. 2006. "Ascription, Choice, and the Construction of Religious Identities in the Contemporary United States." *Journal for the Scientific Study of Religion* 45(1): 23–38.

Charmé, Stuart L. 2000. "Varieties of Authenticity in Contemporary Jewish Identity." *Jewish Social Studies* 6(2): 133–55.

Cohen, Steven Martin, and Arnold M. Eisen. 2000. *The Jew Within: Self, Family, and Community in America*. Bloomington: Indiana University Press.

Ezrahi, Ohad. 2004. "Le-Ra'pe et Ha-Yahadut" [Healing Judaism]. *Haim Aherim* 97: 32–36.

Ezrahi, Ohad. 2007. "Hafestival hagadol mekulam" [The Largest Festival]. In *New Jew: Visual Anthropology at Tribal Festivals in Israel*, ed. Naama Haikin, 42–48. Tel Hai: The Open Photography Museum.

Ezrahi, Ohad. 2008. "Olamot, Neshamot, Elohut." Mahut Hachaim website. http://people.eol.co.il/NewsItem.aspx?id=1166 (accessed November 16 2008).

Foster, Roger. 2016. "Therapeutic Culture, Authenticity, and Neo-Liberalism." *History of the Human Sciences* 29(1): 99–116.

Gauthier, François. 2014. "Intimate Circles and Mass Meetings: The Social Forms of Event-Structured Religion in the Era of Globalized Markets and Hyper-Mediatization." *Social Compass* 61(2): 261–71.

Gauthier, François, Linda Woodhead, and Tuomas Martikainen. 2013. "Introduction: Consumerism as the Ethos of Consumer Society." In *Religion in Consumer Society: Brands, Consumers, and Markets*, ed. Francois Gauthier and Tuomas Martikainen, 1–24. Burlington, VT: Ashgate.

Handler, Richard. 1986. "Authenticity." *Anthropology Today* 2(1): 2–4.

Heelas, Paul. 1996. *The New Age Movement: The Celebration of the Self and the Sacralization of Modernity*. Oxford, UK: Blackwell Oxford.

Hervieu-Léger Danièle. 2000. *Religion as a Chain of Memory*. New Brunswick, NJ: Rutgers University Press.

Huss, Boaz. 2007. "The New Age of Kabbalah: Contemporary Kabbalah, the New Age, and Postmodern Spirituality." *Journal of Modern Jewish Studies* 6(2): 107–25.

Illman, Ruth. 2019. "Researching Vernacular Judaism: Reflections on Theory and Method." *Nordisk Judaistik / Scandinavian Jewish Studies* 30(1): 91–108.

Illouz, Eva. 2008. *Saving the Modern Soul: Therapy, Emotions, and the Culture of Self-Help*. Berkeley: University of California Press.

Kaplan, Dana, and Rachel Werczberger. 2017. "Jewish New Age and the Middle Class: Jewish Identity Politics in Israel Under Neoliberalism." *Sociology* 51(3): 575–91.

Kelman, Ari Y., Tobin Belzer, Ilana Horwitz, Ziva Hassenfeld, and Matt Williams. 2017. "Traditional Judaism: The Conceptualization of Jewishness in the Lives of American Jewish Post-Boomers." *Jewish Social Studies* 23(1): 134–67.

Lindholm, Charles. 2008. *Culture and Authenticity*. Malden, MA: Wiley-Blackwell.

Lindholm, Charles. 2013. "The Rise of Expressive Authenticity." *Anthropological Quarterly* 86(2): 361–95.

Margolin, Ron. 2010. *Inner Religion: The Phenomenology of Inner Religious Life and Its Manifestation in Jewish Sources from the Bible to Hasidic Texts*. Ramat Gan: Bar Ilan University and the Shalom Hartman Institute. [Hebrew]

Meintel, Deirdre. 2014. "Religious Collectivities in the Era of Individualization." *Social Compass* 61(2): 195–206.

Ochs, Vanessa L. 2010. *Inventing Jewish Ritual*. Philadelphia: Jewish Publication Society.

Persico, Tomer. 2014. "Neo-Hasidic Revival: Expressivist Uses of Traditional Lore." *Modern Judaism* 34(3): 287–308.

Possamai, Adam. 2017. *The I-Zation of Society, Religion, and Neoliberal Post-Secularism*. Singapore: Palgrave Macmillan.

Roof, Wade Clark. 1999. *Spiritual Marketplace: Baby Boomers and the Remaking of American Religion*. Princeton, NJ: Princeton University Press.

Rothenberg, Celia E. 2006a. "Hebrew Healing: Jewish Authenticity and Religious Healing in Canada." *Journal of Contemporary Religion* 21(2): 163–82.

Rothenberg, Celia E. 2006b. "Jewish Yoga: Experiencing Flexible, Sacred, and Jewish Bodies." *Nova Religio* 10(2): 57–74.

Rudnyckyj, Daromir. 2009. "Spiritual Economies: Islam and Neoliberalism in Contemporary Indonesia." *Cultural Anthropology* 24(1): 104–41.

Simchai, Dalit, and Avihu Shoshana. 2018. "The Ethic of Spirituality and the Non-Angry Subject." *Ethos* 46(1): 115–33.

Sullivan, Lawrence E. 1986. "Sound and Senses: Toward a Hermeneutics of Performance." *History of Religions* 26(1): 1–33.

Swidler, Ann. 1986. "Culture in Action: Symbols and Strategies." *American Sociological Review* 51(2): 273–86.

Taylor, Charles. 1992. *The Ethics of Authenticity*. Cambridge, MA: Harvard University Press.

Taylor, Charles. 2007. *A Secular Age*. Cambridge, MA: Harvard University Press.

Tucker, James. 2002. "New Age Religion and the Cult of the Self." *Society* 39(2): 46–51.

Turner, Victor. 1979. "Frame, Flow, and Reflection: Ritual and Drama as Public Liminality." *Japanese Journal of Religious Studies* 6(4): 465–99.

Weissler, Chava. 2006. "'Women of Vision' in the Jewish Renewal Movement: The Eshet Hazon ['Women of Vision'] Ceremony." *Jewish Culture and History* 8(3): 62–86.

Werczberger, Rachel. 2011a. "Memory, Land, and Identity: Visions of the Past and the Land in the Jewish Spiritual Renewal in Israel." *Journal of Contemporary Religion* 26(2): 269–89.

Werczberger, Rachel. 2011b. "Self, Identity, and Healing in the Ritual of Jewish Spiritual Renewal in Israel." In *Kabbalah and Contemporary Spiritual Revival*, ed. Boaz Huss, 75–100. Be'er Sheva: Ben-Gurion University Press.

Werczberger, Rachel. 2016. *Jews in the Age of Authenticity: Jewish Spiritual Renewal in Israel*. New York: Peter Lang.

Werczberger, Rachel, and Boaz Huss. 2014. "New Age Culture in Israel: Social, Ideological, and Political Aspects—Guest Editors' Introduction." *Israel Studies Review* 29(2): 1–16.

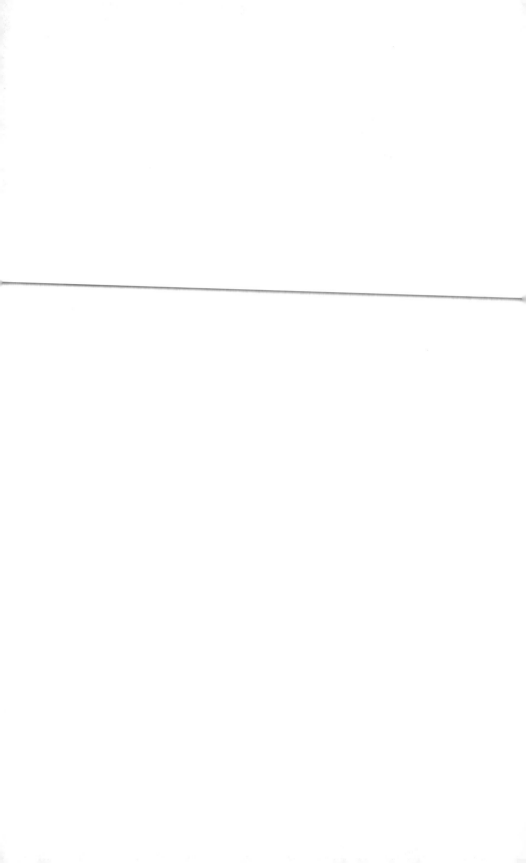

11

"We Also Study in a Yeshiva"

Ethnography in a Secular Yeshiva in Tel Aviv

Shlomo Guzmen-Carmeli

גַּם אֲנַחְנוּ לוֹמְדִים בִּישִׁיבָה

The Hebrew sentence in the accompanying image is a popular sticker in the BINA secular yeshiva. It translates as "We also study in a yeshiva." This is a tongue-in-cheek play on words because the Hebrew *b'yeshiva* can also mean "sitting down"—hence the chair. "The word 'yeshiva' was not coined by the religious world," says Eli, who teaches in the secular BINA yeshiva in Tel Aviv. "But while the religious yeshiva is a defense mechanism that attempts to justify the larger narrative, here in the secular yeshiva we do something different." What is this "something different"? Eli explains, "The focus of our learning is to break stereotypes.[1] If we haven't succeeded in disproving something we learned in kindergarten, we haven't done our work properly. . . . When I explicate the text, is it my purpose to justify the story? To study it? Am I supposed to explain God, does He need a defense attorney? Reading and understanding the text are processes that occur on the day it is read. As

---

1. Throughout the article, the word *learners* is used instead of *students*, and *learning* instead of *studying*. BINA learners do not study in a pursuit of an academic degree but out of the desire to be enriched. Also, in the English-speaking Orthodox Jewish world, "learning" specifically describes those who "learn Torah," as opposed to those who "study" a profession, for example.

far as I am concerned, these things were written for the here and now; it's the living story of our lives. . . . I want to open windows. It's important for me to open as many windows as possible. Don't close them; fresh air only enters when windows are flung open."

The decision to designate the BINA educational institution as a yeshiva and the viewpoint presented by Eli both in the interview and in his classes exemplify the ongoing tension that permeates this institution: a strong desire for continuity and connection to tradition along with the desire for a new, secular reading of canonical Jewish texts. The secular BINA yeshiva located in Tel Aviv is an intriguing institution in the Jewish Israeli renewal movement. The dialectic tension that pervades it is the focus of this chapter, which describes the fieldwork conducted in the yeshiva.

My fieldwork in the secular yeshiva was conducted from October 2010 to June 2011. In addition to the observation sessions, I carried out in-depth interviews with the learners and attended diverse events such as ceremonies, parties, and lectures (usually held outside regular learning days). In this chapter I examine the learning process (*limud Torah*, "study of Torah") in the yeshiva as an act of cultural performance (Schechner 2003). This is the initial stage in the attempt to understand the social significance of the learning and exegesis process in the yeshiva.

The learning activity is a performance that connects the cultural text to a social context and differentiates between theory and reality (Heilman 1983). The learning creates a symbolic syntax that attracts various elements, a system in which people live and that they can relate to, a system that they shape and form.

An analysis of Torah study in the secular yeshiva through the lens of cultural performance reveals that BINA learners subvert the concept of Orthodox sovereignty over the text by using study performances that emphasize the liminal nature of the texts. The secular yeshiva learners undermine traditional exegesis by turning to personalized commentary and by connecting to texts outside the sphere of traditional study. However, similar to their counterparts in Orthodox yeshivas, learners in the secular yeshiva also extract texts from their precarious liminal condition to provide clear ideological commentary that conforms with the secular values of the yeshiva.

The Secular BINA Yeshiva

The BINA yeshiva targets young people, age 17–30, from diverse backgrounds. It offers a broad weekly curriculum. BINA yeshivas stand apart from other pluralistic *batei midrash* (houses of learning, i.e., study halls dedicated to Torah study) operating under the Israeli Jewish Renewal movement[2] because of their extensive learning programs and the commitment they require of their participants (Sheleg 2010). BINA is a unique institution on the Israeli landscape. The names of all those interviewed in the Tel Aviv yeshiva, both teachers and learners, have been changed for the purposes of this study.

BINA was established in 2006 as one of a series of educational initiatives of the kibbutz movement and the Posen Foundation to support secular creativity and research in the years after Rabin's assassination. The yeshiva's goals are the "pursuit of Jewish renewal out of a pluralistic mindset. The pedagogic approach strives to build a free and sovereign Jewish public and community in the State of Israel, one which views Judaism as an open, renewable culture, and views tradition as a source of inspiration, not a source of authority. The yeshiva views itself as a spiritual and cultural center that seeks to create a generation of secular *talmidei chachamim* [Torah scholars] who assume active and influential responsibility in Israeli society."[3]

The discourse conducted between the secular yeshiva and the Orthodox yeshivas was already set in motion by the choice of name. The word *bina* means "wisdom" in Hebrew, but BINA is also a Hebrew acronym for "workshop for the soul of the nation." This phrase was coined by the famous Hebrew poet Chaim Nachman Bialik in his celebrated poem *Hamasmid*, in which he describes his convoluted relationship with the Volozhin yeshiva, a forerunner of the Lithuanian yeshiva movement. The poem criticizes Volozhin but also laments its destruction and seeks to "raise secular nationalism to the level of a new faith for the nation" (Kurzweil 1964, 133).

Similar to the message of *Hamasmid*, BINA derives its inspiration from secular Zionism and the Jewish Enlightenment movement and resurrects

---

2. Unlike the North American Jewish Renewal movement, which stresses Jewish spiritual revival buttressed by neo-Hasidic lore and non-Jewish spiritual techniques, the Israeli Jewish Renewal movement defines itself as "secular" and focuses on the intellectual study of Jewish and Zionist textual canon and on Jewish practice framed in cultural instead of religious terms.

3. From the BINA website, https://www.bina.org.il/en/.

the vision of the Zionist founders. Ronen, a teacher at the yeshiva, expresses this concept as follows:

The wagon was not empty;[4] instead, it was emptied, others emptied it. The first and second generations [of Zionist thinkers] had an ideology; they understood what they were rebelling against, what they were taking from the old culture, what they were renewing. But we have not only forgotten what the rebellion was about, we have also abandoned the ideology that we ostensibly hold. After all, almost all Israelis without exception declare themselves Zionists, but if you ask people what that means, what is the content of their Zionism, they will answer at best in clichés and talk about the flight of [the Israeli] F-15 jets over Auschwitz.[5]

Learning in the yeshiva is described as a process of "repairing" Zionism through a "return to Jewish literature" and contending with what BINA views as the ignorance and apathy prevalent among large sections of the secular public in Israel with regard to their culture. According to BINA attendees, the scholarship in their institution creates a new secular Jewish culture that corresponds with the traditional texts. In contradistinction to the abandoned, neglected *beit midrash* described in *Hamasmid*, BINA seeks to establish a *beit midrash* founded on pluralistic values that bring learners face to face with spiritual Jewish sources for critical learning. The yeshiva's teachers and learners describe Jewish culture as an entity that is undergoing a continuous process of change and formation. The learners regard the yeshiva as an arena for imparting the tradition of knowledge. The teachers aim to develop and renew the Jewish culture that is generated in the encounter between the learners, the text, and the moral paradigm of the yeshiva. They also express their criticism of the Orthodox yeshiva institution.

In overviews and studies dealing with the pluralistic *batei midrash* phenomenon, scholars and other observers have claimed that those attending these institutions are from relatively well-off backgrounds (the middle

4. This is a reference to a well-known metaphor of the Chazon Ish, Rabbi Avrohom Yeshaya Karelitz (1879–1954). In a meeting with David Ben-Gurion in 1952, the Chazon Ish compared Haredi society to a "full wagon," loaded with Torah and mitzvot (commandments), as opposed to the "empty wagon" led by secular Zionism. Thus, according to the rabbi, the "empty wagon must give way to the full wagon," meaning that the secularists must yield and allow Haredi Jews to live in accordance with their beliefs. For a description of this encounter, see Brown (2011).

5. On September 4, 2003, three Israeli Air Force F-15 fighter jets thundered over the Auschwitz death camp in Poland to express the power of the State of Israel as the protector of Jews wherever they may be.

or higher socioeconomic sector) and include a high percentage of youth movement graduates (Hacohen-Wolf and Amzaleg-Bahar 2003). My familiarity with younger members of the Jewish Renewal movement in the BINA research field supports this claim. Most BINA learners are, or once were, connected to youth movements and many (though not all) grew up in upscale neighborhoods. It is interesting to note that I was directed to the oldest, most mature group, composed of army graduates. This group, who join BINA after their army service for a year of Jewish learning, are called *bagatzim* (*bogrei tzava*, or "army graduates"). When I joined the group, it numbered twelve learners; two left after the first semester and two new members joined in the course of the year.

Most of the learners in the yeshiva during the time of my fieldwork were from Ashkenazi backgrounds. Most had served in the past as *madrichim* (counselors) of youth groups affiliated with Israeli left-wing youth movements such as HaShomer Hatzair and Hanoar HaOved VeHalomed. Some maintained their involvement in youth movement activities during their studies in the yeshiva. All the members of the group described their army service as "meaningful"; three had served in the permanent army (*keva*) as officers; all had served in various command posts in the infantry, intelligence, and educational corps.

BINA learners live in an organized social environment. Learning in the yeshiva is subsidized by various nonprofit associations,[6] and the *bagatzim* learn approximately two days a week. The *bagatzim* also participate in various activities in the yeshiva, including ceremonies and evening activities organized by BINA's Mechina students. The Mechina program is designed for younger students who attend the yeshiva before their army service. They come for a year of learning, volunteering, and living together in the low-socioeconomic Shapira neighborhood in southern Tel Aviv.

Although BINA receives much support from other institutions, the choice of secular youths to learn there is somewhat anomalous. The secular

6. The yeshiva receives monetary funding from entities that support the Jewish Renewal movement in Israel and around the world, such as the Posen Foundation, which promotes the concept of Judaism as a culture and encourages various projects and studies dealing with secular Judaism. Other donors are the Keren HaHadasha (Israel New Fund) and the AVI CHAI Foundation. In addition, the yeshiva receives private donations from Israel and abroad and support from the Jewish Federations in New York, Chicago, San Francisco, and Los Angeles. In recent years the yeshiva has also received some support from the Jewish Agency, the Tel Aviv municipality, and the Department of Tarbut Toranit (Torah Culture Department) in the Ministry of Education.

yeshiva is viewed as an atypical venue for the socialization process of secular youths. Members of the *bagatzim* group described the responses of their
friends and families to their decision to enroll for a year of yeshiva learning.
Reactions ranged from amazement over a "waste of time" to apprehension
lest they choose to adopt an Orthodox Jewish lifestyle (*chazara b'teshuvah*,
"a returnee to the faith"). The *bagatzim* describe their choice of BINA as
part of a process of self-searching and formation of their personal identity, a process that for many began during a trip abroad after their army
service (Noy and Cohen 2005). Why did they specifically choose BINA
from the gamut of learning alternatives in Israel's "basket of spiritual goods"?[7]
The learners said that they wanted to learn more about Judaism beyond the
walls of academia, "in an experiential way," but without the mediation of
religious cultural agents. "Without being exposed to sermonizing and indoctrination attempts to become *ba'alei teshuva* [repenters]," in the words of Eyal,
a student in the group. Another reason for choosing BINA is the close affinity
of the social circle of the learners (their youth movements or friends) with
the yeshiva's social network.

Learning for the *bagatzim* is divided into lessons on various subjects
and integrates the learning of texts from different periods: the Bible, the Talmud, Kabbalah, and Hebrew poetry. The learners also become acquainted
with modern philosophy and thought, both Jewish and general. A relatively
large amount of time is devoted to learning Talmud. All the classes share
the same overall structure: An opening lecture presents a specific topic or
text, followed by the group splitting up into *chavrutot* (learning pairs) for
a short period of learning, and a concluding discussion called *asif* (literally
"harvest" but meaning "summary"). The *bagatzim* meet twice a week, on
Sundays and Thursdays, from 8 a.m. to 9 p.m. Meals are served in the breaks
between the lessons.

In the interviews, the learners praised the teaching staff as the highlight of the learning experience in the yeshiva. They were able to develop
close relationships with well-known educators, "stars" in the field of Jewish
renewal in Israel. The members of the yeshiva's teaching staff come from
diverse personal backgrounds and hold different perspectives on faith. Some

7. For more information on available choices regarding the "spiritual basket" in the context
of the *teshuva* (repentance) movement in Israel, see Sharabi (2012). Regarding the proliferation of tracks in spiritual studies in Israel and the world, see, for example, Werczberger
(2011, 23–31).

are formerly religious, from Haredi or national-religious backgrounds, whereas others are secular-from-birth Jews who are or were members of the kibbutz movement. A minority are religious Jews who also hold a wide range of worldviews. But all the lessons share a clear ideological-ethical motif: a desire to study Jewish sources in order to adapt them to pluralist-humanist principles that are viewed as universal values. Learning in the yeshiva is probing and critical in nature, and when the text under discussion does not conform to these values, the discussion may reject the text or try to reread and reformulate it in accordance with the values of the yeshiva, as will be described later.

In total contrast to Haredi yeshivas, BINA is a gender-equality arena; women and men learn and teach side by side. According to Sagiv and Lomsky-Feder (2007), at any given time more women than men are likely to be learning in Jewish renewal programs (see also Hacohen-Wolf and Amzaleg-Bahar 2003). This dovetails neatly with the gender profile in BINA's *bagatzim*, which is made up of eight women and four men.

Learning as Performance

Critical anthropological analyses of "cultural performances" (Schechner 2003, 1–5) in recent years underscore the fact that such performances are always multilayered and filled with contradictions (Alexander 2004; Brown 2011; Gamliel 2000). Learning is an important example of cultural performance because learning includes not only the texts as analyzed in themselves but also the social activities involved in the various methods by which the text is discussed and studied. The learning of texts as cultural performance adds to its learning as literacy (Bielo 2009a, 2009b; El-Or 2002) and as a "reading" (Boyarin 1989, 339–421). The use of religious texts intersects with Jewish orientations such as belief, ideology, and geography. Following the concept of cultural performance, in this context the learning of texts is not viewed merely as an intellectual endeavor. Rather, it is a vital component of Jewish cultural and religious life. Learning texts generates Jewish identity, culture, and consciousness (Boyarin 1989, 1991; Friedman 1987; Goldberg 1987; Heilman 1983; Steiner 1985). To unpack the complexities and contradictions of this cultural performance, I follow both the specific methods of learning and the rules of learning and their violations (Seligman et al. 2008).

This study continues the ethnographic studies that deal with learning in Lithuanian yeshivas and other Haredi learning institutions (Boyarin 1989; Hakak 2004, 2005, 2012; Stadler 2007, 2009), in secular learning institutions (Azulay 2010; Neeman 2011; Sagiv and Lomsky-Feder 2007), and in the open *batei midrash* that are part of the Jewish Renewal movement (Sheleg 2010).

Limud Torah as Performance of Sovereignty

Battles are being waged among "contemporary Judaisms" regarding the way the Torah "should" be studied, between claiming possession of the Torah and excluding it, between preservation and change.[8] It is therefore important to adopt a comparative perspective in examining *limud Torah* in different forums, including the structure of the learning, the form of learning, and how it is carried out. The theoretical prism of cultural performance and ritual exemplified here reveals the symbolic dimensions of the act of learning that links the system of symbols and myths to channels of social communication.

The traditional text is not just a source of inspiration; it is a source of authority with variable contexts. Thus, for example, the text constitutes a source of authority according to Zionist ideology in all its diverse forms, for the privilege of political sovereignty in Eretz Israel (see, e.g., Aran 2013). For the Haredi public, especially the Lithuanian community, the mastery of the text achieved by *talmidei chachamim* (Torah scholars) is what gives them the authority to rule, that is, to render religious halakhic rulings (Brown 2011). In addition to the link between control of the text and sovereignty, studies also discuss the manner in which cultural performances and rituals create sovereignty. For example, Don Handelman discusses the significance of public rituals and describes how Zionist cosmology is shaped and emphasized year after year by using various Jewish symbols in "geography of memory" sites, such as Mount Herzl and Yad Vashem (Handelman 1983). Furthermore, memorial days and national holidays create a

---

8. This is only a superficial reference to the various conflicts and arguments in "contemporary Judaisms" regarding issues related to *limud Torah* and gender, the question of who has authority to explicate the text, and questions related to religious practices, such as who is permitted to read from the Torah, to be called up to the Torah in the synagogue, and more. For more on these issues, see Dagan (2005) and El-Or (2002).

continuum of performative events that are integrated into the traditional time period between Passover and Shavuot. This is a national time system that corresponds with the historical Jewish time continuum, creating one well-consolidated Zionist narrative.

Edna Lomsky-Feder also describes Remembrance Day school ceremonies as events featuring a dialectic between the "other voices" rising from the civil society and the canonical narrative as expressed in the ritual (Lomsky-Feder 2004). This serves to demonstrate the clear connection between the performance of symbolic events and the expression of sovereignty, not only over territory but also over narrative and time. The state creates rituals to express sovereignty (Gellner 1999); the ritualistic act itself is an interpretive procedure that seeks to shape the narrative. Through the cultural performance, cultural positions are expressed in relation to a specific subject. Moreover, creation of a ritual is not only an expression of sovereignty but also the creation of sovereignty. The performance determines not only what must be remembered but also how it should be remembered. When analyzing the text, it is important to scrutinize its content, its sources, and the intricate relationship between "who is the author" and the "death of the author." Thus a somewhat limited emphasis is placed on the analysis of the learning operation as an act of cultural performance, behavior that can be observed, documented, and analyzed. Of course, the text is not a performance in and of itself, but it acquires the dimension of a performance because through it, a social act takes place that is itself performative when it is discussed and studied. The mode of learning is set according to requisite norms that might also be called a series of rules of behavioral performances, according to the terminology of the discussion on ritualistic processes (Turner 1995). It is important to understand the process to properly describe in detail how the learning is accomplished. It is through this learning that the perception of sovereignty is created—personal as well as joint sovereignty of the group that studies the texts. I demonstrate this point by analyzing the cultural performance of *limud Torah* in the secular yeshiva.

Performance of Learning in the Secular Yeshiva

Several seating areas are scattered throughout the secular yeshiva: an old couch, wooden chairs around small tables, and a worn-out armchair at the side of the hall. The activity and learning spaces in the secular yeshiva correspond to the spirit of the place and seek to radiate a homey, informal feeling. The first explanation for the rather slipshod appearance is, of course, the limited budget available to the yeshiva. But the design of the area makes another statement as well: The yeshiva has an ambience that combines the "feel" of a student apartment with an open space for relaxed, easygoing learning. The yeshiva occupies a large rectangular building with an interior courtyard surrounded by rooms: classrooms, offices, a staff room, kitchen, and bathroom. The library is dispersed on various shelves. Expressionist pictures hang at the entrance. The corridors are lined with portraits of Luba Eliav[9] (after whom the Mechina program was named), the poetess Rachel, and Leah Goldberg. Announcements are attached to large corkboards: invitations to cultural events and various events taking place in *batei midrash* of the Jewish Renewal movement in Tel Aviv. Quotes from poems and meditations also appear; any student who is moved by a text is free to display it on the corkboards as well.

The same relaxed attitude is also expressed in the learners' clothing. "No one walks around in brand-name outfits, clothes that shout money or are too elegant—that would be embarrassing," says Gili, a student in the Mechina program. "We wear what's comfortable, but there's style here." And it does seem that despite the variety of clothing, there is some kind of standard. The male yeshiva learners usually wear jeans or shorts, sandals, and short-sleeved shirts from their army service or cut-off, worn-out printed shirts. The female learners' clothing is much more varied: short summer dresses, all kinds of coats, long scarves; it seems that the older the article of clothing, the better. But this does not mean that people in the yeshiva pay no attention to their outward appearance; the contrary is true. The slipshod, disheveled look is carefully chosen, as I gleaned from conversations about shirts purchased in small markets in Europe or a colorful wool scarf found at a bargain price in a vintage store in Tel Aviv.

Despite the casual atmosphere in the institution and the clothing worn by the learners, classes in the yeshiva are not optional; there is a regular time schedule, and the studies necessitate commitment and personal responsibility. This commitment is not dictated by the yeshiva; it is negotiated at the beginning of the school year between the learners in the various frameworks. Thus, for example, in the oldest group (the *bagatzim*), where I conducted

---

9. Aryeh Luba Eliav (1921–2010) was an Israeli parliament member and a writer who won the prestigious Israel Prize in 1988 for his contributions to society.

most of my observations, it was determined that anyone who comes late to a class must wait outside the classroom until the break. Similarly, it was emphasized that full attendance in classes was expected. One group member who did not attend classes regularly received strong social criticism and left after one semester at the yeshiva.

In the next few paragraphs I describe a lesson conducted in the secular yeshiva. Unlike studies in Orthodox yeshivas or classes in academic institutions, learning in the secular yeshiva is informal and open; the experience of learning itself is paramount. This is also expressed in the performance of learning. My analysis of the observation data shows that despite the fact that the *limud* is classified as open, the learning process is actually rather standardized. The following is a description of the learning that took place in the course of a Talmud class on the subject of "Where an ox [belonging to an Israelite] has gored an ox belonging to a Canaanite, there is no liability" (*Bavli, Baba Kama* 38a).[10]

A sign on the door of the *bagatzim* classroom instructs passersby not to knock or disrupt the class. The *bagatzim* sit around the table. Although there are no set rules determining where people are to sit, each learner has a permanent place. Moving to a different spot may disrupt the study routine and provoke a discussion. The teacher does not sit at the head of the table, and the discourse is not formal. On the table is a box of homemade cookies, a pitcher of water, and a number of colorful cups. The class opens with a personal discussion. Ronen, who teaches Talmud in BINA and other Jewish renewal programs, tells the participants about his experiences during the vacation, and group members ask him questions about his family. This class took place in the second semester when the *bagatzim* already knew one another and their teachers. Ronen distributes photocopied pages from *Masechet* (tractate) *Bava Kamma*. He gives the following introduction:

> Today we will discuss material that is rather problematic. There are many things connected to these *halakhot* that make me uncomfortable. The attitude here toward non-Jews is infuriating; the concept of enlightenment is very distant from the texts we'll learn here. But it seems to me that the solution is not to suppress or hide this material

---

10. Here, I use Schechner's model of examining cultural performance events as one segment (Schechner and Appel 1990, 1–7).

but to confront it directly. This way we can change things at the deepest level.

We see that Ronen first explains the context of the discussion and the critical interpretive process required of the learners. Then he briefly outlines the development of the discussion in the Talmud. After this introduction, the learners prepare for a half-hour of discussion in *chavrutot* (study pairs).

The division into *chavrutot* is a permanent fixture of the classes. I join the *chavruta* of Yair and Reut. Yair holds the pages of the *Masechet* with one hand; the other hand grasps a cup of black coffee. Alternately he sips coffee and reads out loud. Reut's *Masechet* pages are perched on her knees; she follows along as she listens to Yair and smokes a Noblesse cigarette.[11] Yair translates the terms from Aramaic, and they try to understand the unfolding discussion in the Talmud. Once they have acquired a basic understanding of the text, Yair and Reut discuss various encounters they have had with non-Jews. Reut tells Yair about a foreign worker from the Philippines who took care of her sick grandmother, and Yair talks about events that took place during his army service. The *chavruta* study that is part of the learning process in various yeshiva classes appears to be a warm-up, a preliminary stage that leads to the heart of the symbolic activity, the performance itself (Schechner and Appel 1990, 1–7). Those who learn in a *chavrutot* explicate the text and connect their discussion to familiar experiences from their own worlds. The Talmud considers the circumstances under which it is permissible to steal from a non-Jew, and Yair tells Reut about a situation in which soldiers stole fruit and shirts from Palestinians during an operational activity in Hebron. The learning is apologetic in nature. Yair and Reut seek to change several things simultaneously: the text, the Jewish Israeliness they perceive as racist, and their personal experiences.

Frequently, the learning in the yeshiva is experienced as a conflictual process in which the learners serve as "active agents of change" (Turner 1987, 24). Cultural performance in the yeshiva is directed toward changing the culture by undermining the traditional interpretations and sometimes

---

11. Noblesse, an Israeli cigarette brand, is a play on words of the French phrase *noblesse oblige*—that people from a noble ancestry have an unwritten obligation to act honorably and generously toward others. In the present context, however, this Israeli cigarette is relatively inexpensive and in the past was distributed freely to kibbutz members. It is associated in Israel with youth, simplicity, and rebellion against authority.

even by undermining the content of the text being studied. I demonstrate this through an analysis of the discussion held in the *asif* (review) part of the class, held after the study in *chavrutot*. The *asif* is the height of the performance. It exemplifies how joint viewpoints are generated that validate the values of the learners, even though they conflict with the text under study.

> EYAL: The statement here is clear, it is permissible to steal from a non-Jew. The moral values that apply to other Jews ("Israel") do not exist when dealing with someone who is not a Jew.
>
> NAOMI: Today we also have a double standard between Jews and Palestinians.
>
> GIDI [a teacher in the yeshiva]: I don't want to get into abstract discussions here where everyone shares what he's thinking. Let's first talk about the text and then discuss it, and see what we can take from it and what we might want to re-write. . . . True, at the onset of the discussion a situation is described in which it is permissible to steal from a non-Jew, but immediately, when the problem of why it is forbidden to steal from a non-Jew becomes clear, a regulation was fixed declaring it to be forbidden.
>
> EYAL: But it [the regulation] was not determined because it's not OK to steal from him, because it's ethically invalid, but only so it shouldn't cause problems.[12]
>
> NAOMI: So are you saying that *hillul Hashem*, a desecration of God's name, is caused because of the "problems" and not because it's a desecration of God's name to steal from a non-Jew?
>
> GIDI: If it had been (from their viewpoint) a *hillul Hashem* to steal from a non-Jew, they would have changed the section. [Instead,] they think it's OK, but they rule otherwise because of fear of what such a ruling could cause. We can write a book on issues

---

12. In fact, the Talmudic discussion concludes on a note of dissatisfaction regarding the Halakha stating that when an ox belonging to an Israelite gores an ox belonging to a Canaanite, there is no liability but that the reverse situation does carry liability. The topic concludes with a story about two Roman soldiers who are sent to examine the Torah of Israel. They decide that it is the truth and object only to the section about the ox that gores. They end with, "We do not tell the rulership about this." The learners discuss the reasons for the dissatisfaction in the Talmud and complain that this does not mean (according to the Talmud) that the religious ruling is erroneous, reflecting an ethical problem, but only dissatisfaction that the Halakha must be kept secret for fear of the non-Jews.

234 Shlomo Guzmen-Carmeli

> like these. The problem is what it would do to anti-Semitism,
> and what it does in our internal discourse. None of those people
> [referring to the learners in Haredi yeshivas] would say, "I rely
> on a system that is distorted." I don't know many people who
> think of themselves as bad people. . . . Our familiarity with this
> text, and the decision that "I do not accept this, here I will write
> a new Halakha," is part of what we seek to do.

The preoccupation with text as exemplified in this discussion is a process. What the learners view as the appropriate culture is created and validated as part of a performance; in the course of this performance, traditional texts are rejected and reformulated. The learning does not validate the existing text; it changes the text and modifies it to fit the culture that the learners seek to create.

Anthropological research describes cultural performances as serving the functions of cultural renewal and cultural strengthening (Beeman 2002, 85–97). The performances are also cultural instruments that uncover, undermine, and flout authority structures and symbol systems. By doing so, these performances reflect and reveal joint truths that are well internalized (see, e.g., Degh 1990, 71–90; Lawless 1996; Rosenberg 1970). Thus learning performances are likely to preserve the existing situation, but they also, as demonstrated in the critical discussion on the Talmud, destroy the social order (which, in this instance, is reflected in the text) and constitute an arena that generates social-cultural change.

Another discussion that took place in the course of a lesson called "View from the Sidelines," exemplifies the interpretive process carried out in the BINA secular yeshiva. The lesson veered from discussions on colonialism to the explanations of terms adopted from postmodern approaches. The subject was the "butcher responsa"[13] of Rav Yosef Mashash,[14] where the rabbi was asked whether it was *halakhically* permissible to purchase and eat meat from animals slaughtered by kosher butchers who publicly desecrated Sabbaths and *yomim tovim* (holidays). The discussion revolved around the halakhic considerations in Rav Mashash's decision to declare the meat

13. Rabbi Yosef Mashash, *Teshuvot Mayim Chayyim Responsa* 143.
14. Rabbi Yosef Mashash (1892–1974) was born in Morocco and served as the chief rabbi of Tlemcen in Algeria. He made aliyah to Israel in 1964 and served as the chief rabbi of Haifa.

kosher, despite the behavior of the butchers. The focus was on the lenient and inclusive Sephardic rabbinic rulings in relation to the stringent, hard-line Ashkenazi rabbinic rulings. The halakhic discussion evolved into a discussion criticizing Ashkenazi Halakha. Amit (one of the *bagatzim*) said, "It always seems important to pass the law, even if people won't observe it and even if you won't be able to enforce it when everyone flouts it. Here they legislated a law that the public can't observe, and he [Rav Mashash] understands that he has to make a change." Amit later remarked:

> This lesson has changed several things for me. I'm thinking about secularism that wouldn't agree to "accept" Judaism, that turned every-thing into all or nothing: This is what triggered the great reaction, the ultra-Orthodox Jewry and *chazara b'teshuvah* [repentance] move-ment that we see around us. It is a shame that secular "Halakha" is not more inclusive like the Sephardim. In this way we lose people. I take this with me as a lesson for life: the need to be tolerant, the need to accept others.

The accepted viewpoint in the secular yeshiva, which views texts as a source of inspiration but not of authority, creates a spontaneous "flow" of ideas (Schechner 2003, 1–7), through which the values and goals of cultural Judaism are consolidated by the learners. Amit's analysis shows that learning a text is a process that can cause a change in the text and a change in the individual studying the text. According to Richard Schechner, when a reader adopts new values in his or her encounter with a text, the performance creates a new culture (Schechner 2002, 37–43). Thus, in the course of the discussion carried out in the *asif* part of the lesson in the yeshiva, a joint perspective is formed by the learners in relation to the text and in relation to the non-Jewish other.

Remarks made by the yeshiva learners show that they want to have a "clean-slate encounter" with the original texts. Thus, for example, Yair describes how he wants to read the Babylonian Talmud without commen-tators and without consulting Rabbi Steinzalt's translation of the text from Aramaic to Hebrew.

> I don't want anyone else to explain the text for me. If my first encoun-ter [with the text] will be via commentary, it will be etched in my

consciousness. . . . The first reading should be me vis-à-vis the text, even if I don't understand everything. . . . What's important to me is what I take away from it, what I understood from the segment.

Thus the learners in the BINA yeshiva seek a clean-slate reading lacking traditional exegesis, as opposed to learners in Orthodox yeshivas who seek "the correct reading of the text" as mediated by traditional commentators.

The learners' sense of sovereignty over the text depends on their ability to link the text to their own inner worlds. The following conversation, which was conducted in the course of a lesson on the Babylonian Talmud's *Masechet Shabbat*, demonstrates this.

> SHARON [a member of the *bagatzim*]: I don't understand these stupid *halakhot*. How can it be that Halakha extends to all these places, to your shoe, the bedroom. All the time, a sense of fear and you need to close all the loopholes, all the holes. A mother can't even braid her daughter's hair on Shabbat!
>
> DORIT [teacher in the yeshiva]: I invite you as a secular Jew to give credit to the fact that many religious people choose this path. . . . What significance does life have for people in a world in which they choose to impose so many limitations on themselves, for example: to tithe their salaries?
>
> SHARON: You don't understand me. I am a secular person and I have *halakhot* in my life and I have commandments. They are simply different ones . . .
>
> DORIT: I hear a lot of critical viewpoints here, and the stance of the condescending secular Jew.
>
> SHARON: The question is: Is Judaism a compass that helps me navigate my life or something that gives me the sense that I'm not to be trusted? Does that sentence you to having your life dictated to you, down to the smallest details? The Torah is mine, but I decide what I take from the whole complex. If you talk about a compass, it's my compass and not the rabbi's.

Yael, another student in the *bagatzim*, has been studying the Zohar with the class. She also indicates that a desire for a personal, emotional study encounter is a precondition for gaining a sense of sovereignty over the text:

"What do we take from this text? I want us to talk about what we acquire here. . . . It's legitimate to stop and think, What is the message of these things that each of us encounter, what we take from them and what we don't take."

These quotes illustrate the tension experienced by the learners, tension based on the desire to become familiar with the texts while sometimes harshly criticizing their contents. The learners want to appropriate the texts for themselves and criticize those who accept the texts literally or based on traditional commentary. The tension is neutralized through new, personal explication of the text. Performance in the yeshiva revolves around the question of *how* they study rather than *what* they study? The performance in the BINA yeshiva has a dimension of uncertainty (which is essential for performance). A discussion on the points at which the performance deviates from the script reveals the social process taking place during the learning and reveals how the text is internalized during the performance. In the course of the debates in the BINA yeshiva, the text being studied comes to "belong" to the learners. The polemics in the course of the learning process create not only understanding but also internalization and parallelism between the script and the performer, which in turn creates sovereignty of the learner over the text under study. In this uncertainty, as expressed in performance, lies an element of danger (Brown 2011). I address this, with regard to the texts being studied in the course of interpretation in the yeshiva, in the next section.

Texts in a Dangerous State

In contrast to Torah study in Orthodox institutions, learning in a secular yeshiva is a direct encounter with the text, in order to allow the learners their unrestricted, personal interpretations. Yet an analysis of learning performance in the yeshiva shows that even in a secular yeshiva, text without interpretation is dangerous. The learner extracts the text from the domains of liminality[15] by aligning it with a humanist-pluralist interpretation that validates the values of the yeshiva—in other words, by averting the dangers embodied in the traditional Orthodox interpretation. Ronen describes the dangers of adopting the traditional interpretation of a text.

---

15. The liminal state, described extensively by Turner (1995), is a stage in the rite of passage that facilitates the potential for change.

That is one of the hardest things for us to explain to someone who comes to the yeshiva for a day. It is also a question that a lot of the families ask the students: Are they are going to become penitents and adopt a religious lifestyle (become a *chozer b'teshuvah*)?[16] Otherwise, why would a secular Jew want to study in a yeshiva? Our fundamental approach is that a yeshiva is an institution that belongs to secular Jews as well. We also learn and our Judaism is not inferior to that of those who are observant, because my secularism is not based on ignorance but on my familiarity with Judaism. . . . Studies here are not meant for *chazara b'teshuvah*, God forbid! . . . As far as I'm concerned, if a student should decide to become religious, if something here in the yeshiva would cause him to wear a *kippah* or grow a beard, that would be an educational failure at the highest level. The aspiration here is to construct an identity that sanctifies equality and pluralism, a secular identity.

Friedman (1987) has analyzed the use of texts in Haredi society. He argues that the text has become a tool in the work of founding and fortifying a "culture of severities" that developed in response to the Enlightenment and modernity. He maintains that the dismantling and reassembly of texts so familiar to us from learning Talmud in *chavrutot* has undergone a change. The *chumrot* (severe religious practices) that the Haredi Jews adopted were more stringent than the customs of their forefathers and the practices mandated by earlier halakhic texts (Soloveitchik 1994). Because the text is sacred and cannot be changed, it is reality that undergoes reinterpretation and readjustment to the sacred, immutable text (Rubin 2011).

Most of the traditional commentators are absent in the course of study at the secular yeshiva. The traditional text is not regarded as sacred, and it is interpreted in accordance with the ideological worldview of the yeshiva. In the course of the performance of sovereignty in BINA, the text—and not the learner—undergoes the liminal rite of passage. Instead of the ideological meaning of traditional religious interpretation, the text assumes a different ideological meaning that is secular, universal, and humanistic and is thus adapted to the values of the yeshiva.

---

16. For concerns about *chazara b'teshuvah*, see Sagiv and Lomsky-Feder (2007, 272).

"The sovereign human being is sovereign over himself," states Ari Elon, a teacher at the BINA yeshiva. "There is no Master of the Universe in his world, and he is not Master of the Universe in anyone else's world. A person who believes in rabbis is not his own master. He creates a rabbi for himself. The rabbi creates a divinity for him" (Elon 1986, 225).[17] This assertion reverberates in the discourse at the BINA yeshiva. Yet an examination of the performance of learning in the secular yeshiva reveals that the process of creating sovereignty over the text and, consequently, sovereignty over the learner's interpretation of his world is not exactly a personal, subjective process. The learners seek to elevate the text under study, so that it assumes a meaningful place in their daily lives. The learning experience, which is described as a deep process of change, is to a large extent a process of preserving and validating the learner's world of values. The encounter with sacred writings is a cultural performance of intersection with the sacred culture. And in this encounter it is clear that sacredness has the upper hand.

The secular yeshiva challenges the Orthodox viewpoint of sovereignty on texts and argues that it, too, has sovereignty on the canonical Jewish texts. Although innovation in Torah study in Orthodox yeshivas is limited to interpretations that are compatible with the existing commentary scheme (Guzmen-Carmeli 2020), the *limud* in the secular yeshiva encourages learners to extract the texts from the realm of traditional commentary and "correct" them while binding them to the personal interpretation of the individual learner. The reading of texts, which places the emphasis on personal and subjective interpretation over the commentaries of traditional text explicators, is upheld as the correct model for Torah study and interpretation. The learners attempt to firmly affix their sovereignty on the text as a resource and transform their choices regarding interpretation into accepted, appropriate, and worthwhile norms. The learner "continues" the text and sharpens his or her sense of personal connection, of having a direct relationship with the text under study; however, this sense of personal interpretation of the text is, of course, the result of cultural construction. The text in the secular yeshiva is read anew through the prism of another rather dogmatic interpretation, the pluralist-humanist point of view. This approach "corrects" the text while adapting it to the spirit of the time in a way that reflects the lives and values of the secular yeshiva learners.

17. Elon's article offers a secular interpretation of the well-known children's song written by Chaim Nachman Bialik.

Following the arguments of Sagiv and Lomsky-Feder (2007), the encounter with the text is an encounter with social significance, part of the symbolic struggle over cultural capital (Bourdieu 1993). There is no danger that secular yeshiva learners will become religious as an extension of their learning. The learning is a complex performative act that extricates the texts from their liminal status, lacking any clear interpretation. Interpretation means control, creating sovereignty for the learners over the studied text. The new generation of secular *talmidei chachamim* rescue the texts from dangerous regions. The learners in the secular yeshiva scrutinize the text as though looking into a mirror, and with the help of the text they create an improved and corrected version of themselves and their community.

Similar to the course of study in the Orthodox yeshivas, we see that what constructs the learning is not the text itself. The text only holds up a mirror for the society that adapts it to a changing cultural context.

References

Alexander, Jeffrey C. 2004. "Cultural Pragmatics: Social Performance Between Ritual and Strategy." *Sociological Theory* 22(4): 527–73.

Aran, Gideon. 2013. *Kookism: The Roots of Gush Emunim, Settler Culture, Zionist Theology, and Contemporary Messianism*. Jerusalem: Carmel.

Azulay, Naama. 2010. "'Hebrews We Are and Our Hearts Will We Worship': The Jewish Renewal Movement in Israeli Secular Society." PhD diss., Bar Ilan University. [Hebrew]

Beeman, William O. 2002. "Performance Theory in an Anthropology Program." In *Performance Studies as a Discipline*, ed. N. Stuckey and C. Wimmer, 85–97. Carbonville: Southern Illinois University Press.

Bielo, James, ed. 2009a. *The Social Life of Scriptures: Cross-Cultural Perspectives on Biblicism*. New Brunswick, NJ: Rutgers University Press.

Bielo, James. 2009b. *Words upon the Word: An Ethnography of Evangelical Group Bible Study*. New York: New York University Press.

Bourdieu, Pierre. 1993. *Sociology in Question*. London: Sage.

Boyarin, Jonathan. 1989. "Voices Around the Text: The Ethnography of Reading at Mesivta Tifereth Jerusalem." *Cultural Anthropology* 4(4): 339–421.

Boyarin, Jonathan. 1991. "Jewish Ethnography and the Question of the Book." *Anthropological Quarterly* 64(1): 14–29.

Brown, Gavin. 2011. "Theorizing Ritual as Performance: Explorations of Ritual Indeterminacy." *Journal of Ritual Studies* 17(1): 3–18.

Dagan, Hagi. 2005. *Judaisms: A Group Portrait.* Tel Aviv: Mapah and Tel Aviv University. [Hebrew]

Degh, Linda. 1990. "Are Sectarian Miracle Stories Contemporary American Folk Legends? A Preliminary Consideration." In *Storytelling in Contemporary Societies,* ed. Lutz Roehrich and Sabine Wienker-Piepho, 71–90. Tubingen: Gunter Narr.

Elon, Ari. 1986. "What Is Up and What Is Down? Only Me, Myself, and You." In *Regard and Revere—Renew Without Fear: The Secular Jew and His Heritage,* ed. Yehoshua Rash, 225–34. Tel Aviv: Sifriat Poalim.

El-Or, Tamar. 2002. *Next Year I Will Know More: Identity and Literacy Among Young Orthodox Women in Israel.* Detroit: Wayne State University Press.

Friedman, Menachem. 1987. "Life and Book Tradition in Ultraorthodox Judaism." In *Judaism Viewed from Within and from Without: Anthropological Studies,* ed. Harvey Goldberg, 235–55. Albany: State University of New York Press.

Gamliel, Tova. 2000. "The Lobby as an Arena in the Confrontation Between Denial and Acceptance of Old Age." *Journal of Aging Studies* 14(3): 251–71.

Gellner, David N. 1999. "Religion, Politics, and Ritual: Remarks on Geertz and Bloch." *Social Anthropology* 7(2): 135–53.

Goldberg, Harvey, ed. 1987. *Judaism Viewed from Within and from Without: Anthropological Studies.* Albany: State University of New York Press.

Guzmen-Carmeli, Shlomo. 2020. *Encounters Around the Text: Ethnography of Judaisms.* Haifa: Pardes and Haifa University Press. [Hebrew]

Hacohen-Wolf, Hagit, and Haya Amzaleg-Bahar. 2003. *Batei Midrash and Learning Communities from the Participants' Points of View: Assessment Study Conducted by the Mitveh Company for the Commission on Jewish Identity and Renewal.* Jerusalem: Mitveh. [Hebrew]

Hakak, Yohai. 2004. *Vocational Training for Ultra-Orthodox Men.* Jerusalem: Floersheimer Institute. [Hebrew]

Hakak, Yohai. 2005. *Spirituality and Worldliness in Lithuanian Yeshivas.* Jerusalem: Floersheimer Institute. [Hebrew]

Hakak, Yohai. 2012. *Young Men in Israeli Haredi Yeshiva Education: The Scholars Enclave in Unrest.* Leiden: Brill.

Handelman, Don. 1983. *Nationalism and the Israeli State.* Oxford, UK: Berg.

Heilman, Samuel C. 1983. *The People of the Book: Drama, Fellowship, and Religion.* Chicago: University of Chicago Press.

Kurzweil, Baruch. 1964. *Our New Literature: Continuation or Revolution?* Tel Aviv: Schocken.

Lawless, Elaine. 1996. *Women Preaching Revolution: Calling for Connection in a Disconnected Time.* Philadelphia: University of Pennsylvania Press.

Lomsky-Feder, Edna. 2004. "The Memorial Ceremony in Israeli Schools: Between the State and Civil Society." *British Journal of Sociology of Education* 25(3): 291–305.

Neeman, Rina. 2011. "Tel-Avivian Prayer: An Israeli Prayer House in Tel-Aviv." *Israeli Sociology* 12(2): 403–31. [Hebrew]

Noy, Chaim, and Erik Cohen, eds. 2005. *Israeli Backpackers: From Tourism to a Rite of Passage.* Albany: State University of New York Press.

Rosenberg, Bruce. 1970. *The Art of the American Folk Preacher.* New York: Oxford University Press.

Rubin, Nissan. 2011. "Sociological-Anthropological Theories for the Interpretation of Texts." In *Halacha, Meta-Halacha, and Philosophy*, ed. Avinoam Roznik, 98–121. Jerusalem: Van Leer Institute. [Hebrew]

Sagiv, Talia, and Edna Lomsky-Feder. 2007. "An Actualization of a Symbolic Conflict: The Arena of Secular 'Batei Midrash.'" *Israeli Sociology* 8(2): 269–300. [Hebrew]

Schechner, Richard. 2002. *Performance Studies: An Introduction.* London: Routledge.

Schechner, Richard. 2003. *Performance Theory.* New York: Routledge.

Schechner, Richard, and Willa Appel, eds. 1990. *By Means of Performance: Intercultural Studies of Theatre and Ritual.* Cambridge, UK: Cambridge University Press.

Seligman, Adam B., Robert P. Weller, Bennett Simon, and Michael J. Puett. 2008. *Ritual and Its Consequences: An Essay on the Limits of Sincerity.* Oxford, UK: Oxford University Press.

Sharabi, Asaf. 2012. "'Teshuvah Baskets' in the Israeli Teshuvah Market." *Culture and Religion* 13(3): 273–93.

Sheleg, Yair. 2010. *The Jewish Renaissance in Israeli Society: The Emergence of a New Jew.* Jerusalem: Israel Democracy Institute. [Hebrew]

Soloveitchik, Haim. 1994. "Rupture and Reconstruction: The Transformation of Contemporary Jewry." *Tradition* 28(4): 64–131.

Stadler, Nurit. 2007. "Ethnography of Exclusion: Initiating a Dialogue with Fundamentalist Men." *Nashim: A Journal of Jewish Women's Studies & Gender Issues* 14(1): 185–208.

Stadler, Nurit. 2009. *Yeshiva Fundamentalism: Piety, Gender, and Resistance in the Ultra-Orthodox World*. New York: New York University Press.

Steiner, George. 1985. "Our Homeland, the Text." *Salmagundi* 66: 4–25.

Turner, Victor. 1987. *The Anthropology of Performance*. New York: PAJ.

Turner, Victor. 1995 [1969]. *The Ritual Process: Structure and Anti-Structure*. New Brunswick, NJ: Transaction.

Werczberger, Rachel. 2011. "When the New Age Entered the Jewish Bookshelf: Jewish Spiritual Renewal in Israel." PhD diss., Hebrew University of Jerusalem. [Hebrew]

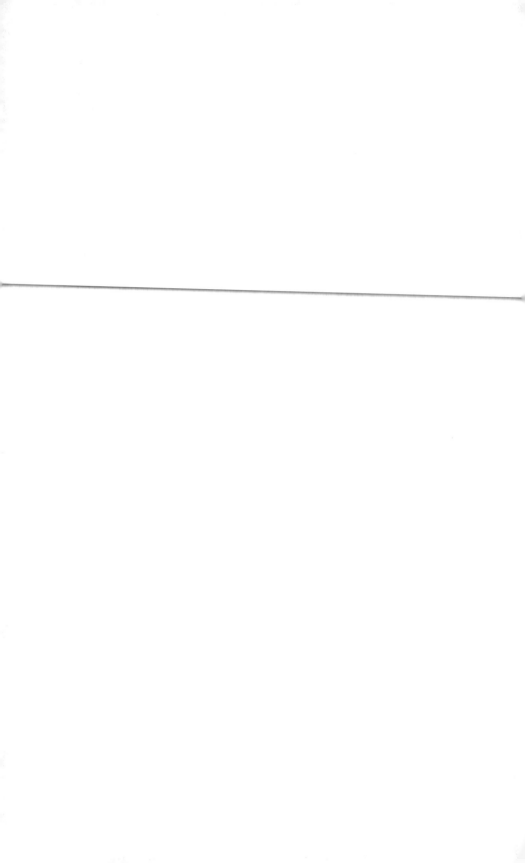

12

On the Altar of *Shekhina*

The Kohenet Hebrew Priestess Institute and the Gendered Politics of Jewish Renewal

Cara Rock-Singer

Don't try to rebuild the temple	*let the light in.*
There's wisdom in destruction.	*Verdant green sprouts*
Let the old ways die.	*rise*
Sit in the rubble	*In place of*
With wonder.	*what no longer*
Look around.	*serves you.*
Listen to your heartbeat.	*Spring is here.*
There's blue sky above	*Let the destruction of the temple*
and possibility	*Remind you how vast the horizon is*
in this mess.	*That the only limits and laws*
See the flowers	*Are the ones you write for yourself*
As they find their way	*Cause breakdown can be a blessing*
Through the cracks.	*And we might just be brave enough*
The cracks that	*to breakthrough.*

—Kohenet Aliza Rivka[1]

I could hear the drumbeat from quite a distance. *Du-du-bump du-du-du-bump du-du-bump du-du-du-bump do-do do-do.* I had just arrived at the Isabella Freedman Jewish Retreat Center in northwestern Connecticut, a site

---

1. This is an allusion to Leonard Cohen's "Anthem."

that was incorporated in 1892 as a vacation society for factory girls threatened by urban pathology (Ufford 1897, 79; Heinze 2004, 91). There, I would join a group of women[2] who had come together to heal from what they saw to be a patriarchal, rational Jewish worship that had taken a wrecking ball to women's embodied spirituality and the divine feminine. The sound intensified as I approached the red yurt. I could begin to make out the words of what would soon become a familiar song. *We embody Shekhina. We embody Shekhina. Dwelling in us the feminine divine. We honor the stories of our foremothers. And the women in our line. Sarah, Rivka, Rakhel, Leah, Dinah, Ruth u' Naomi. Du-du-bump du-du-du-bump du-du-bump du-du-du-bump do-do do-do.* It was an adaptation of a neopagan song, "We all Come from the Goddess" that had been "Jewified," replacing names of different goddesses with biblical women.

In the summer of 2014, as I arrived at the opening circle of the Kohenet Hebrew Priestess Institute to become a participant-observer of its fifth cohort, I was disoriented by the chaos. A woman stood at the entrance and instructed new arrivals to remove our shoes and ritually wash our hands. Then she waved a bundle of burning sage along the length of our bodies and bowed her head to bless us. We sat on the floor in a circle around what seemed like a fancy tablecloth covered with objects, including a giant shofar, scattered around a large copper bowl. Women dressed in flowing bright textiles were dancing and singing. When so moved, dancers would approach a red string hanging down from the rafters and hold it to their belly buttons. I felt like I had stepped into a foreign Judaism, where I could recognize the occasional loan-word or ritual object. Over time, I would learn that what I found in the yurt was not a hodgepodge of traditions or materials but rather a web of allusions and symbols, all organized into a deliberate structure. The dangling string was the goddess's umbilical cord, the bowl was the washbasin (*kior*) of the tabernacle, and the fabric and objects were an altar.

This essay unfolds around the altar, a ritual center for priestesses to tend to the feminine divine. Kohenet participants ritually build altars to organize and orient sacred space and time; to facilitate connection among participants who assemble from across national borders and life stages; to claim continuity across "spiritual geographies" (Bender 2010, 157) that ground

---

2. Although not every participant is woman-identified, I have chosen to honor the feminine identity of the group by referring, in the plural, to women and using feminine pronouns unless I am discussing an individual who does not identify in this way.

Inside the Red Yurt at the Isabella Freedman Jewish Retreat Center in Falls Village, Connecticut, during a Kohenet retreat week. A symbolic umbilical cord is dangling into the washbasin (*kior*) at the center of the altar. Photo by Cara Rock-Singer.

Kohenet's practices in ancestral traditions; and to serve as what Birgit Meyer has termed a "sensational form," a "relatively fixed mode . . . for invoking and organising access to the transcendental, offering structures of repetition to create and sustain links between believers in the context of particular religious regimes" (Meyer 2011, 29). By tracing contestations over whether the altar is an ancient Israelite mode of worship, an appropriation of another culture, or an illicit mode of *avodah zarah* (literally, "foreign worship"), in this essay I examine the gendered politics of authenticity in a Jewish revival.

It was the altar that first drew me into Kohenet's community at the start of my first weeklong retreat.[3] The three teachers, the *rav kohanot*, Rabbi Dr. Jill Hammer, Taya Shere, and Shoshana Jedwab, were sitting at the head of the circle, and Jill began her introductory remarks by placing us in time. She explained that that evening was Rosh Chodesh (the new moon) of the Hebrew month of Av, a low point in liturgical time, as Jews mourned the destruction of the Second Temple and acutely experienced the pain of exile. The *rav kohanot* then convened a ritual to build the sacred space and establish the group as a community. We went around in a circle, taking turns, with each participant introducing herself and presenting her offerings in a prescribed order. The first offering was of water from sacred sources, which we poured into the large copper bowl that was adorned inside with mirrors, an allusion to Exodus 38:8. Participants brought water from all sorts of places, near and far: the rain outside, a river near their home, the Pacific Ocean, and melted snow from Jerusalem. Jill had saved some water from the collection made during this same ritual the previous year. Some women, by motioning with their arms, figuratively offered their tears, the fluids of their bodies, or the fluids made between the bodies of lovers. After pouring the water, each participant placed an object she valued onto the altar. Together, we assembled objects from nature, gifts

---

3. The Kohenet Hebrew Priestess Institute is scaffolded by weeklong retreats, from Monday to Sunday, twice a year, summer and winter. Between retreats, segments of the community can come together at the "Virtual Temple," where there are online courses, message boards, and a "dream basket" for unloading the subconscious. At the end of a cohort's fifth retreat, marking the completion of two years of training, there is an initiation ritual. That ceremony transitions the "seekers" (*dorshot*), who have been studying traditional modes of Jewish women's leadership, into "shrine keepers" (*tzovot*), and the curriculum shifts to preparing to lead prayer services and life-cycle rituals. Ordination takes place at the end of the third year, following the summer retreat. Recently, Kohenet started a second West Coast training program, Kohenet West, which has met at Ananda Ashram Meditation Retreat Center in Northern California.

A Kohenet altar laid out with symbols of the four cardinal directions and the four elements, and populated with community objects. Photo by Cara Rock-Singer.

from loved ones, a handmade goddess sculpture shaped like a vagina, musical instruments, books, and a new stack of business cards that one participant wanted to "charge" with the community's energy. The last step of each introduction was to speak the name one wished to be called by the group. After pronouncing, chanting, singing, or whispering the name with an accompanying hand or body motion, the whole group echoed the motion and sound back three times, mirroring the same affect and energy. Out of bodies, objects, and the energy of the collective, priestesses built a dwelling for *Shekhina*, the feminine divine.

Through collective life, individual *kohanot* produce the sense of the sacred and also learn to imagine ideals through which society is created and recreated (Durkheim 1995 [1912], 425). As a religious project, Kohenet is an experiment in alternative forms of sociality. It seeks to use physical tools and imperfect bodies to build an inclusive and just Judaism, with the hope that its sacred work might eventually establish a City of Goddess in our broken world. As the construction of the altar suggests, the language of building should not be taken *too* metaphorically: Kohenet is invested in revaluing material and its relationship to the spiritual, using "ritual technologies" and "medicines" for healing the ills and easing the pains of modern life (Rock-Singer 2020). In this essay, then, I focus on the altar as a medium for prayer, creating continuity from meeting to meeting, and linking today's *kohanot* with their ancient ancestors.

As a postmodern project of religious revival, Kohenet works to craft tradition through selective archaeological and diasporic logics. Like other Jewish feminist projects working to "remake American Judaism," Kohenet strives to balance radicalism and accommodation, to curtail rabbinic power structures while claiming an authentic alternative tradition (Prell 2007, 9). To do so, Kohenet's leaders and participants reach for "usable pasts" across the depth and breadth of Jewish history (Hyman 1983), understanding their inheritances to include the practices of ancient Israelites and world Jewry alike. Kohenet also reflects broader trends in American Jewish spirituality, mixing the eclectic urban syncretism and political progressivism of countercultural Berkeley, California; the inward-turned Jewish worship that grew up in the context of "late capitalism" in such places as New York's B'nai Jeshurun; and the ritual, ecological, and healing knowledge from journeys through Starhawk's Reclaiming Community, immersions in matriarchal Afro-Brazilian Candomblé tradition, and training in Buddhist-inspired meditation or yoga (Fader 2006; Matory 2005; Pike 2004; Sigalow 2019). By weaving these multiple sources of ritual knowledge and practice into the "text-based monotheism" that emerged after the destruction of the Second Temple in 70 CE, Kohenet seeks to expand the base of "religious power" to include priestesses with a range of ritual expertise (Hammer and Shere 2015, 21–22).

In many ways, Kohenet is a textbook example of the constructive and illustrative period of what Shaul Magid calls "American post-Judaism," defined by progressive politics and metaphysical forms of spiritual seeking (Magid 2013, 7–8). This is hardly coincidental: Many of Kohenet's members are affiliated with the Renewal movement, and some consider themselves to be disciples of the late Rabbi Zalman Schachter-Shalomi (1924–2014). Kohenet has formulated a postrabbinic Judaism by integrating ancient cultic practice with subsequent rabbinic innovation. It has sought to loosen the grip of rationalism, rabbinic authority, and Halakha

(Jewish law) and to offer mystical, experiential, and "soft monotheistic" forms of worship and practice (Dillon 1999, 69).[4] Yet Magid's description is hardly sufficient.

The "post" approach conjures a tenuous distance from a recent past, of life on the teetering edge, of dissolution or a sea change—but from and into what? For whom? Kohenet is being forged by women and gender queer folks whose lives and lineages do not conform to the progressive teleology that has left masculine counterparts unencumbered by romanticism or obligations to authoritative pasts (Magid 2013, 2, 7–9). Kohenet must do the substantial labor of pulling material from often distant and seemingly disconnected pasts, exhuming traditions that had been buried with ancestors, extinguished by the Enlightenment, or smashed like idols. In the (sometimes fumbling) hands of those who were disenfranchised under the rabbinic system, Kohenet is building a Judaism through ritualized practices that leaps off the page and out of the pews, animated by the pleasure and pain of imagining new futures. Kohenet makes palpable the ways that the "post" approach analogizes, too easily allowing power relations to slip into abstraction, through interchangeable prefixes and hyphens (Jakobsen and Pelligrini 2003, 93). Thus Kohenet's rise casts light on the pertinence of gender as an analytic category for understanding "differential hybridity" in the stories of Jewish revivals: As traditions travel and mix, they are *not* reconstituted on equal grounds (Seth 2009, 380; Adams 2001).

Like other contemporary metaphysical movements, Kohenet is aware of the critiques of the "spiritual marketplace" and is sensitive to the violence of cultural appropriation (Bender 2010, 153–57). The frame of spiritual borrowing and religious syncretism, however, is predicated on normative rabbinic Judaism's assumptions about continuity and the boundaries of Jewish community that Kohenet throws into relief (Robbins 2011, 414–15). In reimagining an authentic Jewish tradition, Kohenet is faced with a problem: What is *mine*? Does rabbinic tradition belong to Jewish women, wholly or partly? To rediscover women's inheritances, Kohenet's leaders have performed a selective extraction from the past. They have mined Jewish texts, from the Bible to kabbalistic literature, to locate archetypes of powerful

---

4. *Soft monotheism* is a term, adapted from pagan late antiquity and associated with Christianity, that Jill Hammer has used to describe Kohenet's theology.

women;[5] studied the material remnants of the ancient Near East to under-stand ritual; (re)instated women's practices from early modern Ashkenaz, Sepharad, and the Levant; and connected energetically down ancestral lines to heal past trauma. To reclaim and reconstitute spiritual practices, Kohenet continually negotiates how to relate to the diverse cultures from which the group draws resources.

Kohenet has emerged from the shadow of biblical and then rabbinic traditions that sought to regulate ritual practice and worship of the divine. Specifically, biblical authors and subsequent rabbinic interpreters "fore-ignized" all altars other than those in the Temple in Jerusalem. In the pro-cess, altars became the target of polemical claims to delegitimize competing religious practices, especially improper modes of worship or devotion to other deities. In Jewish thought and contemporary scholarship, the altar remains tainted by association with idolatry, rendering it fundamentally anti-Judaic (see Batnitzky 2000; Halbertal and Margalit 1992). Kohenet rec-ognizes such claims to be "misforeignization," assertions of a singular form of authenticity within a polyvocal tradition (Ballentine 2019, 18–22) that seek to consolidate masculine power in a symbolic center.

In this essay I trace how Kohenet functions as an "altar-native" com-munity predicated on "altarity."[6] First, I position Kohenet within a broader landscape of Jewish feminism, with particular attention to contestations over whether materiality and theology are "not Jewish." I then consider how Kohenet's leaders have defended the altar's Jewish authenticity, invoking dis-courses of memory, narratives of Jewish history, and academic studies of the ancient world. I also examine how Kohenet understands the altar to be like a new Temple, which holds the potential to renew Jewish life through embodied worship, energetic connection, and reorganization of overlapping Jewish traditions. Finally, I return to the contested status of the altar, and hybrid practices more broadly, within a community attuned and sensitive to the stakes and power of a feminist revival.

---

5. The thirteen archetypes are the Shrinekeeper, the Prophetess, the Midwife, the Weaver, the Lover, the Queen, the Shamaness, the Seeker, the Wise Woman, the Fool, the Maiden, the Mother, and the Mourning Woman.

6. As Mark C. Taylor notes, altarity is semantically rich, drawing together "alterity" and "altar" (Taylor 1987, xxviii). Similarly, I combine "alterity," which invokes a commitment to otherness, and "altar," which invokes the site of sacrifice and connection to the divine. I am grateful to Michael Naparstek for helping to clarify and formulate these terms.

"Altarity": Centering the Altar and Kohenet's Place on the Fringes

Over three and a half years of ethnographic work, I heard a range of reactions to Kohenet: excitement, curiosity, ambivalent intrigue, lack of acknowledgment, and accusations of heresy. One ardently feminist, queer rabbi, who is actively working to create inclusive new forms of Jewish community, mentioned to me that she had found herself among like-minded rabbis and rabbinical students in discussing the newly released YouTube video "We Are Kohenet."[7] She recounted several responses, from "It looks sort of cultish"— that outmoded word for new religious movements that is unapologetically used to denigrate—to "*We* had to study for five or six years full-time and be evaluated to prove our knowledge and skills to become clergy." In the latter case, I do not disagree, but is that a sentiment that is shaped by my own lengthy graduate education and dependence on the authority of my institution's diploma? I chalk up the "cult" response to Kohenet's "unholy" trinity[8]—too many gods, too much material, too much sexuality—that threatens its position in Jewish life.

Like a twenty-first-century Jewish exhibition, not at a World's Fair but on the World Wide Web, Kohenet has made use of the "agency of display" (Kirshenblatt-Gimblett 1998, 75) to present its ideal vision of Jewish community: one that celebrates difference, values embodied physical and metaphysical experience, and learns from but is not beholden to the past. "We Are Kohenet" disrupts normative expectations of what Jews and Judaism "look" like (Haynes 2018; Limonic 2019). The video shows women, young and old, Black, Brown, and white, sitting in a circle or dancing freely in the forest. The trees are draped with lush red fabrics, and the women are wrapped in prayer shawls or silk garments; some are holding *siddurim* (prayer books), nestling children, beating drums, or doing needlework. The group is oriented around an altar, whose central point is a spherical rose quartz crystal topped with a small red stone. Even if you do not know the metaphysical properties of rose quartz—unconditional love and mothering—the arrangement is obviously a breast. A braided red and blue umbilical cord, which hangs down from the branches above, is wrapped

---

7. See https://www.youtube.com/watch?v=4HRovbSp4BM.
8. This is an allusion to the "unholy linkage of godlessness, communism, and homosexuality" that cast secular Jews and queers as anti-American during McCarthyism (Jakobsen 2003, 75).

around the maternal figure. The centrality of the reproductive body promises new life, nurtured by a community of women.

A montage of voices answers the question that almost every viewer must be thinking: What in Goddess's name is a Hebrew Priestess!? *We* practice embodied, earth-based spirituality. *We* worship the divine's feminine form and craft ritual to serve as "as a transformative force in Jewish and human life." After characterizing the program as "a clergy training program, a sisterhood, and a movement, changing the face of Jewish leadership," the video ends with an invitation and/or an ascription: "We need you priestessing. We need you, priestess!"

Working at the margins is a veritable feminist tradition, and Jewish feminist history has shown that the radical and peripheral have the potential to move into and transform the mainstream. In February 2015 on the Upper West Side of New York City, I attended an event, "Meet Me Again at Sinai Day of Learning," hosted at B'nai Jeshurun in honor of the twenty-fifth anniversary of Dr. Judith Plaskow's feminist theology *Standing Again at Sinai*. As the event's program booklet declared, Plaskow's groundbreaking work "shook the foundations of Jewish expression with its candid discussion of Jewish feminist theology." As Plaskow later described in an interview, it had been a long road and an uphill battle to write Jewish theology from her perspective as a lesbian woman. On her first day of graduate school in the 1970s, the formidable rabbinic scholar Judah Goldin had admonished Plaskow that "there is no such thing as Jewish theology": "Buber was a poet! Rosenzweig was a philosopher!" Goldin argued. Undeterred, Plaskow became a theologian!

Plaskow developed her theological ideas while participating in B'not Esh, a feminist spirituality collective founded in 1981. B'not Esh applied second-wave feminist consciousness-raising techniques and adapted the *havurah* movement's model of ritual community to explore the possibilities of an authentic Jewish spirituality rooted in women's experience (Plaskow 1990; Ackelsberg 1986; Breitman 1995). *Standing Again at Sinai* expressed painful longing for the Jewish center, represented by the covenant at Sinai, from which women were categorically excluded. Plaskow pinpointed Exodus 19:15 as the root of "the profound injustice of Torah itself": Moses addresses "the people," but he speaks to men, warning them of women's ritual impurity as they prepare to encounter God (Plaskow 1990, 25–26). In systematic theology and spiritual community, Plaskow sought to "reconstruct" a Jewish

world in which gender and sexual identities did not disrupt the possibilities of members' sense of wholeness and inclusion in the Jewish collective
narrative.

Forty years after Plaskow set out to become a feminist theologian,
"Meet Me Again at Sinai" called together a broad-based Jewish feminist
community to reflect on where Jewish feminism had come from and where
it was going. Its list of influential speakers included Letty Cottin Pogrebin, a
founding editor of the secular feminist *Ms.* magazine; Rabba Sara Hurwitz,
the first female Orthodox rabbinic figure ordained in the United States and
co-founder of Yeshivat Maharat, the first Open Orthodox yeshiva to ordain
women as clergy; Joy Ladin, the first openly transgender professor at Yeshiva
University; and Vanessa Hidary, a slam poet whose stage name is The
Hebrew Mamita. The arenas of participation in Jewish feminism were likewise broad: those who had fought for women's ordination across the denominational spectrum; formulated new liturgies with feminine God language;
invented new rituals to honor women's life-cycle events; written scholarship and journalistic reporting; performed social commentary through the
arts; and led nonprofit organizations or synagogues. I was excited to find
Kohenet on the program and interested to see how Kohenet's "full contact
Judaism" would fit into a program that celebrated Plaskow's systematic
theology.

The day's events began with four options for morning prayers, one of
which was Kohenet-style davening led by Rabbi Jill Hammer and her partner, Shoshana Jedwab. I wandered down a fluorescent-lit hallway to find a
plain carpeted room with folding chairs set up in a circle. At the center, Jill
and Shoshana had constructed a fitting altar: a ring of soft, rounded river
stones surrounding what appeared to be a cairn built on top of a mirror.
As Shoshana began to beat her drum, Jill explained that they had built a
mountain—technically, a pile of stones—to ground our prayer. The room
filled with curious faces, young and old, who followed along Kohenet's feminized liturgy from photocopied packets. When it came time for the Amidah,
the core series of prayers that praise, thank, and entreat God for blessings,
Kohenet dispensed with the normative practice of standing in silence and
instead invited the assembled collective to go on a pilgrimage to an imminent, tangible Sinai. Jill posed an orienting question: "What was most difficult there for *you*, as an individual?" She invited the attendees to approach
the assemblage of stones and take one to meditate on silently.

After the service, I lingered to watch as an impressive number of partic-ipants flooded the center to thank Jill and Shoshana. I heard women in their 20s and in their 70s express how excited and moved they had been to not only *stand* at Sinai but to grasp it in their hands. The power that so attracted these women repelled others. I later heard that, though Rabba Hurwitz had appeared on the program, Yeshivat Maharat had declined to officially sponsor the "Meet Me at Sinai" event because of concerns over Kohenet's participa-tion. Some, my source explained, felt that Kohenet's neopagan approach to accessing the divine through the material world crossed into the territory of *avodah zarah* (idol worship). I understood Yeshivat Maharat's refusal to be on the program to be a political statement: Religious convictions aside, the insti-tution was itself vulnerable to accusations that they were a radical and desta-bilizing force within Orthodoxy. Gaining wider acceptance in the centers of Orthodox power required drawing some bright red lines: In a broad-based feminist coalition, if Kohenet was included, Yeshivat Maharat had to bow out.

Other Jewish Memories

Months after the event "at Sinai," I asked Shoshana about the accusations of *avodah zarah*. On her face, I could see her deep pain as she formulated a response. Shoshana grew up as the child of Holocaust survivors in what she describes as a traditionally Orthodox family, and she works as a full-time Jewish day school teacher. For a long time she had been hesitant and uncomfortable with the idea of being a Hebrew Priestess. When her wife, Jill, founded Kohenet with Taya Shere, Shoshana joked, "I'll just be a Levite," the class of Israelites who supported the priests. She would accompany the work of the *kohanot* with her drum or by caring for their daughter while Jill was busy teaching and leading.

Over the years, Shoshana increasingly felt that the solid distinction between right and wrong ways to worship was a gendered double-standard: She brought up the mezuzah, the small scroll hung on the doorposts of houses. Even Maimonides, a symbol of rationalism and one of the most authoritative rabbinic voices, had acknowledged that this object had a dual resonance, serving both as a reminder of the requirements of Halakha and as a magical amulet. She noted a similar doubleness in the way her Orthodox Holocaust-survivor mother observed Shabbat. Her mother would set the candles off in a special place on the table and speak to her dead ancestors as she brought in Shabbat each week. How different were these examples, whose authenticity no one would question, from Kohenet's altar practice? Did they not all facilitate worship of the divine through immanent forms? Kohenet did not promote idol worship. Full stop. Rather, Shoshana explained, Kohenet drew on a range of Jewish traditions to worship the divine.

Shoshana grew firm in her acceptance of the altar as she came to understand it as a symbol of protest against violence. The exclusion of women from religious and public life, the erasure of altars, and—though she did not draw the line explicitly—existential threats to the Jewish people all operated through similar logics: Rivals for power were treated as dangerous others. Shoshana described how it seemed as though someone had taken a "vacuum cleaner . . . on the sacred documents": There were traces here and there, like crumbs scattered throughout biblical and rabbinic texts, that supported her intuition. She offered the examples of Miriam, Devorah, and the "indigenous priest" Jethro, who all had special powers. Later, there was Kabbalah, which was "straight pantheism" and had sparked her interest in physics, astronomy, and the paranormal. "Once you've tasted the *Sefirot* [emanations of God], [once] God as an energetic manifestation—once God is real rather than an idea, once you are not interested in the Aristotelian unmoved mover, you can be accused of all sorts of things!" Shoshana further challenged what she saw to be the role of Greek philosophy in setting the exclusive terms of Jewish tradition.

Shoshana positioned Kohenet's project *within* rather than outside Jewish history. She framed Kohenet as a radical intellectual critique of the Deuteronomic Reform's embrace of the Josianic purge in the seventh century BCE and of its continuing legacies. Shoshana shed light on the gendered violence of King Josiah's reform agenda: He facilitated the burning of statues and shrines to Asherah, the mother goddess, to consolidate his power. Likewise, the accusations that Kohenet practiced *avodah zarah* were a form of "Jewish battering," an attack on people on the edges who challenge the center. Shoshana recounted that at B'nai Jeshurun, the congregation on the Upper West Side where she davened for years, they were inclusive of LGBTQ+ issues and worked for social justice but that "they toed the Deuteronomous line and bashed idolatrous nations. What gives?" There had been enough bloodshed and enough spiritual violence.

If, to adapt Shoshana's metaphor, someone took a vacuum cleaner to the tradition to purge it of evidence of powerful women, women's power, and the feminine divine, Kohenet's response has been an attempt to flick the switch, blowing in reverse, making it all available again. Shoshana wrote a song, "I Remember," that is a midrash put to music. It encapsulates Kohenet's journey to restore women's spiritual leadership through a process of countermemory. Shoshana recounted how the song had been birthed one day when she called out to Jill, who was down the hall in their Upper West Side apartment: "Jill, is there a verse in *Tanakh* [Hebrew Bible] that is entirely written in the feminine?" Jill didn't need to think about it: "Jeremiah 2:2!" she quickly replied. In the verse God reminds Israel of its youth when it had been a more faithful companion.[9] Shoshana flipped the script: Thousands of years later, her people, the *kohanot*, called out longingly to the divine feminine, *Shekhina*, an intimate companion on the journey to liberation:

> *Zacharti lach hesed neuraich*
> *ahavat kelulotaich*
> I remember your love and your kindness
> When you walked with me
> Through desert wilderness
> I remember you
> *Leichteich acharai bamidbar*
> *Leichteich acharai b'eretz lo z'rua*
> How you walked with me
> When you were young and free
> How you walked with me
> Through the sand and sea

The vision of friendship, and perhaps queer love, was in radical contrast to the masculine God who awaited Moses atop Sinai to enter into a covenant of law.

The mountain and the book are the canonical Jewish "sensational forms," mediators of Jewish access to the divine, with a gender and sexual history that often goes unexplored (Meyer 2011, 29). As Shoshana once commented, she had always been uncomfortable with the "phallic nature

---

9. The quoted piece of the verse reads "Zacharti lach hesed neuraich ahavat kelulotaich leichteich acharai bamidbar b'eretz lo z'rua," which translates to "I remember the devotion of your youth, the love you showed me when you walked with me in the desert to a land not yet sown." I have provided a translation here that is based on Shoshana's lyrics but that is closer to an interpretation of the original verse, before it was reinterpreted.

of Sinai," which was only reinforced by the tradition of the weekly Torah reading. Shoshana dissected a system of logic, rooted in the language itself, that un-unmarked the gender of the weekly ritual. "When we take the Torah out, it is a 'She,' since Judaism is gendered," I have written in the notes I took as she spoke. Hebrew, of course, is a gendered language, and I do not know whether "Judaism" was a Freudian slip of my pen or what she actually said. Shoshana continued, describing the choreography of the Torah service: "She comes out of the *aron* [ark]," which is a kind of altar and also the word for "coffin" and "closet" in Modern Hebrew. The Torah is processed and shown off before being "placed on the *bima* [stage or raised platform] and then undressed." Then She is read. As a technology for Jewish continuity, reciting Her words is an act of inculcating people into the communal narrative: It is *reproductive*. Then, after a prayer for the sick, the service climaxes in the *hagbah*: She is held high, and the congregation crowds in close to behold Her words and to affirm the law given to the people by Moses at Sinai, a tradition that began with the scribe and priest Ezra (Nehemiah 8:5).

Rather than treat the Torah as the object of a sexual drama, a positive rite of a masculine cult, Shoshana suggested that we think of Her on Her own terms. "But the Torah talks about itself as a tree!" What would it mean to take Her at Her word? What would it mean to understand this ritualized reading as divinity "cycling through life from the birthing out of the coffin, to the story inside, to the prayer for the sick?" She had done these rituals her entire life, but it was not until recently that she was able to disentangle the medium and the message that normative rabbinic Judaism had "rendered invisible" (Meyer 2009, 12). The altar became an appealing way to queer Jewish worship, allowing practitioners to walk through the world with the divine. To embrace the aesthetics and materiality of the altar was likewise a recognition that the umbilical cord, breast, or *kior* made from women's mirrors were sacred bearers of tradition no less than the mountain and its written word.

Jewish Altar-natives?

From her social location as a rabbi who had been ordained by the Jewish Theological Seminary, Jill felt a responsibility to adjudicate the propriety of altars not only for herself but for the new religious movement she led. In one of our several interviews, I asked Jill about how and why the practice of worshipping at an altar, which strikes so many Jews as a fundamentally and *emphatically* "not-Jewish," became central to Kohenet practice. "In some ways it is connection to other earth-based traditions and goddess traditions," Jill explained, "but [altar practices] are also really a reclaiming of a space-based Jewish ritual technology." Although Jill was initially "freaked out and intrigued" when she first encountered altars in neopagan spaces, she came to understand her nervousness to be a symptom of a Jewish response to exile and destruction. Abraham Heschel's anxieties that American Jewish materiality verged on idolatry led him to develop a temporal theology, but Jill worried that authentic Jewish women's practices had become collateral damage of communal trauma (Heschel 1951; Koltun-Fromm 2015, 52–53).

Jill did historical, anthropological, and textual research to prove that the altar was not an *import* into Judaism but rather an *exile*. She found evidence of altars, or hints of them, in canonical texts from the Bible through the *Zohar*, archaeology from ancient Israelites, Jewish folklore, and practices of non-Ashkenazi communities. Altars were part of not only public spaces, such as the Temple and the *aron* and *bima* in normative American synagogues, but also private spaces, such as in ancient Israelite and modern Yemenite homes. The historical traces and living parallels led her to accept altars as "mine too," a practice that, as a Jew, she owned rather than borrowed and mixed into Jewish worship (Sigalow 2016, 1032–34).

Kohenet's altar-based worship not only challenged theological consensus but also constructed an alternative Jewish lineage that empowered women as religious authorities. Early in our Kohenet training, Jill taught us about the archetype of the *tzovah* (temple keeper), whose ritual technology, the altar, was not only native to Judaism but also essential to the recovery of women's leadership.[10] "Women's leadership didn't start in 1973. There was ancient rock art showing it!" Jill exclaimed. She set out Kohenet's method: "We are going to shift the way we think about ancient Israel," she explained. Because it was not "well documented," we would "have to rely on traces, snippets from the Bible and archaeological evidence about women's work as shrine-keepers." With material and textual evidence, Jill revised the story that rabbinic tradition canonized: "Here's the story: The Temple fell down and then there were rabbis. I'm changing the story!" Jill declared. "Here's my story: There were shrines. Sometimes they had buildings which

---

10. *Shrine* and *altar* were used interchangeably.

were dwelling places for the divine presence. There wasn't only *one* Temple. Until the first exile, there were probably multiple shrines served by different kinds of people, like Samuel and maybe even Miriam, who were not descendants of [the High Priest] Aaron. There's a lot we don't know, but here's the bottom line: There was a diverse priesthood, it included women, and though it is not emphasized, this stuff is in the Bible." One of Kohenet's central missions, Jill explained, was to bring such women's traditions to light: "They should not be invisible to us." She turned on the projector and plugged in her laptop to show us proof, in the form of images, drawn from authoritative academic articles and books.

Although past Jewish revivals, such as Ahad Ha'am's Cultural Zionism, could gain traction without laying claim to the "ontological truth" of the Exodus narrative, Kohenet's revival of a *priestesshood* could not be built from "collective, living myth" (Lederhendler 2001, 5). Since the rise of rabbinic Judaism, there had not been widely or universally accepted Jewish altar practices; many of the examples Jill used were drawn from a particular diasporic community or constructed by analogy, akin to the *bima* or *aron*. To build an ironclad case with the weight of history, Jill grounded her argument for Jewish ownership of altars in "archaeological truth" from the ancient world.

Jill's claims to the past themselves contained complications that went unmarked at Kohenet. Although there is robust consensus among historians of the ancient world that there were altars, not only in the Jerusalem Temple but also in other cultic centers (*even after* the first exile), and even indications of sacrificial rites in Israelite homes, there is no evidence that women presided over or even were involved in such rituals. Accordingly, the association between domestic space and women's authority cannot be assumed in the ancient world (Rosenblum 2013). Adding a critical layer is not meant to delegitimize the project of claiming altar practices as a site of women's spiritual leadership but rather to place Kohenet within another ancient priestly tradition. As anthropologist Nancy Jay has argued, the priesthood was, by design, a form of fictive kinship that established a male lineage with the exclusive authority over the sacrificial rites as a "remedy for having been born of woman" (Jay 1992, xxiii, 30–40). The priestess, akin to the feminist participant in ritual Torah study, performs herself into a lineage whose social structure was formed to exclude those with female reproductive potential (Alexander 2013, 249).

Materializing and Mapping the Sacred Feminine

Rav kohenet Taya, who is Ashkenazi in origin but has immersed herself in Candomblé in Brazil and New Age circles in the United States, feels very much at home with altar practice. When I asked her to explain the purpose of the altar to me, Taya described it as "a map of the embodied sacred" and "a portal for our conversation with spirit." I could tell she was choosing her words carefully, trying not to present the altar *as* the object of worship but rather as a medium that gives shape to worship and displays the community's values. She wove metaphysical traditions about energetic communication into her many descriptive registers (Bender 2010). The altar's objects served as "a communication with spirit about what it is we are activating or honoring or giving attention to," Taya explained. It functions as a social technology to connect "those in our circle [to] what we're valuing or wanting to have witnessed or have worked" and also serves as a record, "an energetic link in connection to that time and space and those we were in circle with." During the description, Taya layered the altar with meanings—a canvas that women populate with their sacred art, a representation of the pedagogical objectives of the week, a statement of intention and attention to the four directions, a form of communication—and finally, she landed on the metaphysical language of energetic connection.

Taya understood the altar to represent a broader lesson about how to revive Jewish life. "I feel like one of the main principles for me around altars is to not let them get stagnant," Taya explained.[11] Whether through moving things around, dusting them, or just "being in presence . . . on a regular basis," altars need to be tended, to continually "support and activate" their "sacred intentions." "What about memory?" I asked. Taya again tread carefully, aware of the ways in which nostalgia operated as a driving force, or form, of American Judaism (Gross 2021). Speaking strictly from her own experience, Taya reflected, "Contemporary Jewish culture for me had become really stagnant because of the immense and intense focus on memory and Jewish cultural memory to the detriment of actually what is

---

11. In fact, over the course of three years of training, I saw the altar practice evolve. When I began, there was one central altar, but over time a number of altars representing different priestess paths were added. The central altar was reserved for marking the cardinal directions, but the peripheral altars were available for community members to place objects. Taya felt that the central altar had become too cluttered and innovated communal practice in response.

relevant now, and it has really taken a recentering for me of what I choose to focus on." Taya explained, "It feels like a radical act, even activism, to be unwilling to be mired in those past stories. I have a desire to be honoring of them, but I'm not willing to let them run my Judaism or my spiritual practice or my choices around that." Translating into a familiar academic language, Taya said that the shift she desired was often talked about in terms of "moving from the people of the book to the people of the body," but she rejected that dichotomy: "It's not about 'not books.' It's much more about not-burdens . . . not needing to hold stories that no longer serve or [are] no longer live." Sensitive to the idioms of the day and the violence of the past, Taya proposed that change to tradition could be approached like a clothing swap rather than a purge.

As Taya spoke, I sensed paradoxes in the logic of the project as far as the metaphor—or media—of "stuff" was concerned. "Was Kohenet not built on the recovery of lost practices?" I asked. "Totally! And even a lot of what we're rediscovering we're rediscovering *because* it was lost. The material has been lost. We wish it hadn't been lost. And so, there's this dual edge around it, and it feels like a dance really of right balance and being careful what we're putting weight on," Taya explained. That messy process of discernment was the fundamental work of how Taya imagined Kohenet's Jewish spiritual leadership.

In the winter retreat, in February 2015, in a workshop on ritual practice, Taya framed her approach to a vibrant, fluid Jewish leadership as a shift from *being* to *doing* Jewish: "My practice life is more exciting than identity because it is active," Taya offered. Ahava, a Jew of Color whose priestess work focused on bridging cultures, raised her hand to ask a question: "Do non-Jewish practices become Jewish by virtue of me doing them?" Taya responded, rejecting Jewish boundary work that often had a hierarchical edge: "I don't like to otherize and say non-Jewish." I could sense Ahava's unease as she tried to articulate a vision of hybridity that honored origins and celebrated encounters (Engler 2009), painting a picture of maps with overlapping and fuzzy borders. Taya quickly cut back in, realizing that razing boundaries could also create vulnerability: "I don't mean to say something culturally appropriative." Zelda, an activist invested in decolonization, offered a third model, one of diplomacy predicated on gift economies. "When I smudge, I do so as a Jew who has received this practice as a gift. I can represent my people and our ancient people that have been lost as an interterritorial ambassador. I consider it a great honor." Zelda approached ritual as an "implicated subject," aware of contested pasts and presents that materialized in Kohenet's worship practices (Rothberg 2019).

It was not only outsiders to the community, such as those who refused to "meet *Kohenet* again at Sinai," who worried about Jewish borderlines (Boyarin 2004). Over the years that I spent in the Kohenet community, we had many conversations about a topic that has been called different things depending on a person's (sometimes multiple) perspective(s): cultural appropriation, colonization, borrowing, mixing, sharing, or honoring. For some with strictly observant backgrounds, altars provoked "idol anxiety"; other participants, conditioned by experiences in families of Holocaust survivors, queer identities, or survivors of trauma, feared being a perpetrator of cultural violence; and those who came from spiritual or neopagan communities were primed to understand cultural borrowing as an unproblematic, even quintessentially human thing to do (Sigalow 2016; Bender and Cadge 2006). The range of responses to and sensitivities about Kohenet's altar practices were intellectual and affective expressions of the hybridity of refraction, tensions over identity and practice *within* the Kohenet community (Engler 2009, 571).

Altars should be understood as "a nexus of competitive ritualizations and/or discursive claims" no less today than among "ancient practitioners and cultural producers" on whom Kohenet bases its claims of authenticity (Ullucci 2015, 388). For those who arrive at Kohenet from neopagan communities, paradoxically, it is easy for the "hyperapparent" altar, which makes tangible the presence of God, to disappear into the very architecture of the community (Meyer 2011, 32–34). As a spiritual technology, the altar does the work of aligning the Goddess, the body, the community, the earth, and the cosmos for worship by a particular community. Dorothy, a Jew-witch in her 70s who had participated in Starhawk's Reclaiming community, was very much at home around an altar, which she felt had organizing, orienting, and balancing effects. Dorothy laid out the chain of associations on which Kohenet's neopagan, earth-based Judaism was built as she described the altar's construction: "Stones in the north, feathers and flying things in the east, fiery things in the south, cups and water vessels in the west." The four elements, she explained, map onto parts of the body and the four kabbalistic worlds, and she began to sing one of the many communal chants Taya had adapted from a pagan song: "Earth my body, water my blood, air my breath, and fire my spirit. Earth, *asiya* [action]; water, *yetzirah* [formation]; air, *briyah* [creation], and fire, *atzilut* [emanation]." It was an invocation of sacred geography, ritualized in the building and disassembly of the altar to open and close retreat time, that conjoined the body with the cosmos. The repetition of the song, like the ritualization of the community, concretized embodied lives into the altar: a new kind of impermanent, decentralized temple that could be made and remade.

Conclusion

In the epigraph that began this essay, the poet invites her reader to recognize the wisdom of destruction: From nature's cycles we can realize the necessity of letting go in order to make room for new life. Situated in overgrown ruins of the Temple, which is both her history and an inhibiting structure, she offers a meditation on writing new rules to best serve the needs of the living. Being with Kohenet made me acutely aware of the strange position of "Western" women as colonizer and colonized, of people who feel the nostalgia but must dig in the dirt and in the margins for the forgotten, destroyed, and censored over hundreds and thousands of years.

The altar is the arena of this contested status. On the one hand, it is a centering device that orients, maps, and organizes sacred space; binds the community together; and connects temporally and spatially distant points in Kohenet's spiritual geography. On the other hand, the altar is a symbol of and a technology that reinforces Kohenet's alterity. The altar thus serves as a window into the gendered politics of Jewish authenticity and, by extension, the gendered limits and possibilities of Jewish revivals.

References

Ackelsberg, Martha. 1986. "Spirituality, Community, and Politics: B'not Esh and the Feminist Reconstruction of Judaism." *Journal of Feminist Studies in Religion* 2(2): 109–20.

Adams, Vincanne. 2001. "The Sacred and the Scientific: Ambiguous Practices of Science in Tibetan Medicine." *Cultural Anthropology* 16(4): 542–75.

Alexander, Elizabeth Shanks. 2013. *Gender and Timebound Commandments in Judaism*. New York: Cambridge University Press.

Ballentine, Debra. 2019. "Foreignization in Ancient Competition." *Journal of Religious Competition in Antiquity* 1(1): 18–36.

Batnitzky, Leora. 2000. *Idolatry and Representation: The Philosophy of Franz Rosenzweig Reconsidered.* Princeton, NJ: Princeton University Press.

Bender, Courtney. 2010. *The New Metaphysicals: Spirituality and the American Religious Imagination.* Chicago: University of Chicago Press.

Bender, Courtney, and Wendy Cadge. 2006. "Constructing Buddhism(s): Interreligious Dialogue and Religious Hybridity." *Sociology of Religion* 67(3): 229–47.

Boyarin, Daniel. 2004. *Border Lines: The Partition of Judeo-Christianity.* Philadelphia: University of Pennsylvania Press.

Breitman, Barbara E. 1995. "Social and Spiritual Reconstruction of Self Within a Feminist Jewish Community." In *Women's Spirituality, Women's Lives*, ed. Judith Ochshorn and Ellen Cole, 73–82. New York: Haworth Press.

Dillon, John. 1999. "Monotheism in the Gnostic Tradition." In *Pagan Monotheism in Late Antiquity*, ed. Polymnia Athanassiadi and Michael Frede, 69–80. New York: Oxford University Press.

Durkheim, Emile. 1995 [1912]. *The Elementary Forms of Religious Life*, trans. Karen E. Fields. New York: Free Press.

Engler, Steven. 2009. "Umbanda and Hybridity." *Numen* 56(5): 545–77.

Fader, Ayala. 2006. "Jewish Spirituality and Late Capitalism." *Jewish Culture and History* 8(3): 40–61.

Gross, Rachel B. 2021. *Beyond the Synagogue: Jewish Nostalgia as Religious Practice.* New York: New York University Press.

Halbertal, Moshe, and Avishai Margalit. 1992. *Idolatry*, trans. Naomi Goldblum. Cambridge, MA: Harvard University Press.

Hammer, Jill, and Taya Shere. 2015. *The Hebrew Priestess: Ancient and New Visions of Jewish Women's Spiritual Leadership.* Teaneck, NJ: Ben Yehuda Press.

Haynes, Bruce D. 2018. *The Soul of Judaism: Jews of African Descent in America.* New York: New York University Press.

Heinze, Andrew R. 2004. *Jews and the American Soul: Human Nature in the Twentieth Century.* Princeton, NJ: Princeton University Press.

Heschel, Abraham Joshua. 1951. *The Sabbath: Its Meaning for Modern Man.* New York: Farrar, Straus & Young.

Hyman, Paula. 1983. "The Jewish Family: Looking for a Usable Past." In *On Being a Jewish Feminist: A Reader*, ed. Susannah Heschel, 19–26. New York: Schocken.

Jakobsen, Janet. 2003. "Queers Are Like Jews, Aren't They? Analogy and Alliance Politics." In *Queer Theory and the Jewish Question*, ed. Daniel Boyarin, Daniel Itzkovitz, and Ann Pellegrini, 64–89. New York: Columbia University Press.

Jakobsen, Janet, and Ann Pelligrini. 2003. *Love the Sin: Sexual Regulation and the Limits of Religious Freedom*. New York: New York University Press.

Jay, Nancy. 1992. *Throughout Your Generations Forever: Sacrifice, Religion, and Paternity*. Chicago: University of Chicago Press.

Kirshenblatt-Gimblett, Barbara. 1998. *Destination Culture: Tourism, Museums, and Heritage*. Berkeley: University of California Press.

Koltun-Fromm, Ken. 2015. *Imagining Jewish Authenticity: Vision and Text in American Jewish Thought*. Bloomington: Indiana University Press.

Lederhendler, Eli. 2001. "Introduction: The 'Problem of Judaism' Today—Beyond Assimilation and Nationalism." In *Who Owns Judaism? Public Religion and Private Faith in America and Israel*, ed. Eli Lederhendler, 3–12. New York: Oxford University Press.

Limonic, Laura. 2019. *Kugel and Frijoles: Latino Jews in the United States*. Detroit: Wayne State University Press.

Magid, Shaul. 2013. *American Post-Judaism: Identity and Renewal in a Postethnic Society*. Bloomington: Indiana University Press.

Matory, J. Lorand. 2005. *Black Atlantic Religion: Tradition, Transnationalism, and Matriarchy in the Afro-Brazilian Candomblé*. Princeton, NJ: Princeton University Press.

Meyer, Birgit. 2009. "Introduction: From Imagined Communities to Aesthetic Formations—Religious Mediations, Sensational Forms, and Styles of Binding." In *Aesthetic Formations: Media, Religion, and the Senses*, ed. Birgit Meyer, 1–30. New York: Palgrave Macmillan.

Meyer, Birgit. 2011. "Mediation and Immediacy: Sensational Forms, Semiotic Ideologies, and the Question of the Medium." *Social Anthropology* 19(1): 23–39.

Pike, Sarah M. 2004. *New Age and Neopagan Religions in America*. New York: Columbia University Press.

Plaskow, Judith. 1990. *Standing Again at Sinai: Judaism from a Feminist Perspective*. San Francisco: Harper & Row.

Prell, Riv-Ellen. 2007. "Introduction: Feminism and the Remaking of American Judaism." In *Women Remaking American Judaism*, ed. Riv-Ellen Prell, 1–23. Detroit: Wayne State University Press.

Robbins, Joel. 2011. "Crypto-Religion and the Study of Cultural Mixtures: Anthropology, Value, and the Nature of Syncretism." *Journal of the American Academy of Religion* 79(2): 408–24.

Rock-Singer, Cara. 2020. "Milk Sisters: Forging Sisterhood at Kohenet's Hebrew Priestess Institute." *Nashim: A Journal of Jewish Women's Studies & Gender Issues* 37(fall): 87–114.

Rosenblum, Jordan D. 2013. "Home Is Where the Hearth Is? A Consideration of Jewish Household Sacrifice in Antiquity." In *"The One Who Sows Bountifully": Essays in Honor of Stanley K. Stowers*, ed. Caroline Johnson Hodge, Saul M. Olyan, Daniel Ullucci, and Emma Wasserman, 153–63. Atlanta: SBL Press.

Rothberg, Michael. 2019. *The Implicated Subject: Beyond Victims and Perpetrators.* Stanford, CA: Stanford University Press.

Seth, Suman. 2009. "Putting Knowledge in Its Place: Science, Colonialism, and the Postcolonial." *Postcolonial Studies* 12(4): 373–83.

Sigalow, Emily. 2016. "Towards a Sociological Framework of Religious Syncretism in the United States." *Journal of the American Academy of Religion* 84(4): 1029–55.

Sigalow, Emily. 2019. *American JewBu: Jews, Buddhists, and Religious Change.* Princeton, NJ: Princeton University Press.

Taylor, Mark C. 1987. *Altarity.* Chicago: University of Chicago Press.

Ufford, Walter Shephard. 1897. *Fresh Air Charity in the United States.* New York: Bonnell, Silver.

Ullucci, Daniel. 2015. "Sacrifice in the Ancient Mediterranean: Recent and Current Research." *Currents in Biblical Research* 13(3): 388–439.

IV
RETROSPECTS

Part IV brings the volume to a close with the voices of two prominent fig-ures in Jewish revival history and scholarship. An active protagonist in the American *havurah* movement, Rabbi Michael Paley reflects on a unique moment in recent Jewish history during which alternative forms of per-formance, experience, devotion, and spirituality first emerged. Paley's life story provides a rare opportunity to share the dramatic dilemmas of young Jewish intellectuals striving to recalibrate Jewish worship with the concerns of the turbulent counterculture of the 1960s. Combining the charismatic fervor of soul searching with the abstract formality of Jewish and non-Jewish philosophy, Paley and his fellows created new postdenominational forms of prayer and study that have left their mark to this day. An ongoing reference in Jewish renewal memory, the *havurah* remains a *model of* cultural critique and a *model for* new types of Jewish intentional communities.

The volume concludes with a postscript by leading anthropologist Jonathan Boyarin. Providing a critical overview of each chapter, he ties together the major concerns of revival activists and scholars—temporality and identity, space and text, form and content. The plurality and breadth of Jewish revival are both its strength and its weakness. Thus the key to the enduring effect of Jewish revival is reflexivity and self-recognition: Revival can be recognized as such because its proponents recognize themselves as revivalists. Coming full circle, Boyarin takes us to the heart of the powerful paradox of revival and renewal movements: By virtue of breaking with the past, they necessarily lay claim to (interrupted) continuities and renewed authenticities.

13

"High Liability Judaism"

A Countercultural Autobiography
of Havurat Shalom

Michael Paley

The counterculture movement of the 1960s played a major role in reviving Jewish American life. From the *havurah* (literally "fellowship") movement of the 1970s to the independent minyanim of the 2000s, postdenominationalism, feminism, and neo-Hasidism revolutionized contemporary notions of Jewishness. "If American Judaism is in a renaissance," Riv-Ellen Prell writes, "it is in part due to countercultural impulses that have taken shape within specific generations living out a Jewish practice in relationship to their own time and on their own terms" (Prell 2007, 38). One of the most influential groups of the 1970s was Havurat Shalom of Somerville, Massachusetts, whose founding members, among them Rabbi Arthur Green[1] and Rabbi Zalman Schachter-Shalomi,[2] would emerge as leading figures in the American renewal scene in the second half of the twentieth century. Rabbi Michael Paley, a member of Havurat Shalom, persistently advocates for the creation of "small, intense communities of social action within Jewish narratives." Recently named by *Newsweek* magazine as one of the fifty most influential rabbis in America, Paley's biography

---

1. Rabbi Arthur (Art) Green (b. 1941) is an American scholar of Jewish mysticism and a key figure in the neo-Hasidic revival. He was a founding dean of the nondenominational rabbinic program at Hebrew College in Boston.
2. Rabbi Zalman Schachter-Shalomi (1924–2014) is considered the spiritual leader and founder of the Jewish Renewal movement.

reflects the ongoing vitality of contemporary Jewish life in North America.

Paley was born in 1952 in Brookline, Massachusetts, and was raised in nearby Chestnut Hill, growing up in what he describes as a "vapid, Torah-less, Jewish suburban environment." Paley became engaged in Judaism early in his life and joined Havurat Shalom in 1968. He went on to attend the Reconstructionist Rabbinical College in Philadelphia and Yeshivat HaMivtar in Jerusalem and studied Jewish and Islamic philosophy and science at Brandeis and Temple University. He was the first *havurah*-ordained rabbi and Rabbi Zalman Schachter-Shalomi's second *musmach* (ordained rabbi). After becoming a rabbi, Paley served as the Jewish chaplain at Dartmouth College, where he founded the Conference for Rural Jews. He was also a dean at Bard College, where he taught Jewish studies, and the university chaplain at Columbia University. Paley founded the Edgar M. Bronfman Youth Fellowship program in Israel, which brings together outstanding students from diverse Jewish backgrounds, and was a vice-president of the Wexner Heritage Program. From 1997 to 2017 he served as the Pearl and Ira Meyer Scholar in Residence and the Director of the Jewish Resource Center at UJA-Federation of New York.

In 2018 Paley moved to Budapest, where he works for the Joint Distribution Committee to organize the Jewish community. "There's only one place to be for the Jewish revival in Eastern Europe and that's Budapest," Paley said in a recent interview. "Hungary was always anti-Semitic. But Hungarian Jews don't want to leave Hungary," he realized. "They want to bring something else to the narrative, a rebirth, a reawakening" (Mark 2018).

The rest of this chapter relays excerpts from Paley's autobiographical narrative (selected by this volume's editors) from a life-story interview he gave to oral historian Jayne Guberman on February 14, 2017, as part of the Jewish Counterculture Oral History Project (Paley 2017).

"Awakening as a Jew"

The Six Day War had the greatest impact of any event in the history of my life, without question. I'm sure I wouldn't be sitting here with you without the Six Day War. In 1966, I went on the UJA bar mitzvah pilgrimage to Israel. My parents were Zionists, after all. So, [we] got on a plane, a bunch of guys and women. It was 1966. It was a really amazing trip, and it engaged me with Israel.

I knew Israel before. I'd been. So to have a war in a place I'd been was much different from kids who were just learning about Israel. But the decisive impact of the Six Day War was that it was a victory. And there had been nothing positive about my Jewish identity up until that moment. It was all post-Holocaust, boring Hebrew schools, bad cooking—that turned out to be only my grandmother. I don't know, what was the good part of Judaism? It was like, nothing. Nothing good about Judaism except that we were all Jews.

I am awakening as a Jew. But I'm not talking personally here; I'm talking historically. Even though I thought Judaism was now engaging, and I liked going to shul [Yiddish for "synagogue"] and things like that, what was Judaism in suburban Boston? In Chestnut Hill, of all places? There was no content to it. I was getting some content, but the environment of Judaism had no success in it. And then all of a sudden, out of nowhere, a miracle. All right, I can give you my demurral on it now, but there's no doubt that at 15 years old, that all of a sudden—I remember, Halloween in October 1967. John Shapiro and I dressed up as Moshe Dayan. We had, some years earlier, dressed up as Castro. So we had army fatigues and a cigar and a beard. So now we used army fatigues and a patch. It was the first Jews we'd ever dressed up as.

The Six Day War was just filled with miracle and pride. And we were the winners. We had come from the Holocaust, and there were Holocaust survivors on our street, and it was devastating. I mean, since the *This Is Your Life* show of Gregor Shelkin—that's my images of Judaism. And all of a sudden, we were the winners. It was revolutionary, absolutely revolutionary. And people were talking about Israel, and talking about Jews, and Jews were now strong. I went to Brookline High School during those years, and it was a totally Jewish existence for me in high school. But all of a sudden, the conversations changed. Everything changed. Everything changed in the Six Day War.

"Civil Rights Was Their Religion"

We were tremendously involved with civil rights because of my parents. My father was the head of the Temple Forum, which was a very fecund place for civil rights leaders, like Martin Luther King, and Thurgood Marshall, and Medgar Evers, James Meredith, and all these people to come and fundraise. And Kivie Kaplan came, and all these people—they all came, and my father was the person that organized this. And so Thurgood Marshall came to our house, and we all met Medgar Evers. I have pictures, you know, of those moments. And then Martin Luther King came to Mishkan Tefila [a prominent Conservative synagogue in Boston], and I went and saw him. I'm young. I'm too young—it's '63–'64, I'm 10, 11, 12 years old—but I'm watching my father, and my identity is being formed by my parents' activism. They're not Freedom Riders, but they're very much engaged. They're on the older side of that. Civil rights was their religion, in some ways. That, I would say, civil rights movement was their Jewish identity, and they did it with all [the] other Jews. That was it.

They did go to demonstrations, but they didn't go to the big ones, not that I know of at least. I don't remember. But because of the money aspect of it, civil rights leaders came to us. I mean, my father—when Thurgood Marshall was the head of the NAACP, civil defense/legal defense fund, he came to our house. Thurgood Marshall. And my father underlined how important of a deal that was. That was really significant in every way. So then when Vietnam came around, my father was for the war in Vietnam—kind of a John F. Kennedy, anticommunist, cold warrior, for the beginning of it. But I was totally radicalized by it.

So when I'm 15 in '67, the Vietnam War is all of a sudden becoming more and more in the news. And by '68, the Summer of Love, I'm the perfect age. There was no Jewish part of the antiwar movement, and there was no antiwar movement part of the Jewish existence. But in 1968, Larry Silverstein, who was then the assistant rabbi at Mishkan Tefila and a graduate student at Brandeis, gave a talk against the war at my cousin Lisa Miller's bat mitzvah. And her grandfather, who was a Gold Star [veteran]—lost his leg in the war, I don't know, maybe he didn't lose it in the war, whatever the story is—just, they were, they went ballistic about that.

"That's How I Got Myself Invited to the *Havurah*"

I was euphoric that finally someone was mentioning the Vietnam War in shul. And so all of a sudden those things came together. And then my Jewish side, and my activist side, which had been totally separate, all of a sudden started to visit each other a little bit. And then in '69, I went to a draft resistance demonstration, in the Chelsea Naval Yard, and I met Michael Brooks, and Art Green, people that were all there. They had, they had *tallisim* [prayer shawls] on. They were wearing—then and even now, I noticed—I went to the demonstration where the rabbis got arrested, last week. All the rabbis that got arrested all wore *tallisim*, you know, and I wore a *tallis*. And in 1968 I just had never seen anybody wearing a *tallis* at a demonstration before. And that's how I got myself invited to the *havurah*.

Michael Brooks said, "Why don't you come for dinner?" Just Shabbos dinner. But he said, "Come first—we're going to have davening [Yiddish for 'praying']." So I said I didn't know what davening meant. So, what does davening mean? He says, "We're going to pray; we're going to pray on Friday night and then we'll have dinner." I said, cool. I was up for anything, I was like, being a hippie. If they said, And we're going to drop acid after that—cool, you know, cool. Then we're going to overthrow the government. Cool. I don't know, I was up for it!

It was the very beginning of the *havurah*. It started in September, I think, of '68. The people coming for dinner that night are Larry Laufman, and, I mean, you know—all these *havurah*, I think Barry Holtz. For me, I'm younger—I'm precocious, let's say that. And so we walk into the davening, and Zalman—first of all, it's in the living room of an apartment in Cambridge, as opposed to Mishkan Tefila.

I think Zalman was wearing a *shtreimel* [a fur hat worn by Hasidic men] but not all the time. And I think he has his kid on his knee. I mean, this is not Mishkan Tefila. This is through the looking glass. This is the Beatles. This is the Moody Blues. This is a totally different experience of Jewish life. He starts off with a *niggun* [Hasidic tune]. I didn't know what a *niggun* was. I only had Junior Congregation. I had done some chanting with Hare Krishna. So, maybe I'd experienced that, you know. And then there was a group called the Electric Prunes. And they did masses, rock masses. So I had gone to a place called The Damaged Angel, on Arlington Street, and they would do chanting there. So I knew something about chanting. I didn't know that it existed in Judaism. And then Zalman just did this *niggun*, for like an hour.

I started to go off and say, "How about the davening? How about the service?" And he said, "This is the service." And I said, "Are we allowed to do that?" He said, "We're in charge." And that was a really important moment. We are in charge. We can do anything we want. My mother had assaulted my grandmother for eating lobster out and being kosher at home. Like, you know, it was black or white, and religion was black, and the rest of the Enlightenment world was white. And all of a sudden we were in charge, we could do anything we want. We can fix it. We can make it spiritual, I don't know.

"I Was Transported Right Through"

This was one hundred percent transporting. Transporting. If I thought that there was the realm of "I and Thou" and I was trapped in the I-It, this was the opening of the door. I was transported right through, right up. I've never been back since then. And my whole life changed then. It has never turned back. I've always been able to open the davening door. Since that time, since that day. Zalman did something for me that was just the great gift of my life. He opened the door to another realm of being. If there's a counterculture for me, it's the next realm of being. It was friendship. It was slow. Remember, in Mishkan Tefila, they were slow. I had dyslexia. I could barely keep up. I could barely read Hebrew. I could barely read English. Now all of a sudden, Zalman's going—he could go on for a minute, or two minutes, one word. Well, I said, by the end of the first minute, I could do the word, repeat it five times. By the fourth or fifth time, it was like—it was like, perfect.

It was intellectual, and it was spiritual. Someone told some Hasidic *may-sehse* [tale] and we talked about politics and about the movement. And it was sexy. I don't want to—I'm in the height of sexy at this time, and I never wanted to leave. And all the people I met that night are still my friends. I never left. I never left. I mean, the funny thing is, it was just one little quirk here. I went away in the end of '68, and I went back to the *havurah* from wherever I'd gone to the mountains. I had this great group I was a part of, and then I couldn't find them! I don't exactly remember how I found—maybe Richie Siegel showed up teaching at Mishkan Tefila. I actually don't remember how I found them, but then they were in Somerville, so that was—then once I found them, it was a better place. Now they had a whole house. So that was—thank God! I was this close to probably becoming a Buddhist.

"I'll Be Kosher Starting Tomorrow"

I became kosher in one day. Like, I went to the *havurah*, and then I said, I think I should become kosher. And then I came home, and I said to my mother, "I've become kosher." And she said, "That's too bad because we have the ham with the pineapple circles." You know, pinned onto it with cloves. And she said, "I know you like that." And I said, "Oh, I do like that. I'll be kosher starting tomorrow." But then I was—I was pretty kosher. I was completely kosher at home, had my own little set of utensils and dishes. But on Sunday, because my grandfather wasn't kosher and they served chicken, I would eat that because I didn't want to tell my grandfather. I was afraid; I was afraid to tell my grandfather I was becoming more and more medieval.

I was going to be a "back to the earth" guy. And for me, Harriet Mann taught a thing called the "food seminar" at the *havurah*. And to raise our consciousness. I think, it even got quoted in the *New York Times* about how kashrut should change—you know, it should be eco-friendly. We raised chickens. We bought chickens, and we raised them in the back of the *havurah*.

Zalman showed us how to slaughter them. So we slaughtered them. I slaughtered one of them, and then we sacrificed them, on a hibachi. Hibachis were all the rage back then, you know, little Japanese hibachis. That was a pivotal experience, and I never ate meat again after that.

I became a vegetarian. And not just a vegetarian, I became a *kana*, a zealot. So if you look in the front page of the *Jewish Catalog*, you'll see a person with a *tallis* over his head, looking out over some space or something like that. And it's me, and you can know that because I started wearing suspenders, because I wouldn't wear a leather belt anymore. And I wouldn't wear leather shoes. Only a baseball glove. Now I wear leather shoes and a belt. But for years and years I wore only suspenders. We were not *frum* [Yiddish for "religious"]. We were in the counterculture. Everything had a rich symbolic meaning, and we'd talk about it for hours. And read about it and think about it. It was fantastic.

"We Were Going to Write a New *Shulchan Aruch*"

I was in my senior year in high school. I needed to learn about Judaism, in a way that I had not learned about Judaism, so I started to go to Maimonides and take classes, including Rav Soloveitchik's *gemara shiur* [a Talmud lesson], and I made lots of progress during that period of time. It was an incredibly "whoa!" movement in my head toward Judaism. I'd learned—I was learning. In that year or two, I was a *masmid* [persistent student]. I was one hundred percent sitting and learning. I'm having just an eye-opening experience for me. These books on the shelf are all of a sudden turning into words and ideas. It was magic! And then I'm going to the *havurah* every morning to study. And I really need to learn, I'm just desperate, really. And I said to Art Green, "I just have to do this everyday, I have to drop out of high school and come and study." So he said, "Well, we don't have an everyday program." So I said, "I need to just come sit here and study everyday." He says, "Well, there is a group that's getting together to study everyday. But they are the radical communitarians." "Well," I said, "I'm a radical communitarian."

So I went to study every day. Every day. I would get up in the morning, I would drive to Somerville, and I would study with them all morning long, and the late afternoon I would go back and take a class at high school. Humash and Rashi and finally Mishnah and Gemara everyday. With these people. Art [Green] on Monday—I'm making up the days. But Art on Monday, and Swersky on Tuesday, Rosenberg on Wednesday, Reimer on Thursday, and Jacobson on Friday. And then sometimes somebody else would come in. It was the only—we were like the Qumran. We thought that we were going to be the *ner tamid* [eternal flame]. We felt that constant study would save the world, along with activism. And so that's who we were. That's really who we were. We were the Qumran cult. And then, no one else in the *havurah* wanted to be the Qumran cult. They wanted to go to graduate school, learn like that. We left, and we moved.

There were teachers, but it was absolutely an egalitarian committed place. We didn't want to do models of the tzaddik [literally, "the righteous one," the charismatic leader of a Hasidic sect], you know. So Art was probably less the guru than he thought and more than we admitted. But he was the brilliant figure. You know, I mean, if you went to the *havurah* on Shabbos morning and the *d'var torahs* [literally, "word of the Torah"] that he would give—just his reading the Torah and then translate, all of a sudden breaking into English during the middle of the learning. Women davening. It was revolutionary. It was never going to be—I don't think that the seminary idea really ever happened. It was a *havurah* and not a seminary.

We were redeveloping, we were rethinking—we were going to write a new *Shulchan Aruch* [Hebrew for "set table"; the *Shulchan Aruch* is the most widely accepted compilation of Jewish law]. This was post-Holocaust. We needed to redo things. The counterculture wasn't the general culture only; it was Jewish culture. So *haver, rav haver* is a phrase you can see in the Gemara, and we were going to be a *haver* [partner]. And it had the Qumran parts to it as well. That class, on Neusner's *Fellowship in Judaism*, I think it's called, it was a significant book for me. Jacob Neusner did not invent the *havurah* as he often said that he did, but he did have an influence on it, you know.

"We Were Fake Europeans"

There was a certain sense that we were in the next cycle of Judaism. What Zalman would come to call the "Third Age." I think Zalman then finally called it the "fourth turning of Hasidism." There's all these kinds of articles and things like that. But what we knew was that American Judaism was much more significant than anyone was giving it credit for, so that when I was growing up, all the teachers were either Israelis or Europeans. And we were Americans. It wasn't all going to end up in Israel, so the *shelilat hagolah*, the negation of the Diaspora, was a significant thing to push against. We were going to live in America. Aliyah, Israel was going to be important to us. [But] it wasn't going to be everything.

It was a huge fight—not clear, but dominant. Within the *havurah*. Bill Novak left the *havurah* over it. It was a significant question. Why didn't we all just move to Israel? You want to start an urban kibbutz, move to Israel. It's the home of the urban kibbutz. We were Americans. That's a significant piece of all this. We were Americans that weren't moving to Israel and remembered Europe, even though we had never been there. We only learned it through Ruth Rubin records. You know. We were fake Europeans. A lot of this was fake European, fake shtetl. We were rebuilding the shtetl. The mystical world that we were interested in transplanting was from this bloody soil of Europe, and we're going to build it again in Somerville, in America, without pogroms. Could you rebuild the shtetl without the pogroms—because it's America? That was the question that hung over the whole experience. It was a very deliberate experience.

The *havurah* was a very intentional community. Everything meant something. We bought Yiddish records. We didn't find old Yiddish people to come and sing to us so we'd learn their *niggunim*. We got records! Because it was America! You learned songs on records. It was—well, I should interpret it. It was a disruptive experience. We were not trying to reignite the shtetl. It was disruption in the middle of it. So we were not getting survivors to come in and live with us so we could once again be Poland or central Ukraine. We're studying Bratislaver texts, but with Art—in translation, with psychology, with history, with modern methodology, with literary criticism. We were not Hasidim of the Bratislaver Rebbe. We were study partners of Arthur Green. And that is a disruptive experience. It was not in a continuity. I think it was intentionally a step removed. It was thankfully a step removed. There are many bad things that happened back there. We were not trying to revive them. We were trying to do this whole thing. We were also positive Jews. We had all grown up as negative Jews, before the Six Day War. We were positive Jews there.

David Roskies wrote this fascinating article called "Creative Betrayal." And that's what we were doing. It was creative betrayal. We were not continuing in that world. We were recreating a world that was a betrayal of the world of Ben-Zion Gold [a Harvard rabbi and Polish Holocaust survivor]. A renaissance in that way. Renaissance. It's a rebirth experience. We were in a rebirth experience. We were not doing something that had no precedent or was radically new. It was just—we were not replicating. It was not new wine in old casks, or old wine in new casks. It was something different. Something new. That's what we thought. And I think we were right.

"Dropping Acid with Zalman"

My senior year, just before I wanted to go to rabbinical school, I had *sefikot b'emunah*, as we call them, you know, doubts in my faith. And I haven't had them that often, to tell you the truth. I don't know, I've had a lot of consistency. So Zalman said, "We're going to go to Brooklyn and we'll see the [Lubavitcher] Rebbe." Zalman was a pretty constant figure in that period. He had a tremendous impact on people's relationship to davening, to spirituality, to mysticism, to all the things that you're talking about. He was just a unique figure. And I don't even mention the acid aspect of it, which was also a part of my spiritual quest. Dropping acid with Zalman in the context of the *havurah*, on two occasions. We used to go and smoke and also, in these cases, drop acid. It was a segment of the *havurah* that was experimenting.

So I go to Brooklyn with a guy called Corey Fischer, who's like an actor, and Charlie Roth. I remember all this really well. It was just this time of year because it was Shabbos Shira. And Zalman's walking—I'm going through Brooklyn with Zalman, and Zalman knows like everybody. He's greeting them. He's giving them hugs. "Meshullam Zalman" they call him—you know, we didn't call him Shullam Zalman, like that. I walked out of the world, you know, into, like, a whole different thing. And then we stayed in someone's apartment. But then we get to the davening Shacharis [morning prayer] on Sunday morning, I think. On 770 [the moniker for the Lubavitcher rebbe house and world headquarters]. You know, if you walk on 770, there's like a big *beit midrash* [study hall] behind, it's right there—in the anteroom. And there's the Rebbe. He's coming in. I think he gives Zalman a hug. I feel Zalman is welcome there, tremendously. But Zalman thinks he's being rejected, so it's not a light moment for Zalman either. He's not doing it just for me. He's doing it, you know—he's going back to Lubavitch.[3]

So then he says something to the Rebbe, and the Rebbe comes over to me, and he wants to know about neutrino spin. Do neutrinos spin and do they spin clockwise or counterclockwise? He asked me to comment on proton decay. And then he starts asking me questions on ionization issues. I knew all the answers to all the questions. They're not hard questions. They're questions that a first- or second-year student would know. He asked them like a thunder. They're coming like waves crashing against my head. It's like, whoo—question after question. I know all the answers. I only say a word or a fragment of a word and then whoo! another question comes. And all of a sudden, I am—I'm in a different space. My head is—I don't know. The world is collapsing on my head, you know. And then he said, "Don't become a Hasid. Go back to the university." And he walks off, like that.

3. Originally a high-ranking Chabad Hasid, Rabbi Zalman Schachter-Shalomi was one of the first two *shlichim* (emissaries) for the Lubavitcher Rebbe. Even after his separation from the mainstream Chabad movement, he was recorded by David Ingber saying, "I'm still Lubavitch, if Lubavitch kept on changing. But Lubavitch stopped changing. But if they had kept on changing, I'd be in the middle of Lubavitch" (in Paley 2017).

The whole thing takes about four or five minutes. And I—I just have to sit there for an hour or whatever it is. It feels like a day. I don't know exactly how long it is—and just kind of recover from that. And I never recovered from that. That was for me a kind of a—the velocity of time changed. That's what I felt. And I was just more awake and more aware, and more engaged. It was just a transformative moment for me. Because it was—it was kind of Buber again. It was seeing that there were realms. We all live in the world of *Asiyah* [doing], the world of activity, and then sometimes we get into the world of *Yetzirah* [creation], the world of forms, and I'm part of a form, and I can see that. But every once in a while, you can get into the world of *Beriyah* [creation], you know, the world of creation, and creativity, and where everything interlocks. And I just got a glimpse of that, and it was only a second, it was enough. And I figured, that was the world of *Beriyah*, that was the physics world. And that he did that through the velocity of his questions. I'm a bit of a mystic, you know. I'm a philosopher in some ways, but I'm a bit of a mystic. And I have felt that in many places, you know. In Assisi I felt it. I felt it in Varanasi, India.

So when I came back to the *havurah* after that, I was much more alert to my experience of experiencing tzaddikim and central figures in the *havurah* as powerful men. And before that, I had put almost everything into the community and into the transformative nature of the learning. But now I began to deal with rebbes. And there were a number of rebbes in the *havurah*, and that was at very least, destabilizing to me. Because I just hadn't prepared myself. I was a kid, you know, and I was part of the *hevrah*. The *hevrah* was everything. We talked about the *hevrah*. And I'm a good hevrahman. Now all of a sudden I had, you know, big figures—Art and Zalman and to a certain degree Eddie and Hillel. They were people that weighed in. And then it seems to me—after the Rebbe, I kind of felt, whoa, who am I to be here? I hadn't known that before. I was naïve. And so for me as a 16- and 17-year-old, to walk into this heavy group of people, you know—it's unnatural that it could have happened. It's not obvious. I should have been intimidated or silenced or I don't know! Certainly not part of it, and I was part of it because I didn't know. When I come back from the Rebbe, all of a sudden I'm writing papers and things like that. No papers at the *havurah*. *Havurah* is a dyslexic dream. You know, it's all oral, and it's slow, and it's deep, and it's abiding. And all of a sudden it's people telling me I'm right about this and wrong about that.

"The Habits of the *Havurah*"

The *havurah* was a place of deep intentionality and deep leaderless society. And in a leaderless society, [a] 17-year-old could say whatever the hell they wanted, and that was cherished, because, after all—leaderless. We're not going to be leaders with you here! Even if what I said was stupid most of the time, they were at least committed to it, and maybe I was cute enough, or whatever. They—and the habits of the *havurah* were started by some of those people.

For example, the way we do the Birkat [Birkat Hamazon, the prayer at the end of the meal], we wouldn't do this song; we did others. It was *havurah n'vorech* [Fellows, let's bless] instead of *rabotai n'vorech* [My rabbis, let's bless]. These are little changes, but it was—I can say it better. We sat in a circle, right? And even at the dinner table, we sat in a circle, around the dinner table. And it was different than a guy at the *bima* leading the davening. If you have a guy standing up, leading the davening, and facing away from the community, you're leading it toward God. If you sit around in a circle, both the prayer and at the dinner, you are davening to each other. And you're caring a lot about what other people are thinking about you, and what you're thinking about them. You are working through the interpersonal all the time. And the interpersonal has marshals and sheriffs. So, people who are going to come in and say, you're behaving badly here, or you're always late and we can't count on you, or you get to teach a class, and you don't get to teach a class. And that was the tension of the *havurah*. The Dorton people felt betrayed by that. And in some ways, I felt betrayed by that also, but because I was part of the Dorton group. Every morning, you know, we used to daven; we started to daven every morning. I used to cry—I used to literally break into tears in the davening in the morning. Because I was moved by the whole thing. I felt my life being rescued before my very eyes. But then the *havurah* was filled with wonderful people, you know. And so—but there was a hierarchy there. And the hierarchy was in an aristocracy, and we knew what the aristocracy was. Learning, you know. If you were there in the first year—memory and Jewish skills. Memory was very important. Memory of the old country. You know, Yerushalmi's *Zakhor*. He wrote it after the *havurah*, but it's a good book. If you had this kind of communal sense of memory that you could access the fragmented past—Zalman wrote a book. I think it's called *Future of a Fragmented Scroll*. This is all part of this, you know.

We had agenda-less meetings. We had a thing called the agenda-less meeting, and that was when we attacked each other. In a kind of *musar* [ethics] way, you know. "You're really pissing me off!" "You're taking up too much air time!" It was a criticism circle. In the name of community. Not just openness. Openness would just be, "I'm telling you what I really think." That would be honesty. Honesty and openness often go together. This was very much, "We are the group of people. We have a special spiritual mission. We need to—and we need to be together in it." And therefore we are going to criticize each other to be together. And you could get hurt in those meetings! Yeah. And you could hurt people in the meetings! I think I did a little bit of both. Yeah. I regret them, a little bit. But it was like a little communist, you know. Not commune-ist. Communist. Re-education circles.

"Eros and Shabbos"

One of the things that I learned in the *havurah*, and which I think about and affects me a lot, is the male nature of this community engaging in highly intense relationships and trying to deny the eros of them—when the eros is going to come for sure. And I was a tender boy at the time, and that was the first time that I was ever exposed to that. So remember, at the end of every davening we would hug each other hard. Hard. Not just like, little clamshell hugs. Bearhugs, you know! We touched each other a lot, and we were of that age, and there were some people that were quite open to that experience. And I wasn't one of them, but I was swept up in it to a degree that I would not have expected in the rest of my regular life.

We had crushes on each other, we did. But we had more than crushes, you know. We were highly engaged with each other. The Gemara is written by people who are highly engaged with each other. It's written, those are the stories. And you don't have very much of erotica in there, but you have a little bit. We're in a post-Freudian world. We know about eros. There was eros. And Shabbos—I learned this about Romemu [a Jewish renewal community based in New York City]. I learned it about BJ [B'nai Jeshurun] at a certain time, I learned about Lincoln Square another time. These are good pickup joints, as well. And if you really wanted to get laid, you could probably do it at the *havurah*, you know. On a Friday night. I was—I responded to that in a very clear way. I got married at age nineteen. To my high school girlfriend. After long reflection on that, I think that was really a part of it. If you learn with a person the way we learned with each other, for long enough, and it's not that long, you fall in love. That's the facts. It happened at Brovenders, it happened at Dartmouth when I was at Dartmouth. It happens all the time. You fall in love. And sometimes the person's appropriate, sometimes the person's not. I fell in love with these people. And I fell in love with them in a way that I had an activity that could sustain it. And the erotic dimension of it was also there, and it made the whole thing much more fraught.

We just did want to tear down the walls between us. That's what the meetings were. You can read about it in the manual of discipline in the Qumran texts. They had it, too. You know? So if you sit and you have the meals—I can remember the meals. String beans with mushroom soup on it, the little crinkly onions, fried onions. I can remember who brought the bulgur wheat, and we all went to the co-op and things like that. But that was all a—that was all a staging area for very intense meetings that had intense results to them. There is no communal experience—and we were a communal experience, more than Fabrangen, more than the New York Havurah—we were a communal experience, we were in each other's faces.

"The Beginning of Sexual Liberation"

In the beginning, they were everybody's wives and girlfriends. And it was the post–birth control era. The beginning of sexual liberation. So, yeah, I always say this as a joke. But my theory of divine providence is that God comes to Adam and Eve and says, "Okay, you sinned. You have to be good now for 5,000 years." And God comes back to us in 1968 and says, "All right, for the next fifteen years, have a fantastic time." I use another word usually. And I was exactly the right age for the fantastic time. Thank you, God. You know, so—I mean, really! And people took full advantage of that. I think it was one of the only times in human history that you go to some woman at the end of davening and say, "Would you like to sleep with me?" And they'd say, "Okay!" "It won't mean anything. I might not even remember your name." "Okay! You know, it's only rubbing. It's the afternoon. I'm happy. Sure, sure it's Shabbos, why not? Let's go, let's go!" Really, like that. But that also led to lots of other things, and people felt, you know, bruised up by that.

In the third year of the *havurah*, Sharon Strassfeld came. That was a big change. She could really daven. We didn't have anybody that could really daven before that. We didn't have any women, sorry, I don't know why I said it that way. The women just became a thing of the *havurah*, that it should be egalitarian. In the beginning, we just didn't have any liabilities. It wasn't like you couldn't get an *aliyah* [*la-torah*; an invitation to give the blessing before the reading of the Torah] if you were a woman. But remember, most of us are coming from suburban synagogues where women didn't have *aliyot*. Even in 1968. I'd never seen a woman have an *aliyah*. Not that I'd never seen people daven while sitting on a cushion on the floor. Everything was new. But that just didn't occur to me, that you could do that. And that people were changing the liturgy. It was a pre-feminist moment. Stonewall had been what, fifteen minutes before. We didn't know that women were supposed to be equal. It just never occurred to people. It was pre-feminist. But it was then feminist. That phrase—it was just a bunch of guys with their girlfriends and their wives—I remember that phrase. Don't worry. I repent! I'm sorry! It was stupid. We should have done it right away. We didn't know. I didn't know.

We went to Weiss's Farm, in Somerville, New Jersey, I think, or some-place in New Jersey—and like a fight broke out, you know, about it. And the Fabrangen was much more progressive. This was '70, '71. Because Fabrangen came to that retreat, and we went back and talked about it on our own retreat. I think the one at Camp Ramah. And we let a lot of women into the *havurah* because we thought we had to let a lot of women into the *havurah*, and some of the women were, you know—it wasn't such an easy process. I remember we let Alex Orr in, but the difference between Alex Orr and Art Green was really big. Some of the women that came in, even though we wanted to have more women members, they weren't studying; they weren't being the Hasidim. They were feminists, and that was their agenda. I think what Green says is right. It was a pre-feminist moment, and there was loss in it as it became feminized.

After '70, '71, all the women in the *havurah* were feminists, and most of the men were struggling to become more feminist. But we were still trying to preserve the neo-Hasidic aspects of it. We didn't call it neo-Hasidic of course. We just called it Hasidic, or whatever, mystical. But we were doing it, you know. And not to put too fine a point on it, some of the texts of Rebbe Nachman and the Besht [the Ba'al Shem Tov], they were sexist. And the *Zohar* is a deeply misogynist book, you know, with all of its God is the *Shekhina* and women—it has all these horrible, anti-feminist, sexist pieces to it. Deeply. And yet we wanted to study the *Zohar*. So how did that make any sense?

I remember we did a seminar on feminism. There were some people who were very much against the feminization of the *havurah*. They felt that once it started to go in that direction, that would become a women's movement collective, and it would stop being the *havurah*. That would become the dominant issue. That would become the only issue that we considered and that we would be able to address. It was a real fear. And the lesbian aspects of it also were a piece of that. We were challenged, a little bit. If the women's issue became the issue of the *havurah*, as opposed to the mystical issue, then we would become like a feminist—on the vanguard of Jewish feminism. And we weren't cut out for that, because we didn't have enough women involved, and we just weren't cut out for it. We thought we were making this other kind of contribution, and it was an important contribution, and so that's it, you know. And we couldn't just say, oh, goodbye, we're now only going to be feminists as our calling card. We didn't want to do anything wrong about feminism. We weren't trying to, you know, squash anybody, but I'm just trying to be honest and tell you that this is the piece. Study was still very much in the epicenter of *havurah* life, and all of a sudden the feminist critique came into the study. For a very self-conscious group, it was a lack of self-consciousness. But you could say [that] about a number of other topics as well, but feminism the most, the most important: gay, anti-Zionist, and communitarian. There were a lot of anti-Zionists in the group, political lefties, and we just didn't want to do that. So we marginalized those people. That's the fact.

There was a moment, and I was one of the people involved. I was always more political then, and I'm more political now, than a lot of the other people. But we were going to be neo-Hasidim. I want to keep on saying that, because that's the fact of the matter. These were things that came up in Jewish life and that were crucial, but that wasn't our countercultural moment. Our countercultural moment was postdenominationalism, learning as a way of expressing Judaism as opposed to davening. And the elevation of spirituality. And it wasn't going to be feminism. We weren't against it. We tried to accommodate it. It wasn't going to be politics. We were political, we rung our hands and gnashed our teeth, but that was what it was going to be. And so anything else that was distracting from that were distractions. It wasn't that it was bad. It was just distractions. And we all felt it was crucial. I can remember having conversations, that if any one of those aspects of the agenda became the central part of the agenda, then the *havurah* that we knew was over.

"The Do-It-Yourself Jewish Kit"

It was the second year of the *havurah*, that's what we called it, the second year of the *havurah*. As opposed to the New York Havurah, and Fabrangen, we did have membership, right. And you could get rejected. And the *b'rit* [covenant] was somewhere around all that. There were conditions to being in the *havurah* because we wanted to make it an intentional community. But yes, I also had interviews with the *havurah* members. But I don't feel that they were tense for me. I was already very much part of the group. But we were rejecting people right and left. Just—we should be clear about that—it was a closed group. And lots of people got injured by not being admitted to the *havurah*. There's a famous case of a couple that now lives in Houston—I think he might have died—he was going to Harvard Business School, you know. And so we said, "We're not going to have a guy from Harvard Business School in the *havurah*." So we just, "You're not our kind of guy. You're in Harvard Business School." And I remember Sharon was going to quit over that, "What does that mean? This guy does business school, that's enough of a reason not to have them?" And it was something like that. It was kind of a manifesto of ideology that if you didn't feel part of that, then you really weren't in the *havurah*. The *havurah* became pretty well-known all of a sudden. We felt ourselves to be slightly famous, you know? Not famous like famous, but famous. The *havurah* started having lots of people come on Shabbos morning. Friday night was only for the members and some fellow travelers. I always went on Friday night, I think even before I was a member. But it was small. And then everybody, everybody went to somebody's house for dinner and if you didn't get invited to dinner, you could invite yourself to dinner. That was the rule. So, you know, "I'd like to come to your house for dinner." Okay, they couldn't say no. Everybody had to live within walking distance. We were Shabbat inviters.

It was all fake in some ways. No one really had grown up in this way. Green didn't grow up in this way. Zalman didn't grow up in this way. Epi was the repository of authentic dinners. When I was very young, Brooks and Feld, people like that, would invite me over. I learned a lot about it. To do it myself, was like, a real thing. And then people would come and criticize me. They would come and tell me, "You know, you don't say the Birkat right. These are not the tunes we use. You don't sing enough after. You don't sing enough before." I would ask, and people would, in no uncertain terms, tell me how to do it.

So, we were the inviters because we had a family and they were the single guys; they would come. But I set up my apartment so I could do all this stuff, you know? Long table, and more chairs than most people would have. We'd bake our own challahs. You know, we were the do-it-yourself Jewish kit. So I was very much interested in the *niggunim*, and I—you would come to my house on a Friday night, and we'd sing a lot. A lot. Sometimes we'd have home and homes. You know, come to my house on Friday night, I'll come to your house Shabbos lunch.

Shabbos lunch was a thing. We would gather in the foyer of the *havurah* and we would gather into little groups that you were then going to escort home. Some families that we went to—some couples, everyone would bring a story and a little talking point. And other people, they'd let the conversation go. Wherever it would go. But many people did not. You—*parashah*, we did; someone brought a text. You know, as I got more learned and things, I brought better texts, I think. We would pick texts out, study them in the afternoon.

"Nothing Like Davening on a Friday Night with the *Havurah*"

Nothing like davening on a Friday night with the *havurah*. Nothing like it. It was wonderful. Almost without failure, every week, it was great. The singing was great. We knew each other. I'll just say two things about it. I remember years later, like in the early '80s, Dovid and Shayna came to Hanover where I was the rabbi, and they come to Friday night dinner. Friday davening. And I had, based on the *havurah*, built a davening for the Dartmouth Hillel that was like the davening at the *havurah*. We knew each other well. Many of the people became rabbis from that group. Nancy Flam became the head of the Spirituality Institute, and David Seidenberg just wrote a book on ecology and Kabbalah, and Shirley Idelson became the Dean of Students at Hebrew Union College. It was [a] very talented group of people that went on. Rob Eshman is now the editor of the *Jewish Journal* in L.A. They were all at my table, in my little davening at Dartmouth Hillel. And David was in tears at the end of it. He says, "That's what it felt like." I did the whole thing—flickering candles, not electric lights. I let them burn out, the whole thing. That was amazing. That was a spiritual experience.

They were neo-Hasidic. They were really neo-Hasidic in that way. They were intense, and they were literate, and they were vibrant. Very fresh. Something very fresh about it. Green used music and many people used music, and I didn't use music. At Shabbat dinner. I did not. I was *frum*-er. I became *frum*-er and remained *frum*-er than most of the people. But I sang, and sang and sang. Oh yeah, singing. But he—he put records on. Bach's B minor Mass, *Missa Luba* once, *niggunim* from the Mojitz album. Recorded music. That's what I meant. But I didn't—I only sang. I sang my heart out! I love singing. I loved it then and I love it now. I still sing on Friday night. I still sing. Between when we wash our hands and before we sing the Motzi [the blessing over the bread] I sing three or four *niggunim*. I am committed to it.

My mother died eight years ago, and Ebn Leader came to my mother's apartment, and the Reimers and Greens and Lehmanns and Novaks and Polens—Nehemia and Lauri Polen, and all these people. And it was Hanukkah. And he led the davening, and my brother and sister and I just cried and cried and cried. And I really—my brother-in-law, who is not religious, he came over to me and said, "Well, I just didn't know that's what davening was. Who would know that? Anybody would want to do that every day. You would never not want to do that." And I said, "That's it." Because as soon as—forty years with all those people, forty-five, whatever it is—we were sitting on the floor again. The prayers mean something. Prayers don't mean anything in most shuls. You can't say what the prayers mean, and what they're about, how they work. In the *havurah*, the prayers worked. We knew what they were about. It's remarkable. Almost no minyan does that. The prayers were one hundred percent mirrors. So what we looked like that day when we looked into the prayers is how we saw ourselves differently each time. They were—they were self-expression and also communal cohesion experiences. We were having a different davening. We were experimenting, we were getting to know each other through the liturgy. It was a ritual. It's different. We used *Nusach Sefard*, so it has more mystical elements, *keter yitnu*, you know, crown of God, like that. So the mystical elements in our things were both innovative, because they weren't using that at Mishkan Tefila. They didn't even know what that was at Mishkan Tefila. And yet, there was this fidelity to a tradition. So we were *frum* about some things, and we were completely nothing about other stuff.

"I Was Innovative. I Really Worked Hard on It"

We prepared the davening, we really prepared. I led the davening a lot. I was pretty young, I think I was maybe in the third year when I decided I'd do it. And I wasn't innovative in the beginning, but then I was innovative. I really worked hard on it. Well, you know, there's a phrase—*Af tikon teivel, bal timot* ["He sets the world in his course and does not let it shake"]. It's from Psalm 29:93. And so I used that once. I used it as kind of a mantric element. So at the end of every one of the songs, and even the pieces of the Baruchu and the Shema and the Amidah, I used the phrase *af tikon* so that people— and I would yell it sometimes, and I would whisper it, and sometimes I would repeat it many times—*af tikon*—like thirty or forty times, like that. So it was—and it was at a time in which I felt that the whole *havurah* was particularly shaky and insecure. We had just, it was just after the '73 war, I think, and it was maybe about the '73 war. So that would be like an example of something that I did. But of course it changed the whole davening, because it's a phrase that you're using in a repetitive way. I just kind of remember that being successful. I never did it after that.

And then "Tzadik Katamar" we used to do, we did it big band—"tza-dik ka-taa-mar yifrach—da na na na." Then we'd do trombones and things like that. We'd march around, you know, because it was—yeah, we'd march around. One time I came and there were tables in the basement. In the prayer room, you know, and everybody's wearing hats. It was very creative. You could do that. Kazoos, people would bring kazoos. No musical instruments. Maybe that's not right. Maybe Novak played the guitar. He's a really good guitar player. Yes, maybe there were musical instruments. Yes, I'm sure that there were, because Zalman had once said that the reason we don't do musical instruments is *zichron hurban ha-bayit*, the recollection of the destruction of the Temple. And he said, "If we keep on recollecting the destruction of the Temple, don't worry, we'll be destroyed completely." We should stop mourning the past and start rebuilding the future.

"We Learned About Each Other. And That Was Transformative"

The role of learning was to meet each other. It was the best use of traditional texts that I've ever experienced. It wasn't to learn and know more. It was to know each other. We would sit and learn. People would prepare a lot. George Savran would teach Bible classes. He would prepare four or five hours for every hour that he would teach, but even so, in that group, in that circle, on the second floor when we would sit around that table, we learned about each other. And that was transformative, and I think it has the best chance of being transformative of Jewish lives in the future. We should stop being a shul-based community. We should start being a learning-based community. And you can see it anyway—the Limud and all sorts of other learning programs are wildly more successful than shuls. We were post-denominational. That was crucial. Because Reform, Conservative, Ortho-dox, they were answering nineteenth-century questions. We were trying to answer twenty-first-century questions: What did Judaism need to revive itself? What did Judaism need to survive? What did Judaism need to bring more people into a pluralistic community? What should Judaism obviously do about issues of gender and issues of nationalism? Community is not pos-sible if you're only focused on yourself. And community is critical. I think we achieved community because we weren't focused only on ourselves. Not everybody. There were some people that were focused on themselves. But a lot were not focused on themselves. A lot. More than you can imagine.

It was a dazzling time. I stand with my understanding of the learning, there, and I don't think it's romanticized. I can think of too many examples of going through it. I remember in Shir ha-Shirim [Song of Songs]—"Love is as strong as death is," and working on that sentence week after week, just so much. My whole experience of love and even of finality and mor-tality, it was just—and that wasn't based on my knowing the Mishnah, you know. I learned the Mishnah later on; you could do it. This was not about acquiring knowledge. This was about noetic knowledge, you know. It was more precious and different. You want to learn Mishnah? Go to Brandeis. So my pedagogic style is to teach not just up, but I hope even kind of at a soaring level. And that's the *havurah*. It was serious, it was intricate, it was delicate. Otherwise—I don't want to hear the same story over and over. Even the Torah can get boring if you don't do something new with it. We just change the lens, you know.

Tikkun Olam

I actually think the *havurah* invented the phrase *tikkun olam* [repair of the world]. I think it comes from Arthur Waskow in 1973. Michael Stanislawski did a little study tracking the phrase *tikkun olam*. You know, if you had said to me in 1970 or 1971, "Well, here's a number of phrases. Which one do you think will make it in the Jewish community?" I do not think I would have rated *tikkun olam*, which is a mystical understanding of collecting the *nitzotzot* [sparks] and—I mean, really? That's going to be—Obama stands in front of the Jewish community and says "You know, I believe in *tikkun olam*." Really? Does he have any idea? It's crazy, but there it was. So then that did have an enormous impact. On the walls of the UJA right now is our commitment to *tikkun olam*.

I didn't really buy into *tikkun olam* that way. I can't say—you know, when I go to the demonstration on the refugees, things like that, yes, I'm doing that with a Jewish motivation. I have become a Jewish cosmopolitan. I've become a Jewish cosmopolitan with good, solid progressive credentials, and even at my work in the UJA, which some people think is establishment but I believe is actually a shockingly progressive organization. I think a lot of the motivation comes out of Jewish texts including *Ahavat Israel*, so— it is a lens through which I see the world, *Ahavat Israel*, and I am not going to let go of that lens. So even though I have some sympathy with BDS [boycott, divestment, sanctions], and I have some sympathy with Jewish Voices for Peace, things like that, I'm an *Ahavat Israel* guy—love Jews, love the Jewish people.

My social action comes out of my Jewish values. And I'm not able or willing to take some of my Jewish values and take them out so I can just have progressive values. When I was a rabbi in central New Hampshire, in Vermont, there was this guy that would come to the classes that I gave named Bernie Sanders. Bernie Sanders, he's gone on! He was then running for mayor of Burlington. And he ran for president. And I voted for him—because I support him. But he studied a text called *The Non-Jewish Jew* by Isaac Deutscher, in which he basically claimed that these are progressive values, these are Russian Revolution progressive values and they have nothing to do with Judaism. Judaism is a recalcitrant and, you know, reactionary tradition. It's not a stupid argument. [Yet] I reject it. I still think of Shabbos as a general strike. I still think of anti-slavery, anti-genocide issues. I feel motivated by my Jewish values, including *ahavat tzion*.

"I Want to Be a Pluralistic, Postdenominational Rabbi"

I'm the first *havurah*-ordained rabbi. I'm just sure that that's true. I got ordained at a *havurah* national conference, and I got ordained by *havurah* members. So what could be more than that? After the level and intensity of the study at the *havurah*, as well as the lack of papers and evaluation devices, let's say that, but not entirely that, I just decided to do it myself, you know. And I was going to decide to become a rabbi under my own terms, as opposed to JTS [Jewish Theological Seminary] or RRC [Reconstructionist Rabbinical College] or YU [Yeshiva University] or anybody else. I left RRC close to the end. Close to the end doesn't even capture how close to the end it was. I decided I didn't want RRC. I think I left in January of the last year that they were going to make me go to RRC. Saying "that they were going to make me go into RRC" gives you a little hint of my disdain for it at that moment. But I didn't want to be a Reconstructionist rabbi, and I didn't want to be an Orthodox rabbi because I'm not Orthodox. I didn't want to be Conservative; I'm certainly not Conservative. Reform I didn't even know very much about. So I wanted to be a pluralistic, postdenominational rabbi for small, intense communities. And so that is what I became.

I studied with Zalman, I studied with Allen Lehmann, I studied with Norbert Samuelson—Reform—Norbert, and Conservative/Reconstructionist—Allen Lehmann, and Orthodox/Renewal—Zalman, and Brovender Orthodox, and Seyyed Hossein Nasr—Muslim. And all of those people came to my *smicha* [ordination]. So in 1981–82 I had already taken a *bechina* [exam] for the *rabbanut* [rabbinate], and I had done well enough at it so that I could have been what's called a *rav u'manhig* [rabbi and leader of a congregation]—which is enough, you know. You can then come back to America and call yourself a rabbi.

I wanted to be the student of Zalman. I wanted to be a pluralistic person. I wanted to be a Jew, a rabbi for the Jewish community. And so I became Zalman's second *musmach*. But the first *musmach*, Danny Siegel, was his *talmid*, his acolyte, his disciple. I'm not Zalman's disciple. Zalman is one of my great teachers. But I did not intend to become Zalman. David Ingber, maybe, he wants to continue the Zalman legacy. Most of the Renewal people that I know of, some of whom are extraordinarily talented, want to become like Zalman—are devout Zalman disciples, want to further his work. I don't. I want to further the work of the pluralistic Jewish community. So I only worked in pluralistic programs—Bronfman and Dorot and Hillel, Wexner and Limmud FSU—all these things, they're all pluralistic programs. And I want to turn the Jewish community toward study, because study is a unifying activity, and it should be serious, transformative, elevating study. So that is what I did. At my *smicha*, I got Zalman and Allen and Brovender and Norbert and Seyyed Hossein Nasr to come in front of all these people and ask me questions.

This was at the summer institute in Hartford, Connecticut. And for three hours they asked me questions. Just in front of about 150, 200 people. I just strived to answer as many as I could. I mean, Allan, at one point looked at me and said, "Can you recite a Gemara and teach it to us? You know enough Gemara?" And I said, "Oh, no, no." And he said, "Well, try!" And I did! It was an unparalleled experience. And there's a phrase in my *smicha* that says, "We are sure that his fear of sin will take precedence over his own wisdom." And I appreciate that line. What it means to me is that it's not about me. It's not about my own view. It's not about the Conservative Jewish view or the Reform Jewish view. I'm afraid of sin. I'm afraid of going off the *derech* [the path], so I'm trying to bring everyone together on the *derech*. That's what I thought the *havurah* was really about—the *derech*, however defined. I mean, right now they say, "He's off the *derech*." That means he's not Haredi anymore. Forget about the Haredi part, but there is a Jewish way, and I want to be part of the Jewish way. I think I'm a true product of the *havurah* in that way: pluralism, community, learning, social action, social responsibility, love. I don't think I've sold out about it.

"High-Liability Judaism"

Tefilah [prayer] is my encounter with God. I'm not going to design a community which is going to exclude the majority of people because they can't get into prayer. It's a highly poetic, subtle, complex, and exquisite experience, which I'm highly committed to, and I do it a lot. If I think about the hours of my life that I spend in *tefilah*, it would be an enormous number of them. I'm not going to exclude a wide population of Jews from things I said. I think if I talk about pluralistic and educational, and socially active and socially responsible, everybody should be able to do that. Everyone. And that's what I want. And in that I want to have my own prayer life, and my own spiritual search, which I've been persistent in. I teach *tefilah*, but I don't mostly lead *tefilah*, but I do teach it. It's a wonderful intellectual, liturgical exercise.

Spirituality was at the heart of what the *havurah* experience was, in many ways. And certainly, for Havurat Shalom in particular, in comparison to both Fabrangen and the New York Havurah. I am sorry that Art didn't build a movement. Zalman tried to build a movement. Art didn't build a movement. So it is a wonderful relic. I feel honored to have been a part of it. I feel thrilled. I feel it's divine providence that I was part of it, but Art didn't build a movement. Someone in this very room said that they like Musar, but Musar is a little group, and Hasids is a big group. So what you can say about Musar is that it didn't really build a movement, you know?

There's no *havurah* movement. I think there's a series of *havurah* ideas. And I believe in them, and I love them. Learning, postdenominationalism, pluralism, sense of community, social responsibility, social activism—all within a Jewish narrative. Because I think we are part of a long story, and we have lots of literary creations—Torah, Mishnah, Gemara, Achronim, Rishonim, Midrash—which are curriculum for who we are. And if you learn those stories and the narrative so the story and narrative clicks, it will teach you certain things. And those things are not well replicated in the rest of society. We want people to prosper, even with money. Most religions are poverty oriented. We want people to have universal intellect. Most people don't do that. But I believe in those things. We are global citizens. Most people are more and more xenophobic and turn inward. We are big about *tzedakah* [charity]. We believe in generosity to each other. Most people do not believe in generosity and do not practice generosity. Now everybody has little pieces of those. We keep them balanced. Anytime you go out of balance on those things, then the whole narrative structure falls apart. I think these are the narrative structures that the *havurah* has tried to prosper, as opposed to some other things. And if we build big edifices so we can all sit in shul together, I think that was a dead end. I think that was a mistake. I really do. The UJA right now is trying to prop up synagogues and make them exciting and dynamic institutions again. I'm hoping that they go the way of other Jewish institutions and new institutions come. I don't believe in those institutions. I like little minyanim.

The independent minyanim of today are the legacy of the *havurot*. Including the "partnership minyan," the Orthodox partnership ones. These are *frum*, egalitarian minyanim. Mechitza, but women lead the davening and give *d'vrei torah*. So that's very attractive to me. If my friends didn't go to Minyan M'at, so I would hang out with them and sing and drink once a week, I would go to a partnership. It would be a very amenable thing for me to do. In Israel, a lot of the minyanim in Israel, like the Hartman minyan and Leader minyan. Shlomo [Carlebach] has been great at giving musical voice to something enthusiastic in davening. All these things. But these are all small, intense groups. The building of big prayer halls so everybody can pray was, I think, a mistake. I'm a minyan guy.

This is high-liability Judaism. You have to really engage yourself, something to give and something to lose. Whereas you go into a big synagogue, nobody knows and nobody cares. It's not that they don't care, but it's just—that's just not what they're about. So I'm not against them, but I don't think they are the vehicle that will take us to the future. And the *havurah* was, I think, one of the sparks of the turn toward these vehicles, at least in the non-Orthodox world. In the non-Orthodox world, taking lessons from the Orthodox world, very early on, because Zalman and Art and a few others could actually read Orthodox texts. This is significant and transformative. Maybe even salvific.

"I Still Think That God Needs Us Jews"

We're almost fifty years after the founding of the first *havurah*, and for me the lesson is that it gives secular Jews a way about going about being Jewish—small, intense communities of social action and social responsibility with Jewish narratives. This is what secular Jews can do, and most Jews are secular, you know. I'm not so worried about the people that go to Reform or Conservative movements, but they're rapidly shrinking. They want to. They're good people. They're well-meaning. They don't know how. I wouldn't know how to tell them to do it either for the middle of the twenty-first century. But these small communities of secular Jews, and you can see them in lots of places now—Moishe Houses, and Hillel next, and the Beis, all these things. They're all kind of a reformulation of the *havurah* so that people who come from a secular Jewish perspective will know what to do, where to belong. Even the Jewish community centers. Right after you leave, a guy from Kraków's going to come and we're going to talk about a secular Jewish community of Kraków, because the religious communities are boring and no one can bear them. I don't know if rabbis are going to be the heads of the

Jewish world or the Jewish people in the next generation. I think that they won't be. But communal organizers, and community leaders, I think, will be. So that's my thought about it. And I hope to go to Europe and form those kinds of communities. Lay leaders are very important now. They didn't used to be so important. Now they're very important. That was a real departure from all the other things, but that's what I think.

What would victory be for us? Okay, we did good. We lasted three thousand years. We had good values. We brought lots of Nobel prize winners, enough, goodbye. Let's all intermarry and go back into the gene pool and see you later. It's not a stupid idea! Simon Rawidowicz has the great article "Israel the Ever-Dying People." That's his strategy for innovation. I kind of like the idea that many of us think that this is it, that we're in the last generation of Jews. It's a good strategy—because if you're the last generation, go for broke. It's a very good innovation strategy.

I still think that God needs us Jews in the world because of Torah. I have to say this in a shorter way. In the book of Exodus, in chapter 19, there is a mission statement, which I believe is *am segulah, goy kadosh*, and *mamlechet kohanim*. So *am segulah*, you know, is we're the treasured people. We have a lot of memory, because we're old, and we've been at it for a long time. And you should have a people that has a long memory. And to be assigned to everybody else, *am segulah* and then *goy kadosh*—we should be a little distinctive. Separated. A little holy, something, we care about these things. But the real one for me is *mamlechet kohanim*, we should be the conduit of blessing into the world, and I believe that we can be the conduit of blessing into the world. And the world has to know that it can permanently change. I'm optimistic. I'm extremely optimistic, I'm an optimistic person, and I'm optimistic now because I think the world can change because we are the *mamlechet kohanim*, the kingdom of priests. And the kingdom of priests means we have to be open to the blessing coming through us. We have to be careful that we don't burn up as the blessing comes through. And it's a precarious job. And I do think that the *havurah* tried to be *mamlechet kohanim*. I do think it—one of the first things the *havurah* did; people don't talk about this—is we got rid of the Kohen/Levi/Israel *aliyot*. We didn't do Kohen anymore, because we were egalitarians. Not just them, but everybody. Just because your father's a Kohen doesn't mean you get to be a Kohen! You're not going to get your first *aliyah*. We're not doing that anymore. We're all in this. We are the *mamlechet kohanim*. That's what I feel. We need Hasidim, we need friars, we need Reform Jews, we need secular Jews, we need Bundists, we need BDS, we need scholars. We need 'em all because we're the *mamlechet kohanim*. That's what the *mamlechet kohanim* does. And I think there's still blessing pouring itself into the world. The *Shefa* [divine flow] of God is still pouring God into the world. I'm still a religious guy, you know. Even though I say the other stuff. I myself am a religious guy, and I feel that, I feel that all the time, even right now, that God is pouring Godself into the world, and I want to make sure there's a conduit to bring that blessing into the world. I think that's us. It's worth the effort.

References

Mark, Jonathan. 2018. "Federation's Rabbi Sailing Off to Newest Challenge." *New York Jewish Week*, January 9. https://jewishweek.timesofisrael.com/federations-rabbi-sailing-off-to-newest-challenge/ (accessed April 27, 2021).

Paley, Michael. 2017. "Interview with Michael Paley." By Jayne Guberman. *Oral Histories* 6. https://repository.upenn.edu/jcchp_oralhistories/6.

Prell, Riv-Ellen. 2007. "Independent Minyanim and Prayer Groups of the 1970s: Historical and Sociological Perspectives." *Zeek, A Jewish Journal of Thought and Culture* 2007 (spring): 33–38.

14

After-Word, On-Word, Back-Word

Jonathan Boyarin

These concluding reflections can be only a highly selective engagement with moments in this rich collection of texts. The contributors taught me much (hence "after-word") and reminded me how powerfully my own explorations and constructions of Jewishness have focused on the obsolete and the residual as opposed to the emergent. I recall being caught up short years ago on first reading Matti Bunzl's *Symptoms of Modernity* and being told that my ethnography of elderly Polish Jews in Paris was "dominated by the paradigm of mournful nostalgia" (Bunzl 2004, 6). He was right, of course. These necessarily fragmentary comments, then, likely reflect to some extent my own continuing orientation toward recuperation of Jewish pasts in order to sustain them as *living past* and not just as they may be deployed for reimagining the present and future (hence "back-word"). They are also intended to foster continuing discussions that may sharpen some of the provocative explorations and insights contained in this book (hence "on-word").

A number of years ago I gave a talk about Jewishness and memory to a rather small group of mostly young adults at the Upper West Side "Jewish continuity" institution known as Makor. During the question and answer session, one young woman asked me a bit plaintively and perhaps a bit impatiently, "Does being Jewish *always* have to be grounded in loss?" My baseline assumption is that the answer is yes, but the question certainly brought me up short. Keen awareness of this dilemma—the power of Jewish memories, especially of loss, along with the suppression of creativity and the conservation of internal hierarchies that they can feed—is displayed in

Cara Rock-Singer's chapter here about the Kohenet movement. Taya Shere explains that "contemporary Jewish culture for me had become really stagnant because of the immense and intense focus on memory and Jewish cultural memory to the detriment of actually what is relevant now." Perhaps, rather than being pushed to decide *for* or *against* memory, this challenge might for now best lead me to stress how much my own sense of the dynamism of Jewish memories was fostered by the marginality of the Lower East Side Jewish worlds in which I spent so much time recuperating those memories.

Nevertheless Taya's question suggests that there may well be a privileged relationship between patriarchy and rhetorics of loss. Like other spaces of Jewish revival and renewal explored in this volume, the Kohenet insistence is that recuperations not come at the expense of subservience. But also like other spaces here, some forms of subservience (such as sexism) may be more evident than others. I find it telling that aspects of the Kohenet ritual bricolage recall Zionist historiography by effectively telescoping Jewishness, making a magical shortcut, a *kefitsas haderekh*, back to presumed biblical Israel era worship at high places. To be sure, Rock-Singer focuses specifically on the use of altars here, but her essay, taken on its own, would suggest that an alternative strategy not explored by the Kohenet movement (at least on the evidence here) is the recuperation of their great-grandmothers' Jewishness. If so, that leap over more immediate ancestry is facultative rather than necessary to the Kohenet movement, and it appears that integration of more immediate ancestral practices also happens among the *kohanot* now (Kafrissen 2021).

I am stuck, perhaps in defense of the past as well, on this volume's reference in the subtitle to "a transnational age." This is hardly the first time that the Jewish world has been "transnational"; one might rather say, reflecting the spirit of a recent exhibit at the Jüdische Museum Hohenems on early modern Jews as "the first Europeans," that Jews were transnational before nationalism. Tellingly, in fact, it turns out that some of the formations of renewal and revival explored in this volume—the Hungarian case in particular—seem not so much to be exploring the viability of communal and "religious" forms that are altogether new at the turn of the third Christian millennium as to be testing the continued viability of forms that flourished before World War II, such as a Jewishly grounded, noninstitutionalized, cosmopolitan artistic-social sphere. It seems not by accident that the headquarters of these loose Judapest groups (when not online) have been located in former Jewish quarters.

Despite the lucid overviews of Asher Biemann and Shaul Magid, there is room for a lot more discussion and clarification of the key terms, work that can only be signposted here. Biemann offers us a fantastic quote from Martin Buber about the idea of Jewish renaissance as a move away "from the dialectical petrification of scholasticism to a broad and soulful perception of nature, from mediaeval asceticism to a warm, flowing feeling of life, from the constraints of narrow-minded communities to the freedom of the personality." So much is captured in this quote of the baseline assumptions about "traditional" (i.e., early modern) forms of communal organization and authority under pre-nation-state Jewish communal semiautonomy. That is, the aura of stultification of postwar suburban Conservative Judaism that Michael Paley recalls (and, yes, that I recall as well and have similarly documented and, as Paley rightly mentions, is captured with devastating accuracy in the Coen brothers' *A Serious Man*) is part and parcel of a larger background stereotype of rabbinic Judaism as being "stuck in the Middle Ages," constrained, dry, repressive. Much as this characterization of the European "mediaeval" proper has been criticized by contemporary medievalists through the lens of larger critiques of linear temporality and progressivism (Biddick 2003; Davis 2008), it is important to stress within the framework of this overview of "revival" that Jewishness (despite and with all the repressions that the attempt to sustain autonomy under liberal modernization entails) was in fact not necessarily moribund.

More needs to be teased out about the relation between notions of "revival" and "renewal" and what they respectively assume about the past, that is, morbidity and obsolescence. Of course, as discussed in more than one essay, "Jewish renewal" was the name given to a certain cluster of highly conscious and highly voluntaristic prayer settings (especially), often combining motifs attributed to Eastern European Jewish Hasidism with elements of New Age spirituality and sociality (such as the open sexuality recalled by Michael Paley). It was also a revival in the important sense (here again, consistent with the rhetoric of Buber and Rosenzweig, and we could add Gershom Scholem and so many others of their generation) that American Judaism was understood as being in the process of dying at its own hand. But are we then going to conclude, without more (and through a kind of parody of) rabbinic logic that what Rabbi Joel Teitelbaum accomplished in New York City after World War II, bringing together a diverse and fragmented population of Holocaust survivors, most of whom had never set foot in the town of Satu Mare, as a tightly bound community of "Satmar Hasidim," inextricably both a material and a spiritual community—that this was somehow *not* a project of "renewal" or "revival"? (Curiously, it seems one would not know about these people, to the extent they were traditionalist Hungarian Jews before and after the genocide, on the basis of Daniel Monterescu and Sara Zorandy's reference to "already assimilated Hungarian Jewry" after World War II.)

Similar to the rhetoric of Buber and others about the morbidity and obsolescence of the Central European Judaism of his day, early in the twentieth century, outside Jewish observers (other than Buber, of course) often understood the Hasidism of their day to be a relic, a husk, debased and corrupted and destined for oblivion. Zealous defender of the liveliness of the past that I am, I seek out through the essays traces of those older stereotypes. Certainly, the extensive and approving citation of Daniel Elazar that comes at the end of Zvi Gitelman's essay—to wit, that "a Jewishness based on identity rather than an assumed way of life complicates matters for Jewish survival, but, at the same time, seems to be the only way to achieve Jewish survival in our times"—can only be sustained if one also assumes that Orthodox and traditionalist formations either are destined to disappear or are somehow not really Jewish. As of 2021, either assertion seems bizarre. To be sure, Polish Hasidism was horrendously reduced in numbers by Nazi genocide, and Hungarian Hasidism was fragmented. But are not the Hasidic villages of Kiryas Joel (now the town of Palm Tree, after Rabbi Teitelbaum) or New Square (after the "old" town of Skvira) evidence of Jewish revival as well as, and alongside, a felt and enforced imperative of demographic survival?

I am suggesting that, when the framework is cultural and spiritual creativity in the present, it becomes especially imperative to avoid the assumption of an unchanging baseline called tradition. The essay by Shaul Magid, who knows better than most of us how dynamic Eastern European Hasidism actually was, goes far in this direction, especially with his invocations of Buber. But I query Magid's dichotomy between survival and revival. True, Magid underscores the provisionality of the dichotomy. But his agenda is clear: The emphasis on survival and its successor term, continuity, is a form of ethnic (as opposed to statist) biopolitics grounded in fear. I share his basic critique of this form of what others call biological Judaism. He provocatively suggests that such fear is hardly traditional by citing the rabbinic dictum of *netsakh yisroel*, the divine assurance of the people's perpetuity. One might add, in response to sociologists' and demographers' repeated warnings that there aren't enough Jews, How many Jews would be enough? How many do we need? And even, What are we, chopped liver? Yet it is not clear to me, for example, why Adin Steinsaltz's claim that "a Jew is . . . one who wants his or her grandchildren to be Jewish" is an expression of fear; why can't it be an expression of desire? Nor is it clear that, when Ruth Ellen Gruber describes "refound Jews in Eastern Europe" as "well aware that the proof of the success of their revival [rests] . . . with their children and grandchildren," that awareness should be dismissed as grounded in a retrograde and fearful attempt to avoid institutional change.

Thus, although Magid's dichotomy between survival and renewal is useful to a point—I too, once wore a *kippah* not to indicate my fealty to Halakha but rather to proclaim to the world my Jewishness—I do not see that the dichotomy maps usefully onto one between the material and the spiritual. Such a dichotomy has never seemed particularly "Jewish" to me, and it only seems intuitively obvious in our times as a result of the process of "religionization" that Hannah Tzuberi cites. Even though I recognize that certain forms of idealistic dualism are powerful strands in Jewish thought and poetics, as in the case of Satmar Hasidism mentioned earlier, I find that communal formations and rhetorics of what Jews should do and feel usually tend to come as a package.

If evidence were needed for the notion that the organic metaphor of bodily survival can easily be applied to what we call spiritual matters as to demographics, we need look no further than the epigraph to Rachel Werczberger's essay, where Rabbi Ohad Ezrahi describes Judaism as so sick that it is at risk of dying in our midst. This is an old trope, fully in line with Maskilic and Zionist (including, of course, Maskilic-Zionist) critiques of Diaspora Judaism. So I do not see this as particularly countercultural in the Israeli context. On the contrary, it seems that in the Israeli context as well, to quote Tzuberi on Germany, this "narrative of a 'Jewish revival' . . . does unacknowledged work for the continuing project of national unification and sovereignty, shunning those conceptions of culture and cultural identity that potentially destabilize state power."

Similarly, and granted that (despite my comments earlier) the introduction to this volume recognizes "Orthodox revival" and that two relevant case studies—that of Mizrahi Breslover Hasidim and of various rabbinic groups in Paris—are presented here, the following quote from Amos Oz and Fania Oz-Salzberg that is deployed in the introduction should not be accepted on its own terms but as fully contingent and ideologically loaded in its suggestion that contemporary Orthodox or Haredi Jews are still somehow past-oriented: "For many generations Jews stood in the river of time with their faces to the past and their back to the future, until the modern age arrived, shook them and turned them to the opposite direction." This assertion naturalizes a highly contingent linear temporality. It is not necessarily the case that our ancestors were faced with the either-or choice of being oriented toward the past or toward the future. Indeed, in their everyday lives probably most of them were primarily oriented toward their immediate surroundings and prospects, and articulations of grand sacerdotal narratives were left to the elites. Nor are even Jewish ideologies of temporality generally constrained by the progressive movement from past through present toward future. For example, the contemporary Bobover Hasidic girls studied by Ayala Fader (2009) are told that they should follow their great-grandmothers' modest ways precisely to help bring the Messiah. Is this an orientation toward the past or toward the future? The question makes little sense.

Analogously, we should be wary of associating renewal with freedom and tradition with constraint, seductive as those associations are. Shlomo Guzmen-Carmeli hints at, perhaps more indirectly than he might have, a critique of the "free" stance in relation to the text on the part of the learners at the BINA secular yeshiva. What they share with Orthodox students is, curiously, the notion that there should be a clear congruence between our values as readers and interpreters and our values with respect to the text to which we devote ourselves. Put overly simplistically, the Orthodox response is that we should conform ourselves to the text, whereas the BINA response is that we should conform the text to us. In neither case (again, on the evidence presented here; I'm not saying all yeshiva settings necessarily preclude the possibility) does there seem to be an anthropological or cultural-historical recognition of the rabbis' *difference* from us, so that intense study of texts could be a process of intertemporal encounter, even a degree of identification without merger, rather than solely an attempt to make perfect the ideological and self-disciplinary fit between putative ancestry and descent.

Otherwise we wind up with two poles of fantasized identification, with the text as constructed over time or with the self as sovereign. This latter option is made explicit in Guzmen-Carmeli's quote from BINA teacher Ari Elon: "The sovereign human being is sovereign over himself." This is a remarkable statement of Kantian and masculinist faith. Given this form of faith, it is understandable that the BINA yeshiva walks a fine line between valorizing the text as worthy of study and denigrating the yeshivish culture that is the dominant world in which the text is valorized. Hence, as Guzmen-Carmeli quotes, the intended outcome is not at the student's discretion: God forbid they should become religious! Rather, "the aspiration here is to construct an identity that sanctifies equality and pluralism, a secular identity."

Turning to the Hungarian case, I note that much of what Monterescu and Zorandy describe is what was happening in the first decade of the twenty-first century. That was when the unification of Europe seemed on a much more firm trajectory than it does now. Viktor Orbán, for instance, is mentioned briefly, but one would want to know more about whether Hungary's Jews are largely staying there, whether the freer and intercultural spaces opened up around the noninstitutional Jewish organizations continue to operate, and so on. But what I do *not* want to do by pointing to the increasing fragility of European unity and the turn toward *völkisch* nationalism is reinforce the assumption that Europe's Jewishness is destined to oblivion. After all, the trope of the disappearance of the Jews, powerful as it is, is millennial and, in its origins, not Jewish at all. I am reminded here of a story that Nicole Lapierre tells in her book *La silence de la mémoire* (1989): The last Jew in a certain town in Poland decides that he's had enough and he's going to leave. All the other last Jews in town get together to give him a going-away party.

The Paris case is in some ways the most specifically grounded study here in communal space and, accordingly, not entirely clear with respect to the categories of survival, revival, or renewal. More interesting at any rate is the depiction of the unusual and dynamic intersection of built environment, competing religious authority, and symbolic space that it sketches. The work by Charlotte Fonrobert on the *eruv* that Lucine Endelstein cites emphasizes the *eruv* not so much as a legal fiction but rather as a form of creating Sabbath community. In an intriguing contrast, Endelstein shows how in the 19th arrondissement of Paris, rather than neatly demarcating between an external, non-"Shabbatical" world and a unified "Shabbatical" one inside, *eruvim* "enclose" large numbers of people who are completely unaware of their existence. Even more telling, competing *eruvim* overlap, honored by different subgroups among the observant Jewish population whose dwellings they surround.

One of the most significant contributions of this volume is the meditations almost all of the contributions offer—sometimes explicitly, sometimes not—on the question of authenticity (see Boyarin 2017). As Magid explains, this had been a key value for Buber. Werczberger similarly emphasizes that authenticity is a key value of New Age Judaism, including in Israel. But what is "authentic" about the idea that Judaism was "impaired" following the destruction of the Second Temple in 70 CE and the presumptive exile of all the Jews living there? The theme of authenticity could be traced in more detail through other essays here. For example, Gitelman's data raise the question of whether Chabad's missionary efforts in the former Soviet Union, regardless of how successful they are or are not, present a renewed opportunity for the missionary's targets to connect with an "authentic" Judaism. Rock-Singer poses the question of authenticity as well in her study of Kohenet altars.

I have in effect suggested that there are not only liberations but also suppressions involved in at least some of these projects of revival. A good place to look here, I think, would be the case of Mizrahi Breslover. While Nissim Leon appropriately points out that joining a group such as the Breslov Hasidim may be attractive as a way to become Haredi without surrendering Mizrahi ways, it certainly entails surrounding the "traditional" Mizrahi ethos, which, for example, easily encompasses the combination of traditional synagogue services on Shabbat morning with television on Shabbat afternoon. To give up that possible combination is a form of *loss*. On the other hand, perhaps the Mizrahi Breslov synthesis or compromise with the attractions of Haredi totalism could also be understood as a (covert?) project of Mizrahi continuity rather than renewal.

Hannah Tzuberi's essay lucidly shows how the German state's ultimate retention of control over "who is a Jew" in Germany clashes with any residual notion of communal Jewish autonomy. She offers us the term *religionization* to indicate a process by which particular groups can safely be integrated into the individualist ethos of the collective state, their particular differences effectively neutralized. Is it not the Liberal Jews, whom the German state insisted on recognizing as such, who would likely conform more to Magid's pole of survival, whereas those affiliated with the Central Council of Jews in Germany would more likely be associated with the pole of renewal? In this case, then, it is precisely the formation that would be classified as Jewish renewal—significantly, those whose Jewishness is defined as religion—that confirms the authority of the German state. In this case at least, it would seem to be, if anything, the older, more Orthodox, more Eastern European origin, and more "ethnic" Jewish formation that would be in resistance to the state, not the emergent revival or renewal group. In a larger frame, the analogy of the German state's encouragement of Jewish immigration to conservationist efforts at "reforestation" strikingly and disturbingly emphasizes the highly constrained degree of agency within which any putatively autonomous efforts at renewal take place. Indeed, Tzuberi underscores that "restitution was premised on the incorporation of Jews (or an image of Jews) as part of an injured *German* collective."

Similarly in Poland, there is a kind of Jewish revival or renewal that largely implicates non-Jews, but in Poland this seems much less a state project and more a project of the collective that sees itself as Polish nationals. The analogy to phantom limb pain and to the associated necessity of "knowledge of the prior existence of the limb" is powerful; it suggests Jewish renewal as something like a psychoanalytic working-through. But the relation between temporality and personhood—here figured specifically as Polish personhood—is complicated by the rhetoric of "us." Geneviève Zubrzycki quotes one young woman: "This [Jewish] culture was taken away from us. . . . Finding some of it again today is a bit like finding pieces of ourselves." What comes across is not just a question of appropriation—since when did Jewish culture "belong" to Poland, and who other than Polish Jews have the *right* to complain of its being stolen as an incidental effect of genocide? What is more striking and pertinent here is the way that the non-Jewish Polish collectivity becomes hypostatized through a period of roughly a century: from the time we "had" Jewish culture, to its theft by the Nazis and the Communists, to "our" reclamation of it today. As Zubrzycki rightly concludes, this is indeed a project of remaking Polishness—one that, for all its ambiguities, I cannot fail to welcome.

Of course, this volume makes no pretense to being a catalogue of formations of Jewish revival. I have already suggested that it is not clear why contemporary Hasidic (not just neo-Hasidic!) groups should not fall under this rubric. And not only Hasidic: The Misnagdic or Lithuanian-style Beth Medresh Govoha in Lakewood, New Jersey, claims more than 6,000 students, far larger than any such yeshiva in Eastern Europe before World War II. One could, I suppose, make a coherent argument that the notion of revival is so broad (and the forms of rupture so diverse, so powerful, and so ubiquitous) that even institutional forms that existed before World War II participate, necessarily, in projects of revival. It would be a shame to go that route, because there is indeed a critical insight that is made available by the gathering of cases and articulations presented here. To some extent, as Biemann reminds us, revivals and renewals can be recognized as such because they recognize *themselves* as such. But to the extent that they claim the mantle of authenticity, they necessarily lay claim to (interrupted) continuities as well.

I could easily imagine a sequel to this volume. It might, for example, include studies of the transformations and revivals, in many forms, of Yiddish after World War II. It might consider the phenomenon of a "new new Jewish left," around the banner of *Jewish Currents* magazine and elsewhere. It would, I think, also have to consider such movements or phenomena as the Temple Mount Faithful or the Israeli settlers known as the Hilltop Youth. At some point, it might be worthwhile to consider what aspects of Jewish life should *not* be thought of as revivals or renewals in some form. I think we would find them rather exotic.

References

Biddick, Emily 2003. *The Typological Imaginary: Circumcision, Technology, History.* Philadelphia: University of Pennsylvania Press.

Boyarin, Jonathan 2017. "In Search of Authenticity: Issues of Identity and Belonging in the Twentieth Century." In *The Cambridge History of Judaism*, vol. 8, *The Modern World, 1815–2000*, ed. Mitchell B. Hart and Tony Michels, 942–64. Cambridge, UK: Cambridge University Press.

Bunzl, Matti 2004. *Symptoms of Modernity: Jews and Queers in Twentieth-Century Vienna*. Berkeley: University of California Press.

Davis, Kathleen 2008. *Periodization and Sovereignty: How Ideas of Feudalism and Secularization Govern the Politics of Time*. Philadelphia: University of Pennsylvania Press.

Fader, Ayala. 2009. *Mitzvah Girls: Bringing Up the Next Generation of Hasidic Girls in Brooklyn*. Princeton, NJ: Princeton University Press.

Kafrissen, Rokhl. 2021. "Magical Thinking." *Tablet*, March 11. https://www.tabletmag.com/sections/community/articles/magical-thinking-rokhls-golden-city.

Lapierre, Nicole 1989. *La silence de la mémoire*. Paris: Plon.

Contributors

ASHER D. BIEMANN is professor of religious studies at the University of Virginia, where he teaches modern Jewish thought and intellectual history. He is the author of a critical edition of Martin Buber's *Sprachphilosophische Schriften* (2003), *The Martin Buber Reader* (2001), *Inventing New Beginnings: On the Idea of Renaissance in Modern Judaism* (2009), and *Dreaming of Michelangelo: Jewish Variations on a Modern Theme* (2012), which appeared in German as *Michelangelo und die jüdische Moderne* (2016). Together with Richard I. Cohen and Sarah E. Wobick-Segev, he has edited *Spiritual Homelands: The Cultural Experience of Exile, Place, and Displacement Among Jews and Others* (2020). He is currently completing a book titled *Enduring Modernity: Judaism Eternal and Ephemeral*.

JONATHAN BOYARIN is the Diann G. and Thomas A. Mann Professor of Modern Jewish Culture at Cornell University. His work centers on Jewish communities and the dynamics of Jewish culture, memory, and identity. He has investigated these fields in a range of ethnographic projects set in Paris, Jerusalem, and the Lower East Side of New York City. Much of his work is in interdisciplinary critical theory, almost always from the perspective of modern Jewish politics and experience. He has extended these interests into comparative work on diaspora, the politics of time and space, and the ethnography of reading. He is also a Yiddish translator. His most recent book is *Yeshiva Days: Learning on the Lower East Side* (2020).

LUCINE ENDELSTEIN is a researcher at the Centre National de la Recherche Scientifique and a member of Laboratoire Interdisciplinaire Solidarités, Sociétés, Territoires (UMR 5193). She teaches at the University of Toulouse Jean Jaurès and at the Institute of Political Studies of Toulouse. Her work focuses on migration and mobility, religion, and the city. She is co-editor of the *Archives de Sciences Sociales des Religions* special issue "Jewish Worlds in Motion: Borders, Porosities, Circulations" (2017) and the author of a number of articles on Jewish renewal and urban change in France. She recently co-directed *Le petit commerce dans la ville-monde* (2020) and *Secondary Effects: Living in the Time of Covid-19* (2022).

ZVI GITELMAN is professor emeritus of political science and Preston Tisch Professor Emeritus of Judaic Studies at the University of Michigan. He has written or edited nineteen books, the most recent being *The New Jewish Diaspora: Russian-Speaking Immigrants in the United States, Israel, and Germany* (2016). His 2012 book *Jewish Identities in Postcommunist Russia and Ukraine: An Uncertain Ethnicity* drew on two large surveys that he conducted with two colleagues in Russia. His current research is on the political uses of history in postcommunist states and on World War II in the USSR.

RUTH ELLEN GRUBER has written on Jewish heritage issues for more than three decades and currently runs the website www.jewish-heritage-europe.eu. Her books include *Jewish Heritage Travel: A Guide to Eastern Europe* (1992), *Virtually Jewish: Reinventing Jewish Culture in Europe* (2002), *Upon the Doorposts of Thy House: Jewish Life in East-Central Europe, Yesterday and Today* (1994), and *Letters from Europe (and Elsewhere)* (2008). The recipient of a Guggenheim Fellowship, Poland's Knight's Cross of the Order of Merit, and other awards and honors, she was the Distinguished Visiting Chair in Jewish Studies at the College of Charleston, South Carolina, in 2015.

SHLOMO GUZMEN-CARMELI is a lecturer in the Department of Sociology and Anthropology at Bar-Ilan University, Israel. His research interests include text and society, the ethnography of Jewish communities, the anthropology of knowledge and learning, the anthropology and sociology of religion and Judaism, the anthropology of medical research, separatist communities, and ritual healing. His book *Encounters Around the Text: Ethnography of Judaisms* (2020) won the Bahat Grant Prize for outstanding academic manuscript in 2017.

NISSIM LEON is an associate professor in the Department of Sociology and Anthropology at Bar-Ilan University. His research interests include modern

Judaism, ultra-Orthodox communities, religious fundamentalism, nationalism, collective memory, and the politics of the middle class. He is the author of *Harediyut Rakah: Religious Renewal in Oriental Jewry in Israel* (2010) and *Mizrachi Ultra-Orthodoxy and Nationalism in Israel* (2016); and a coauthor of *The Herut Movement's Central Committee and the Mizrachim, 1965–1967* (2011) and *A Flock with No Shepherd: Shas Leadership the Day After Rabbi Ovadia Yossef* (2018).

SHAUL MAGID is professor of Jewish Studies at Dartmouth College and Kogod Senior Research Fellow at the Shalom Hartman Institute of North America. Author of many books and essays, his latest books are *The Bible, the Talmud, and the New Testament: Elijah Zvi Soloveitchik's Commentary to the Gospel* (2019), *Piety and Rebellion: Essay in Hasidism* (2019), and *Meir Kahane: The Public Life and Political Thought of an American Jewish Radical* (2021). He is presently working on the political theology of Joel Teitelbaum of Satmar.

DANIEL MONTERESCU is professor of urban anthropology and food studies at the Central European University, Vienna. He has a PhD from the University of Chicago and has held fellowships and visiting professorships at École des Hautes Études en Sciences Sociales, Paris; the European University Institute, Florence (Marie Curie); The Technion, Haifa; Aix-Marseille Université; and Kyoto University. He is the author of *Jaffa Shared and Shattered: Contrived Coexistence in Israel/Palestine* (2015), coeditor of Food, and Settler Colonialism (2022) and coauthor of *Twilight Nationalism: Politics of Existence at Life's Edge* (2018). He is the principal investigator of the Gerda Henkel Stiftung grant "Lost Cities: The Social Life of Ruins in Israel/Palestine, 1882 to the Present" and is currently completing a book manuscript *Food and Borders*.

RABBI MICHAEL PALEY is a senior scholar and director of the Tarbut Fellowship at the American Joint Distribution Committee, the leading global Jewish humanitarian and relief organization. For more than two decades he was the scholar in residence for the UJA-Federation of New York. He has held positions at Bard College, Columbia University, where he was the first rabbi to be appointed University Chaplain, and Dartmouth College. A teacher and religious leader, he was a student of Rabbi Zalman

Schachter-Shalomi and Seyyed Hossein Nasr, an early leader of the *havurah* and Jewish renewal movement and a longtime facilitator of Jewish-Islamic relations.

CARA ROCK-SINGER is an assistant professor of religious studies at the University of Wisconsin–Madison, where she is also affiliated with the Center for Jewish Studies, the Holtz Center for Science and Technology Studies, and the Department of Gender and Women's Studies. Her research and teaching center on the relationships among gender, Judaism, and science in the contemporary United States. Her book project *Gestating Judaism: The Corpuses and Corporalities of American Jewish Feminisms* sheds new light on the role of women in producing American religion and on the embodied politics of reproducing and reviving tradition.

HANNAH TZUBERI studied Jewish studies and Islamic studies at Freie Universität Berlin (FU Berlin) and was a research assistant at the Institute for Jewish Studies (FU Berlin). Currently she is a postdoctoral researcher in a collaborative research project "Beyond Social Cohesion: Global Repertoires of Living Together (RePLITO)" at FU Berlin, directed by Professor Schirin Amir-Moazami. She is the co-editor of the *Jewish Studies Quarterly* special issue "Jewish Friends: Contemporary Figures of the Jew" (2020) and is working on a book project titled *Reviving Judaism, Reviving the Nation: Post-Holocaust Imaginaries of the (German) Nation-State*. Her research interests include contemporary European Jewry, nation building, collective memory, and religion and secularism.

RACHEL WERCZBERGER is a senior lecturer at Hadassah Academic College. Her research interests include Jewish renewal and revival, New Age culture and contemporary spiritualities, and authenticity and religion under neoliberalism. Her book *Jews in the Age of Authenticity: Jewish Spiritual Renewal in Israel* was published in 2016. Her current research project focuses on the everyday religious and spiritual experiences of Israeli Jews.

SARA ZORANDY received a master's degree in history, with a specialization in Jewish studies, from the Central European University. She is a conference interpreter and independent researcher. She wrote her thesis on the changing Hungarian Jewish identity after the Six-Day War and has conducted in-depth interviews with Hungarian Jews for the Hungarian Jewish cultural quarterly *Múlt és Jövő*. Her main academic interest lies in observing and mapping alternative Jewish communities operating alongside yet independently of the established institutions in Hungary.

GENEVIÈVE ZUBRZYCKI is a professor of sociology and a faculty associate of the Frankel Center for Judaic Studies at the University of Michigan. She is the author of *The Crosses of Auschwitz: Nationalism and Religion in Post-Communist Poland* (2006), *Beheading the Saint: Nationalism, Religion, and Secularism in Quebec* (2016), and *Resurrecting the Jew: Nationalism, Philosemitism, and Poland's Jewish Revival* (2022).

Index

Note: Page numbers appearing in italics refer to photographs.

CPSIA information can be obtained
at www.ICGtesting.com
Printed in the USA
LVHW030207241122
733821LV00004B/86

9 780814 349175